D0151687

WITHDRAWN-UNL

# Communications and Networks

# Communications and Networks
## A Survey of Recent Advances

Edited by
Ian F. Blake  H. Vincent Poor

With Contributions by
J. Abrahams  I.F. Blake  H. Derin
A. Ephremides  A.H. Haddad  Y.F. Huang
Y-C. Jenq  M.E. Kanefsky  S.A. Kassam  C.C. Lee
H.V. Poor  P.F. Swaszek  S. Tantaratana
D. Tjøstheim  J.K. Wolf  E.Wong  K.Yao

With 58 Illustrations

A Dowden & Culver Book

Springer-Verlag
New York  Berlin  Heidelberg  Tokyo

Ian F. Blake
Department of Electrical Engineering
University of Waterloo
Waterloo, Ontario N2L 3G1
Canada

H. Vincent Poor
Department of Electrical
 and Computer Engineering
University of Illinois at Urbana-
 Champaign
Urbana, IL 61801
U.S.A.

Library of Congress Cataloging-in-Publication Data
Main entry under title:
Communications and networks.
  Bibliography: p.
  Includes index.
  1. Signal theory (Telecommunication)—Addresses,
essays, lectures.  2. Coding theory—Addresses, essays,
lectures.  3. Estimation theory—Addresses, essays,
lectures.  I. Blake, Ian F.  II. Poor, H. Vincent.
TK5102.5.C617  1986        001.64′4        85-4667

© 1986 by Springer-Verlag New York Inc.
All rights reserved. No part of this book may be translated or reproduced in any
form without written permission from Springer-Verlag, 175 Fifth Avenue, New
York, New York 10010, U.S.A.

Printed and bound by R.R. Donnelley & Sons, Harrisonburg, Virginia.
Printed in the United States of America.

9 8 7 6 5 4 3 2 1

ISBN 0-387-96253-0 Springer-Verlag New York Berlin Heidelberg Tokyo
ISBN 3-540-96253-0 Springer-Verlag Berlin Heidelberg New York Tokyo

In appreciation of John B. Thomas
on the occasion of his sixtieth birthday and his thirtieth
year of teaching at Princeton University.

# CONTENTS

# LIST OF CONTRIBUTORS

JULIA ABRAHAMS
Department of Electrical and Computer Engineering, Carnegie-Mellon University, Pittsburgh, Pennsylvania

IAN F. BLAKE
Department of Electrical Engineering, University of Waterloo, Waterloo, Ontario, Canada

HALUK DERIN
Department of Electrical and Computer Engineering, University of Massachusetts, Amherst, Massachusetts

ANTHONY EPHREMIDES
Department of Electrical Engineering, University of Maryland, College Park, Maryland

A.H. HADDAD
School of Electrical Engineering, Georgia Institute of Technology, Atlanta, Georgia

Y.F. HUANG
Department of Electrical Engineering, University of Notre Dame, Notre Dame, Indiana

YIH-CHYUN JENQ
Tektronix Research Laboratories, Beaverton, Oregon

MORTON E. KANEFSKY
Department of Electrical Engineering, University of Pittsburgh, Pittsburgh, Pennsylvania

SALEEM A. KASSAM
Moore School of Electrical Engineering, University of Pennsylvania,
Philadelphia, Pennsylvania

C.C. LEE
Department of Electrical Engineering and Computer Science, Northwestern
University, Evanston, Illinois

H. VINCENT POOR
Department of Electrical and Computer Engineering, University of Illinois
at Urbana-Champaign, Urbana, Illinois

PETER F. SWASZEK
Department of Electrical Engineering, University of Rhode Island,
Kingston, Rhode Island

SAWASD TANTARATANA
AT&T Bell Laboratories, Holmdel, New Jersey

DAG TJØSTHEIM
Department of Mathematics, University of Bergen, Bergen, Norway

JACK KEIL WOLF
Department of Electrical Engineering and Computer Sciences, University of
California at San Diego, La Jolla, California

EUGENE WONG
Department of Electrical Engineering and Computer Sciences, University of
California at Berkeley, Berkeley, California

KUNG YAO
Department of System Science, University of California at Los Angeles,
Los Angeles, California

# INTRODUCTION

The areas of communications, computer networks, and signal processing have undergone rapid development over the past several years. The advent of VLSI circuitry and increasingly sophisticated computer hardware and software techniques have made possible the construction of systems and signal processors for communications applications not contemplated only a short time ago. The increasing complexity of communication systems, both by themselves and in land-based or satellite networks, has created a greater need for finding useful mathematical techniques for their analysis. The rapidly evolving technologies involved continue to find exciting new areas for application, and it remains a challenge for researchers to keep abreast of developments.

In this volume researchers from a broad cross section of the areas of communications, signal processing, and computer networks have been invited to contribute articles to assist readers in learning about the current state of research and future research directions in their area. The authors were not given tight guidelines for their contributions and thus the character and emphasis of each chapter differs. Although the scope of the areas considered is necessarily limited in a volume of this size, the coverage here is quite broad and it is hoped that the reader will find the contents of this volume to be interesting, useful, and informative.

This volume has a strong emphasis on the methods of random processes, treating both their structure and their applications in communication systems and networks. The chapters in this book are organized into two parts. The first part is comprised of nine chapters treating a number of aspects of the problems of signal detection and estimation as well as several topics of interest dealing with the structure of random processes. The second part of this volume contains eight chapters covering a broad variety of topics in the general areas of coding, networks, and signal processing. Of course, the boundary between the areas covered in these two parts is not sharp; however, this division is a convenient one for the purposes of organization.

In Chapter 1, the difficult problem of determining the level and boundary crossing properties of random processes is considered by Abrahams, and recent significant contributions to the problem by mathematicians, scientists, and engineers are reviewed. The extensive bibliography and descriptive character of this chapter makes this difficult problem accessible to the specialist and nonspecialist alike. The second chapter, by Haddad, considers the problem of the joint estimation and detection in stochastic systems with modeling uncertainties. In such problems the estimation of either parameters or states of a system is often of subsidiary interest to the detection problem, and a number of approaches to this problem that are useful in applications are reviewed here.

The next five chapters consider further various aspects of signal detection and estimation theory. In Chapter 3, Huang explores the use of series expansions of probability distributions to obtain an approach for analyzing the performance and robustness of signal detection and estimation schemes for non-Gaussian environments. These methods are quite recent and represent a useful addition to the methodology for dealing with the non-Gaussian noise environments arising in many modern applications. In the next chapter, Kassam considers optimum methods for the quantization of signal-detection data for the detection of certain types of signals, both deterministic and stochastic, in noise. This chapter surveys a number of recent results on this problem, and the results presented allow for the optimization of the analog-to-digital conversion function in several detection frameworks, including both baseband and narrowband models. The related problem of parameter estimation using discrete-time and digitized observations is considered by Lee in Chapter 5. Lee develops a general method for performing this function, and presents a practical algorithm for its implementation. In Chapter 6, Poor surveys techniques for designing signal-detection systems to be robust against (i.e., insensitive to) modeling errors. The method discussed includes both nonlinear methods for robustness against uncertainty in the probabilistic description of interfering noise as well as linear methods for guarding against uncertain spectral behavior in signals or noise. Recent developments in the area of sequential detection are surveyed by Tantaratana in Chapter 7. Since the last major survey of this area a number of important developments have emerged, including methods for robust and nonparametric sequential detection, efficiency analysis of sequential detectors, and methods for sequential detection in dependent noise environments. These and related methods are discussed in this chapter.

The next two chapters by Tjøstheim and Wong, respectively, consider fundamental structural problems in random processes of importance in many problems of communication theory. In Chapter 8, Tjøstheim surveys models for nonlinear time series, some of which arise out of dynamical systems and others out of nonlinear random vibration and control theory. These models can describe the behavior of many phenomena more accurately than the conventional linear models. The contribution of Wong discusses ideas for defining a natural Markov property for multiparameter processes, a problem of surprising difficulty relative to the analogous one-parameter case. Among the several issues considered in this setting are ways of defining multiparameter analogs to such models as Brownian motion and the Ornstein-Uhlenbeck process.

The second part of the volume treats a more diverse selection of topics from communication systems, image and signal processing, and computers networks. The first article in this part, by Blake, reviews the recent approaches to digital communications in the presence of intentional interference. In particular, the important case of frequency-hopped systems in the presence of tone and partial band jamming is surveyed. The application of Markovian fields to image processing is viewed in the next chapter by Derin, which provides an interesting perspective on the contributions of Wong and Kanefsky (discussed below). The next two chapters provide insight into the behavior of computer networks under a variety of protocols and performance criteria. These chapters will provide the reader with a basic understanding of the key issues in modern networks research. In the first of these (Chapter 12) Ephremides describes the routing problem in computer networks, treating such issues as centralized versus distributed routing algorithms and static versus dynamic algorithms. In Chapter 13, Jenq analyzes three of the more popular network protocols, those of slotted ALOHA, CSMA, and CSMA-CD, and compares their performance from the viewpoints of channel utilization, packet delay, stability, and retransmission control. In Chapter 14, Kanefsky discusses the use of predictive source encoding in the two-dimensional coding of images, a method that provides for both efficiency and self-error correction. Procedures for performing image compression in this way are considered and their performance is analyzed in the context of binary or facsimile data. The problem of vector quantization of signals has received a considerable amount of attention over the past few years, and in the next chapter Swaszek summarizes the key results in this area. In Chapter 16, Wolf considers the variety of applications of the Chinese Remainder Theorem in communications, and he illustrates this interesting topic by considering certain classes of codes and a cryptographic problem from this perspective. The volume concludes with a consideration by Yao of a new approach to the classical problem of detecting sinusoids in noise under the assumption that their amplitudes and frequencies are deterministic but unknown. In particular, Yao adapts the so-called Pisarenko method of frequency estimation to this problem, and discusses the performance and computational issues arising therefrom.

As can be seen from the variety of topics discussed, this volume will introduce the reader to key ideas in a broad spectrum of research areas within the general field of communications, networks, and signal processing. The aim of this volume is to provide the readers convenient access to recent results and research directions in these areas, and it is hoped that the timely articles it contains will be both useful and informative to this end.

As a final comment, we note that all the authors of these articles are among the many former doctoral students of Professor John B. Thomas of Princeton Univesity, to whom this volume is respectfully dedicated.

# PART I


# SIGNAL DETECTION, ESTIMATION,

# AND RANDOM PROCESSES

# A Survey of Recent Progress on Level-Crossing Problems for Random Processes

**Julia Abrahams**

*Department of Electrical and Computer Engineering*
*Carnegie-Mellon University*
*Pittsburgh, Pennsylvania*

## 1.1 Introduction

Since Blake and Lindsey's [19] comprehensive survey of results and techniques for level-crossing problems for random processes appeared in 1973, a number of interesting new results addressing both classical and new problem areas have been developed. As there are many diverse areas of application of

This work was supported in part by NSF Grant ECS-8204559. Much of this work was done while the author was with the Statistics and Probability Program, Office of Naval Research, Arlington, VA 22217.

level crossing results, the theoretical literature is fairly widely dispersed. The present survey is intended to be an update of Blake and Lindsey's and is intended to be similar to theirs with an emphasis on explicit analytical results for continuous parameter processes. As they discussed many of the techniques and methods available in an accessible tutorial fashion, the present survey will be confined to an overview of the results that are available.

The problems of interest concerning the process $x(t)$ include finding the probability that $x(t)$ first crosses a constant level $a$, or a curve $a(t)$, during the time $(T, T + dT)$, the probability that $x(t)$ does not cross the fixed level during an interval of length $T$, and the probability distribution of the maximum of $x(t)$ over an interval of length $T$. These problems are closely related and are called the *one-sided barrier problem* in [19]. The *two-sided barrier problem* concerns the probability that $x(t)$ firsts exits a region $(a, b)$ during $(T, T + dT)$, and related probabilities, including the probability distribution of the difference between the maximum of $x(t)$ over an interval and its global minimum. The *zero-crossing problem* concerns the probability distribution of the time between zero crossings and of the number of zero crossings during an interval. Analogous level-crossing questions are most often solved for moment information only. These problems have all been discussed in [19] for scalar processes $x(t)$, and the more recent results for these problems will be described in Section 1.2. As in [19], most results are known for processes with some Markov-like property and which are generally Gaussian as well. A few new results concern vector processes, and these will be described in Section 1.3. Here the geometry of the region from which the vector process leaves introduces a family of different problems. An area of recent intensive investigation has been the geometry of random fields, and a thorough discussion of this area and a review of the literature has been provided in the book of that title by Adler [6]. Section 1.4 will discuss the problem of finding the distribution of the maximum of a random field over some subset of its parameter space.

This survey omits mention of any of the vast literature involved with closely related problems. The emphasis of this survey naturally reflects the background and biases of the author. Every attempt has been made to treat completely the literature relating to the problems discussed.

## 1.2 Level-Crossing Probabilities

Recent results related to the one-sided barrier problem are discussed in Section 1.2.1, the two-sided barrier problem, in Section 1.2.2, the zero-crossing problem, in Section 1.2.3, and the nonzero level-crossing problem, in Section 1.2.4. A few miscellaneous results that pertain to other aspects of the level-crossing problem for scalar processes are addressed in Section 1.2.5.

### 1.2.1 One Sided Barriers

As discussed in Blake and Lindsey [19], finding the probability distribution of the first crossing time or first passage time to a constant level or barrier is equivalent to finding the probability distribution of the maximum of the process over a fixed interval. There are very few known results.

Although general methods for the Markov case are known, it is difficult to obtain explicit solutions, and in fact the Wiener process with drift appears to be the only Gaussian-Markov process for which a complete solution is available. Transformations of this result can be used for related processes such as the Brownian bridge or the log-normal process discussed in [27]. Shepp [93] has also found an expression for the joint density of the maximum over an interval and its location for the Wiener process with drift. A clear treatment of classical approaches to the first passage time problem for diffusions appears in Ricciardi's monograph [86], and a recent paper by Barndorff-Nielson, et al. [18] provides the explicit, generalized inverse-Gaussian, first-passage-time density for a family of diffusions, apparently the only such density known more explicitly than to within its Laplace transform. All first-passage-time density functions for diffusions are infinitely divisible, as discussed by Bondesson [20].

The conditionally Markov idea of Mehr and McFadden [19, ref. 82] can be used to generate new solutions from known Markov process solutions, especially in the Gaussian case, but in view of the scarcity of Markov solutions, the conditionally Markov idea has provided only solutions for Slepian's [19, ref. 111] process and some nonstationary extensions of it, including Slepian's process with drift [2]. The method requires the length of the interval over which the maximum is taken to be fixed in relation to the correlation function parameters. Depending on the shape of the correlation function away from the origin (where it is triangular), different special case methods have been used to obtain maximum distributions for long intervals. See Shepp [19, ref. 104], Shepp and Slepian [94], and Cressie and Davis [36].(The list of known results for the distribution of the maximum of a process which appears in [94, 36] and is repeated in [6, p. 159] incorrectly includes processes for which only zero-crossing results are known. However, the distribution of the maximum of a random sinusoid is known [58, p. 154].). Bar-David [13,15] and Bar-David and Anaton [16] have considered Slepian's triangular autocorrelation function process for short intervals with a triangular or particular ramp mean. Additional results related to Slepian's process have been given by Ein-Gal and Bar-David [44]. The conditionally Markov property has been studied to some degree motivated by, but independently of, its application to level-crossing problems. The following references pertain to conditionally Markov or to the related reciprocal processes without including new level crossing results [50,51,5,35,30,72,3,31,32].

A new non-Markov stationary Gaussian process for which the distribution of the maximum over the unit interval has been found is the Brownian bridge from which its integral over the unit interval has been subtracted. This result has been derived by Darling [39]. Since the process has a correlation function which decays quadratically around the origin, this result may be useful in refining maximum distribution inequalities based on comparisons of correlation functions, an application to which Slepian's process has been put.

The first-passage-time distributions have been obtained for several processes with extreme value distribution marginals [21, 43]. The processes are themselves obtained by a limiting operation based on the pointwise maximum of a sequence of independent processes.

A number of additional results which result in statistical information about first passage times without providing explicit distribution information are also available. Formulas for evaluating the distribution of the supremum of the Wiener process with mean $f(t)$ under general conditions on $f(t)$ are derived by Park and Skoug [80], who also refer to earlier results obtained for this type of problem. The expressions obtained generally involve infinite series from which numerical results can be obtained. In the case of piecewise linear mean, the result is reasonably explicit. Park and Beekman [79] have studied extensions of this problem, formulated in terms of barrier-crossing probabilities, for the case of stochastic barriers described by certain compound Poisson processes. Ricciardi and Sato [87] have recently developed a series approach for a stationary Gaussian process with time-varying boundary, and they evaluate the first few terms explicitly. Keilson and Ross [52] have developed an infinite series expansion in terms of zeros and residues of the parabolic cylinder function for the first-passage-time density function of the Ornstein-Uhlenbeck process from which numerical values have been tabulated. In addition, expressions for the symmetric two-sided barrier problem are given as well as some low-order moment expressions for both problems. The approach is the classical one of Darling and Siegert [19, ref.31]. Extensions to this work appear in [33]. Daniels [38] employs a similar approach for the Ornstein-Uhlenbeck process with U-shaped mean.

Tsurui and Osaki [97] have found the first-passage-time density for a Poisson process with exponential decay to within its Laplace transform together with its expected value. This process is included in the class of processes for which the expected level-crossing rate was studied by Bar-David and Nemirovsky [17].

If $T(a)$ is used to denote the first time that a random process reaches the level $a > 0$, then $T(a)$ may be regarded as a random process with "time" parameter $a$ when the first-passage process is well defined. The properties of the first-passage process for the Wiener process or Wiener process with positive drift have been studied by Wasan [98] and Buckholtz and Wasan [22]. Since this process has stationary independent increments, the distribution of its supremum may be found by classical methods [19, ref. 2].

Much work has been concerned with the asymptotic properties of maximum distributions, as the interval over which the maximum is taken becomes infinite, and of level crossing distributions, as the level becomes infinite. The reader is referred to the work of Leadbetter, *et al.* [58] for a discussion of these kinds of problems.

## 1.2.2 Two-Sided Barriers

A few explicit expressions are known for the probability distribution of the range, the difference between the maximum and the minimum, and for the maximum in absolute value of particular random processes. Nadler and Robbins [74] treat the range of the Wiener process with drift by finding the joint distribution of maximum and minimum. Their work builds on Anderson's [8] results for the probability that a Wiener process stays between two ramp boundaries during an interval. See also [53]. It appears straightforward to use these results for the Wiener process with drift to generate results for the range and maximum absolute value of Slepian's process. Kennedy [54] has found expressions for the range distribution and maximum absolute value distribution for the Brownian bridge by demonstrating relationships between this process and two other Markov, non-Gaussian processes, Brownian excursion and Brownian meander, whose supremum distributions are found by Kennedy. These processes and their supremum distributions have been studied by a number of authors. See [37] for a discussion of work related to Brownian excursion and Brownian meander.

An interesting observation by Piterbarg and Prisyazhnyuk [85] is that the range of a process is equivalent to the maximum of the field of its increments. Perhaps this approach will lend itself to additional exploitation.

## 1.2.3 Zero Crossings

Explicit results concerning the distribution of the length of the interval between zero crossings have been obtained by Rickard [88] for a particular non-Gaussian process, the smoothed random telegraph signal. The method is a classical one and requires expressions for particular moments, such as the mean zero crossing rate, found earlier by Pawula [82] and Rickard and Pawula [89]. The mean zero crossing rate has also been found for a class of non-linearly filtered random telegraph signals by Pawula [83]. Mean nonzero level crossing rates have also been found by these authors.

The zero crossing interval distribution for a particular Gaussian process was found by Wong [19, refs. 128,129]. Recently the author [1] was able to generalize Wong's method to find the distribution of the time to first zero for a particular class of second order Markov Gaussian processes, of which Wong's process is the only stationary member. Wong's original result used McKean's [19, ref.79] analysis of the first passage time to zero of the integrated Wiener process. Goldman [45] was able to obtain some expressions pertaining to the first passage time to nonzero levels of this process.

Aside from these special case solutions, a few more general aspects of the intervals between zero crossings have been investigated. de Maré [64] proves that the zero crossing intervals of a stationary Gaussian process are in general dependent although there does exist a Gaussian process whose stream of zero crossings has the same covariance structure as a Poisson process. This result answers a question of McFadden's and extends one of his results [19, refs. 73,75]. A related question is to characterize the set of correlation functions of unit processes, or processes taking on values ±1 exclusively. A recent paper by Martins de Carvalho and Clark [68] refers to the earlier literature on this problem. In view of the use of unit processes to investigate zero crossings and vice versa, it is interesting to note that Masry's [69] paper on unit process correlation functions independently rederives one of McFadden's [19, ref.73] results on the distribution of intervals between zero crossings. Bar-David [14] discusses another general result: sample functions of a Gaussian process cannot be recovered from their zero crossings.

## 1.2.4 Level Crossings

Although most results on the distribution of length of the interval between nonzero level crossings or number of nonzero level crossings per interval, called the *level crossing rate*, give moment information rather than complete distribution information, an interesting paper by Sharpe [92] is an exception. Sharpe considers an inverse to the usual problem and constructs a process with a given family of mean level-crossing rates for which the exact level-crossing rate distribution may be found for all levels. The process is non-Gaussian and is specified by the joint distribution of the point processes generated by crossings of all levels.

Mean level-crossing rates for a number of different non-Gaussian processes obtained by transformations of Gaussian processes have also been given explicitly by Hasofer [49], Orsingher [75,77], and Khimenko [55]. The special case of the chi-squared process seems to have been studied independently by Barakat [11], Bahuguna, *et al.* [10], and Ebeling [42].

A general integral expression, called a generalized Rice's function, for cross moments of all orders involving crossing rates of different levels is given by Marcus [63] for an extremely general class of processes. Explicit evaluation of this expression is intractable in most cases. The special case of crossing rate moments involving only one level was known earlier; see Marcus's discussion. These moments can be used to evaluate the terms of a Rice [19, ref. 93] or Longuet-Higgins [19, ref. 69] infinite series expansions for the level-crossing interval distribution of a stationary Gaussian process, as pointed out by Leadbetter [57]. Cariolaro [28] has developed a series of this type in the nonstationary Gaussian case, and he has performed some evaluation of the terms. Miroshin [71,73] considers questions related to the convergence of these kinds of series expansions.

A general expression for the moments of the level crossing interval distribution in terms of other related probabilities and moments has been developed by Attia [9]. In [29], Cariolaro has developed a general expression for the joint distribution of the number of up-crossings and the number of downcrossings of a fixed level in an interval in terms of their marginal distributions.

## 1.2.5 *Other Results*

In this section, miscellaneous topics that do not fit conveniently into any of the previous sections on scalar random processes will be mentioned.

Groeneboom [47] derives the density of the time of occurrence of the maximum over all time of the Wiener process or Brownian bridge with drift. A particular Wiener process with drift is also studied in this context by Pflug [84].

Barbé [12] addresses the question of finding a measure of level-crossing activity which is more convenient than the mean level-crossing rate.

Masry [70] shows that two jointly Gaussian processes have the same curve crossings for any fixed curve if and only if their sample paths are indistinguishable. This is not true if the processes are only individually Gaussian.

Slepian [19, ref.113] studied the effect of conditioning a stationary differentiable Gaussian process to have fixed up- and down-crossings by deriving a representation for the conditioned process. Orsingher [77] attempts this problem for the lognormal process, unfortunately incorrectly. It does not appear that Slepian's method is helpful for memoryless transformations of Gaussian processes. de Maré [66] examines the nondifferentiable version of Slepian's problem. Lindgren [59] conditions a stationary Gaussian process to have a fixed maximum and derives a representation for the conditioned process. These representations provide insight into the behavior of the sample paths near crossings or maxima. See also de Maré's [67] discussion of other results of this type as well as Lindgren's [62] overview, which includes the extension of these representations, the Slepian model processes, to vector processes and fields.

Some recent work has addressed the interesting problem of predicting the occurrence of a catastrophe, such as a high level crossing or a local maximum, during some future period based on observations of the process and possibly of some additional related processes, such as the derivative of the process. The development of predictor performance criteria, design of optimal predictors, and analysis of predictor performance have been addressed by Lindgren [61] and de Maré [67] in recent years. They make use of representations of processes in the neighborhood of a catastrophe developed in the references just mentioned. This class of prediction problems seems very important for applications and promising for further investigation.

Another interesting problem concerns the prediction of a process from observations of its zero crossings. Slepian [95] derives a solution for the Ornstein-Uhlenbeck process, and de Maré [65] addresses the simpler linear interpolation problem.

## 1.3 Vector Processes

Although problems concerned with the exit of a vector process from some region of space and associated probabilities can sometimes be conveniently reformulated in terms of a scalar process and its level-crossing probabilities, this is not always the case. One example of the former is the chi-squared process, whose level crossings are equivalent to the sphere crossings of a stationary vector Gaussian process with independent identically distributed components; see Lindgren [60] and Sharpe [91]. Another example is the work of DeLong [40] on sphere crossings for vector Brownian motion with drift; he has obtained an infinite series expression for the distribution of the supremum over the unit interval of the Euclidean norm of this vector process. Other work on sphere crossings for vector Brownian motion appears in [90,99,100]. Sphere crossings for the vector Brownian bridge in the two-dimensional case were studied by Kiefer [56].

Orsingher [76] considers the sample path behavior of a bivariate Gaussian process after conditioning on crossing events in the plane. This represents a two-dimensional generalization of Slepian's [19, ref. 113] work.

The straightforward but computationally difficult work of Buckholtz and Wasan [23] on the transition probabilities of a vector diffusion with absorbing barriers yields what appears to be the only explicit first-passage-time density function results for a vector process. Their results are for two-dimensional Brownian motion and the first time that process reaches a boundary consisting of two intersecting lines, or equivalently for two correlated one-dimensional Brownian motions and the first time either of them reaches a fixed level.

The crossing of a square root boundary by the Wiener process is of particular interest because it is closely related to the crossing of a constant level by the Ornstein-Uhlenbeck process. DeLong [41] has studied the multivariate version of this problem and has found the probability distribution of first crossing time to within its Mellin transform, and from this moment information can be obtained. The method is a multivariate analog of a classical one. Similar work by Haake, *et al.* appears in [48].

## 1.4 Random Fields

The random field problem most amenable to special-case explicit solution seems to be that of finding the distribution of the maximum of a random field over some subset of the parameter space, for example, the unit "cube". Bounds on this probability are given [6] for the unit cube problem and two different Gaussian fields, the Brownian sheet or Yeh-Wiener process and a multidimensional generalization of Slepian's process called the *Slepian field*. The results found in Adler [6] are upper and lower bounds for the Brownian sheet due to Goodman [46] in the two-parameter case and an upper bound for the Slepian field due to Cabaña and Wschebor [25]. Recently, Cabaña and Wschebor's upper bound for the Slepian field has been improved by Adler [7] in the two-parameter case, and Adler has also found a lower bound for the same process. Furthermore, Goodman shows that his bounds are asymptotically tight, while Cabaña and Wschebor point out how their result can be used to bound maximum distribution probabilities for other fields whose covariance can be bounded by the Slepian field covariance. Zincenko's [101] expression for the exact distribution of the maximum of the Brownian sheet is known to be incorrect.

A series of results pertaining to the distribution of the maximum of a two-parameter field along the boundary of the unit square are also known, and these expressions can be used to derive lower bounds to the maximum distribution over the entire unit square for the corresponding field. Paranjape and Park [78] considered the Yeh-Wiener process as did Chan [34], while Park and Skoug [81] were able to derive an expression for the maximum distribution on the boundary and additional bounds for the two-parameter Yeh-Wiener process with drift. Park and Skoug [81] also obtain results pertaining to the two-parameter Brownian bridge. Recently, the author [4] has obtained an expression for the distribution of the supremum of the two-parameter Slepian process on the boundary of the unit square.

Some other results on particular random fields which provide bounds of various sorts are given in [96,24,26].

**1.5 Comments**

It is hoped that this survey has been helpful in calling to the attention of interested readers the existence of some widely scattered results. It has been written as an update to Blake and Lindsey's excellent survey which describes many of the approaches to level-crossing problems in a clear tutorial fashion. Although it is disappointing that powerful general methods for level crossing problems continue to be unavailable, it is encouraging that so many interesting special case results have been obtained during the period of this survey.

**References**

[1] J. Abrahams, The zero-crossing problem for some nonstationary Gaussian processes, *IEEE Trans. Inform. Theory,* Vol. IT-28, pp. 677-678, 1982.

[2] J. Abrahams, Ramp crossings for Slepian's process, *IEEE Trans. Inform. Theory,* Vol. IT-30, pp. 574-575, 1984.

[3] J. Abrahams, On Miroshin's second-order reciprocal processes, *SIAM J. Appl. Math.,* Vol. 44, pp. 190-192, 1984.

[4] J. Abrahams, Distribution of the supremum of the two parameter Slepian process on the boundary of the unit square, *Stoch. Proc. Appl.,* to be published.

[5] J. Abrahams and J.B. Thomas, Some comments on conditionally Markov and reciprocal Gaussian processes, *IEEE Trans. Inform. Theory,* Vol. IT-27, pp. 523-525, 1981.

[6] R.J. Adler, *The Geometry of Random Fields,* New York, NY: Wiley, 1981.

[7] R.J. Adler, The supremum of a particular Gaussian field, *Ann. Probab.,* Vol. 12, pp. 436-444, 1984.

[8] T.W. Anderson, A modification of the sequential probability ratio test to reduce the sample size, *Ann. Math. Statist.,* Vol. 31, pp. 165-197, 1960.

[9] F.A. Attia, On the level-upcrossings of stochastic processes, *Anal.*

*Numer. Theor. Approx.,* Vol. 8, pp. 127-135, 1979.

[10] R.D. Bahuguna, K.K. Gupta and K. Singh, Expected number of intensity level crossings in a normal speckle pattern, *J. Opt. Soc. Am.,* Vol. 70, pp. 874-876, 1980.

[11] R. Barakat, The level-crossing rate and above-level duration time of the intensity of a Gaussian random process, *Inform. Sci.,* Vol. 20, pp. 83-87, 1980.

[12] A. Barbé, A measure for the mean level-crossing activity of stationary normal processes, *IEEE Trans. Inform. Theory,* Vol. IT-22, pp. 96-102, 1976.

[13] I. Bar-David, Radon-Nikodym derivatives, passages and maxima for a Gaussian process with particular covariance and mean, *J. Appl. Prob.,* Vol. 12, pp. 724-733, 1975.

[14] I. Bar-David, Sample functions of a Gaussian process cannot be recovered from their zero-crossings, *IEEE Trans. Inform. Theory,* Vol. IT-21, pp. 86-87, 1975.

[15] I. Bar-David, A sample path property of matched-filter outputs with applications to detection and estimation, *IEEE Trans. Inform. Theory,* Vol. IT-22, pp. 225-229, 1976.

[16] I. Bar-David and D. Anaton, Leading edge estimation errors, *IEEE Trans. Aero. Elec. Sys.,* Vol. AES-17, pp. 579-584, 1981.

[17] I. Bar-David and A. Nemirovsky, Level crossings of nondifferentiable shot processes, *IEEE Trans. Inform. Theory,* Vol. IT-18, pp. 27-34, 1972.

[18] O. Barndorff-Nielsen, P. Blaesild and C. Halgreen, First hitting time models for the generalized inverse Gaussian distribution, *Stoch. Proc. Appl.,* Vol. 7, pp. 49-54, 1978.

[19] I.F. Blake and W.C. Lindsey, Level crossing problems for random processes, *IEEE Trans. Inform. Theory,* Vol. IT-19, pp. 295-315, 1973.

[20] L. Bondesson, Classes of infinitely divisible distributions and densities, *Z. Wahr. Verw. Geb.,* Vol. 57, pp. 39-71, 1981.

[21]    B.M. Brown and S.I. Resnick, Extreme values of independent stochastic processes, *J. Appl. Prob.,* Vol. 14, pp. 732-739, 1977.

[22]    P.G. Buckholtz and M.T. Wasan, Characterization of certain first passage processes, *Sankhya-Ser. A,* Vol. 38, pp. 326-339, 1976.

[23]    P.G. Buckholtz and M.T. Wasan, First passage probabilities of a two dimensional Brownian motion in an anisotropic medium, *Sankhya-Ser. A,* Vol. 41, pp. 198-206, 1979.

[24]    E.M. Cabana, On the transition density of multidimensional parameter Wiener process with one barrier, Universidad Simon Bolivar, Dept. of Math. and Comp. Sci. Report No. 78, 1982.

[25]    E.M. Cabana and M. Wschebor, An estimate for the tails of the distribution of the supremum for a class of stationary multiparameter Gaussian processes, *J. Appl. Prob.,* Vol. 18, pp. 536-541, 1981.

[26]    E.M. Cabana and M. Wschebor, The two-parameter Brownian bridge: Kolmogorov inequalities and upper and lower bounds for the distribution of the maximum, *Ann. Probab.,* Vol. 10, pp. 289-302, 1982.

[27]    R.M. Capocelli and L.M. Ricciardi, On the inverse of the first passage time probability problem, *J. Appl. Prob.,* Vol. 9, pp. 270-287, 1972.

[28]    G.L. Cariolaro, A systematic approach to the problem of crossings by a random process, *Alta Frequenza,* Vol. 41, pp. 606-622, 1972.

[29]    G.L. Cariolaro, Number of crossings by a random process and related distributions, *Alta Frequenza,* Vol. 43, pp. 303-305, 1974.

[30]    J.-P. Carmichael, J.-C. Massé and R. Theodorescu, Processus gaussiens stationnaires réciproques sur un intervalle, *C. R. Acad. Sci. Paris-Ser. I,* Vol. 295, pp. 291-293, 1982.

[31]    J.-P. Carmichael, J.-C. Massé and R. Theodorescu, On second order reciprocal stationary Gaussian processes, Université Laval Dept. of Math. Preprint 1984.

[32]    J.-P. Carmichael, J.-C. Massé and R. Theodorescu, On multivariate reciprocal stationary Gaussian processes, Université Laval Dept. of Math., Report No. 84-5, 1984.

[33]    G. Cerbone, L.M. Ricciardi and L. Sacerdote, Mean, variance and skewness of the first passage time for the Ornstein-Uhlenbeck process, *Cybernetics and Systems,* Vol. 12, pp. 395-429, 1981.

[34]    A.H.C. Chan, Some lower bounds for the distribution of the supremum of the Yeh-Wiener process over a rectangular region, *J. Appl. Prob.,* Vol. 12, pp. 824-830, 1975.

[35]    S.C. Chay, On quasi-Markov random fields, *J. Multivar. Anal.,* Vol. 2, pp. 14-76, 1972.

[36]    N. Cressie and R.W. Davis, The supremum distribution of another Gaussian process, *J. Appl. Prob.,* Vol. 18, pp. 131-138, 1981.

[37]    E. Csáki and S.G. Mohanty, Excursion and meander in random walk, *Canad. J. Statist.,* Vol. 9, pp. 57-70, 1981.

[38]    H.E. Daniels, The minimum of a stationary Markov process superimposed on a U-shaped trend, *J. Appl. Prob.,* Vol. 6, pp. 399-408, 1969.

[39]    D.A. Darling, On the supremum of a certain Gaussian process, *Ann. Probab.,* Vol. 11, pp. 803-806, 1983.

[40]    D.M. DeLong, Some asymptotic properties of a progressively censored nonparametric test for multiple regression, *J. Multivar. Anal.,* Vol. 10, pp. 363-370, 1980.

[41]    D.M. DeLong, Crossing probabilities for a square root boundary by a Bessel process, *Commun. Statist.-Theor. Meth.,* Vol. A10, pp. 2197-2213, 1981.

[42]    K.J. Ebeling, Statistical properties of spatial derivatives of the amplitude and intensity of monochromatic speckle patterns, *Optica Acta,* Vol. 26, pp. 1505-1521, 1979.

[43]    W.F. Eddy and J.D. Gale, The convex hull of a spherically symmetric sample, *Adv. Appl. Prob.,* Vol. 13, pp. 751-763, 1981.

[44]    M. Ein-Gal and I. Bar-David, Passages and maxima for a particular Gaussian process, *Ann. Probab.,* Vol. 3, pp. 549-556, 1975.

[45]    M. Goldman, On the first passage of the integrated Wiener process, *Ann. Math. Statist.,* Vol. 42, pp. 2150-2155, 1971.

[46] V. Goodman, Distribution estimates for functionals of the two-parameter Wiener process, *Ann. Probab.*, Vol. 4, pp. 977-982, 1976.

[47] P. Groeneboom, The concave majorant of Brownian motion, *Ann. Probab.*, Vol. 11, pp. 1016-1027, 1983.

[48] F. Haake, J.W. Haus and R. Glauber, Passage-time statistics for the decay of unstable equilibrium states, *Physical Rev. A*, Vol. 23, pp. 3255-3271, 1981.

[49] A.M. Hasofer, The upcrossing rate of a class of stochastic processes, in *Studies in Probability and Statistics*, E.J. Williams, Ed., New York, NY: North-Holland, pp. 153-159, 1974.

[50] B. Jamison, Reciprocal processes: the stationary Gaussian case, *Ann. Math. Statist.*, Vol. 41, pp. 1624-1630, 1970.

[51] B. Jamison, Reciprocal processes, *Z. Wahr. Verw. Geb.*, Vol. 30, pp. 65-86, 1974.

[52] J. Keilson and H.F. Ross, Passage time distributions for Gaussian Markov (Ornstein-Uhlenbeck) statistical processes, *Selected Tables in Mathematical Statistics*, Vol. 3, pp. 233-327, 1975.

[53] D.P. Kennedy, Limit theorems for finite dams, *Stoch. Proc. Appl.*, Vol. 1, pp. 269-278, 1973.

[54] D.P. Kennedy, The distribution of the maximum Brownian excursion, *J. Appl. Prob.*, Vol. 13, pp. 371-376, 1976.

[55] V.I. Khimenko, The average number of trajectory overshoots of a non-Gaussian random process above a given level, *Radiophysics and Quantum Electronics*, Vol. 21, pp. 819-823, 1978 (English 1979).

[56] J. Kiefer, K-sample analogues of the Kolmogorov-Smirnov and Cramèr-V. Mises tests, *Ann. Math. Statist.*, Vol. 30, pp. 420-447, 1959.

[57] M.R. Leadbetter, Point processes generated by level crossings, in *Stochastic Point Processes*, P.A.W. Lewis, Ed., New York, NY: Wiley, pp. 436-467, 1972.

[58] M.R. Leadbetter, G. Lindgren and H. Rootzén, *Extremes and Related Properties of Random Sequences and Processes*, New York, NY:

Springer-Verlag, 1983.

[59]   G. Lindgren, Some properties of a normal process near a local maximum, *Ann. Math. Statist.*, Vol. 41, pp. 1870-1883, 1970.

[60]   G. Lindgren, Extreme values and crossings for the $\chi^2$-process and other functions of multidimensional Gaussian processes with reliability applications, *Adv. Appl. Prob.*, Vol. 12, pp. 746-774, 1980.

[61]   G. Lindgren, Model processes in nonlinear prediction with applications to detection and alarm, *Ann. Probab.*, Vol. 8, pp. 775-792, 1980.

[62]   G. Lindgren, Use and structure of Slepian model processes for prediction and detection in crossing and extreme value theory, University of Lund and Lund Institute of Technology Dept. of Math. Stat. Report No. 1983:4, 1983.

[63]   M. Marcus, Level crossings of a stochastic process with absolutely continuous sample paths, *Ann. Probab.*, Vol. 5, pp. 52-71, 1977.

[64]   J. de Maré, When are the successive zero-crossing intervals of a Gaussian process independent?, University of Lund and Lund Institute of Technology Dept. of Math. Stat. Report No. 1974:3, 1974.

[65]   J. de Maré, Reconstruction of a stationary Gaussian process from its sign changes, *J. Appl. Prob.*, Vol. 14, pp. 38-57, 1977.

[66]   J. de Maré, The behaviour of a non-differentiable stationary Gaussian process after a level crossing, *Stoch. Proc. Appl.*, Vol. 6, pp. 77-86, 1977.

[67]   J. de Maré, Optimal prediction of catastrophes with applications to Gaussian processes, *Ann. Probab.*, Vol. 8, pp. 841-850, 1980.

[68]   J.L. Martins de Carvalho and J.M.C. Clark, Characterizing the autocorrelations of binary sequences, *IEEE Trans. Inform. Theory*, Vol. IT-29, pp. 502-508, 1983.

[69]   E. Masry, On covariance functions of unit processes, *SIAM J. Appl. Math.*, Vol. 23, pp. 28-33, 1972.

[70]   E. Masry, A note on Gaussian processes and zero-memory non-linear transformations, *J. Appl. Prob.*, Vol. 14, pp. 857-861, 1977.

[71]  R.N. Miroshin, Convergence of Rice Longuet-Higgins series for a Wong process, *Theory Prob. Appl.*, Vol. 21, pp. 863-866, 1976 (English 1977).

[72]  R.N. Miroshin, Second-order Markov and reciprocal stationary Gaussian processes, *Theory Prob. Appl.*, Vol. 24, pp. 845-852, 1979 (English 1980).

[73]  R.N. Miroshin, Convergence of Longuet-Higgins series for stationary Gaussian Markov processes of first order, *Theory Prob. Appl.*, Vol. 26, pp. 97-117, 1981.

[74]  J. Nadler and N.B. Robbins, Some characteristics of Page's two-sided procedure for detecting a change in a location parameter, *Ann. Math. Statist.*, Vol. 42, pp. 538-551, 1971.

[75]  E. Orsingher, Level crossings of transformations of stationary Gaussian processes, *Metron,* Vol. 37, pp. 81-100, 1979.

[76]  E. Orsingher, Planar Gaussian motions generated by crossing events, *Pub. Inst. Stat. Univ. Paris,* Vol. 25, pp. 61-86, 1980.

[77]  E. Orsingher, Upcrossings and conditional behavior of the lognormal process, Boll.*Un. Mat. Ital.,* Vol. 18-B, pp. 1017-1034, 1981.

[78]  S.R. Paranjape and C. Park, Distribution of the supremum of the two-parameter Yeh-Wiener process on the boundary, *J. Appl. Prob.,* Vol. 10, pp. 875-880, 1973.

[79]  C. Park and J.A. Beekman, Stochastic barriers for the Wiener process, *J. Appl. Prob.,* Vol. 20, pp. 338-348, 1983.

[80]  C. Park and D.L. Skoug, Wiener integrals over the sets bounded by sectionally continuous barriers, *Pacific J. Math.,* Vol. 66, pp. 523-534, 1976.

[81]  C. Park and D.L. Skoug, Distribution estimates of barrier-crossing pro-babilities of the Yeh-Wiener process, *Pacific J. Math.,* Vol. 78, pp. 455-466, 1978.

[82]  R.F. Pawula, Statistical geometry of the smoothed random telegraph signal, *Int. J. Control,* Vol. 16, pp. 629-640, 1972.

[83]  R.F. Pawula, The probability density and level-crossings of first-order nonlinear systems driven by the random telegraph signal, *Int. J. Control*, Vol. 25, pp. 283-292, 1977.

[84]  G. Pflug, A statistically important Gaussian process, *Stoch. Proc. Appl.*, Vol. 13, pp. 45-57, 1982.

[85]  V.I. Piterbarg and V.P. Prisyazhnyuk, Exact asymptotic behavior of the probability of a large span of a stationary Gaussian process, *Theory Prob. Appl.*, Vol. 26, pp. 468-484, 1981 (English 1982).

[86]  L.M. Ricciardi, *Diffusion Processes and Related Topics in Biology*, New York, NY: Springer-Verlag, 1977.

[87]  L.M. Ricciardi and S. Sato, A note on first passage time problems for Gaussian processes and varying boundaries, *IEEE Trans. Inform. Theory*, Vol. IT-29, pp. 454-457, 1983.

[88]  J.T. Rickard, The zero-crossing interval statistics of the smoothed random telegraph signal, *Inform. Sci.*, Vol. 13, pp. 253-268, 1977.

[89]  J.T. Rickard and R.F. Pawula, The zero crossing variance of the smoothed random telegraph signal, *Int. J. Control*, Vol. 21, pp. 743-752, 1975.

[90]  V. Seshadri and K. Lindenberg, Extrema statistics of Wiener-Einstein processes in one, two, and three dimensions, *J. Statist. Phys.*, Vol. 22, pp. 69-79, 1980.

[91]  K. Sharpe, Some properties of the crossings process generated by a stationary $\chi^2$ process, *Adv. Appl. Prob.*, Vol. 10, pp. 373-391, 1978.

[92]  K. Sharpe, Level crossings of a constructed process, *J. Appl. Prob.*, Vol 16, pp. 206-212, 1979.

[93]  L.A. Shepp, The joint density of the maximum and its location for a Wiener process with drift, *J. Appl. Prob.*, Vol. 16, pp. 423-427, 1979.

[94]  L.A. Shepp and D. Slepian, First-passage time for a particular stationary periodic Gaussian process, *J. Appl. Prob.*, Vol. 13, pp. 27-38, 1976.

[95]  D. Slepian, Estimation of the Gauss-Markov process from observation of its signs, *Stoch. Proc. Appl.*, Vol. 14, pp. 249-265, 1983.

[96]    P.T. Strait, Level crossing probabilities for a multiparameter Brownian process, *Pacific J. Math.,* Vol. 65, pp. 223-232, 1976.

[97]    A. Tsurui and S. Osaki, On a first-passage problem for a cumulative process with exponential delay, *Stoch. Proc. Appl.,* Vol. 4, pp. 79-88, 1976.

[98]    M.T. Wasan, On an inverse Gaussian process, *Skand. AktuarTidskr.,* Vol. 51, pp. 69-96, 1968.

[99]    J.G. Wendel, Hitting spheres with Brownian motion, *Ann. Probab.,* Vol. 8, pp. 164-169, 1980.

[100]   W. Zikun, Last exit distributions and maximum excursion for Brownian motion, *Scientia Sinica,* Vol. 24, pp. 324-331, 1981.

[101]   N.M. Zincenko, On the probability that a Wiener random field exceeds a certain surface, *Theor. Probability and Math. Statist.,* Vol. 13, pp. 65-72, 1977.

# 2

# On Detection-Estimation Schemes
# for Uncertain Systems

**A.H. Haddad**

*School of Electrical Engineering*
*Georgia Institute of Technology*
*Atlanta, Georgia*

## 2.1 Introduction

Combined detection-estimation schemes for stochastic signals have been considered as early as the mid-1960s (see, e.g., [1-5]). In general three basic problems may be classified as joint detection-estimation problems: (1) It is desired to detect a signal when some or all of its parameters or model are unknown. The result is a decision-directed estimation where the ultimate interest is in the detection outcome, while the estimate of the parameters or states may only be a by-product, which need not be obtained. In many robust detection problems, these variables are not estimated explicitly, and the concern is in making the detector performance insensitive to the unknown variables. (2) It is desired to estimate a signal in the presence of several uncertainties which take on discrete (finitely many) values. In this case, the resulting estimator is concerned primarily with the estimate of the signal attributes, and the detection of the precise mode of uncertainty governing the signal model is a by-product of the estimation process. In most cases, one is satisfied with the estimation outcome without explicitly identifying or detecting the modes involved. (3) A truly joint estimation-detection scheme is concerned with detecting the presence of a signal and estimating its parameters at the same time, and the performance criterion used in such a case is a coupled one yielding a detector and estimator which depend on each other. The first problem is not discussed here, and only a brief exposition of the third problem will be given. The main part of this chapter is concerned with the joint detection-estimation schemes for estimation purposes. The discussion of the third problem will be limited to its relationship to the estimation problem.

The motivation for the detection-estimation problem for signals or systems with uncertainties stems from two different sources. The first is naturally defined, in the sense that it is desired to estimate a signal which may or may not be present [1,4,5]. In this category we may include cases when it is not clear which of several signals are present, and whose estimate is desired, as in multiple-target tracking. The second is more artificial, and considers the problem of estimating the state of signals or systems when there is structural or parametric uncertainty, and the uncertainty is then formulated as taking on discrete values. The rationale for the discrete values or finite state modeling of the uncertainty is used to avoid two of the drawbacks of the major approaches to estimation under uncertainty. The first is the minimax case, which is both difficult to derive and which sometimes yields a conservative estimate [6,7]. It essentially minimizes the worst-case error under the uncertainty, so that the resulting scheme is robust for small observation records but yields poor performance under large observation data. The other approach is the adaptive approach (e.g., see [8-11]), which requires complete identification of the underlying parameter values or systems model so that they can be used in the estimation scheme. Most schemes (using a variety of performance criteria) are based on the premise that the observation time is sufficient for the convergence of the identification part of the scheme, and hence assuming the parameters are constant or slowly varying, the estimation scheme will perform as an optimal one for the remaining time. Another drawback of adaptive estimation is the fact that the approaches are mostly adhoc, thus requiring an art in the design and running phases, just as is the case in the use of the extended Kalman filter as an adaptive estimator. The finite hypothesis case used in the formulation considered in this chapter is a compromise that tends to have robustness properties for the small-sample case while maintaining some form of convergence for the large-sample case, and thus it is expected to be especially suitable for intermediate cases not sufficient for complete identification. They are also suitable for moderate time variation in the parameters that cannot be handled by the standard adaptive schemes.

A complete survey of combined detection-estimation schemes would be very lengthy. Hence our scope is limited to the highlights of the results concentrating on one aspect of the problem. We start with a brief review of the joint detection-estimation problem placed in historical perspective, then concentrate on such schemes for systems with unknown parameters, generalized to the case of time- varying parameters, and continue with Markov models with unknown transition probabilities.

## 2.2 Joint Detection-Estimation

The first estimation-detection scheme for the estimation of signals with one of M possible models was derived by Magill [2]. Simply stated, the objective was to estimate the state $\underline{x}(t)$ of a linear system (i.e., Gaussian signal) observed in white Gaussian noise, where the system could have one of $M$ possible models (all Gaussian, with different means and covariances). Consequently, under the hypothesis $H_i$ that the $i$th model is true, one can obtain the minimum-mean-squared-error (MMSE) estimate of $\underline{x}(t)$ given the observations $Y(t) = \{\underline{y}(\tau), 0 \le \tau \le t\}$, as

$$\hat{\underline{x}}_i(t) = E\{x(t)|Y(t), H_i\} \tag{2.1}$$

where $\underline{y}(t)$ is the observation process. If the observations are now given by

$$y(t) = C\underline{x}(t) + \underline{w}(t), \quad 0 \le t \tag{2.2}$$

where $\underline{w}(t)$ is white with covariance parameter $R$, the optimal MMSE estimate is given by the weighted sum

$$\underline{\hat{x}}(t) = E\{\underline{x}(t)|Y(t)\} = \left[\sum_{i=1}^{M} \Lambda_i(t)\right]^{-1} \sum_{i=1}^{M} \underline{\hat{x}}_i(t)\Lambda_i(t) \tag{2.3}$$

where the $\Lambda_i(t)$ are the generalized likelihood functions given by

$$d \ln\Lambda_i(t) = \underline{\hat{x}}_i^T(t)R^{-1}\left[d\underline{z}(t) - 1/2 \ \underline{\hat{x}}_i(t) \ dt\right] \ \Lambda_i(0) = p_i. \tag{2.4}$$

Here $p_i$ is the prior probability that $H_i$ is true (at $t = 0$),

$$d\underline{z}(t) = C\underline{x}(t) \ dt + d\underline{W}(t) \equiv y(t) \ dt \tag{2.5}$$

where $\underline{W}(t)$ is the Brownian motion giving rise to $\underline{w}(t)$, and the integral (2.4) is to be interpreted in the Itô sense. The use of detection-estimation to denote such a scheme is motivated by the use of the likelihood function, which may also be used to detect which of the models is the appropriate one, in addition to estimating the state of the signal. While this is the first estimation-detection scheme, which serves as the basis for most of the schemes requiring estimation only to follow, its basic premise for estimating the signal with unknown parameters required additional elaboration to achieve some optimality criterion. The impetus for the study of the performance criteria that led to the more extended schemes was given by the first paper describing a truly joint detection and estimation system. This system was considered by Middleton and Esposito [1] and later extended in [3-5] to cover different cost criteria, multiple hypotheses, and more expanded objectives such as prediction. The work of Middleton and Esposito will not be described in detail, as it does not directly relate to all the schemes reviewed in the sequel. However, the work considers the detection of a signal which may or may not be present, as well as the estimation of its state. The cost function used involves both the detection cost and the estimation cost, and may be expressed as:

$$E\{C_{1,1}(\underline{x},\underline{\hat{x}}) + C_{0,1}(\underline{x}) + C_{1,0}(\underline{\hat{x}}) + C_{0,0}\} \tag{2.6}$$

where $\underline{\hat{x}}$ is a functional of the observation $Y(t)$, and the cost functions $C_{i,j}(*,*)$ are defined as follows:

$C_{0,0}$ = the cost of correctly rejecting $H_1$

$C_{0,1}$ = the cost of incorrectly rejecting $H_1$

$C_{1,0}$ = the cost of estimating the signal and accepting $H_1$ when $H_0$ is true

$C_{1,1}$ = the cost of estimating the signal when it is indeed present

Here, the hypotheses $H_0$ and $H_1$ denote the absence or presence, respectively, of the signal $\underline{x}(t)$ in the observations $\underline{y}(t)$.

The resulting scheme depends on whether these costs are strongly or weakly coupled. Overall, it results in an estimate that is a function of the decision rule, and similarly the decision rule for the detector depends on the estimation error and not just the likelihood function. However, in the extreme cases of constant $C_{i,j}$ or quadratic but equal $C_{i,j}$, the scheme reduces to pure detection or pure estimation respectively. Further generalization of this scheme was made by incorporating composite hypotheses and prediction in [4,5,13]. Also, modified cost functions were shown to yield an estimate which included a hard nonlinear weighting using the likelihood functions. In general, if, in addition to $H_0$, we have two signal models represented by $H_i$, $i = 1,2$, we may choose the costs as

$$C_{i,j} = K_{i,j} + \begin{cases} C_\alpha \|\underline{x} - \underline{\hat{x}}\|^2 & i = j \\ C_\beta \|\underline{x} - \underline{\hat{x}}\|^2 & i \neq j \end{cases} \tag{2.7}$$

where $C_{i,j}$ is the cost of the detection-estimation when $H_i$ is accepted, while $H_j$ is true. In this case, the estimate $\underline{\hat{x}}(t)$ may be expressed as

$$\underline{\hat{x}}(t) = g(\Lambda)\underline{\hat{x}}_1(t) + [1 - g(\Lambda)]\underline{\hat{x}}_2(t) \tag{2.8}$$

where

$$\Lambda = \Lambda_2/\Lambda_1 \qquad\qquad (2.9a)$$

and

$$g(\Lambda) = \frac{C_\alpha}{C_\alpha + C_\beta\Lambda}\mu(\eta - \Lambda) + \frac{C_\beta}{C_\beta + C_\alpha\Lambda}\mu(\Lambda - \eta). \qquad (2.9b)$$

Here $\eta$ is the detection threshold, $\mu(\cdot)$ is the unit step function, and $\Lambda$ is the standard likelihood ratio. If $C_\alpha = C_\beta$, the estimate (2.8) reduces to the standard MMSE estimate as in (2.3), while if $C_\beta = 0$, the estimator includes a hard decision, namely, that $\hat{x}_i$ is used when $H_i$ is accepted by the detector.

This joint detection-estimation scheme is rather specialized, and while it provided motivation for other approaches studied for the estimation problem, it really may be considered an offshoot outside the mainstream of the work to follow. Its contribution provided a sound basis for the generalization of Magill's work to more general cases. In particular, it provided the motivation for considering the estimation problem when the signal is observed in uncertain environments, namely, the signal may or may not be present in some observation samples. This problem was first considered by Nahi [14] and later generalized to Markov changes in the observation parameters [15-18]. This avenue of research is complemented by the work that follows from Magill's formulation involving signal models with uncertain parameters including both the time-invariant ones as well as the time-varying ones. The remainder of this chapter is concerned with these two types of problems involving various levels of generalization.

## 2.3 Estimation-Detection Schemes for Unknown Constant Parameters

As stated in Section 2.1, the problem of recursive estimation of the state of a dynamic linear system with unknown parameters can be formulated as either an adaptive linear estimation problem, or as a nonlinear filtering problem by using state augmentation. The approach to be described here uses quantized parameter values to yield a detection-estimation problem. The problem may be formulated for the continuous-time case as follows:

$$\dot{\underline{x}}(t) = A(\underline{\theta})\underline{x}(t) + B(\underline{\theta})\underline{v}(t), \quad t > t_0, \quad \underline{x}(t_0) = \underline{x}_0 \qquad (2.10a)$$

$$\underline{y}(t) = C(\underline{\theta})\underline{x}(t) + \underline{w}(t), \quad t \geq t_0, \qquad (2.10b)$$

where $\underline{x}(t)$ and $\underline{y}(t)$ are the state and observation vectors, respectively, and $\underline{v}(t)$ and $\underline{w}(t)$ are independent white Gaussian noise vectors with covariance parameters $Q$ and $R$, respectively. The parameter vector $\underline{\theta}$ is assumed to be unknown and to belong to a compact set $\Omega$. It is desired to estimate the state $\underline{x}(t)$ from the past observations $Y(t) = \{\underline{y}(\tau), t_0 \leq \tau \leq t\}$.

As discussed above, only the formulation that yields a combined detection-estimation structure will be considered here. Lainiotis [9,11] was among the first to derive such a structure by considering a quantized formulation of the parameter description, resulting in a scheme based on Magill's [2]. Further extensions will be noted in the sequel. In the quantized description the parameters are assumed to take only a finite number of values in $\Omega$, namely

$$\underline{\theta} \in \{\underline{\theta}_1, \underline{\theta}_2, \ldots, \underline{\theta}_M\}$$

and a prior probability, $p_i$, is assigned to each value. The problem becomes one of estimating $\underline{x}(t)$ when its model is one of $M$ possible hypotheses, and the resulting estimate is given by the weighted sum (2.3) involving the conditional estimates $\hat{\underline{x}}_i(t)$ and the generalized likelihood functions $\Lambda_i(t)$, which can also be considered as the likelihood ratios of the hypotheses $H_i$ with respect to the null hypothesis $H_0$ obtained by setting $C \equiv 0$. The expressions for the estimators and likelihood functions may be explicitly obtained in this case by means of Kalman filters and correlators as follows:

$$\dot{\hat{\underline{x}}}_i(t) = A_i \hat{\underline{x}}_i(t) + K_i[\underline{y}(t) - C_i \hat{\underline{x}}(t)], \quad \hat{\underline{x}}_i(t_0) = E[\underline{x}_0] \qquad (2.11a)$$

where

$$K_i = P_i C_i^T R^{-1} \qquad (2.11b)$$

$$\dot{P}_i = A_i P_i + P_i A_i^T + B_i Q_i B_i^T - K_i R K_i^T, \quad P_i(t_0) = \text{Cov}(\underline{x}_0) \qquad (2.11c)$$

and

$$\frac{d}{dt}\ln\Lambda_i(t) = \underline{\hat{x}}_j^T C_i^T R^{-1}[\underline{y}(t) - 1/2C_i\underline{\hat{x}}_j(t)], \quad \Lambda_i(t_0) = p_i. \quad (2.11d)$$

Properties of this scheme such as convergence to the nearest-neighbor value of the parameter have been derived, and extensions to a variety of conditions such as discrete-time, initial condition uncertainty, and nonlinear problems have been considered [19-25].

There are two difficulties with the above formulation: the first is the dependence on the priors in the selection of the quantized values, and the second is the lack of a systematic procedure for the selection of quantized values for $\underline{\theta}$. Two approaches have been proposed to circumvent these difficulties; the first approach uses a weighted min-max criterion [13] and the second uses an incremental mean-squared error criterion [26]. The use of these criteria avoids the problem of arbitrary selection of the quantized values of $\underline{\theta}$. The weighted min-max MSE criterion assumes that $\Omega$ is subdivided into $M$ compact subsets $\Omega_i$ rather than consisting of $M$ discrete elements. Initially, the parametric uncertainty is restricted to be in $R$ and $Q$ only, however, it may be further generalized to the other system matrices. The primary rationale for this restriction is the desire to consider the relative signal-to-noise ratio which is represented by $Q$ and $R$ as the major source of uncertainty. This approach proposed in [13] and further extended in [27,28], defines a conditional mean-squared error (CMSE) as

$$L(\underline{\hat{x}}, Y, \underline{\theta}) = E\{\|\underline{x} - \underline{\hat{x}}\|^2 | Y, \underline{\theta}\} \quad (2.12)$$

and selects as the optimal estimator the one that minimizes the maximum value of L over all $\Omega_i$:

$$\min_{\underline{\hat{x}}} \max_{\underline{\theta}\in\Omega_i} L(\underline{\hat{x}}, Y, \underline{\theta}), \quad i = 1,2,\ldots,M. \quad (2.13)$$

Since a solution may not exist for this multiple-objective criterion, it is substituted with a weighted CMSE given by

$$\min_{\underline{\hat{x}}} \sum_{i=1}^{M} \max_{\underline{\theta}_i\in\Omega_i} [\lambda_i' L(\underline{\hat{x}}, Y, \underline{\theta}_i)] \quad (2.14)$$

where

$$\lambda_i' = \lambda_i \left[ \sum_{j=1}^{M} \lambda_j \Lambda_j(t)/\Lambda_i(t) \right]^{-1}, \quad \sum_{i=1}^{M} \lambda_i = 1, \quad \lambda_i > 0 \qquad (2.15)$$

and where $\Lambda_i$ is the likelihood function defined in (2.11d). Here $\underline{\theta}_i$ denotes a general value of $\underline{\theta}$ restricted to $\underline{\theta} \in \Omega_i$, so that $\Lambda_i$ is in general a function of all $\underline{\theta}$ values, with the maximization performed with respect to $\underline{\theta} \in \Omega_i$, while holding $\underline{\theta} \in \Omega_j$, $j \neq i$ fixed. The structure of the estimator is thus constrained to the form

$$\hat{\underline{x}} = \sum_{i=1}^{M} \lambda_i' \hat{\underline{x}}_i(t) \qquad (2.16)$$

where $\hat{\underline{x}}_i$ is as given in (2.11) for some $\underline{\theta}_i \in \Omega_i$, and the $\underline{\theta}_i$ are chosen so as to maximize

$$L_i \equiv \lambda_i E\{ \|\underline{x} - \hat{\underline{x}}\|^2 | \ Y, \underline{\theta}_i \}. \qquad (2.17)$$

A scalar case is considered in [27] while a general recursive solution to the maximization problem of $L_i$ to derive $\underline{\theta}_i$ is given in [28]. The advantage of the approach is in reducing the conservatism of the min-max solution for large sample sizes while retaining the robustness properties for small sample sizes. Again, convergence properties have been investigated to justify the approach in the limiting case of large sample sizes and stable systems [28]. This approach still involves a large number of assumptions such as the selection of the subsets $\Omega_i$ and the choice of the weighting factors $\lambda_i$. The incremental mean-squared error (IMSE) criterion [26] attempts to remove some of these assumptions and provides a coherent framework for the combined detection-estimation scheme for systems with unknown parameters.

The IMSE formulation uses the same model as the original problem (2.10) in this section, and even allows for nonlinearities instead of the $A, B, C$ matrices provided they yield a process with finite variance. The parameter vector is again restricted to a compact set $\Omega$ without any additional prior distributions. Let $\hat{\underline{x}}_0(t)$ be the optimal estimate of $\underline{x}(t)$ under the MMSE criterion, assuming the value of $\underline{\theta}$ is known, i.e., the resulting MMSE estimate is the best achievable even if all the information is provided. When using any other estimator $\hat{\underline{x}}(t)$, the MSE should be compared to that of the full-information

MMSE estimate, and thus yields the definition of the IMSE [26]:

$$L(\hat{\underline{x}},\underline{\theta}) = E\{\|\hat{\underline{x}}(t) - \underline{x}(t)\|^2 - \|\hat{\underline{x}}_0(t) - \underline{x}(t)\|^2 | Y, \underline{\theta}\} \qquad (2.18)$$

where

$$\hat{\underline{x}}_0(t) = E\{\hat{\underline{x}}(t)| Y, \underline{\theta}\}. \qquad (2.19)$$

The objective is to find $\hat{\underline{x}}(t)$ that maximizes the following performance index:

$$\max_{\underline{\theta}\in\Omega} E\{L(\hat{\underline{x}},\underline{\theta})|\underline{\theta}\}. \qquad (2.20)$$

The major result of [26] is that the estimator that minimizes the worst-case IMSE is given by an expression of the form

$$\hat{\underline{x}}(t) = \left[\sum_{i=1}^{M} \hat{\underline{x}}_i(t)\Lambda_i(t)\right]\left[\sum_{j=1}^{M} \Lambda_j(t)\right]^{-1} \qquad (2.21)$$

for some finite $M$, where $\hat{\underline{x}}_j$, $\Lambda_i$ are as in (2.11), and where the $\{\underline{\theta}_j\}$ are points of positive support of the worst-case distribution of $\underline{\theta}$ on $\Omega$, and the $\{p_i\}$ are the values associated with this distribution. It should be noted that $\underline{\theta}_j$ and $p_i$, which appear in the formulation of $\hat{\underline{x}}$ and $\Lambda_i$, are generated so as to yield the minimum of the max IMSE. The primary importance of this result is that it provides a justification for the quantization approach discussed earlier, and can lead to an interactive design technique for the selection of $M$, the number of quantization levels, $\underline{\theta}_j$, the quantum values, and $p_i$, the corresponding prior probabilities. Since the performance index is monotonic with $M$, provided that the $\underline{\theta}_j$ and $p_i$ are selected optimally, one can select the appropriate value of $M$ either by checking the acceptability of the worst-case IMSE or by comparing the upper and lower bounds of the resulting IMSE, as they are an indication of the possible improvement available with increasing $M$. The approach may be extended to systems with unknown order by using a singular perturbations approach [29] that yields additional complexity reductions, and to systems with uncertainties occurring at unknown times [30].

## 2.4 Estimation-Detection Schemes for Markov Parameters

The preceding section considered the estimation problem for systems with uncertain but constant parameters. The extension to the time-varying parameter case can be performed either by assuming slowly changing parameters, and applying the constant-parameter scheme or by assuming that the parameters vary according to a Markov process model. The motivation for this case stems from the original paper on the estimation of a signal which may or may not be present, by considering the uncertain observations case when each observation may or may not contain the signal, as was first considered by Nahi [14]. It was later extended to the case of Markov models for these observations, namely

$$\underline{x}(t_{k+1}) = A\underline{x}(t_k) + B\underline{v}(t_k) \tag{2.22a}$$

$$\underline{y}(t_k) = \gamma_k C\underline{x}(t_k) + \underline{w}(t_k) \tag{2.22b}$$

where $\{\gamma_k\}$ is an independent sequence of random variables taking on the values of 0 or 1. Additional contributions to the solution of this problem were made in [31-37] covering both different suboptimal schemes and different aspects of the problems such as filtering or smoothing. These contributions were generalized to include the cases of Markov sequence models for the $\{\gamma_k\}$. A natural generalization of such models is to assume that the parameter variations occur in the covariances of the noise processes (both input and observations) and in other parts of the system model. The first contribution to the general switched environment case, namely that in which the noise covariance may be switching according to a Markov chain rule among $M$ possible values, was made by Ackerson and Fu [17]. The problem has wide applications in systems whose exact model variations are not known. Contributions in this area can be classified into two types: The first is involved with generalizing the switching model to include more systems and observation parameters, and the second is involved with various suboptimal approximations for the solution of the estimation problem (see e.g., [38-42]).

The problem considered by Ackerson and Fu and by others may be stated in a reasonably general form as

$$\underline{x}(t_{k+1}) = A(\underline{\theta})\underline{x}(t_k) + B(\underline{\theta})\underline{v}(t_k) \tag{2.23a}$$

$$\underline{y}(t_k) = C(\underline{\theta})\underline{x}(t_k) + D(\underline{\theta})\underline{w}(t_k), \qquad k = 0,1,2,... \tag{2.23b}$$

where $D(\underline{\theta})$ is introduced to account for the possible variations in the observations noise covariance. This is a discrete-time version of the original problem formulated in Section 2.3, with the additional assumption that $\underline{\theta}$ is not constant, taking one of $M$ values $\{\underline{\theta}_1, \underline{\theta}_2,...,\underline{\theta}_M\}$, but that it switches among these values according to a Markov rule:

$$P\{\underline{\theta}(t_{k+1}) = \underline{\theta}_j | \underline{\theta}(t_k) = \underline{\theta}_i\} = \Pi_{ij} \tag{2.24}$$

where the transition matrix $\Pi$ is assumed known. For simplicity of notation, the explicit dependence of the matrices and $\underline{\theta}$ on $t_k$ is omitted. In this case, the optimal solution is again a combined detection-estimation structure as the one shown in Section 2.3, except that at time $t_k$, the number of possible hypotheses (or models) is $M^{k+1}$ where one hypothesis is matched to each possible sequence of $\{\underline{\theta}(t_i), i = 0,1,...,k\}$. Given each sequence the problem is conditionally Gaussian, and the optimal filter is the usual Kalman filter. The weighted sum of these filters is determined by the likelihood functional for each of these sequences. The problem is that in the recursive evaluation of each likelihood functional from $(k-1)$ to $k$, the number increases from $M^k$ to $M^{k+1}$ since each of the $M^k$ sequences at $t_{k-1}$ can have $M$ possible transitions. The same applies to the evaluation of the filters, as each of the $M^k$ filters gives rise to $M$ new ones. The resulting estimation-detection structure is valid in principle and is relatively simple to derive, but the memory requirements and the computational requirements increase exponentially. Consequently, the major contributions in the area have been related to suboptimal schemes that do carry some of the detection-estimation features. Two major suboptimal schemes were proposed by Ackerson and Fu [17] and Akashi and Kumamoto [40]. In the first, the *a posteriori* density of the estimates at the time $t_k$ is assumed to be Gaussian, which of course can be a very poor approximation if the transition probabilities are high. In the second, only a random sample of the $M^{k+1}$ sequences are taken, and the resulting estimator-detector uses those random samples as representatives of the entire system. The disadvantage of the first scheme stems from the adhoc nature of the assumptions, and the second scheme suffers from the relatively large computational requirements that characterize random sampling. A third alternative based on the multitarget tracking approaches [43] has been considered in [44]. In this approach, the number of filters in the detection-estimation is either held fixed or upperbounded by $\tilde{M}$. The sequences are selected based on the following criteria:

1. The most likely *a posteriori* sequences are kept, and all others are rejected at each time instant $t_k$.

2. Sequences are merged into one if the Bhattacharyya distance [45] between their conditional density functions is less than a given threshold.

3. A particular sequence is retained if its contribution to the estimate or error covariance of that estimate is sufficiently different from that of the other sequences.

The selection of $\tilde{M}$ is made based on performance analysis which may be implemented in an interactive computer-aided design mode. It may be based on the number of states as well as on the average number of jumps between states during a given observation interval. Such a selection is extremely simplified in the asymptotic cases of very fast transitions or very slow transitions. An example is provided in [44] to illustrate the performance of this latter scheme as compared with the other suboptimal schemes. The primary advantage of this approach is its systematic implementation, in that if one value of $\tilde{M}$ is not satisfactory, a larger value may be selected within the computational constraints.

Additional generalization of this scheme has been to the case of unknown transition probabilities $\Pi_{ij}$, which is a reasonable assumption, since the motivation for using a Markov parameter model was the fact that the exact behavior of the parameter variations was not known. Hence, it is rather naive to assume that the transition probabilities of such changes are known. The modification resulting from this additional restriction is to assume that $\Pi$ belongs to a finite set $\{\Pi_i, \ i = 1, 2, \ldots, K\}$. The structures originally used for this problem are the same as the ones for the Markov jump parameters case; however, an additional $K$ estimators-detectors are required at each stage to take care of the $K$ possible values of the transition probabilities. The case considered first concentrated on parametric uncertainties in the observation noise process either in the form of uncertain observations [46] or in the form of unknown noise covariance [47]. These restrictions were intended to allow the proof of convergence of the schemes to the appropriate values of the unknown transition matrices. In [48] Tugnait generalized the schemes to include uncertainties in all the systems matrices $(A,B,C,D)$. Furthermore, the finite possible values taken by $\Pi$ assumed earlier is replaced by assuming that $\Pi$ is a function of a parameter that may take values in a compact subset of a finite-dimensional Euclidean space. Under conditions of ergodicity, distinguishability, and identifiability, the convergence of the resulting schemes is proved in [48].

Extensions to nonlinear systems have been made in [42-49] as well as applications to the estimation and control of a variety of applications, such as aircraft control [50], tracking of manoeuvreing targets [51-53], and systems subject to failure [54-56], among others.

## 2.5 Detection-Estimation Schemes for Incident Processes

In this section some observations are made on another class of detection-estimation problems resulting from an incident process that is itself a Markov or Poisson process. All the systems described above are distinguished by having a Gaussian model that can switch among a finite or countably infinite number of possible models. The class discussed here involves a departure from that basic assumption and assumes that the linear system model is driven primarily by Poisson inputs, so that the resulting signal is not Gaussian except in the limit as the input rate becomes very high. The structure for an optimal estimation scheme for such systems is no longer given by the combined detection-estimation structure. Here an adhoc use is made of a different type of detection-estimation structure for low input rate. In this case, in each observation interval the incidence of an input is first detected and then an estimate of its timing and amplitude is used to compute the estimate of the system state [57]. Initial contributions to this problem were made by Kwakernaak [58,59] who derived representations for the optimal filters. In [57], a detection-estimation scheme is used to detect the incidence of an input which is then used to derive the estimate of the state. The approach is motivated by failure detection schemes used to estimate the state of the linear system subject to failures as reviewed by Willsky [55]. The scheme can, of course, diverge if an incidence is not detected, especially if the system is not stable (such as in trajectory tracking problems). In [60] the assumption of an additional Wiener process input is also made, and the scheme is modified by including delays in order to improve the estimate as well as to reduce the probability of divergence. It should be noted that the approach may be used in a combined detection-estimation scheme for the estimation problem when the incidence rate is unknown; two schemes may be used, one for the low rate, as above, and the second for high incidence rate (singular perturbation techniques may be applied asymptotically for fast incident process), and the two are then combined in a detection-estimation structure as discussed in this chapter. This aspect of the detection-estimation approach is discussed here very briefly as it is tangential, even though related to, the major thrust of this chapter.

## 2.6 Summary and Conclusions

This chapter provided a brief survey of detection-estimation structures that are utilized for the state estimation of systems subject to structural or parametric uncertainties. The primary emphasis was on the progress of the multimodel formulation from the constant parameter case to the Markov jump parameters with unknown transition probabilities. The chapter was related to two major problems in detection-estimation: the joint detection-estimation problem as formulated in [1] and the incident process problem as discussed in [57].

Additional related references may be found in earlier survey papers on combined detection-estimation schemes [11,12] and [61,63]. Further motivation and applications to tracking and control may be found throughout the cited references.

# References

[1]  D. Middleton and R. Esposito, Simultaneous optimum detection and estimation of signals in noise, *IEEE Trans. Inform. Theory,* Vol. IT-14, pp. 434-444, 1968.

[2]  D.T. Magill, Optimal adaptive estimation of sampled stochastic processes, *IEEE Trans. Auto. Contr.,* Vol. AC-10, pp. 434-439, 1965.

[3]  D.G. Lainiotis, Joint detection, estimation and system identification, *Inform. Contr.,* Vol. 19, pp. 75-92, 1971.

[4]  A. Fredricksen, D. Middleton and V.D. VandeLinde, Simultaneous signal detection and estimation under multiple hypotheses, *IEEE Trans. Inform. Theory,* Vol. IT-18, pp. 607-614, 1972.

[5]  D.W. Kelsey and A.H. Haddad, Detection and prediction of a stochastic process having multiple hypotheses, *Inform. Sci.,* Vol. 6, pp. 301-311, 1973.

[6]  J.O. Pearson, Estimation of uncertain systems, in *Control and Dynamic Systems,* Vol. 10, C.T. Leondes, ed., New York, NY: Academic Press, 1973.

[7]  J.A. D'Appolito and C.E. Hutchinson, A minimax approach to the design of low sensitivity state estimators, *Automatica,* Vol. 8, pp. 599-608, 1972.

[8]  R.K. Mehra, Approaches to adaptive filtering, *IEEE Trans. Auto. Contr.,* Vol. AC-17, pp. 693-698, 1972.

[9]  D.G. Lainiotis, Optimal adaptive estimation: Structure and parameter adaptation, *IEEE Trans. Auto. Contr.,* Vol. AC-16, pp. 160-170, 1971.

[10]  Y. Bar-Shalom, Optimal simultaneous state estimation and parameter identification in linear discrete-time systems, *IEEE Trans. Auto. Contr.,* Vol. AC-17, pp. 308-319, 1972.

[11]  D.G. Lainiotis, Partitioning: A unifying framework for adaptive systems, I: Estimation, *Proc. IEEE,* Vol. 64, pp. 1126-1142, 1976.

[12]  D.G. Lainiotis, Partitioning: A unifying framework for adaptive systems, II: Control, *Proc. IEEE,* Vol. 64, pp. 1182-1198, 1976.

[13]  D.W. Kelsey and A.H. Haddad, A note on detectors for joint minimax detection-estimation schemes, *IEEE Trans. Auto. Contr.,* Vol. AC-18, pp. 558-559, 1973.

[14]  N.E. Nahi, Optimal recursive estimation with uncertain observations, *IEEE Trans. Inform. Theory,* Vol. IT-15, pp. 457-462, 1969.

[15]  A.G. Jaffer and S.C. Gupta, Optimal sequential estimation of discrete processes with Markov interrupted observations, *IEEE Trans. Auto. Contr.,* Vol. AC-16, pp. 471-475, 1971.

[16]  Y. Sawaragi, T. Katayama and S. Fujishige, Adaptive estimation for a linear system with interrupted observation, *IEEE Trans. Auto. Contr.,* Vol. AC-18, pp. 152-154, 1973.

[17]  G.A. Ackerson and K.S. Fu, On state estimation in switching environments, *IEEE Trans. Auto. Contr.,* Vol. AC-15, pp. 10-17, 1970.

[18]  M.T. Hadidi and S.C. Schwartz, Linear recursive state estimators under uncertain observations, *IEEE Trans. Auto. Contr.,* Vol. AC-24, pp. 944-948, 1979.

[19]  D.G. Lainiotis, Partitioned estimation algorithms, I: Nonlinear estimation, *Inform. Sci.,* Vol. 7, pp. 203-255, 1974.

[20]  D.G. Lainiotis and S.K. Park, On joint detection, estimation and system identification: Discrete data case, *Int. J. Control,* Vol. 17, pp. 609-633, 1973.

[21]  A.H. Haddad and J.B. Cruz, Jr., Nonlinear filtering for systems with random models, *Proc. 2nd Symposium on Nonlinear Estimation Theory,* pp. 147-150, 1971.

[22]  D.G. Lainiotis, Partitioned linear estimation algorithms: Discrete case, *IEEE Trans. Auto. Contr.,* Vol. AC-20, pp. 255-257, 1975.

[23]  L.A. Liporace, Variance of Bayes estimates, *IEEE Trans. Inform. Theory,* Vol. IT-7, pp. 665-669, 1971.

[24]  R.M. Hawkes and J.R. Moore, Performance of Bayesian parameter estimators for linear signal models, *IEEE Trans. Auto. Contr.,* Vol. AC-21, pp. 523-527, 1976.

[25]  R.M. Hawkes and J.R. Moore, Performance bounds for adaptive estimation, *Proc. IEEE,* Vol. 64, pp. 1143-1150, 1976.

[26]  A.V. Sebald and A.H. Haddad, Robust state estimation in uncertain systems: Combined detection estimation with incremental MSE criterion, *IEEE Trans. Auto. Contr.,* Vol. AC-22, pp. 821-825, 1977.

[27]  R.A. Padilla and A.H. Haddad, On the estimation of uncertain signals using an estimation-detection scheme, *IEEE Trans. Auto. Contr.,* Vol. AC-21, pp. 509-512, 1976.

[28]  J.K. Tugnait and A.H. Haddad, On state estimation for linear discrete-time systems with unknown noise covariances, *IEEE Trans. Auto. Contr.,* Vol. AC-24, pp. 337-340, 1979.

[29]  A.V. Sebald and A.H. Haddad, State estimation for singularly perturbed systems with uncertain perturbation parameter, *IEEE Trans. Auto. Contr.,* Vol. AC-23, pp. 464-469, 1978.

[30]  A.V. Sebald and T. Takenawa, Optimal state estimation in the presence of deterministic perturbations of uncertain structure occurring at unknown times, *Proc. 18th IEEE Conf. Dec. Contr.,* pp. 488-493, 1979.

[31]  A.G. Jaffer and S.C. Gupta, On estimation of discrete processes under multiplicative and additive noise conditions, *Inform. Sci.,* Vol. 3, pp. 267-276, 1971.

[32]  M. Askar, H. Derin and H.O. Yurtseven, Recursive estimation of Gauss-Markov process using uncertain observations, *Proc. Twelfth Annual Asilomar Conf. on Circ. Syst. and Comp.,* California, pp. 731-735, 1978.

[33]  M. Askar and H. Derin, A recursive algorithm for the Bayes solution of the smoothing problem, *IEEE Trans. Auto. Contr.,* Vol. AC-26, pp. 558-561, 1981.

[34]  M. Askar and H. Derin, Recursive algorithms for Bayes smoothing with uncertain observations, *Proc. 1983 ACC,* San Francisco, CA, pp. 108-110, 1983.

[35]  R.A. Monzingo, Discrete linear recursive smoothing for systems with uncertain obsesrvations, *IEEE Trans. Auto. Contr.,* Vol. AC-26, pp.

754-757, 1981.

[36]   A.G. Jaffer and S.C. Gupta, Recursive Bayesian estimation with uncertain observation, *IEEE Trans. Inform. Theory,* Vol. IT-17, pp. 614-616, 1971.

[37]   R.A. Monzingo, Discrete optimal linear smoothing for systems with uncertain observations, *IEEE Trans. Inform. Theory,* Vol. IT-21, pp. 271-275, 1975.

[38]   J.K. Tugnait, On identification and adaptive estimation for systems with interrupted observations, *Automatica,* Vol. 19, pp. 61-73, 1983.

[39]   C.B. Chang and M. Athans, State estimation for discrete systems with switching parameters, *IEEE Trans. Aero. Elec. Sys.,* Vol. AES-14, pp. 418-425, 1978.

[40]   H. Akashi and H. Kumamoto, Random sampling approach to state estimation in switching environments, *Automatica,* Vol. 13, pp.429-434, 1977.

[41]   A. Wernerson, On Bayesian estimators for discrete-time linear systems with Markovian parameters, *Proc. 6th Symposium on Nonlinear Estimation Theory and Its Applications,* San Diego, CA, pp. 253-263, 1975.

[42]   H.F. Van Landingham, R.L. Moose and W.H. Lucas, Modelling and control of nonlinear plants, *Proc. 17th IEEE Conf. Dec. Contr.,* pp. 337-341, 1979.

[43]   Y. Bar-Shalom, Tracking methods in a multi-target environment, *IEEE Trans. Auto. Contr.,* Vol. AC-23, pp. 618-626, 1978.

[44]   J.K. Tugnait and A.H. Haddad, A detection-estimation scheme for state estimation in switching environments, *Automatica,* Vol. 15, pp. 477-481, 1979.

[45]   T. Kailath, The divergence and Bhattacharyya distance measures in signal selection, *IEEE Trans. Comm. Tech.,* Vol. COM-15, pp. 52-60, 1967.

[46]   J.K. Tugnait and A.H. Haddad, State estimation under uncertain observations with unknown statistics, *IEEE Trans. Auto. Contr.,* Vol. AC-24, pp. 201-210, 1979.

[47]  J.K. Tugnait and A.H. Haddad, Adaptive estimation in linear systems with unknown Markovian noise statistics, *IEEE Trans. Inform. Theory*, Vol. IT-26, pp. 66-78, 1980.

[48]  J.K. Tugnait, Adaptive estimation and identification for discrete systems with Markov jump parameters, *IEEE Trans. Auto. Contr.*, Vol. AC-27, pp. 1054-1065, 1982.

[49]  R.L. Moose, H.F. Van Landingham and D.H. McCabe, Applications of adaptive state estimation theory, *Proc. 19th IEEE Conf. Dec. Contr.*, pp. 568-575, 1980.

[50]  M. Athans *et al.*, The stochastic control of F-8C aircraft using a multiple model adaptive control (MMAC) method: Part I; Equilibrium flight, *IEEE Trans. Auto. Contr.*, Vol. AC-22, pp. 768-780, 1977.

[51]  C.M. Brown, Jr. and C.F. Price, A comparison of adaptive tracking filters for targets of variable maneuverability, *Proc. IEEE Conf. Dec. and Contr.*, pp. 554-563, 1976.

[52]  R.L. Moose, An adaptive state estimator solution to the maneuvering target problems, *IEEE Trans. Auto. Contr.*, Vol. AC-20, pp. 359-362, 1975.

[53]  J.S. Thorp, Optimal tracking of maneuvering targets, *IEEE Trans. Aero. Elec. Sys.*, Vol. AES-9, pp. 512-519, 1973.

[54]  J.D. Birdwell, D.A. Castanon and M. Athans, On reliable control system designs with and without feedback reconfigurations, *Proc. 17th IEEE Conf. Dec. Contr.*, pp. 419-426, 1979.

[55]  A.S. Willsky, A survey of design methods for failure detection in dynamic systems, *Automatica*, Vol. 12, pp. 601-611, 1976.

[56]  A.K. Caglayan, Simultaneous failure detection and estimation in linear systems, *Proc. 19th IEEE Conf. Dec. and Contr.*, pp. 1038-1041, 1980.

[57]  S.P. Au and A.H. Haddad, Suboptimal sequential estimation-detection scheme for Poisson driven linear systems, *Inform. Sci.*, Vol. 16, pp. 95-113, 1978.

[58]  H. Kwakernaak, Filters for systems excited by Poisson white noise, *Control Theory, Numerical Methods, and Computer Systems Modelling*

*(Lecture Notes in Economics and Math. Systems,* Vol. 107), A. Bensoussan and J.L. Lions, Eds., Berlin, Germany: Springer-Verlag, 1975.

[59] H. Kwakernaak, An estimate of the variance reduction in filtering for linear systems excited by Poisson white noise, *Dep. Appl. Math.,* Twente Univ. Technol., Enschede, The Netherlands, Memo. 56, October, 1974.

[60] S.P. Au, A.H. Haddad and H.V. Poor, A state estimation algorithm for linear systems driven simultaneously by Wiener and Poisson processes, *IEEE Trans. Auto. Contr.,* Vol. AC-27, pp. 617-626, 1982.

[61] A.H. Haddad and J.K. Tugnait, On state estimation using detection-estimation schemes for uncertain systems, *Proc. JACC,* pp. 514-519, Denver, CO, 1979.

[62] J.K. Tugnait, Detection and estimation for abruptly changing systems, *Automatica,* Vol. 18, pp. 607-615, 1982.

[63] D.G. Lainiotis, Estimation: A brief survey, *Inform. Sci.,* Vol. 7, pp. 197-202, 1974.

# 3

# Series Expansions in Statistical Theory of Detection and Estimation

**Y.F. Huang**

*Department of Electrical Engineering*
*University of Notre Dame*
*Notre Dame, Indiana*

## 3.1 Introduction

Methods of series expansions have been used extensively in many areas of science and engineering. In particular, since the early part of the century, they have been used in the study of approximations to distribution functions and in the study of approximations to quantiles, especially for complicated distributions. These approximations are of great importance in the general theory of statistical inference so that one can evaluate (approximately) the performance and/or robustness of some standard tests of hypotheses and of optimal estimators.

In the context of detection and estimation, applications of series expansions may date back to the early 1960s, since when the statistical theory of detection and estimation has been studied intensively. Among others, Marcum [1] and Swerling [2] both employed the Edgeworth series expansions, for the underlying probability density functions (p.d.f.), to obtain approximations to error probabilities. Schwartz [3] discussed a Bayesian detection algorithm with the knowledge of a convergent series expansion for the test statistic. The decision is based on a truncated version of this series. Later, Bodharamik *et al.* [4] considered the problem of designing Neyman-Pearson (N-P) optimal detectors based on Gram-Charlier series expansions for the p.d.f.'s of noise. Eastwood and Lugannani [5] derived approximate likelihood ratio detectors, based on a generalization of Schwartz's method, for problems in which the received processes are linear.

Recently, Huang and Thomas [6] investigated sensitivity of the linear detector and the sign detector to noise skewness using the Cornish-Fisher (C-F) expansion for the test statistics. Furthermore, they proposed a modified scheme such that the resulting performance is asymptotically insensitive to noise skewness [7]. Other applications of series expansions include obtaining approximations for the first-order p.d.f. of man-made noise [8]. Also, Freedman [9] considered generalized Gram-Charlier expansions for the p.d.f. and derived recursive formulas for the associated coefficients.

The main concerns in the studies of detection and estimation lie not only on the simplicity of analysis and implementation, but also on the robustness of performance. Parametric schemes often suffer from difficulties of analysis, implementation, and robustness, especially when the underlying noise distribution is complicated, e.g., non-Gaussian. Nonparametric schemes, although they provide a uniform performance over a broad class of distributions, often have unsatisfactory (or suboptimal) performance at the true model. This is simply because implementation of nonparametric schemes usually does not utilize thoroughly the available information of the input model. Furthermore, many nonparametric schemes preclude real-time processing of data as well as estimation for continuous-time problems. Canonical examples of such schemes include those resulting from rank order statistics (see, e.g., [10,11]).

Robust schemes may be more appealing when compared to the prescribed ones. The fundamental concepts of robust schemes are

1. They should be insensitive to small model deviations.

2. They possess optimal or suboptimal properties at the assumed model.

A great many contributions involving different robust schemes have evolved in the literature. Among many contributors, Huber's work [12,13], which is based on a minimax approach, was one of the most important. Analysis and implementation of these schemes, however, still are rather complicated. Another disadvantage is that the $\varepsilon$-contaminated mixture noise model used therein has a limitation on the maximum allowable degree of contamination. This in turn implies the existence of a lower bound on the signal strength. El-Sawy and Vandelinde [14] addressed this problem with a consideration of sequential detection of weak signals in the presence of additive noise.

The primary purpose of this chapter is to study the prescribed difficulties encountered in signal detection and estimation problems. The approach used here involves methods of series expansions. The striking feature of this approach is that, instead of assuming a known p.d.f. of the underlying noise process, one only assumes knowledge of its statistical moments, particularly the first few moments. Thus the resulting schemes will be applicable to a class of noise distributions, as opposed to a particular distribution. Furthermore, the first few moments are, in general, easier to obtain with better accuracy compared to the p.d.f. In addition, if the underlying noise is nearly Gaussian, the resulting schemes will be simple modifications of the optimal schemes corresponding to the Gaussian case. This usually implies simplicity of analysis and implementation.

Of particular interest here are the applications of the Edgeworth expansions and the C-F expansions. In this chapter, two different ways of applying series expansions will be considered. In the first of these, we consider expansions for the distribution or its quantiles of the test statistic. To obtain better results, asymptotic expansions are employed and thus normalized test statistics are considered. This approach leads to asymptotically optimal schemes which are applicable to a broad class of noise distributions. The second approach is to use series expansions to obtain approximations for the underlying p.d.f. Then approximately optimal schemes are derived based on these approximations. These schemes are also applicable to a class of noise distributions, as they are derived from the knowledge of the first few moments.

This chapter is organized as follows: The next section discusses valid asymptotic expansions for distribution functions of sequences of statistics and the corresponding expansions for quantiles of the distributions. Section 3.3 introduces the concept of equivalence classes identified by these asymptotic expansions. Section 3.4 presents Edgeworth expansions and C-F expansions in terms of the statistical moments of the underlying distributions and of the Gaussian distribution function. Conditions for the validity of these expansions are also discussed. Section 3.5 considers application of these expansions to the problem of obtaining approximate parametric signal detection schemes in nearly- Gaussian noise. Section 3.6 discusses briefly estimation problems in the same context. Section 3.7 concludes the chapter.

## 3.2 Valid Asymptotic Expansions

The objective of this section is to discuss asymptotic expansions for the approximations to the distribution or its quantiles of a sequence of statistics. In the theory of statistical inference, the following problem has been extensively studied: Given a sequence of statistics $\{T_i\}$, $i = 1,2,...,M$, consider the evaluation of the distribution function of $T_M$, which is denoted by $F_M$. A standard approach is to consider an asymptotic expansion valid to $r+1$ terms defined as follows:

*Definition 1*: Suppose there exists a sequence of functions $A_0(x), A_1(x),...,A_r(x)$ satisfying the following condition:

$$\left| F_M(x) - \sum_{i=0}^{r} A_i(x) M^{-i/2} \right| = o(M^{-r/2}). \qquad (3.1)$$

Then the series $\sum_{i=0}^{r} A_i(x) M^{-i/2}$ is said to be an asymptotic expansion valid to $r+1$ terms for the distribution function $F_M$. Furthermore, if

$$\sup_{x} \left| F_M(x) - \sum_{i=0}^{r} A_i(x) M^{-r/2} \right| = o(M^{-r/2}), \tag{3.2}$$

then the expansion is said to be uniformly valid to $r+1$ terms.

This definition was first formalized by Wallace [15], who defined the error term to be $O(M^{-r/2})$. The definition used here is in accordance with Erdelyi [16] and Bickel [17]. Note that the basic difference between $o(M^{-r/2})$ and $O(M^{-r/2})$ is on the rate of convergence. The notation $o(M^{-r/2})$ stands for a function which converges to zero faster than $M^{-r/2}$ while $O(M^{-r/2})$ converges to zero no slower than $M^{-r/2}$. Requiring the error term to be $o(M^{-r/2})$ tightens the approximations.

Expansions of the form of (3.1) are, in general, known as Edgeworth expansions. Note that an asymptotic expansion valid to one term is just the ordinary limit theorem. For example, if $r=0$ and $A_0(x)$ is a cumulative normal distribution function, then (3.1) is just the Central Limit Theorem (CLT). This basic approximation can usually be improved significantly by adding one or two terms in the expression. The interests in this chapter are restricted to expansions in terms of known distribution functions and statistical moments of the underlying distribution.

Another type of expansion which is of particular interest here is an expansion of the form $F_M^{-1}$, i.e., an expansion of the quantiles. One of the most commonly used is the Cornish-Fisher expansion [18], which is the counterpart of the Edgeworth expansion. A general form of the C-F expansion for a random variable $X$, in terms of the standard normal variable $Z$, is

$$\text{CF}(X) = \mu_0 + \sigma Z + \frac{\mu_3}{\sigma^2}(Z^2 - 1) + \cdots \tag{3.3}$$

where $\mu_0 = E(X)$, $\sigma^2 = E((X-\mu_0)^2)$ and $\mu_3 = E((X-\mu_0)^3)$. Based on this equation, one can define asymptotic expansions for quantiles (or for test statistics) in accordance with Definition 1.

*Definition 2*: Let $\{T_i, i = 1,2,...,M\}$ be a sequence of statistics. Let $\{Z_i, i = 0,1,2,...,r\}$ be a sequence of random variables. If

$$\left| T_M - \sum_{i=0}^{r} Z_i M^{-i/2} \right| = o(M^{-r/2}) \quad \text{w.p.1} \tag{3.4}$$

holds for $T_M$, then the series $\sum_{i=0}^{r} Z_i M^{-i/2}$ is called an asymptotic expansion valid to $r + 1$ terms for $T_M$.

Suppose that $T_M$ is the normalized sum of a sequence of i.i.d. random variables. If $r = 0$ and $Z_0$ is a normal random variable, then (3.4) is clearly compatible with the CLT. Again, as mentioned previously, adding one or two terms to $Z_0$ can improve the expansion significantly. Typically, it can correct skewness or kurtosis. In this chapter, our interest is mainly restricted to Edgeworth and C-F expansions in which $A_0(x) = \Phi(x)$, the standard normal distribution. In other words, we are primarily concerned with the situations in which the true distribution is "nearly Gaussian".

It is appropriate to remark here that another problem which is related to the study of the statistical approximations and which has been studied extensively is that of obtaining a suitable bound for $\sup_x |F_M(x) - A_0(x)|$. This is equivalent to considering the problem of the rate of convergence in the basic approximation, namely, $A_0(x)$. One such bound is the well-known Berry-Esseen bound [19]. The Berry-Esseen bound is of the order $O(M^{-1/2})$ and is dependent on the first three moments of the underlying distribution, when they exist. Clearly, when more terms are added, such bounds can be improved.

## 3.3 An Equivalence Class

A relation $R$ defined on a set $S$ is said to be an equivalence relation if it is reflexive, symmetric, and transitive [20]. Specifically, $R$ is an equivalence relation if for any element $x$ and $y$ in S, we have

1.   $x \ R \ x$ (reflexivity)

2.   $x \ R \ y \implies y \ R \ x$ (symmetry)

3.   $x \ R \ y$ and $y \ R \ z \implies x \ R \ z$ (transitivity).

Based on an equivalence relation, one can then define an equivalence class as follows:

*Definition 3*: Let $R$ be an equivalence relation defined on a set $S$. Given any element $x \in S$, let $E_x = \{y: yRx\}$. Then $E_x$ is said to be an equivalence class of $S$ under $R$.

It can be seen clearly that if two elements $y$ and $z$ both belong to $E_x$, then $y \ R \ z$, i.e., y is equivalent to $z$ under $R$. Consequently, for any two elements $x$ and $y$ of $S$, $E_x$ and $E_y$ are either identical or disjoint. Thus the set $S$ is the union of disjoint classes under $R$.

As noted previously, knowledge of the first few moments identifies a class of distributions. From (3.2) and (3.4), it can be shown that these two equations both lead to respective equivalence classes. To start with we define a relation, $\overset{r}{=}$, between two sequences of statistics.

*Definition 4*: Let $\{T_i\}$ and $\{T_i'\}$ be two sequences of statistics. Let $F_M(x)$ and $F_M'(x)$ be the distribution functions of $T_M$ and $T_M'$, respectively. Then, given a positive integer $r$,

$$T_i \overset{r}{=} T_i' \text{ if } \sup_x |F_M(x) - F_M'(x)| = o(M^{-r/2}).$$

It is easy to verify that $\overset{r}{=}$ is an equivalence relation. Reflexivity and symmetry are trivial. Let $\{T_i\} \overset{r}{=} \{T_i'\}$ and $\{T_i'\} \overset{r}{=} \{T_i''\}$. Then

$$\sup_x |F_M(x) - F_M'(x)| = o(M^{-r/2})$$

and

$$\sup_x |F_M(x) - F_M''(x)| = o(M^{-r/2}).$$

Thus

$$\sup_x |F_M(x) - F_M''(x)| \leq \sup_x |F_M(x) - F_M'(x)|$$

$$+ \sup_x |F_M'(x) - F_M''(x)| = o(M^{-r/2}).$$

Thus $\{T_i\} \overset{r}{=} \{T_i'\}$ and $\{T_i'\} \overset{r}{=} \{T_i''\}$ implies $\{T_i\} \overset{r}{=} \{T_i''\}$. Hence transitivity holds and $\overset{r}{=}$ is an equivalence relation. It can be clearly seen that if $\{T_i\} \overset{r}{=} \{T_i'\}$ for some $r$, then $\{T_i\} \overset{r'}{=} \{T_i'\}$ for any $r' \le r$. Therefore, the smaller $r$ is, the larger the equivalence class will be. When $r = 0$, this equivalence relation identifies a class which is as large as that obtained from the CLT. This relation also suggests a way to define the term "nearly Gaussian" in a more precise sense. The following Lemma is a straightforward result.

*Lemma 1:* Let $\{T_i\}$ and $\{T_i'\}$ be two sequences of statistics. Suppose that $\{T_i\}$ and $\{T_i'\}$ both have their respective asymptotic expansions uniformly valid to $r+1$ terms, where $r$ is a nonnegative integer. Then $\{T_i\} \overset{r}{=} \{T_i'\}$ if the difference between their respective expansions is $o(M^{-r/2})$.

*Proof:* Let $F_M$ and $F_M'$ be the distribution functions of $T_M$ and $T_M'$, respectively. Let $\sum_{i=0}^{r} A_i(x)M^{-i/2}$ and $\sum_{i=0}^{r} A_i'(x)M^{-i/2}$ be their corresponding uniformly valid asymptotic expansions. Thus

$$\sup_x \left| F_M(x) - \sum_{i=0}^{r} A_i(x)M^{-i/2} \right| = o(M^{-r/2})$$

and

$$\sup_x \left| F_M'(x) - \sum_{i=0}^{r} A_i(x)M^{-i/2} \right| = o(M^{-r/2}).$$

So

$$\sup_x |F_M(x) - F_M'(x)|$$

$$\le \sup_x \left| F_M(x) - \sum_{i=0}^{r} A_i(x)M^{-i/2} \right| + \sup_x \left| F_M'(x) - \sum_{i=0}^{r} A_i'(x)M^{-i/2} \right|$$

$$+ \sup_x \left| \sum_{i=0}^{r} A_i(x)M^{-i/2} - \sum_{i=0}^{r} A_i'(x)M^{-i/2} \right| = o(M^{-r/2})$$

Therefore, $\{T_i\} \overset{r}{=} \{T_i'\}$, and the lemma is established.

From Lemma 1 it is obvious that if two sequences of statistics have the same uniformly valid asymptotic expansion, then they are equivalent under the relation defined in Definition 4. With this equivalence relation, (3.2) thus identifies a class of distributions. Since the true underlying distribution always belongs to this class, (3.2) identifies a nonempty class of distributions. By the same token, one can verify that (3.4) also identifies a nonempty equivalence class under the equivalence relation, Definition 4. In fact, if the sequence of random variables in (3.4) is chosen to be compatible with the sequence of distributions in (3.2), the equivalence classes identified by (3.2) and (3.4) will be identical.

It should be remarked that the statistical moments associated with the corresponding distribution functions in the equivalence class may not be identical. However, they are "equivalent" as their difference is in the order of $o(M^{-r/2})$ or less. Similar arguments can be applied to the cumulants.

### 3.4 Edgeworth Expansions and Cornish-Fisher Expansions

The general form of Edgeworth expansions and Cornish-Fisher expansions have been presented in Section 3.2. In this section these expansions are presented in terms of normal distributions and normal random variables. Thus the resulting expansions are suitable for sequences of statistics which are "nearly Gaussian". Data from many natural environments often exhibit non-but-nearly-Gaussian properties such as skewness, leptokurticity, and platykurticity (see, e.g., [21-25]). In practice, signal processors often side-step the need of considering non-Gaussianness by appealing to the Central Limit Theorem. However, this procedure often leads to erroneous conclusions. Furthermore, as discussed previously, an expansion of one or two more terms will improve the approximation significantly. Most significantly, it may correct the skewness.

Consider a sequence of observations $\{X_i\}$, $i = 1,2,...,M$. Assume that $\{X_i\}$ is an i.i.d. sequence. Let $F_M$ be the distribution function for the normalized statistic,

$$Y_M \triangleq \frac{1}{\sigma M^{1/2}} \sum_{i=1}^{M} (X_i - \mu)$$

where $\mu = E(X_1)$ and $\sigma^2 = E((X_1 - \mu)^2)$. Then the Edgeworth expansion for $F_M$ is given by

$$F_M(x) = \Phi(x) - \lambda_3\frac{\Phi^{(3)}(x)}{\sigma M^{1/2}} + \frac{1}{M}\left[\frac{\lambda_4\Phi^{(4)}(x)}{24} + \frac{\lambda_3^2\Phi^{(6)}(x)}{72} + \cdots \right] \quad (3.5)$$

where $\lambda_i = \kappa_i/\sigma^i$ for $i \geq 3$ and $\kappa_i$ is the $i$th cumulant. Moreover, $\Phi(x)$ is the standard normal distribution and $\Phi^{(r)}(x)$ denotes the $r$th derivative of $\Phi(x)$ with respect to $x$. Cramer [26] showed that the series is a uniformly valid asymptotic expansion provided that one higher cumulant exists than any used in any partial sum, and that the characteristic function $\psi(\omega)$ of $X_1$ exists and satisfies the condition

$$\lim_{|\omega|\to\infty} \sup |\psi(\omega)| < 1. \quad (3.6)$$

The equation (3.6) is satisfied if the distribution of $X_1$ has an absolutely continuous part. Now if the distribution for the sample mean $\overline{X} = \frac{1}{M}\sum_{i=1}^{M} X_i$ is of interest, it can be obtained from (3.5) by a proper transformation.

The C-F expansion for $\overline{X}$, corresponding to (3.5) is

$$\overline{X} = \mu + \frac{\sigma}{M^{1/2}}Z + \frac{\mu_3}{6\sigma^2 M}(Z^2 - 1) + o(M^{-1}). \quad (3.7)$$

It can be shown that (3.7) is an asymptotic expansion valid to three terms for $\overline{X}$, provided that the moments of $X_1$ up to the fourth order exist [7]. This expansion is particularly applicable when approximations to quantiles of a distribution are needed. Typically, one can use the expansion as an approximation to some test statistic, (e.g., $\overline{X}$), in a standard optimal test.

It should be noted that Edgeworth expansions and C-F expansions are known to have some deficiencies which occur in describing the tails of the underlying distribution. The expansions (of finite terms) for $F_M(x)$ may not be valid distribution functions. Specifically, the total probability it ascribes to the range of $X$ may not be equal to 1 and, furthermore, it may have negative values, especially in the tail part. Finally, the monotonicity property may also be violated. Accordingly, the approximations for quantiles (C-F expansions) are not always monotonic in the probability level. Fortunately, when the underlying distribution is nearly Gaussian, these deficiencies are usually not pronounced.

### 3.5 A Signal Detection Problem

#### 3.5.1 Problem Formulation

In this section a binary communication problem of deciding whether or not a signal is present will be considered. This decision will be based on a sequence of observations, which are noise contaminated. The problem can be formulated as a simple binary hypothesis testing problem, namely,

$$H_0: X_i = N_i, \quad i = 1, 2, \ldots, M$$

versus $\qquad\qquad\qquad\qquad\qquad\qquad\qquad\qquad$ (3.8)

$$H_1: X_i = N_i + s, \quad i = 1, 2, \ldots, M.$$

For simplicity it is assumed here that the signal is a positive constant and $\{X_i\}$ is an i.i.d. sequence. Furthermore, the noise is assumed to be nearly Gaussian. The term "nearly-Gaussian" is defined more precisely as follows:

*Definition 5*: Nearly-Gaussian Sequence (NGS): A sequence of random variables is said to be an NGS if its sample mean has an asymptotic expansion valid to three terms as given in (3.7).

As discussed previously, this definition identifies an equivalence class of noise distributions which includes skewed distributions. As a matter of fact, the approach to be discussed in the next section is particularly appealing when skewed noise is encountered.

One classical way to solve the problem (3.8) is to consider parameteric schemes. In other words, assume that the statistical distributions of the observation sequence can be characterized by a finite set of parameters. A typical example is the optimal N-P detector. However, implementation of parametric schemes requires a rather complete knowledge of the underlying process. This knowledge is, in general, hard to obtain or to verify its accuracy. For example, the p.d.f.'s under both hypotheses are supposed to be known in order to implement the N-P optimal detector. This, in turn, implies a potential sensitivity to the accuracy of the presumed model. Another difficulty is that when the underlying process is non-Gaussian, implementation and analysis of the N-P optimal detector will become very complicated.

The purpose of this chapter is to use methods of series expansions to circumvent these difficulties. The goal is to design approximately optimal parametric schemes such that:

1.  The information required to implement the resulting scheme is relatively easy to obtain and its accuracy can be justified easily.

2.  The performance is insensitive to small model deviations, and it should be asymptotically optimal in a class of noise distributions and optimal at the presumed model.

The approach used here is to employ the asymptotic expansions discussed in the preceding section. Note that this approach requires knowledge of statistical moments (or cumulants) of the underlying process. In general, as compared to the p.d.f., statistical moments are easier to obtain with better accuracy. Furthermore, use of moment information only allows the applicability of the resulting scheme to a broad class of noise distributions.

### 3.5.2 The Cornish-Fisher Expansion and Signal Detection

This section considers an example of employing the C-F expansion to resolve the signal detection problem (3.8) in nearly Gaussian skewed noise. It is well known that when the noise is Gaussian, the N-P optimal test statistic is given by

$$T(X) = \sum_{i=1}^{M} X_i.$$

One can see that this test statistic can be normalized by the sample size M without affecting the detector performance, provided that the threshold is adjusted correspondingly. Hence the test statistic to be considered here is the sample mean of the observation sequence, namely,

$$T_n(X) = \frac{1}{M} \sum_{i=1}^{M} X_i. \tag{3.9}$$

To obtain better approximations, the asymptotic C-F expansion is used and hence $T_n(X)$ is appropriate. As discusssed in [6], the detectors using $T_n(X)$, or equivalently $T(X)$, as the test statistic are sensitive to noise skewness. It was shown that the false-alarm rate and the probability of error both increase when the noise skewness increases, while the probability of detection is relatively unchanged.

Consider the C-F expansion for $T_n(X)$, as in (3.7), with the assumption that $\{X_i\}$ is an i.i.d. sequence and $E\{X_1|H_0\} = 0$:

$$T_n(X) = \frac{\sigma}{M^{1/2}} Z + \frac{\mu_3}{6\sigma^2 M}(Z^2 - 1) + o(M^{-1}) \qquad \text{w.p.1.} \tag{3.10}$$

Let $\xi = \mu_3/\sigma^3$ be the skewness measure for the distribution of $X_1$. The equation (3.10) can thus be written as

$$T_n(X) = \frac{\sigma}{M^{1/2}} Z + \frac{\xi\sigma}{6M}(Z^2 - 1) + o(M^{-1}) \qquad \text{w.p.1.} \tag{3.11}$$

If the distribution of $X_1$ is symmetric (with respect to its mean), then $\xi = 0$. This expansion is thus in accordance with the CLT. Nevertheless, the remainder term is $o(M^{-1})$, rather than $o(M^{-1/2})$. On the other hand, if $\xi \neq 0$, the expansion of (3.10) will provide a more accurate approximation for $T_n(X)$. As a matter of fact, it can be shown that the skewness measure of $T_n(X)$, $\xi_n$, is given by

$$\xi_n = \frac{\mu_3}{M^{1/2}\sigma^3} = O(M^{-1/2}).$$

Thus it is clear that the detector performance is affected by noise skewness.

Detection of signals in skewed noise has not been discussed extensively in the literature. Kassam *et al.* [27] considered a mixture noise model which allows an arbitrary tail behavior but requires a symmetric contaminated-nominal central part. Dwyer [28] addressed the problem of extracting signals from under-ice noise, which has an asymmetric distribution. However, in the context of the theory of statistical inference, there has been some work on studying the effects of population skewness on hypothesis testings or estimation. Among many others, Johnson [29] investigated the effect of population skewness on the $t$-variable and proposed a procedure to reduce this effect. Carrol [30] examined the effect of skewness of error on estimating location and intercept in regression problems.

One of the major difficulties in studying signal detection in skewed noise is that, in general, a skewness measure does not appear explicitly in standard test statistics. The advantage of employing asymptotic expansions for the test statistic, in terms of its moments (or cumulants), is that the test statistic is expressed explicitly as a function of skewness measure with a good approximation, provided that the sample size is sufficiently large, as shown in (3.11).

In order to eliminate the skewness effect, an obvious way is to obtain a test statistic that is independent (or asymptotically independent) of the skewness measure. Observing (3.11), one can see that this can be achieved by eliminating the terms which involve the skewness measure in the expansion. Keeping in mind that simple test statistics are of particular interest, we consider the following test statistic:

$$T_m(X) = c + T_n(X) + \rho T_n^2(X). \qquad (3.12)$$

Substituting (3.11) into (3.12) yields

$$T(X) = c + \frac{\sigma}{M^{1/2}}Z + \frac{\xi\sigma}{6M}(Z^2 - 1) + \frac{\rho\sigma^2}{M}Z^2 + o(M^{-1}) \qquad \text{w.p.1.}$$

The constants c and $\rho$ should be chosen such that the terms involving $\xi$ can be eliminated. Thus

$$\rho = -\xi/6\sigma \quad \text{and} \quad c = \xi\sigma/6M. \qquad (3.13)$$

The test statistic $T_m(X)$ now becomes

$$T_m(X) = \frac{\sigma}{M^{1/2}}Z + o(M^{-1}) \qquad \text{w.p.1} \qquad (3.14)$$

which is asymptotically Gaussian.

The resulting test statistic now is asymptotically independent of the skewness measure. Notice that, although the constants $c$ and $\rho$ are dependent on $\xi$, the effects of skewness essentially vanish due to adequate choices of $c$ and $\rho$. The optimality of $T_m(X)$ can now be stated formally in the following theorem.

*Theorem 1:* The statistic given in (3.12) with coefficients identified by (3.13) is "equivalent" to the N-P optimal test statistic for the class of noise distributions defined by Definition 5.

Theorem 1 can be proved straightforwardly with Lemma 1 along with Definition 5. The fundamental concept here is that of the equivalence class described in Section 3.3. Notice that, when the underlying noise is truly Gaussian, the test statistic $T_m(X)$ is identical to $T_n(X)$, the N-P optimal statistic.

To further verify the optimality of the modified detector, a numerical example is given here. Monte Carlo simulation is performed to evaluate its false-alarm rate, and to compare with the sample-mean detector. The noise model used here is a Gaussian model perturbed by a nonzero skewness. The skewness measure ranges from zero to one.

The results are shown in Figures 3.1 and 3.2. Note that the false alarm rate of the sample mean detector increases as the skewness measure increases. On the other hand, the false-alarm rate of the modified scheme stays roughly unchanged, an indication of its insensitivity to noise skewness. Figure 3.3 shows the p.d.f. of the skewed noise (with $\xi = 0.925$) as well as that of the Gaussian noise. Although the difference between these two p.d.f.'s is hardly distinguishable from the figure, the difference in their false-alarm rate is clear. From Figure 3.1, the false-alarm rate of the sample mean detector increased 50% at $\xi = 0.925$. In Figure 3.2, one can see that it increased more than 200%. These results show the necessity of taking into account the noise skewness in studying signal detection problems.

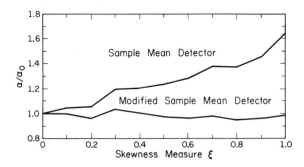

*Figure 3.1\** *Comparison of the sample-mean detector and the modified sample-mean detector using Monte Carlo simulation.* [$\alpha/\alpha_0$ *is the rate of change of false-alarm probability,* $\alpha_0$ *is. the false-alarm probability of the sample-mean detector in Gaussian noise,* $\alpha_0 = 10^{-3}$, $\xi$ *is the skewness measure* ($\xi = \mu_3/\sigma^3$) *and the number of runs is* $10^6$.]

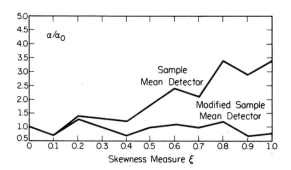

*Figure 3.2 A comparison of the sample-mean detector and the modified sample-mean detector using Monte-Carlo simulation (same as Fig. 3.1 except that* $\alpha_0 = 10^{-4}$).

---

\*(From the *J. Acoust. Soc. Amer.*, Vol. 69, 1983 [7])

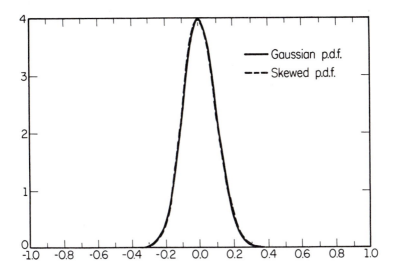

*Figure 3.3 Comparison of the Gaussian p.d.f. and the skewed p.d.f. Skewness measure $\xi$ = 0.925. ( -------, Gaussian p.d.f.; ......., skewed p.d.f.)*

### 3.5.3 Edgeworth Expansions and Signal Detection

In many practical situations, the noise p.d.f. is not known completely. In other cases, the knowledge of the p.d.f. is not well justified. One often has to estimate some unknown parameters of the p.d.f. in order to implement signal detection and estimation schemes. Thus the p.d.f.'s used in the design, analysis, and implementation of detection and estimation schemes are only approximations to the real ones. In this section, Edgeworth expansions will be employed to obtain approximations to the noise p.d.f. Optimal detection schemes will then be derived based on these approximations.

Consider the detection problem defined in Section 3.6. Let $f_0(x_i)$ and $f_1(x_i)$ be the p.d.f. of $X_i$ under $H_0$ and $H_1$, respectively. It is assumed here that the first six moments of the underlying noise p.d.f. are known. The first step here is to obtain Edgeworth expansions to represent $f_0(x_i)$ and $f_1(x_i)$, respectively. Since nearly-Gaussian noise is considered, these expansions are given in terms of the Gaussian density function and the Hermite polynomials

$$f_j(x_i) = a_j(x_i)[1 + c_3 H_3(x_i) + c_4 H_4(x_i) + c_6 H_6(x_i) + \cdots ] \quad (3.15)$$

where

$$a_j(x_i) = \frac{1}{\sqrt{2\pi}\sigma} \exp\left[-\frac{1}{2\sigma^2}(x_i - \mu_j)^2\right], \quad j = 0,1$$

and $H_r(x_i)$ are the Hermite polynomials. It is clear that $\mu_0 = 0$ and $\mu_1 = s$. The Hermite polynomials are orthogonal polynomials and are derived from the Gaussian density functions, namely

$$H_r(x) = (-\sigma)^r e^{(x-\mu)^2/2\sigma^2} \frac{d^r}{dx^r}\left[e^{-(x-\mu)^2/2\sigma^2}\right]. \quad (3.16)$$

Thus

$$H_0(x) = 1$$

$$H_1(x) = \frac{x - \mu}{\sigma}$$

$$H_2(x) = \frac{(x - \mu)^2}{\sigma^2} - 1$$

$$H_3(x) = \frac{(x - \mu)^3}{\sigma^3} - 3\frac{x - \mu}{\sigma}$$

.
.
.

etc.

The rate of convergence of the series in (3.15) depends on the smoothness and integrability properties of $f(x)$ [31]. Other properties of this expansion are discussed in more detail in [32]. The coefficients $c_r$ in (3.15) are given by

$$c_r = \frac{1}{r!} \int_{-\infty}^{\infty} f(x) H_r(x) \, dx \qquad (3.17)$$

and are clearly functions of the moments (or cumulants).

Applying (3.15) to form the likelihood ratio yields

$$L(x) = \prod_{i=1}^{M} \frac{f_1(x_i)}{f_0(x_i)}$$

$$= e^{Ms^2/2\sigma^2} \prod_{i=1}^{M} e^{x_i s/\sigma^2} \frac{1 + c_3 H_3(x_i-s) + c_4 H_4(x_i-s) + c_6 H_6(x_i-s)}{1 + c_3 H_3(x_i) + c_4 H_4(x_i) + c_6 H_6(x_i)}$$

where $H_r(x_i)$, $r = 0,3,4,6$, can be obtained from (3.16) with $\mu = 0$. The log-likelihood ratio is

$$\gamma(x) = \ln L(x)$$

$$= -\frac{Ms^2}{2\sigma^2} + \frac{s}{\sigma^2} \sum_{i=1}^{M} x_i$$

$$+ \sum_{i=1}^{M} \ln \frac{1 + c_3 H_3(x_i-s) + c_4 H_4(x_i-s) + c_6 H_6(x_i-s)}{1 + c_3 H_3(x_i) + c_4 H_4(x_i) + c_6 H_6(x_i)}. \qquad (3.18)$$

The coefficients $c_r$ are obtained from (3.17) with $f(x) = f_0(x)$. This is clearly the well-known linear detector with an additive nonlinearity [4]. By adjusting the threshold appropriately, one can rewrite (3.18) as

$$\gamma_1(x) = \sum_{i=1}^{M} x_i + NL_1(x_i,s) \qquad (3.19)$$

where

$$NL_1(x_i,s) = \frac{\sigma^2}{s} \ln \left[ \frac{1 + c_3 H_3(x_i-s) + c_4 H_4(x_i-s) + c_6 H_6(x_i-s)}{1 + c_3 H_3(x_i) + c_4 H_4(x_i) + c_6 H_6(x_i)} \right].$$

It is seen that the resulting detector is simply a modified linear detector. The nonlinear term is clearly due to deviation from the Gaussian model. When the noise is truly Gaussian, the nonlinear term will vanish. Note that this scheme is derived merely from the knowledge of the first few moments of the noise together with the assumption that it is nearly Gaussian. Implementation of this scheme is less complicated than the conventional N-P optimal detector because the required knowledge is simply the first few moments, which are easier to obtain and can be better justified as compared to the p.d.f. Furthermore, when the noise statistics change, the corresponding moments can be adjusted relatively quickly (adaptive schemes).

To evaluate the performance of the modified detector, one may consider the Chernoff bound on the error probabilities. In [4], the bound was evaluated for several communication systems such as ASK, FSK, and PSK. Another approach is to consider the asymptotic relative efficiency (ARE). Huang [33] derived a locally optimal detector based on the use of the Edgeworth series to represent the noise p.d.f. The resulting detector has the folowing test statistic

$$\gamma_2(x) = \sum_{i=1}^{M} (x_i + NL_2(x_i)) \tag{3.20}$$

where

$$NL_2(x_i) = \frac{4c_4 H_3(x_i) + 6c_6 H_6(x_i)}{1 + c_4 H_4(x_i) + c_6 H_6(x_i)}.$$

This is also a simple modified linear detector with the nonlinearity resulting from non-Gaussianness. It was found that the ARE, when compared to the linear detector, is inversely proportional to $Var\ [\gamma_2(x)|H_0]$.

## 3.6 Series Expansions in Estimation

This section discusses applications of series expansions to the study of signal estimation. The objective here is only to give a brief overview of the existing literature, rather than to address the problem in detail. In general, this problem can be cast as a parameter estimation problem in the theory of statistical inference. Specifically, let $\{P_\theta : \theta \in \Theta\}$, $\Theta \subset R$, be a parameterized family of distributions. The problem is to estimate the parameter vector $\theta = (\theta_1, \theta_2, ..., \theta_p)$ based on the received samples. Since the parameter $\theta$ characterizes the signal, estimating $\theta$ is equivalent to estimating the signal characteristics.

A canonical parameteric approach to this problem is the maximum likelihood estimation. Let $p(x; \theta)$ be a p.d.f. of $P_\theta$ for a given $\theta$. The method of maximum likelihood is to obtain an estimate $\hat{\theta}(x) \in \Theta$ which maximizes $p(x; \theta)$. In other words, $\hat{\theta}(x)$ is the vector in $\Theta$ which is "most likely" to have produced the received samples. Nevertheless, the maximum-likelihood estimate (MLE) may not exist. Furthermore, if the MLE does exist, it may not be unique. However, the MLE frequently provides consistent estimation. Another feature of the MLE is that it is invariant under functional transformations. In particular, if $\hat{\theta}(x)$ is an MLE of $\theta$, then $f(\hat{\theta}(x))$ is an MLE for $f(\theta)$, for any function $f$.

It can be seen that the methodologies described in the preceding section can be applied in parallel here. One can either obtain expansions for some standard statistics occurring in the procedure of MLE or derive the MLE based on expansions of the underlying p.d.f. It should be remarked that this problem has been studied by many statisticians. Among others, Linnik and Mitrofanova [34] obtained asymptotic expansions for the distribution of the MLE. Mitrofanova [35] later extended the results for vector parameters. A good overview on this subject is given by Pfanzagl [36]. Furthermore, Skovgaard [37] discussed the method of computing the Edgeworth expansions of the distributions of MLE in the non-i.i.d. errors case.

### 3.7 Conclusion

Applications of series expansions to study signal detection and estimation have been discussed in this chapter. In particular, Edgeworth expansions and the related expansions such as C-F expansions are considered. These expansions are used to derive signal detection and estimation schemes. The main feature of this methodology is that the resulting schemes are applicable to a class of input models, as opposed to a particular one. Furthermore, the required knowledge is merely the first few moments of the underlying noise distribution. This is a more realistic requirement than knowledge of the p.d.f.

Two approaches have been considered. One is to obtain expansions for some statistic and the other is to use expansions to represent the noise p.d.f.

Under the nearly Gaussian assumption, these two approaches both lead to simple modified schemes. It has been shown that the resulting schemes are less sensitive to model deviations, than are the corresponding optimal schemes. These approaches can be extended to studying detection of random signals and estimation of their parameters.

## References

[1] J.I. Marcum, A statistical theory of target detection by pulsed radar, *IRE Trans. Inform. Theory*, Vol. IT-6, pp. 59-267, 1960.

[2] P. Swerling, Probability of detection for fluctuating targets, *IRE Trans. Inform. Theory*, Vol. IT-6, pp. 269-308, 1960.

[3] S.C. Schwartz, A series technique for the optimum detection of stochastic signals in noise, *IEEE Trans. Inform. Theory*, Vol. IT-15, pp. 362-369, 1969.

[4] A. Bodharamik *et al.*, Optimal detection and signal design for channels with non- but near-Gaussian additive noise, *IEEE Trans. Comm.*, Vol. COM-20, pp. 1087-1096, 1972.

[5] L.F. Eastwood and R. Lugannani, Approximate likelihood ratio detectors for linear processes, *IEEE Trans. Inform. Theory*, Vol. IT-23, pp. 482-489, 1977.

[6] Y.F. Huang and J.B. Thomas, Sensitivity of some optimal detectors to noise skewness, *Proc. of the 1982 Intl. Conf. Comm.*, pp. 2H.1.1-2H.1.5, 1982.

[7] Y.F. Huang and J.B. Thomas, Signal detection in nearly-Gaussian skewed noise, *J. Acoust. Soc. Amer.*, Vol. 74, pp. 1399-1405, 1983.

[8] D. Middleton, Man-made noise in urban environments and transportation systems: Models and measurements, *IEEE Trans. Comm.*, Vol. COM-21, pp. 1232-1241, 1973.

[9] R.S. Freedman, On Gram-Charlier approximations, *IEEE Trans. Comm.*, Vol. COM-29, pp. 122-125, 1981.

[10] J.B. Thomas, Nonparametric detection, *Proc. IEEE*, Vol. 58, pp. 623-

631, 1970.

[11] V.G.Hansen, Detection performance of some nonparametric rank tests and an application to radar, *IEEE Trans. Inform. Theory*, Vol. IT-16, pp. 309-318, 1970.

[12] P.J. Huber, Robust estimation of a location parameter, *Ann. Math. Statist.*, Vol. 35, pp. 73-101, 1964.

[13] P.J. Huber, A robust version of the probability ratio test, *Ann. Math. Statist.*, Vol. 36, pp. 1753-1758, 1965.

[14] A.H. El-Sawy and V.D. Vandelinde, Robust sequential detection of signals in noise, *IEEE Trans. Inform. Theory*, Vol. IT-25, pp. 346-353, 1979.

[15] D.L. Wallace, Asymptotic approximation to distributions, *Ann. Math. Statist.*, Vol. 29, pp. 635-654, 1958.

[16] A. Erdelyi, *Asymptotic Expansions*, New York, NY: Dover, 1956.

[17] P.J. Bickel, Edgeworth expansions in nonparametric statistics, *Ann. Math. Statist.*, Vol. 2, pp. 1-20, 1974.

[18] E.A. Cornish and R.A. Fisher, Moments and cumulants in the specification of distributions, Paper 30 in R.A. Fisher, *Contributions to Mathematical Statistics*, New York, NY: Wiley, 1950.

[19] W. Feller, *An Introduction to Probability Theory and Its Applications*, Vol. II, 2nd ed., New York, NY: Wiley, 1971.

[20] H.L. Royden, *Real Analysis*, 2nd ed., New York, NY: The Macmillan Co., 1972.

[21] A.R. Milne and J.H. Ganton, Ambient noise under Arctic sea ice, *J. Acoust. Soc. Amer.*, Vol. 36, pp. 855-863, 1964.

[22] R.F. Dwyer, FRAM II single channel ambient noise statistics, *101st Meeting of Acoust. Soc. Amer.*, May, 1981.

[23] M.E. Frazer, Some statistical properties of lake surface reverberation, *J. Acoust. Soc. Amer.*, Vol. 64, pp. 858-868, 1978.

[24] G.R. Wilson and D.R. Powell, Experimental and modeled density estimates of underwater acoustic returns, *Signal Processing in the Ocean*

*Environment Workshop*, Maryland, May, 1982.

[25] F.W. Machell and C.S. Penrod, Probability density functions of ocean acoustic noise processes, *Proc. of the Office of Naval Research Workshop on Signal Processing,* 1982.

[26] H. Cramer, *Mathematical Methods of Statistics,* Princeton, NJ: Princeton University Press, 1946.

[27] S.A. Kassam, G. Moustakides and J.G. Shin, Robust detection of known signals in asymmetric noise, *IEEE Trans. Inform. Theory,* Vol. IT-28, pp. 84-91, 1982.

[28] R.F. Dwyer, A technique for improving detection and estimation of signals contaminated by under-ice noise, Naval Underwater Systems Center, Tech. Document 6717, July, 1982.

[29] N.J. Johnson, Modified T-test and confidence intervals for asymmetrical populations, *JASA,* Vol. 73, pp. 536-544, 1978.

[30] R.J. Carroll, On estimating variances of robust estimators when the errors are asymmetric, *JASA,* Vol. 74, pp. 674-679, 1979.

[31] S.C Schwartz, Estimation of probability density by an orthogonal series, *Ann. Math. Statist.,* Vol. 38, pp. 1261-1265, 1967.

[32] M. Kendall and A. Stuart, *The Advanced Theory of Statistics,* Vol. 1, 4th ed., New York, NY: Macmillan, 1977.

[33] Y.F. Huang, On series expansions and signal detection, *Proc. 17th Annual Conf. Inform. Sci. and Sys.,* Johns Hopkins University, pp. 534-538, 1983.

[34] Y. V. Linnik and N.M. Mitrofanova, Some asymptotic expansions for the distribution of the maximum likelihood estimate, *Sankhya Ser. A,* Vol. 27, pp. 73-82, 1965.

[35] N.M. Mitrofanova, An asymptotic expansion for the maximum likelihood estimate of vector parameters, *Theor. Prob. Appl.,* Vol. 12, pp. 364-372, 1967.

[36] J. Pfanzagl, Asymptotic expansions in parametric statistical theory, Chapter 1 in *Developments in Statistics,* Vol. 3, (P.R. Krishnaiah, Ed.),

New York, NY: Academic Press, 1980.

[37]  I.M. Skovgaard, Transformations of an Edgeworth expansion by a sequence of smooth functions, *Scand. J. Statist.*, Vol. 8, pp. 207-217, 1981.

# 4

# Optimum Data Quantization in Signal Detection

**Saleem A. Kassam**

*Department of Electrical Engineering*
*University of Pennsylvania*
*Philadephia, Pennsylvania*

## 4.1 Introduction

The need to use quantized data in signal detection can arise in many situations. If remotely acquired data is to be transmitted to a central processing facility, for example, data rate reduction may be highly desirable or necessary. Similarly, storage of data for off-line processing may also require quantization into a relatively small number of levels, especially if one is dealing with a large volume of data. The use of quantized data often results in more robust

This work was supported by the Air Force Office of Scientific Research under Grant AFOSR 82-0022.

systems which are not very sensitive in their performance to deviations of the actual noise density functions from those assumed in their design. Finally, the use of quantized data can allow simple adaptive schemes to be implemented to allow the system to retain good detection performance even when the noise characteristics can vary considerably over time.

The problem of optimum approximation of analog data using a multilevel or digital representation with a finite number of bits per analog sample is an old problem with well-known solutions. Classic among these is the solution of Max [1], which gives the optimum quantizer minimizing the *mean squared error* (MSE) between the analog sample and its quantized version. If $Y$ is an analog quantity whose observed value is governed by some probability density function (p.d.f.) $f_Y$, Max's solution allows us to obtain the optimum $M$-level quantizer $q$ which minimizes the MSE $e(q;f_Y) = E\{[Y - q(Y)]^2\}$. Let $l_j$ be the output level of the quantizer $q$ when the input is in the interval $(t_{j-1}, t_j]$. For $M$-level quantization we have $t_M = \infty$; we always set $t_0 = -\infty$. The necessary conditions on the levels $l_j$ and breakpoints $t_j$ for $q$ to minimize $e(q;f_Y)$ are obtained by differentiation, and are

$$t_j = \frac{l_j + l_{j+1}}{2}, \quad j = 1, 2, \ldots, M-1 \tag{4.1}$$

and

$$l_j = \frac{\int_{t_{j-1}}^{t_j} y f_Y(y) \, dy}{F_Y(t_j) - F_Y(t_{j-1})}, \quad j = 1, 2, \ldots, M \tag{4.2}$$

where $F_Y$ is the cumulative distribution function (c.d.f.) of $Y$. Equations (4.1) and (4.2) must be solved simultaneously, which can be accomplished using iterative techniques, to obtain a minimum MSE quantizer (assuming that $f_Y$ is sufficiently regular so that the necessary conditions are also sufficient for local minimization).

In the detection context it is not at all clear how we can use a *distortion* criterion such as the MSE as a basis for optimum quantizer design. To begin with, the probability density function of an observation $X_i$ depends on whether the null or the alternative hypothesis is true. Since our objective is to use the quantized data in a signal detector, the quantizer should be chosen to extract information most relevant in the detection problem. It is therefore more appropriate to use as a quantization performance criterion some measure of the *detection* performance obtained with the quantized data, and to design optimum systems based on such a criterion.

For this purpose we will assume as our basic structure the system of Figure 4.1, in which instantaneously quantized data $q(X_i)$ are used to form a detection test statistic. If the quantizer $q$ is an $M$-interval quantizer, it is determined by its breakpoints $t_j$ and output levels $l_j$. In an actual system the quantizer may, for example, be located at the point of data acquisition and the detector may be physically removed from it. The quantized data may then be transmitted over a communication link as a sequence of binary digits, and the output levels $l_j$ would be reconstructed at the detector. The communication link may contain or be completely replaced by digital storage. From this we see that in general the essential quantization operation is that of *data reduction*, which corresponds to the assignment of the input $X_i$ to one of the $M$ intervals $(t_{j-1}, t_j]$ of the input partitioning determined by the quantizer breakpoints. The detector, presented with such reduced data, may implicitly reconstruct output levels $l_j$ for the reduced observations and use them in computing a test statistic. This was the assumption made in starting with the structure of Figure 4.1.

There are some quite specific assumptions that we will proceed under throughout this chapter. One of these is that all data on which our detectors operate are obtained as *discrete* sequences of observation components, as opposed to being continuous-time waveforms. To obtain explicit, useful, and canonical results, we shall need the more stringent assumption that the discrete-time additive noise observation components are *independent* random variables. This usually requires that the noise process be "white" relative to the signal process. There do exist many applications where this assumption is at least approximately true; for example, the matched filtered outputs in a pulse train detection problem may often be taken to satisfy this requirement of independence. With the same objective of obtaining explicit, useful, and

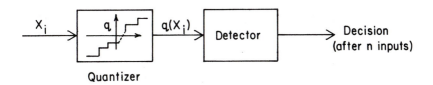

Quantizer

*Figure 4.1 Structure of a quantizer-detector.*

canonical results, we shall concentrate on *locally optimum* and *asymptotically optimum* detection schemes. The criteria of local and asymptotic optimality are appropriate when the signal to be detected is weak; one can argue that this is indeed the appropriate situation to consider, since strong signals can be detected by any reasonable ad hoc system.

We shall in this chapter consider three major types of signal detection problems, which between them allow formulation of a wide range of detection problems arising in applications. Our focus will be on the detection of a *completely known low-pass deterministic signal* in additive noise. For this problem we may describe our observation vector $\underline{X} = (X_1, X_2, \ldots, X_n)$ of real-valued components $X_i$ by

$$X_i = \theta s_i + W_i, \quad i = 1, 2, \ldots, n. \tag{4.3}$$

Here the $W_i$ are random noise components and the $s_i$ are the known values of the signal components. The signal amplitude $\theta$ is either zero (the observations contain no signal) or positive, and the requirement is to decide on the basis of $\underline{X}$ whether we have $\theta = 0$ or whether we have $\theta > 0$. With $f$ the specified common univariate p.d.f. of the i.i.d. noise components $W_i$, our detection problem is that of choosing between a null hypothesis $H_1$ and an alternative hypothesis $K_1$ on the joint p.d.f. $f_{\underline{X}}$ of the observation components $X_i$, $i = 1, 2, \ldots, n$, stated as

$$H_1 : \quad f_{\underline{X}}(\underline{x}) = \prod_{i=1}^{n} f(x_i) \tag{4.4}$$

$$K_1 : \quad f_{\underline{X}}(\underline{x}) = \prod_{i=1}^{n} f(x_i - \theta s_i) \tag{4.5}$$

with $\underline{s}$ specified and any $\theta > 0$. Here $\underline{s} = (s_1, s_2, \ldots, s_n)$ is the vector of signal components.

We shall also briefly discuss the detection of completely known *narrowband* deterministic signals in additive *narrowband* noise as a variant of the above formulation. In addition we will summarize results, corresponding to those on completely known deterministic signal detection, for detection of *random-phase deterministic narrowband signals* in additive noise, and for detection of *random nondeterministic signals* in additive noise. The formulation of these problems as statistical hypothesis-testing problems similar to the one above for the completely known deterministic low-pass signal detection problem will be given in Sections 4.4 and 4.5.

## 4.2 Preliminaries

As has been stated in Section 4.1, we will be concerned with the derivation of locally optimum and asymptotically optimum quantized-data detection systems. To explain the relationship between locally optimum and asymptotically optimum detectors we will here focus on the known-signal detection problem of testing $H_1$ versus $K_1$ for the joint p.d.f. of $\underline{X}$.

### 4.2.1 Local Optimality

A *locally optimum* (LO) or locally most powerful detector for testing $H_1$ versus $K_1$ is one which maximizes the *slope* of the detector power function at the *origin* ($\theta = 0$), from amongst the class of all detectors which have its false alarm probability. Let $D_\alpha$ be the class of all detectors of size $\alpha$ for $H_1$ vs $K_1$. Formally, an LO detector $D_{LO}$ of size $\alpha$ is a detector in $D_\alpha$ which satisfies

$$\max_{D \in D_\alpha} \frac{d}{d\theta} p_d(\theta|D)|_{\theta=0} = \frac{d}{d\theta} p_d(\theta|D_{LO})|_{\theta=0} \qquad (4.6)$$

where the power function is

$$p_d(\theta|D) = P\{D \text{ accepts } K_1 \mid \theta \text{ is the signal amplitude}\}. \qquad (4.7)$$

Under appropriate regularity conditions on the noise marginal p.d.f. $f$ (its absolute continuity, and integrability of its derivative $f'$), the generalized Neyman-Pearson lemma can be applied [2] to obtain the test statistic of the LO detector for $H_1$ vs $K_1$. This is well known to be

$$\lambda_{LO}(\underline{X}) = \sum_{i=1}^{n} s_i g_{LO}(X_i) \qquad (4.8)$$

where $g_{LO}$ is the LO function

$$g_{LO}(x) = \frac{-f'(x)}{f(x)}. \qquad (4.9)$$

This LO test statistic is a special case of the *generalized correlator* (GC) test statistic

$$T_{GC}(\underline{X}) = \sum_{i=1}^{n} a_i g(X_i) \qquad (4.10)$$

in which a set of constants $a_i$ is correlated with a set of transformed data $g(X_i)$.

### 4.2.2 Asymptotic Optimality

In the case of non-Gaussian noise an LO detector will generally not be a uniformly most powerful (UMP) detector. For some *particular* value $\theta_0 > 0$ for $\theta$ we can find the *optimum* (Neyman-Pearson) detector $D_{NP}$ of size $\alpha$; let its power function be explicitly written as $p_d(\theta|\theta_0, D_{NP})$. Then in general we will have

$$p_d(\theta_0|D_{LO}) < p_d(\theta_0|\theta_0, D_{NP}) \qquad (4.11)$$

for $0 < \alpha < 1$, and this will be true for $\theta_0$ arbitrarily small.

Let us call the function of $\theta_0$ on the right-hand side of (4.11) the *envelope power function*, which is therefore the function $p_d(\theta|E)$ defined by

$$p_d(\theta|E) = p_d(\theta|\theta,D_{NP}).$$  (4.12)

The envelope power function now becomes the standard against which the performances of other detectors are compared. In using an LO detector we can be assured only that $p_d'(0|D)$ is maximized. In justifying the use of an LO detector we have mentioned that the case of weak signals implied by the condition $\theta\to 0$ is an important case in practical applications. On the other hand, note that for any *fixed* sample size $n$, the power or detection probability approaches the value $\alpha$ (the false-alarm probability) for $\theta\to 0$. Thus while the condition $\theta\to 0$ is of considerable interest, it is generally used *in conjunction with* an assumption that $n\to\infty$. We will now consider the combined asymptotic assumption $\theta\to 0$ and $n\to\infty$, and explain that in general the LO detector has an optimality property for this asymptotic case.

Consider a *sequence* of hypothesis testing problems,

$$\{H_{1n} \text{ versus } K_{1n}, \ n = 1,2,\dots\},$$

where $H_{1n}$ is simply an explication of the fact that $H_1$ of (4.4) is applicable for the case of $n$ independent observations governed by the noise p.d.f. The sequence of alternatives $\{K_{1n}, \ n = 1,2,\dots\}$ is described by

$$K_{1n} : f_{\underline{X}}(\underline{x}) = \prod_{i=1}^{n} f(x_i - \theta_n s_i), \quad n = 1,2,\dots, \quad \theta_n > 0, \ \theta_n\to 0.$$  (4.13)

We shall be interested in particular types of sequences $\{\theta_n, \ n = 1,2,\dots\}$ converging to zero. For example, we could have $\theta_n = \gamma/\sqrt{n}$ for some fixed $\gamma > 0$, so that $n\theta_n^2$ remains fixed at $\gamma^2$ as $n\to\infty$. In the *constant signal case* ($s_i = 1$, all $n$) this models a sequence of detection problems with increasing sample sizes and decreasing signal amplitudes in such a way that the *total signal energy* $\theta_n^2 \sum_{i=1}^{n} s_i^2 = n\theta_n^2$ remains fixed. In the time-varying signal case, the condition that $\dfrac{1}{n} \sum_{i=1}^{n} s_i^2$ converges (without loss of generality, to unity) as $n\to\infty$ allows a similar interpretation to be made in the asymptotic case $n\to\infty$.

The idea of considering formally a *sequence* of hypothesis-testing problems $\{H_{1n}$ *versus* $K_{1n}, n = 1,2,... \}$ is the following: if we can find a corresponding *sequence* $\{D_n, n = 1,2,... \}$ of detectors which in the limit $n \to \infty$ has some optimality property, then for sufficiently large finite $n$ the use of $D_n$ will give approximately optimum performance. We will say that a sequence of detectors $\{D_{AO,n}, n = 1,2,... \}$ is *asymptotically optimum* (AO) at level $\alpha$ for $\{H_{1n}$ *versus* $K_{1n}, n = 1,2,... \}$ if

$$(1) \quad \lim_{n \to \infty} E\{\delta_{AO,n}(\underline{X})|H_{1n}\} = \lim_{n \to \infty} p_d(0|D_{AO,n}) \le \alpha \quad (4.14)$$

and

$$(2) \quad \lim_{n \to \infty} [p_d(\theta_n|E_n) - p_d(\theta_n|D_{AO,n})] = 0. \quad (4.15)$$

Here $\delta_{AO,n}(\underline{X})$ is the test function for the detector $D_{AO,n}$; thus $\delta_{AO,n}(\underline{X}) = P\{D_{AO,n}$ accepts $K_{1n}$ when $\underline{X}$ is observed$\}$. Note that we have used $E_n$ instead of $E$ in the envelope power function, to show dependence on $n$.

Condition (1) above will obviously be satisfied if each detector $D_{AO,n}$ in the sequence is a size-$\alpha$ detector. According to condition (2), an AO sequence of detectors has a sequence of power values, for the alternatives $K_{1n}$ defined by the $\theta_n$, which is in the *limit as* $n \to \infty$ equal to the power of the optimum detector. If $\{\theta_n, n = 1,2,... \}$ defines a sequence of alternatives for which the sequence of optimum size-$\alpha$ detectors is *consistent*, then $\lim_{n \to \infty} p_d(\theta_n|E_n) = 1$. In this case *any* other sequence of detectors which is simply consistent (and has asymptotic size $\alpha$) will be an AO sequence. Thus it will be of most interest to consider cases for which $\alpha < \lim_{n \to \infty} p_d(\theta_n|E_n) < 1$.

Let us assume that in addition to the regularity conditions we have stated above, $f$ is such that

$$I(f) \triangleq \int_{-\infty}^{\infty} \left[ \frac{f'(x)}{f(x)} \right]^2 f(x) \, dx < \infty. \quad (4.16)$$

$I(f)$ is called Fisher's information for location shift. Furthermore, let the sequence of known signal components $\{s_i, i = 1,2,... \}$ be uniformly bounded, i.e. $0 \le |s_i| \le U_s$ for some finite constant $U_s$, and let

$$0 < \lim_{n \to \infty} \frac{1}{n} \sum_{i=1}^{n} s_i^2 = P_s^2. \tag{4.17}$$

Consider alternatives $K_{1n}$ in which $\theta_n = \gamma/\sqrt{n}$ for any fixed $\gamma > 0$. Then it can be shown that the sequence of Neyman-Pearson optimal detectors and the sequence of LO detectors both have asymptotically normally distributed test statistics. In particular, we can show that for size-$\alpha$ detectors,

$$\lim_{n \to \infty} P_d \left( \frac{\gamma}{\sqrt{n}} \mid D_{LO,n} \right) = \lim_{n \to \infty} P_d \left( \frac{\gamma}{n^{1/2}} \mid E_n \right)$$

$$= 1 - \Phi[\Phi^{-1}(1 - \alpha) - \gamma P_s \sqrt{I(f)}] \tag{4.18}$$

where $\Phi$ is the standard normal c.d.f. Thus the sequence $\{D_{LO,n}, \ n = 1,2,...\}$ is an AO sequence of detectors. A rigorous proof of (4.18) can be based on LeCam's lemmas, as described by Hajek and Sidak [3].

The seqence of LO detectors is not the only sequence of detectors which is AO for $\{H_{1n} \ versus \ K_{1n}\}$. The sequence of Neyman-Pearson optimum detectors also constitutes an AO sequence, and many other sequences of detectors may be defined which are AO.

### 4.2.3 Asymptotic Relative Efficiency

Consider the GC test statistic $T_{GC}(\underline{X})$ of (4.10). We have noted that the LO detector test statistic is a special case of this, and we also know that the sequence of LO detectors for $\{H_{1n} \ versus \ K_{1n}\}$ with $\theta_n = \gamma/\sqrt{n}$ is an AO sequence of detectors. Let $\{D_{GC,n}, \ n = 1,2,...\}$ be a sequence of size-$\alpha$ GC detectors based on some fixed characteristic g and some fixed sequence of coefficients $\{a_i, \ i = 1,2,...\}$. It will be useful to have available for our performance comparisons in the next section a simple measure of the asymptotic performance of such a sequence of GC detectors, which may then be used in comparing the asymptotic performances of two GC detectors. Let us assume that the coefficient sequence satifies the conditions imposed on the signal sequence, with $U_a$ and $P_a$ now the finite constants corresponding to $U_s$ and $P_s$

for the signal sequence. Furthermore, let $g(X_i)$ have zero mean and finite variance under $H_{1n}$. Then it can be shown that

$$\lim_{n \to \infty} P_d \left( \frac{\gamma}{\sqrt{n}} | D_{GC,n} \right) = 1 - \Phi \left[ \Phi^{-1}(1 - \alpha) - \gamma \frac{P_{as}}{P_a} E(g,f) \right] \quad (4.19)$$

where

$$P_{as} = \lim_{n \to \infty} \frac{1}{n} \sum_{i=1}^{n} a_i s_i \quad (4.20)$$

and

$$E(g,f) = \frac{- \int_{-\infty}^{\infty} g(x) f'(x) \, dx}{\left[ \int_{-\infty}^{\infty} g^2(x) f(x) \, dx \right]^{1/2}}$$

$$= \frac{\int_{-\infty}^{\infty} g(x) g_{LO}(x) f(x) dx}{\left[ \int_{-\infty}^{\infty} g^2(x) f(x) \, dx \right]^{1/2}}. \quad (4.21)$$

The quantity $E_{GC}$ defined by

$$E_{GC} = \frac{P_{as}^2}{P_a^2} E^2(g,f) \quad (4.22)$$

is called the *efficacy* of the sequence of GC detectors. Its maximum value is clearly $P_s^2 I(f)$, the efficacy of any AO sequence of detectors. If we always pick $a_i = s_i$, $i = 1, 2, \ldots$, then the efficacy $E_{GC}$ becomes

$$E_{GC} = P_s^2 E^2(g,f). \quad (4.23)$$

The *asymptotic relative efficiency* (ARE) of two sequences of GC detectors, based on characteristics $g_1$ and $g_2$, is then the ratio of efficacies

$$\text{ARE}_{GC1,GC2} = \frac{E^2(g_1 f)}{E^2(g_2 f)} \tag{4.24}$$

and the ARE of a sequence of GC detectors relative to a sequence of AO detectors is

$$\text{ARE}_{GC,AO} = \frac{E^2(g f)}{I(f)}. \tag{4.25}$$

## 4.3 Optimum Quantization in Known Low-Pass Signal Detection

We are now ready to derive data quantization schemes for completely known low-pass deterministic signal detection. To begin with we will consider $M$-interval quantizers, and then generalize the results to $M$-level or $M$-region quantization.

### 4.3.1 M-Interval Quantization

Let us begin by assuming that the breakpoints $t_j$, $j = 0,1,...,M$, are specified (with $t_0 = -\infty$ and $t_M = \infty$) for $M$-interval quantization. The reduced data due to this input partitioning of the $X_i$ into $M$ intervals may be represented as the $M$-component row vector $\underline{Z}_j$ defined by

$$Z_{ij} = \begin{cases} 1, & t_{j-1} < X_i \le t_j, & j = 1,2,...,M \\ 0, & \text{otherwise,} & j = 1,2,...,M. \end{cases} \tag{4.26}$$

Thus each $\underline{Z}_j$ has a single nonzero entry of "1" in the position corresponding to the input interval in which $X_i$ lies. Let $\underline{Z}$ be the $n \times M$ *matrix* of the $n$ row vectors $\underline{Z}_j$. The joint probability density function of the components of $\underline{Z}$ can easily be seen to be

$$P_{\underline{Z}}(\underline{z} | \theta) = \prod_{i=1}^{n} \prod_{j=1}^{M} [P_{ij}(\theta)]^{z_{ij}} \tag{4.27}$$

where

$$P_{ij}(\theta) = P\{t_{j-1} < X_i \le t_j\}$$

$$= F(t_j - \theta s_i) - F(t_{j-1} - \theta s_i). \qquad (4.28)$$

From the generalized Neyman-Pearson lemma we find that the LO detector $D_{LO}$ based on the reduced data $\underline{Z}$ uses the test statistic

$$\lambda_{LO}(\underline{Z}) = \frac{\frac{d}{d\theta}P_{\underline{Z}}(\underline{Z}|\theta)|_{\theta=0}}{P_{\underline{Z}}(\underline{Z}|\theta)|_{\theta=0}}$$

$$= \sum_{i=1}^{n} s_i \sum_{j=1}^{M} \left[ \frac{f(t_{j-1}) - f(t_j)}{F(t_j) - F(t_{j-1})} \right] Z_{ij}. \qquad (4.29)$$

In view of the definition of the $Z_{ij}$, we can express $\lambda_{LO}(\underline{Z})$ in the form

$$\lambda_{LO}(\underline{Z}) = \sum_{i=1}^{n} s_i q_{\underline{t},LO}(X_i) \qquad (4.30)$$

where $q_{\underline{t},LO}$ is the $M$-interval quantizer with the breakpoints vector $\underline{t} = (t_1, t_2, \ldots, t_{M-1})$, with the $j$th output level $l_j$ for input in $(t_{j-1}, t_j]$ being given by

$$l_j = \frac{f(t_{j-1}) - f(t_j)}{F(t_j) - F(t_{j-1})}, \quad j = 1, 2, \ldots, M. \qquad (4.31)$$

We see that $q_{\underline{t},LO}$ represents the locally optimum assignment of output levels in quantization with a given breakpoints vector $\underline{t}$. Furthermore, note that the quantized-data test statistic of (4.30) is also a special case of a GC test statistic.

To complete the specification of the LO quantization we need to determine the locally optimum choice for the breakpoints $t_1, t_2, \ldots, t_{M-1}$ for a given number of input intervals. This becomes rather difficult to carry out in general for any noise density function $f$ and sample size $n$. As an alternative, we can look for the *asymptotically optimum* values for the $M - 1$ breakpoints for the sequence of hypothesis-testing problems $\{H_{1n}$ versus $K_{1n}, n = 1, 2, \ldots\}$ with $\theta_n = \gamma/\sqrt{n}$. We can obtain the AO breakpoints by maximizing the efficacy of the detector based on $\lambda_{LO}(\underline{Z})$ of (4.30).

Consider the quantizer-correlator (QC) statistic

$$T_{QC}(\underline{X}) = \sum_{i=1}^{n} s_i q(X_i) \tag{4.32}$$

where $q$ is any $M$-interval quantizer defined in terms of a breakpoints vector $\underline{t}$ and a levels vector $\underline{l} = (l_1, l_2, ..., l_M)$. Assume without loss of generality that $q(X_i)$ has mean zero under $H_{1n}$. Then the efficacy $E_{QC}$ for a QC detector can be written as

$$E_{QC} = P_s^2 \frac{\left\{ \sum_{j=1}^{M} l_j [f(t_{j-1}) - f(t_j)] \right\}^2}{\sum_{j=1}^{M} l_j^2 [F(t_j) - F(t_{j-1})]}. \tag{4.33}$$

From this we find that the efficacy $E_{QC,LO}$ of the QC detector using the LO output levels for a given breakpoints vector $\underline{t}$ is, from (4.31) and (4.33),

$$E_{QC,LO} = P_s^2 \sum_{j=1}^{M} \frac{[f(t_{j-1}) - f(t_j)]^2}{F(t_j) - F(t_{j-1})}. \tag{4.34}$$

Before continuing let us observe that although the $l_j$ of (4.31) were obtained as the LO levels for given $\underline{t}$, they should also be the AO levels for a given $\underline{t}$ vector for detectors of the QC type using $T_{QC}(\underline{X})$ as test statistics. That this is indeed so can be verified by seeking the levels $l_j$ which maximize the general efficacy expression $E_{QC}$.

Continuing with maximization of $E_{QC,LO}$ with respect to the breakpoints, from the necessary conditions

$$\frac{\partial}{\partial t_j} E_{QC,LO} = 0, \quad j = 1, 2, ..., M-1 \tag{4.35}$$

for AO breakpoints maximizing $E_{QC,LO}$, we find that

$$g_{LO}(t_j) = \frac{1}{2} \left\{ \frac{f(t_{j-1}) - f(t_j)}{F(t_j) - F(t_{j-1})} + \frac{f(t_j) - f(t_{j+1})}{F(t_{j+1}) - F(t_j)} \right\}, \quad j = 1, 2, ..., M-1 \tag{4.36}$$

must be satisfied by the AO breakpoints. Here $g_{LO}(t_j)$ is $-f'(t_j)/f(t_j)$. Using (4.31), this last result becomes

$$g_{LO}(t_j) = \frac{l_j + l_{j+1}}{2}, \quad j = 1,2,...,M-1. \tag{4.37}$$

The equations (4.37) and (4.31) for the levels must be solved simultaneously for the output levels and breakpoints of an AO quantization of data. These two sets of equations provide a total of $2M - 1$ conditions which can be solved, generally numerically, for the $M$ output levels and $M - 1$ breakpoints $t_1, t_2,...,t_{M-1}$ for an AO quantizer.

A very interesting comparison can be made between these results and those on minimum MSE quantization summarized in the introduction. Observe that the levels of (4.31) may be expressed as

$$l_j = \frac{\displaystyle\int_{t_{j-1}}^{t_j} g_{LO}(x)f(x)\,dx}{F(t_j) - F(t_{j-1})}, \tag{4.38}$$

the average value of $g_{LO}$ on $(t_{j-1}, t_j]$. Comparing (4.1) and (4.2) to (4.37) and (4.38), we see immediately that the quantizer which minimizes the MSE between the quantizer characteristic and the *locally optimum nonlinearity* $g_{LO}$ under the null hypothesis is also an asymptotically optimum quantizer. Notice that once (4.37) and (4.38) have been solved simultaneously for the AO quantizer parameters, the levels may be scaled and shifted by fixed scale and shift constants without changing the asymptotic optimality of the quantization; one would simply modify the detector threshold in the same way. The particular solution of the simultaneous equations (4.37) and (4.38) is the one giving also a quantizer which is the *best fit*, in the MSE sense, to $g_{LO}$ under noise-only conditions. Only in the case of Gaussian noise, for which $g_{LO}(x) = x/\sigma^2$ where $\sigma^2$ is the noise variance, do we find that the AO and minimum MSE (Max) quantizers have the same set of breakpoints and that the output levels of the minimum MSE quantizer are also AO output levels.

The normalized efficacy $\tilde{E}_{QC,LO} = E_{QC,LO}/P_s^2$ may be written as

$$\tilde{E}_{QC,LO} = \int\limits_{-\infty}^{\infty} q_{\underline{t},LO}(x)g_{LO}(x)f(x) \ dx \qquad (4.39)$$

so that from the Schwarz inequality

$$\tilde{E}_{QC,LO}^2 \leq \int\limits_{-\infty}^{\infty} q_{\underline{t},LO}^2(x)f(x) \ dx \ I(f)$$

$$= \tilde{E}_{QC,LO}I(f) \qquad (4.40)$$

leading to

$$\tilde{E}_{QC,LO} \leq I(f). \qquad (4.41)$$

This is as expected, $I(f)$ being the maximum value of the efficacy, obtained for an unconstrained AO detector, for this detection problem. We also find that for increasing $M$, $\tilde{E}_{QC,LO}$ approaches $I(f)$ for sequences of breakpoint vectors $\underline{t}$ which imply an increasingly finer input partitioning. In particular, this is true for the AO partitioning satisfying (4.36) for each $M$.

Numerical results for the class of generalized Gaussian p.d.f.'s [4] show that one can expect fairly high asymptotic efficiency relative to the *unconstrained* AO detectors for our problem with only four-interval quantization. For Gaussian noise p.d.f., for example, the ARE of the AO QC detector relative to the unconstrained detector turns out to be 0.88. Results given in [5,6] indicate that such high relative efficiencies are generally preserved for finite sample sizes and finite signal amplitudes. Bushnell and Kurz [7] have given some analyses and numerical performance results for quantization in finite sample-size detection of constant signals. For the time-varying signal case the optimization of local or asymptotic performance seems to provide the best approach to the quantizer design problem, provided that the weak-signal assumption is reasonable.

Other studies on optimum quantization for known-signal detection have been carried out by Groeneveld [8], Ching and Kurz [9], Kurz [10], Poor and Thomas [11,12], Poor and Alexandrou [13], Varshney [14] and Lee and Thomas [15]. Among the earliest contributions to optimum quantization for weak-

signal detection are those of Hansen [16], Baronkin [17], and Levin and Baronkin [18]. Finite sample-size quantizer optimization results have recently been
given by Nutall [19], who considered a multi-input detector with an additive
signal possibly present in one of the inputs. Poor and Thomas [20] have also
considered asymptotically *robust* quantization for the known-signal detection
problem. Quantization for sequential signal detection has been considered by
Tantaratana and Thomas [21].

### 4.3.2 M-Region Generalized Quantization

So far we have constrained ourselves to a consideration of multilevel
quantization of the input data with the usual interpretation that quantization
involves partitioning the range of real values of the input into some number $M$
of *intervals*. We may describe this operation more explicitly as *M-interval partitioning*, with an output level assigned to each input interval. Such a quantization scheme does not optimally utilize the allowable number $M$ of distinct output levels in approximating $g_{LO}$, because the regions of the input partitioning
are constrained to be intervals. Since it is the number of distinct output levels
which determine the data compression value of a quantizer, we shall now consider *generalized* quantization based on *M-region partitioning*, in which the
regions of the input partitioning are not constrained to be intervals.

Let $\{A_j, \quad j = 1,2,...,M\}$ denote the partitioning of the real line
$R = (-\infty,\infty)$ into disjoint subsets $A_j$ for an $M$-region quantization. For a
*given* partitioning, it is easy to obtain the LO levels for the $M$-region quantization. Following the development for the LO levels of (4.31) we find that the
LO levels for $M$-region quantization are given by

$$l_j = \frac{-\int\limits_{A_j} f'(x) \; dx}{\int\limits_{A_j} f(x) \; dx}$$

$$= \frac{\int\limits_{A_j} g_{LO}(x)f(x)\ dx}{\int\limits_{A_j} f(x)\ dx}, \quad j = 1, 2, \ldots, M. \tag{4.42}$$

This result should be compared to that of (4.38), where $A_j = (t_{j-1}, t_j]$.

In the same way, it is easy to establish the counterparts for the efficacies $E_{QC}$ and $E_{QC,LO}$. We find, in particular,

$$E_{QC,LO} = P_s^2 \sum_{j=1}^{M} \frac{\left[\int\limits_{A_j} g_{LO}(x)f(x)\ dx\right]^2}{\int\limits_{A_j} f(x)\ dx}. \tag{4.43}$$

Consider the MSE $e(g_{LO}, q; f)$ between $g_{LO}(X_i)$ and $q(X_i)$ under the noise-only hypothesis,

$$e(g_{LO}, q; f) = \sum_{j=1}^{M} \int\limits_{A_j} [g_{LO}(x) - l_j]^2 f(x)\ dx. \tag{4.44}$$

This can easily be expressed as

$$e(g_{LO}, q; f) = I(f) - 2 \sum_{j=1}^{M} l_j \int\limits_{A_j} g_{LO}(x)f(x)\,dx + \sum_{j=1}^{M} l_j^2 \int\limits_{A_j} f(x)\,dx. \tag{4.45}$$

From this it follows that the $M$-region generalized quantizer minimizing $e(g_{LO}, q; f)$ is also the AO $M$-region generalized quantizer maximizing $E_{QC,LO}$; for optimum levels in (4.45), which are given by (4.42), we have $e(g_{LO}, q; f) = I(f) - \tilde{E}_{QC,LO}$. These observations allow us to complete specification of the AO quantizer. Let $l_j$, $j = 1, 2, \ldots, M$ be a *given* set of distinct levels, and assume without any loss of generality that we have $l_1 < l_2 < \cdots < l_M$. For $e(g_{LO}, q; f)$ to be a minimum, the regions $A_j$ must be such as to contain the subsets $\tilde{A}_j$ defined by

$$\tilde{A}_j = \{x \mid P_j(x) < P_i(x),\ i \neq j\} \tag{4.46}$$

where $P_j(x) = [g_{LO}(x) - l_j]^2$. Defining

$$\tilde{t}_j \triangleq \frac{l_j + l_{j+1}}{2}, \quad j = 1, 2, \ldots, M-1 \tag{4.47}$$

we find that $\tilde{t}_1 < \tilde{t}_2 < \cdots < \tilde{t}_{M-1}$, so that by considering the cases $i > j$ and $i < j$ separately in (4.46) we get the result

$$\tilde{A}_j = \{x \mid \tilde{t}_{j-1} < g_{LO}(x) < \tilde{t}_j\} \tag{4.48}$$

with $\tilde{t}_0 \triangleq -\infty$ and $\tilde{t}_M \triangleq \infty$. Assuming that the set of points at which $g_{LO}(x)$ is equal to the $\tilde{t}_j$, $j = 1, 2, \ldots, M-1$, has probability zero, we finally get

$$A_j = \{x \mid \tilde{t}_{j-1} < g_{LO}(x) \leq \tilde{t}_j\}, \quad j = 1, 2, \ldots, M. \tag{4.49}$$

Note that the $A_j$ above are the optimum regions giving the quantizer best fitting $g_{LO}$ under $H_{1n}$ for a given set of levels $l_j$. We *cannot* conclude that they are also the AO choice of regions maximizing $E_{QC}$ for the *given* levels. However, the set of $2M - 1$ *simultaneous* equations (4.42) and (4.47) together with (4.49) for the levels and regions are the necessary conditions for maximization of $E_{QC}$.

With the $A_j$ defined according to (4.49) and the $\tilde{t}_j$ any increasing sequence of constants, the levels $l_j$ of (4.42) will turn out to form an increasing sequence, for $j = 1, 2, \ldots, M$. If $g_{LO}$ is a monotonic function the optimum regions will clearly turn out to be intervals, and a restriction to quantizers based on $M$-interval partitioning is justified. Otherwise, for a given $M$ the AO $M$-region quantizer will have better asymptotic performance than the AO $M$-interval quantizer.

We can give an interesting interpretation to the above AO $M$-region quantization scheme. The quantizer can be implemented as shown in Figure 4.2, with each $X_i$ first transformed into $g_{LO}(X_i)$, which then forms the input to an $M$-interval quantizer with breakpoints vector $\underline{\tilde{t}} = (\tilde{t}_1, \tilde{t}_2, \ldots, \tilde{t}_{M-1})$ and output levels $l_1, l_2, \ldots, l_M$. We have, of course, the relationship (4.47) between the $\tilde{t}_j$ and the levels $l_j$, so that the $M$-interval quantizer in Figure 4.2 satisfies the condition that the output level $l_j$ for the $j$th interval $(\tilde{t}_{j-1}, \tilde{t}_j)$ lies in this interval. This suggests a suboptimum scheme in which the $M$-interval quantizer is replaced by a *uniform* quantizer. The resulting scheme may then be optimized by picking the uniform quantizer step-size and saturation levels optimally for given $M$. It is interesting to note that Poor and Rivani [22] arrived at such a scheme, using a uniform quantization of the LO transformed data $g_{LO}(X_i)$, as a special case of a more general system employing an odd nonlinear function g before a uniform quantizer (for the case of symmetric f and symmetric quantization).

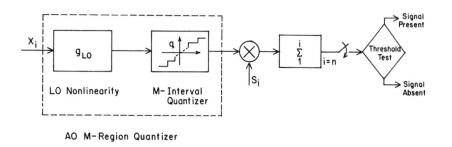

AO M-Region Quantizer

*Figure 4.2 Asymptotically optimum M-region quantizer-detector for a known signal.*

### 4.4 Optimum Quantization in Narrowband Signal Detection

We will now consider the case where the signal and noise are both narrowband processes. We will first give the results for the LO detection for completely known as well as for random-phase narrowband signals, and then briefly consider envelope quantization.

*4.4.1 Asymptotically Optimum Detection of Narrowband Signals in Narrowband Noise*

*Coherent Narrowband Signals*

In the continuous-time domain the general representation of a completely known narrowband signal waveform observed in additive noise is

$$X(t) = \theta v(t) \cos [\omega_0 t + \phi(t)] + W(t). \qquad (4.50)$$

Here $v(t)$ and $\phi(t)$ are known amplitude and phase modulations which occupy a narrow band of frequencies around the carrier frequency $f_0 = \omega_0/2\pi$ and $\theta$ is, as before, the overall signal amplitude. The noise process $W(t)$ will be assumed to be stationary, zero-mean, bandpass white noise, with a power spectral density which is a constant, $N_0/2$, over a band of frequencies $(f_0 - B/2, f_0 + B/2)$ and zero outside. The signal bandwidth $B_s$ will be assumed to be no larger than $B$. We are interested, of course, in testing $\theta = 0$ versus $\theta > 0$.

The noise process $W(t)$ can be expressed in terms of its low-pass in-phase and quadrature components $W_I(t)$ and $W_Q(t)$, respectively, and we get the representation

$$X(t) = [\theta s_I(t) + W_I(t)] \cos \omega_0 t + [\theta s_Q(t) + W_Q(t)] \sin \omega_0 t$$

$$\triangleq X_I(t) \cos \omega_0 t + X_Q(t) \sin \omega_0 t \qquad (4.51)$$

where

$$s_I(t) = v(t) \cos \phi(t) \qquad (4.52)$$

and

$$s_Q(t) = -v(t) \sin \phi(t). \qquad (4.53)$$

Assuming that the components $X_I(t)$ and $X_Q(t)$ are available over some time-interval $[0, T]$, we can sample their waveforms at a uniform rate of $1/\Delta$ to obtain a set of in-phase observations $X_{Ii}$, $i = 1,2,...,n$ and a set of quadrature observations $X_{Qi}$, $i = 1,2,...,n$, where $X_{Ii} = X_I(i\Delta)$, $X_{Qi} = X_Q(i\Delta)$ and $n\Delta = T$.

We will now assume that the in-phase noise components $W_{Ii}$, $i = 1,2,...,n$, form a sequence of i.i.d. random variables, governed by a common univariate density function $f_L$. Similarly, we will assume that the quadrature noise components are i.i.d. and governed by the same univariate noise density function $f_L$. The restriction that the sampling period $\Delta$ be such as to result in independent samples is necessary to obtain analytical results for non-Gaussian noise processes. If the noise bandwidth $B$ is several times larger than the signal bandwidth $B_s$ such a sampling rate would be quite realistic to use. From general results on representation of narrowband noise processes we know that the in-phase and quadrature processes $W_I(t)$ and $W_Q(t)$ are *uncorrelated*. For non-Gaussian noise processes, however, independence of the in-phase and quadrature component samples at any time instant cannot be reasonably assumed. We will therefore assume here that $W_{Ii}$ and $W_{Qi}$ have, for each $i$, some common bivariate density function $f_{IQ}$. To complete our description of the statistics of the noise components, we will assume that the two-dimensional noise samples $(W_{Ii}, W_{Qi})$, $i = 1, 2, \ldots, n$, form a set of i.i.d. random vectors governed by the common probability density function $f_{IQ}$, for which the marginal densities are $f_L$.

Let $\underline{X}_I = (X_{I1}, X_{I2}, \ldots, X_{In})$ be the vector of in-phase observations, and let $\underline{X}_Q$ be the vector of quadrature observations. To detect signal presence $(\theta > 0)$ the LO detector can easily be shown to use the LO test statistic

$$\lambda_{LO}(\underline{X}_I, \underline{X}_Q) = \sum_{i=1}^{n} s_{Ii} g_{LO,I}(X_{Ii}, X_{Qi}) + \sum_{i=1}^{n} s_{Qi} g_{LO,Q}(X_{Ii}, X_{Qi}) \qquad (4.54)$$

where

$$g_{LO,I}(u,v) = \frac{-\dfrac{\partial}{\partial u} f_{IQ}(u,v)}{f_{IQ}(u,v)}, \qquad (4.55)$$

$g_{LO,Q}(u,v)$ being defined with $\dfrac{-\partial}{\partial u}$ replaced by $\dfrac{-\partial}{\partial v}$. Here $s_{Ii}$ and $s_{Qi}$ are, of course, the in-phase and quadrature signal sampled values.

Consider the special case in which $f_{IQ}$ is *circularly symmetric*, so that

$$f_{IQ}(u, v) = h(r)|_{r=(u^2+v^2)^{1/2}} \qquad (4.56)$$

for some function $h$. In terms of the $R_i = (X_{Ii}^2 + X_{Qi}^2)^{1/2}$, the observation *envelopes* at the sampling instants, we can express $\lambda_{LO}(\underline{X}_I, \underline{X}_Q)$ as

$$\lambda_{LO}(\underline{X}_I, \underline{X}_Q) = \sum_{i=1}^{n} \tilde{g}_{LO}(R_i)[s_{Ii}X_{Ii} + s_{Qi}X_{Qi}]$$

$$= \sum_{i=1}^{n} R_i \tilde{g}_{LO}(R_i)\left[s_{Ii}\frac{X_{Ii}}{R_i} + s_{Qi}\frac{X_{Qi}}{R_i}\right], \qquad (4.57)$$

with

$$\tilde{g}_{LO}(r) = \frac{-h'(r)}{rh(r)}$$

$$= -\frac{1}{r}\frac{d}{dr} \ln [h(r)] . \qquad (4.58)$$

This leads us to define a *generalized narrowband correlator* (GNC) test statistic $T_{GNC}(\underline{X}_I, \underline{X}_Q)$ as one in which $\tilde{g}_{LO}$ above is replaced by some arbitrary function $\tilde{g}$. The normalized efficacy $\tilde{E}_{GNC}$ can be shown to be [23]

$$\tilde{E}_{GNC} = \pi \frac{\left[\int\limits_{0}^{\infty} r^2\tilde{g}(r)h'(r)\ dr\right]^2}{\int\limits_{0}^{\infty} r^3\tilde{g}(r)^2h(r)\ dr} \qquad (4.59)$$

for the GNC test statistic and circularly symmetric noise p.d.f. $f_{IQ}$. This may be expressed as

$$\tilde{E}_{GNC} = \frac{1}{2} \frac{\left[\int\limits_{0}^{\infty} r\tilde{g}(r)r\tilde{g}_{LO}(r)f_E(r)\ dr\right]^2}{\int\limits_{0}^{\infty} r^2\tilde{g}(r)^2f_E(r)\ dr} \qquad (4.60)$$

where $f_E(r) = 2\pi rh(r)$ is the noise envelope p.d.f.

The *linear narrowband correlator* (LNC) test statistic is obtained with $\tilde{g}(r)$ a constant, and is the LO statistic for Gaussian noise. With $\tilde{g}(r) = 1/r$ we get the *hard-limiter narrowband correlator* (HNC) statistic, for which effectively only unit amplitude normalized in-phase and quadrature observation samples are utilized in forming the statistic.

*Incoherent Narrowband Signals*

If an additional random, uniformly distributed, phase component $\psi$ is present in the signal term in (4.50), we have the *incoherent* narrowband signal detection problem. The LO detector statistic for this problem can be obtained for circularly symmetric noise probability density function $f_{IQ}$ after some tedious though straightforward manipulations as

$$\lambda_{LO}(\underline{\tilde{X}}) = \frac{1}{2} \sum_{i=1}^{n} |\tilde{s}_i|^2 \tilde{l}_{LO}(|\tilde{X}_i|)$$

$$+ \frac{1}{2} \left| \sum_{i=1}^{n} \tilde{g}_{LO}(|\tilde{X}_i|) \tilde{s}_i \tilde{X}_i^* \right|^2 \tag{4.61}$$

where for convenience we are using the complex quantities defined by

$$\tilde{s}_i = s_{Ii} + j s_{Qi} \tag{4.62}$$

and

$$\tilde{X}_i = X_{Ii} + j X_{Qi}, \tag{4.63}$$

and where

$$\tilde{l}_{LO}(r) = \frac{d^2}{dr^2} \ln [h(r)] + \frac{1}{r} \frac{d}{dr} \ln [h(r)]. \tag{4.64}$$

For AO detection one can drop the first term on the right-hand side of (4.61), which may be described as a *generalized envelope correlator* (GEC) statistic. The other term is a quadrature GNC/envelope detector statistic. It can be shown that with $\tilde{g}_{LO}$ replaced by any $\tilde{g}$, the generalized efficacy of the detector based on the resulting quadrature GNC/envelope detector statistic is also given by (4.60), within a multiplicative constant.

*Noncoherent Pulse Trains*

Let us now consider as a special case the detection of a *noncoherent* narrowband pulse train in additive narrowband noise. Here each pulse is modeled as an *incoherent* narrowband signal, with the absolute phases $\psi_i$ for the individual pulses modeled as independent uniformly distributed random variables.

Suppose the receiver front end is constrained to be a quadrature matched filter matched to the basic pulse shape $v(t)\cos[\omega_0 t + \phi(t)]$. Although this is not the optimum scheme for non-Gaussian noise, it is very frequently encountered as a simple predetection processing element. Denote by $Z_{Ii}$ and $Z_{Qi}$ the in-phase and quadrature components of the outputs of the quadrature matched filter; the index $i$ now indicates the outputs at the end of the $i$-th pulse period. The components $Z_{Ii}$ and $Z_{Qi}$ may be described by

$$Z_{Ii} = \theta e_i \cos \psi_i + U_{Ii} \tag{4.65}$$

$$Z_{Qi} = -\theta e_i \sin \psi_i + U_{Qi} \tag{4.66}$$

for $i = 1,2,\ldots,n$, where $e_i$ is the known pulse amplitude of the $i$-th pulse and the $(U_{Ii}, U_{Qi})$ form an i.i.d. sequence of bivariate noise components. The above is obtained under the usual assumptions made in narrowband signal detection. Noting that the $(Z_{Ii}, Z_{Qi})$ also form a sequence of independent random vectors and using the result (4.61) for $n = 1$, we can easily show that the LO statistic for our noncoherent pulse train detection problem uses $\underline{Z}_I = (Z_{I1}, Z_{I2}, \ldots, Z_{In})$ and $\underline{Z}_Q = (Z_{Q1}, Z_{Q2}, \ldots, Z_{Qn})$ as

$$\lambda_{LO}(\underline{Z}_I, \underline{Z}_Q) = \frac{1}{2} \sum_{i=1}^{n} e_i^2 \left[ \frac{h''(R_i)}{h(R_i)} + \frac{h'(R_i)}{R_i h(R_i)} \right]$$

$$\triangle \sum_{i=1}^{n} e_i^2 \tilde{p}_{LO}(R_i) \tag{4.67}$$

where $R_i = (Z_{Ii}^2 + Z_{Qi}^2)^{1/2}$, this time under the assumption that $(U_{Ii}, U_{Qi})$ has a circularly symmetric probability density function described by $h$. Thus the LO detector is now a generalized envelope correlator (GEC); it reduces to the square-law detector for Gaussian noise. It can be established that the normalized efficacy for the GEC statistic using any $\tilde{g}$ in the place of $\tilde{p}_{LO}$, for this detection problem, is

$$\tilde{E}_{GEC} = \frac{1}{4} \frac{\left[ \int\limits_{0}^{\infty} \tilde{g}(r)\tilde{p}_{LO}(r)f_E(r) \, dr \right]^2}{\int\limits_{0}^{\infty} \tilde{g}^2(r)f_E(r) \, dr}. \tag{4.68}$$

This result should be compared to (4.60).

### 4.4.2 Asymptotically Optimum Envelope Quantization

Both for simplified implementation and to obtain a GNC detection scheme which has characteristics in between that of the LNC detector and that of the HNC detector, we can use a piecewise-constant quantizer characteristic $\tilde{q}$ in place of $R_i\tilde{g}(R_i)$ to obtain specifically the *quantizer narrowband correlator* (QNC) detector test statistic. For $M$-interval envelope quantization we can define $\tilde{q}$ in terms of output levels $l_1, l_2, \ldots, l_M$ and input breakpoints $t_0, t_1, \ldots, t_M$ with $t_0 \triangleq 0$ and $t_M \triangleq \infty$ and $t_j \leq t_{j+1}$.

Now, from (4.60), the normalized efficacy $\tilde{E}_{QNC}$ of the QNC detector is

$$\tilde{E}_{QNC} = \frac{1}{2} \frac{\left[ \sum\limits_{j=1}^{M} l_j \int\limits_{t_{j-1}}^{t_j} r\tilde{g}_{LO}(r)f_E(r) \, dr \right]^2}{\sum\limits_{j=1}^{M} l_j^2 [F_E(t_j) - F_E(t_{j-1})]} \tag{4.69}$$

where $F_E$ is the c.d.f. corresponding to $f_E$. For a *given* set of breakpoints we can obtain the LO levels as we did in the low-pass signal case. These are also the levels maximizing $\tilde{E}_{QNC}$. It is easy to show that a set of levels maximizing $\tilde{E}_{QNC}$ can be defined as

$$l_j = \frac{\int\limits_{t_{j-1}}^{t_j} r\tilde{g}_{LO}(r)f_E(r) \, dr}{F_E(t_j) - F_E(t_{j-1})}, \quad j = 1, 2, \ldots, M \tag{4.70}$$

and that the resulting maximum $\tilde{E}_{QNC}$ for given breakpoints is

$$\tilde{E}_{QNC,LO} = \frac{1}{2} \sum_{j=1}^{M} \frac{\left[ \int\limits_{t_{j-1}}^{t_j} r\tilde{g}_{LO}(r)f_E(r) \; dr \right]^2}{F_E(t_j) - F_E(t_{j-1})}. \tag{4.71}$$

We can further optimize the quantizer design and get an AO QNC detector by maximizing $\tilde{E}_{QNC,LO}$ with respect to the breakpoints $t_j$. It is possible to show that this AO quantization is also a "best-fit" quantization under noise-only conditions of the LO characteristic $r\tilde{g}_{LO}(r)$. It is interesting to compare these results with those for low-pass signals.

An AO quadrature QNC/envelope detector statistic for envelope-quantized *incoherent* narowband signal detection can be obtained using exactly the same quantization scheme as the one above, in view of the fact that the generalized efficacy in this case is a constant multiple of $\tilde{E}_{QNC}$ of (4.60).

Turning to the GEC detector for the noncoherent pulse train, we find that for a *quantizer envelope correlator* (QEC) detector in which $\tilde{g}$ is taken to be $\tilde{q}$, the normalized efficacy is given by

$$\tilde{E}_{QEC} = \frac{1}{4} \frac{\left[ \sum\limits_{j=1}^{M} l_j \int\limits_{t_{j-1}}^{t_j} \tilde{p}_{LO}(r)f_E(r) \; dr \right]^2}{\sum\limits_{j=1}^{M} l_j^2 [F_E(t_j) - F_E(t_{j-1})]} \tag{4.72}$$

which is (within a constant multiple) $\tilde{E}_{QNC}$ of (4.69) with $\tilde{p}_{LO}$ replacing $r\tilde{g}_{LO}(r)$. Let us consider the special case of Gaussian noise, for which the noise envelope p.d.f. is Rayleigh (with some scale parameter $\sigma^2$). In this case the AO envelope quantizer parameters can be obtained from the simultaneous equations

$$h_j = \frac{u_{j-1}e^{-u_{j-1}} - u_j e^{-u_j}}{e^{-u_{j-1}} - e^{-u_j}}, \quad j = 1,2,...,M \tag{4.73}$$

and

$$u_j = \frac{h_j + h_{j+1}}{2} + 1, \quad j = 1, 2, \ldots, M-1 \tag{4.74}$$

where $h_j = \sigma^2 l_j$ and $u_j = t_j^2/(2\sigma^2)$. If we take the square root of the ARE of the AO QEC detector relative to the AO GEC detector as being the asymptotic loss, we find that for $M = 4$ and Gaussian noise this loss is only about 0.25 dB. Details of such numerical results, as well as finite-sample-size performance comparisons, have been given by Cimini and Kassam [24]. The paper by Cimini and Kassam also considers the more general case where $f_{IQ}$, the p.d.f. of $(Z_{Ii}, Z_{Qi})$, is not circularly symmetric and also where the quantization is not restricted to $M$-interval envelope quantization. The results of these considerations are counterparts of the results on generalized $M$-region quantization in Section 4.3. We note in passing that earlier work on this detection problem was done by Hansen [16,25] and Levin and Baronkin [18]. In addition, let us also note that it is possible to extend the above analysis for AO quantization and show that the results hold for the independent amplitude fluctuation case in noncoherent pulse train detection.

Our analyses so far of quantized data detection systems have given us very similar general results for the different situations we have considered (low-pass signal, coherent and incoherent narrowband signal, noncoherent pulse-train). We shall obtain another basically similar set of results for the random signal detection problems we will consider in the next section.

## 4.5 Optimum Quantization in Random Signal Detection

In many applications involving detection of random signals, the observations are obtained simultaneously from a number of receivers forming an *array*. The detection problem then becomes that of detecting a random signal which is *common* to each receiving element, embedded in noise processes at the receiving elements which are uncorrelated with each other and with the signal process. A typical example of this type of application is an underwater hydrophone array used in a passive sonar system to detect the presence of, and to locate, sources of random signals.

Let $\underline{X}_j = (X_{j1}, X_{j2}, \ldots, X_{jn})$ be the vector of $n$ observation components

obtained at the $j$th element of a receiving array of $L$ elements. At each time
index $i$ the observations $X_{ji}$, $j = 1,2,...,L$, across the array may have a
common random signal $S_i$ in additive noise components $W_{ji}$. Our observation
model is thus

$$X_{ji} = \theta S_i + W_{ji}, \quad j = 1,2,...,L, \quad i = 1,2,...,n. \tag{4.75}$$

The assumptions we will make about the signal and noise quantities in our
model are:

1.  The noise components $W_{ji}$ are i.i.d. random variables with a known common p.d.f. The noise components have zero means and variances $\sigma^2 = 1$.
2.  The signal process $\{S_i\}_{i=1}^n$ is zero mean and stationary and has a variance $\sigma_s^2 = 1$. The known autocovariance function of the signal process is $r_S(i)$, $i = 0, \pm 1,....$
3.  The signal and noise processes are independent.

The assumption that the signal and noise variances are unity is not restrictive
since the parameter $\theta$ controls the SNR, which is now simply $\theta^2$.

### 4.5.1 Locally Optimum and Asymptotically Optimum Detection of Random Signals

Let $\underline{X}$ now denote the $L \times n$ matrix of row vectors $\underline{X}_j$, $j = 1,2,...,L$.
Under some regularity conditions on $f$, it can be shown that the LO test
statistic for this detection problem is

$$\lambda_{LO}(\underline{X}) = \sum_{i=1}^n \sum_{j=1}^L h_{LO}(X_{ji})$$

$$+ \sum_{i=1}^n \sum_{m=1}^n r_S(m - i) \sum_{j=1}^L g_{LO}(X_{ji}) \sum_{p=1}^L g_{LO}(X_{pm}) \tag{4.76}$$

where

$$g_{LO}(x) = -\frac{f'(x)}{f(x)} \tag{4.9}$$

and

$$h_{LO}(x) = \frac{f''(x)}{f(x)} - g_{LO}^2(x). \qquad (4.77)$$

If the signal is "white", so that $r_S(i) = 0$ for $i \neq 0$, the LO statistic simplifies to

$$\lambda_{LO}(\underline{X}) = \sum_{i=1}^{n} \left\{ \sum_{j=1}^{L} h_{LO}(X_{ji}) + \left[ \sum_{j=1}^{L} g_{LO}(X_{ji}) \right]^2 \right\}, \qquad (4.78)$$

an alternative expression for which is

$$\lambda_{LO}(\underline{X}) = \sum_{j=1}^{L} \left[ \sum_{i=1}^{n} \frac{f''(X_{ji})}{f(X_{ji})} \right] + 2 \sum_{j=1}^{L} \sum_{p=j+1}^{L} \left[ \sum_{i=1}^{n} g_{LO}(X_{ji}) g_{LO}(X_{pi}) \right]. \qquad (4.79)$$

The first term in $\lambda_{LO}(\underline{X})$ above is a generalized measure of the *energy* received by the array. To appreciate this better, assume that $f$ is a symmetric function. Then $f''/f$ is also an even function. For example, for unit-variance Gaussian noise we have

$$\frac{f''(x)}{f(x)} = x^2 - 1. \qquad (4.80)$$

The second term in (4.79) is a generalized measure of the *correlation* between observations in different channels of the array. This second term is a sum over distinct pairs of channels of a *generalized cross-correlation* (GCC) statistic, and responds only to a *common* signal or at least to signals which are spatially correlated across the array elements. This is a major reason why it is useful to employ only the GCC part of the LO statistic in applications involving detection as well as location of signal sources.

Of course when only one receiver is present ($L = 1$) the system can only act as a signal detector. In this case the LO test statistic of (4.78) reduces to

$$\lambda_{LO}(\underline{X}_1) = \sum_{i=1}^{n} e_{LO}(X_{1i}) \qquad (4.81)$$

where

$$e_{LO}(x) = h_{LO}(x) + g_{LO}^2(x)$$

$$= \frac{f''(x)}{f(x)}. \tag{4.82}$$

For the *generalized energy* (GE) detector using statistic

$$T_{GE}(\underline{X}_1) = \sum_{i=1}^{n} e(X_{1i}), \tag{4.83}$$

the efficacy $E_{GC}$ for random signal detection ($L = 1$) is, assuming that $E\{e(X_{1i})|\theta = 0\} = 0$,

$$E_{GE} = \frac{1}{4} \frac{\left[\int\limits_{-\infty}^{\infty} e(x)f''(x)\ dx\right]^2}{\int\limits_{-\infty}^{\infty} e^2(x)f(x)dx}$$

$$= \frac{1}{4} \frac{\left[\int\limits_{-\infty}^{\infty} e(x)e_{LO}(x)f(x)\ dx\right]^2}{\int\limits_{-\infty}^{\infty} e^2(x)f(x)\ dx}. \tag{4.84}$$

This is maximized for $e = e_{LO}$.

Consider next the *generalized cross-correlation array* (GCA) statistic

$$T_{GCA}(\underline{X}) = 2\sum_{j=1}^{L} \sum_{p=j+1}^{L} \left(\sum_{i=1}^{n} g(X_{ji})g(X_{pi})\right)$$

$$= 2\sum_{j=1}^{L} \sum_{p=j+1}^{L} T_{GCC}(\underline{X}_j, \underline{X}_p) \tag{4.85}$$

where the characteristic $g$ is assumed to satisfy the condition $E\{g(X_{ji})|\theta = 0\} = 0$. For $L = 2$ this is a GCC statistic. It can be established that the efficacy $E_{GCA}$ of the GCA detector for random signal detection is

$$E_{GCA} = \frac{1}{2}L(L-1)\frac{\left[\int_{-\infty}^{\infty} g(x)f'(x)\ dx\right]^4}{\left[\int_{-\infty}^{\infty} g^2(x)f(x)\ dx\right]^2}. \qquad (4.86)$$

It is interesting to note that

$$E_{GCA} = \frac{1}{2}L(L-1)E_{GCC}$$

$$= \frac{1}{2}L(L-1)\tilde{E}_{GC}^2 \qquad (4.87)$$

where $\tilde{E}_{GC}$ is the normalized efficacy of a GC detector for $H_1$ versus $K_1$. Thus $E_{GCA}$ is maximized with $g = g_{LO}$, which gives the AO GCA statistic. When $g(x) = x$ the GCA statistic becomes a linear cross-correlation array (LCA) statistic, whereas for $g(x) = \text{sgn}(x)$ we get the polarity coincidence array (PCA) statistic which has been used for nonparametric detection.

### 4.5.2 Asymptotically Optimum Quantization

We will now consider asymptotically optimum quantization schemes for the two special cases of random signal detection schemes we have discussed, one for the single-channel case $(L = 1)$ and the other based on the statistic for $L > 1$.

#### Quantizer Energy Detector $(L = 1)$

In the generalized energy (GE) detector test statistic $T_{GE}(\underline{X}_1)$ of (4.83) let us now require the function $e$ to be some $M$-interval quantizer characteristic $q$ defined by $q(x) = l_j$ for $t_{j-1} < x \le t_j$, $j = 1,2,...,M$, with $-\infty \triangleq t_0 \le t_1 \le \cdots \le t_M \triangleq \infty$. Using this function for $e$ in the efficacy expression (4.84), the efficacy $E_{QE}$ of the quantizer energy detector is obtained as

$$E_{QE} = \frac{1}{4} \frac{\left\{ \sum\limits_{j=1}^{M} l_j [f'(t_j) - f'(t_{j-1})] \right\}^2}{\sum\limits_{j=1}^{M} l_j^2 [F(t_j) - F(t_{j-1})]} \tag{4.88}$$

provided that $q(X_{1i})$ is constrained (without loss of generality) to have zero mean value under the null hypothesis. This means that we require

$$\sum_{j=1}^{M} l_j [F(t_j) - F(t_{j-1})] = 0. \tag{4.89}$$

Now the result (4.88) for $E_{QE}$, with the constraint of (4.89), is exactly of the form of that for $E_{QC}$ given by (4.33). Thus we may conclude that the AO quantizer parameters must satisfy

$$l_j = \frac{f'(t_j) - f'(t_{j-1})}{F(t_j) - F(t_{j-1})}, \quad j = 1, 2, \ldots, M \tag{4.90}$$

and

$$e_{LO}(t_j) = \frac{l_j + l_{j+1}}{2}, \quad j = 1, 2, \ldots, M-1 \tag{4.91}$$

where $e_{LO}$ is the nonlinearity of (4.82). The very similar general form of this result and the previous quantization results we have discussed is quite apparent. Once again it is possible to show that the AO levels of (4.90) are also the LO levels for a given set of breakpoints, and that the LO and AO quantizer parameters are also those which minimize the mean-squared error between $e_{LO}(X_{1i})$ and $q(X_{1i})$ under the null hypothesis. Finally, generalized $M$-level quantization can be considered, as was done in Section 4.3.2 for the known signal detection problem.

For numerical results for the class of generalized Gaussian densities the reader is referred to the paper by Alexandrou and Poor [26]. Let us now turn to an investigation of quantization for the GCC statistic, for which the results are somewhat novel.

*Multilevel and Quantizer Cross-Correlators.*

The generalized cross-correlation array test statistic of (4.85) can be viewed as a sum over distinct channel pairs of a generalized cross-correlation two-input statistic, and we will therefore restrict attention to the two-input GCC statistic $T_{GCC}(\underline{X}_j,\underline{X}_p)$.

There are two ways of introducing data quantization into this test statistic. The GCC function $g$ can, in one approach, be constrained to be an $M$-interval quantizer function and the quantizer parameters may then be sought to result in an AO quantizer cross-correlator (QCC). It turns out that the AO quantizer parameters are exactly those for AO quantization for the known-signal detection problem, for the same noise density function. This is a consequence of the results (4.86) and (4.87). Thus all the results pertaining to maximization of $\tilde{E}_{QC}$ in Section 4.3 are applicable in the present case. This also includes results on $M$-level generalized quantization.

The second approach to introducing quantization for $T_{GCC}(\underline{X}_j,\underline{X}_p)$ is more general, and is based on the interpretation that $T_{GCC}(\underline{X}_j,\underline{X}_p)$ is the sum of *weighted bivariate data,*

$$T_{GCC}(\underline{X}_j,\underline{X}_p) = T_{GCC}(\underline{X}_{jp})$$

$$= \sum_{i=1}^{n} v(X_{ji},X_{pi}) \qquad (4.92)$$

with $\underline{X}_{jp}$ representing the vector of bivariate components $[(X_{j1},X_{p1}),(X_{j2},X_{p2}),\dots,(X_{jn},X_{pn})]$ and $v$ some real-valued function of two inputs. We may then require $v$ to be an $M$-level function $q$ with constant values over subsets of $\mathbb{R}^2$. For this purpose let $q$ be the function

$$q(x_1,x_2) = l_j \quad \text{for } (x_1,x_2) \in A_j, \quad j = 1,2,\dots,M \qquad (4.93)$$

where $\{A_j\}_{j=1}^{M}$ is a partition of $\mathbb{R}^2$. Let $E\{v(X_{ji},X_{pi})|\theta = 0\} = 0$; then for the test statistic of (4.92) the efficacy is

$$E_{GCC} = \frac{\left[ \int\limits_{-\infty}^{\infty} \int\limits_{-\infty}^{\infty} v(x_1,x_2)f'(x_1)f'(x_2)\ dx_1\ dx_2 \right]^2}{\int\limits_{-\infty}^{\infty} \int\limits_{-\infty}^{\infty} v^2(x_1,x_2)f(x_1)f(x_2)\ dx_1\ dx_2} . \qquad (4.94)$$

Recall that with $v(x_1,x_2) = \text{sgn}\ (x_1x_2) = \text{sgn}\ (x_1)\cdot\text{sgn}\ (x_2)$ in (4.92) the test statistic becomes the *polarity coincidence correlation* (PCC) statistic. With the multilevel function $q$ in place of $v$, it is reasonable to call the resulting statistic a *multilevel coincidence correlation* (MCC) detector. Carrying this nomenclature to its logical extension, the test statistic of (4.92) should be called a *generalized coincidence correlation* detector; the abbreviation for this is also GCC. In a coincidence correlator the value of the output corresponding to any input depends on the set of some input partition which the input value happens to fall in, or coincide with. In a generalized coincidence correlator there may be an uncountably infinite number of sets forming an input partition.

Using the result (4.94), we find that for an $M$-level MCC detector the efficacy is

$$E_{MCC} = \frac{\left[ \sum\limits_{j=1}^{M} l_j \int\limits_{A_j} f'(x_1)f'(x_2)\ dx_1\ dx_2 \right]^2}{\sum\limits_{j=1}^{M} l_j^2 \int\limits_{A_j} f(x_1)f(x_2)\ dx_1\ dx_2} . \qquad (4.95)$$

Once again we find a very close correspondence between this result and that for the efficacy $E_{QC}$ of a quantizer correlator known-signal detector. Proceeding exactly as we did in Section 4.3, we find that the AO levels and the AO partitioning maximizing $E_{MCC}$ can be obtained as

$$l_j = \frac{\int\limits_{A_j} g_{LO}(x_1)g_{LO}(x_2)f(x_1)f(x_2)\ dx_1\ dx_2}{\int\limits_{A_j} f(x_1)f(x_2)\ dx_1\ dx_2} , \qquad j = 1,2,...,M \qquad (4.96)$$

and

$$A_j = \{(x_1,x_2)|\tilde{t}_{j-1} < g_{LO}(x_1)g_{LO}(x_2) \leq \tilde{t}_j\}, \quad j = 1,2,...,M \quad (4.97)$$

provided that $g_{LO}(X_{ji})g_{LO}(X_{pi})$ has zero probability of being equal to any one of the $\tilde{t}_j$. Here the $\tilde{t}_j$ are, as before, defined by

$$\tilde{t}_j \triangleq \frac{l_j + l_{j+1}}{2}, \quad j = 1,2,...,M - 1 \quad (4.98)$$

where the $l_j$ are the AO levels of (4.96)

When $f$ is a symmetric function so that $g_{LO}$ is an odd function we find that any subset $A_j$ of an AO partition always contains complementary pairs $(x_1,x_2)$ and $(-x_1,-x_2)$ of bivariate points. For symmetric $f$ it is reasonable to require *a priori* that the partition $\{A_j\}_{j=1}^M$ be *symmetric*. This means we can consider $2M$-level partitioning with a partition $\{A_j, j = \pm 1, \pm 2, ..., \pm M\}$ such that (2) if $(x_1,x_2)$ is in $A_j$, then so are $(x_2,x_1)$ and $(-x_1,-x_2)$; (2) if $(x_1,x_2)$ is in $A_j$, then $(-x_1,x_2)$ is in $A_{-j}$. This particular case of symmetric partitioning was investigated by Shin and Kassam [27]. The AO MCC detector has subsets $A_j$ in its input partition which are bounded by level curves of the AO function $g_{LO}(x_1)g_{LO}(x_2)$. For unit-variance Gaussian noise, for example, these level curves are hyperbolas $x_1x_2 = $ constant. This suggests that simple-to-implement sub-optimum MCC test statistics may be obtained by constraining the level curves to be of specified shapes; for example, in the first quadrant of $R^2$ we can consider the level curves min $\{x_1,x_2\} = $ constant, for which the best choice of the constants can be made. Such constrained MCC schemes were also considered by Shin and Kassam [27].

Finally, as an indication of how well MCC and QCC detectors can perform, let us mention some numerical values. The optimum four-level MCC detector for Gaussian noise (unit variance) has an efficacy of 0.79; for eight levels this increases to 0.935, approaching the value of unity for the LCC detector as $M \to \infty$. For the QCC detector employing four-level quantizers at *each* input the best efficacy is 0.78; for eight-level quantizers this becomes 0.93.

Although we will not develop it here, it should be mentioned that it is possible to consider narrowband random signal detection and derive AO quantization schemes in the narrowband case also, with results which are related to those obtained above and to those for the deterministic narrowband signal detection problems in Section 4.4.


## 4.6 Conclusion

In this chapter we have tried to bring out the similarities in the treatments of, and results on, locally and asymptotically optimum data quantization in three major types of signal detection problems. These are the detection of known low-pass signals, the detection of deterministic narrowband signals, and the detection of random signals, in additive noise.

One very interesting motivation for considering quantization of the data is that it is possible to obtain simple *nonparametric* detection schemes, based on the use of conditional tests, for symmetrically quantized data. Details on such schemes may be found in [5,27]. Space limitations have also not allowed us to include a discussion on *maximum-distance* quantization, for which we refer the reader to [11]. In detectors such as the QC detector of Section 4.3 we did not consider quantization or finite-bit representations of the coefficients $a_i$. Some work on this has been done by Kassam and Lim [28] and more recently by Chen and Kassam [29].

One of the main restrictions that we worked under is the statistical independence of the noise samples in our detection schemes. Poor and Thomas [30] have considered optimum quantization for detection of known signals in additive correlated noise, but more general situations remain to be investigated.

Finally, let us mention one possible direction for further work in this area. This is the application of block quantization concepts to obtain more efficient schemes than the memoryless schemes that have been considered so far.

## References

[1]  J. Max, Quantizing for minimum distortion, *IRE Trans. Inform. Theory,* Vol. IT-6, pp. 7-12, 1960.

[2]  E.L. Lehmann, *Testing Statistical Hypotheses,* New York, NY: Wiley ,

pp. 83-88, 1959.

[3]   J. Hajek and Z. Sidak, *Theory of Rank Tests,* New York, NY: Academic Press, Chap. 6, 1967.

[4]   S.A. Kassam, Optimum quantization for signal detection, *IEEE Trans. Comm.,* Vol. COM-25, pp. 479-484, 1977.

[5]   S.A. Kassam and J.B. Thomas, Generalizations of the sign detector based on conditional tests, *IEEE Trans. Comm.,* Vol. COM-24, pp. 481-487, 1976.

[6]   S.A. Kassam, The performance characteristics of two extensions of the sign detector, *IEEE Trans. Comm.,* Vol. COM-29, pp. 1038-1044, 1981.

[7]   W.J. Bushnell and L. Kurz, The optimization and performance of detectors based on partition tests, *Proc. 12th Allerton Conf. Circ. and Sys.,* pp. 1016-1023, 1974.

[8]   R.A. Groeneveld, Asymptotically optimum group rank tests for location, *J. Amer. Stat. Assoc.,* Vol. 67, pp. 847-849, 1972.

[9]   Y.-C. Ching and L. Kurz, Nonparametric detectors based on $m$-interval partitioning, *IEEE Trans. Inform. Theory,* Vol. IT- 18, pp. 251-257, 1972.

[10]  L. Kurz, Nonparametric detectors based on partition tests, in *Nonparametric Methods in Communications,* P. Papantoni-Kazakos and D. Kazakos, Eds., New York, NY: Marcel Dekker, Chap. 3, 1977.

[11]  H.V. Poor and J.B. Thomas, Applications of Ali-Silvey distance measures in the design of generalized quantizers for binary decision systems, *IEEE Trans. Comm.,* Vol. COM-25, pp. 893-900, 1977.

[12]  H.V. Poor and J.B. Thomas, Optimum quantization for local decisions based on independent samples, *J. Franklin Inst.,* Vol. 303, pp. 549-561, 1977.

[13]  H.V. Poor and D. Alexandrou, A general relationship between two quantizer design criteria, *IEEE Trans. Inform. Theory,* Vol. IT-26, pp. 210-212, 1980.

[14]  P.K. Varshney, Combined quantization-detection of uncertain signals,

*IEEE Trans. Inform. Theory,* Vol. IT-27, pp. 262-265, 1981.

[15] C.C.Lee and J.B. Thomas, Detectors for multinomial input, *IEEE Trans. Aero. Elec. Sys.,* Vol. AES-19, pp. 288-296, 1983.

[16] V.G. Hansen, Weak-signal optimization of multilevel quantization and corresponding detection performance, *NTZ Commun. J.,* Vol. 22, pp. 120-123, 1969.

[17] V.M. Baronkin, Asymptotically optimum grouping of observations, *Radio Eng. Electron. Phys.,* Vol. 17, pp. 1572-1576, 1972.

[18] B.R. Levin and V.M. Baronkin, Asymptotically optimum algorithms of detection of signals from quantized observations, *Radio Eng. Electron. Phys.,* Vol. 18, pp. 682-689, 1973.

[19] A.H. Nutall, Detection performance characteristics for a system with quantizers, OR-ing, and accumulator, *J. Acoust. Soc. Amer.,* Vol. 73, pp. 1631-1642, 1983.

[20] H.V. Poor and J.B. Thomas, Asymptotically robust quantization for detection, *IEEE Trans. Inform. Theory,* Vol. IT-24, pp. 222-229, 1978.

[21] S. Tantaratana and J.B. Thomas, Quantization for sequential signal detection, *IEEE Trans. Comm.,* Vol. COM-25, pp. 696-703, 1977.

[22] H.V. Poor and Y. Rivani, Input amplitude compression in digital signal detection systems, *IEEE Trans. Comm.,* Vol. COM-29, pp. 707-710, 1981.

[23] J.W. Modestino and A.Y. Ningo, Detection of weak signals in narrowband non-Gaussian noise, *IEEE Trans. Inform. Theory,* Vol. IT-25, pp. 592-600, 1979.

[24] L.J. Cimini and S.A. Kassam, Data quantization for narrowband signal detection, *IEEE Trans. Aero. Elec. Sys.,* Vol. AES-19, pp. 848-858, 1983.

[25] V.G. Hansen, Optimization and performance of multilevel quantization in automatic detectors, *IEEE Trans. Aero. Elec. Sys.,* Vol. AES-10, pp. 274-280, 1974.

[26] D. Alexandrou and H.V. Poor, The analysis and design of data

quantization schemes for stochastic signal detection systems, *IEEE Trans. Comm.*, Vol. COM-28, pp. 983-991, 1980.

[27] J.G. Shin and S.A. Kassam, Multilevel coincidence correlators for random signal detection, *IEEE Trans. Inform. Theory*, Vol. IT-25, pp. 47-53, 1979.

[28] S.A. Kassam and T.L. Lim, Coefficient and data quantization in matched filters for detection, *IEEE Trans. Comm.*, Vol. COM-26, pp. 124-127, 1978.

[29] C.-T. Chen and S.A. Kassam, Optimum quantization of FIR Wiener and matched filters, *Proc IEEE Intl. Conf. on Comm.*, pp. F6.1.1-F6.1.4, 1983.

[30] H.V. Poor and J.B. Thomas, Memoryless quantizer-detectors for constant signals in $m$-dependent noise, *IEEE Trans. Inform. Theory*, Vol. IT-26, pp. 423-432, 1980.

# 5

# Digital Parameter Estimation

C.C. Lee

*Department of Electrical Engineering
and Computer Science
Northwestern University
Evanston, Illinois*

## 5.1 Introduction

This chapter is concerned with problems of parameter estimation using discrete-time and *digitized* samples–that is the received random process is converted into a sequence of digital numbers based on which parameter estimation is to be performed. As digital facilities have become dominant in the area of signal processing, such an approach is advantageous and timely. A parameter estimator will be called digital if it involves input quantization.

When the random process is digitized, so is the statistical model governing it [1]. Consequently, the estimator structure is invariant to the original statistical environment. This chapter considers only the case where the input process is stationary, white, and follows a continuous probability distribution with an *arbitrary* density $f(x|\theta)$, where $\theta$ is the parameter to be estimated. Let $(X_1, X_2, \ldots, X_n)$ be the input discrete-time samples. Suppose that each $X_i$ is properly scaled and then rounded into a binary word of $b$ bits and let $M = 2^b$. Let $\{w_1, w_2, \ldots, w_M\}$ denote those possible digital values each of which is associated with a probability

$$
\begin{aligned}
p_k(\theta) &= \text{Prob } \{D(X_i) = w_k | \theta\} \\
&= \int_{a_{k-1}}^{a_k} f(x|\theta) \, dx, \qquad k = 1, 2, \ldots, M
\end{aligned}
\tag{5.1}
$$

where $D(X_i)$ means "the digitized value of $X_i$" and $\{a_i\}$ are digitization thresholds. Also, let $n_k$ be the number of samples $X_i$ such that $D(X_i) = w_k$. Then, *whatever* the nature of $f(\cdot)$, the digitized samples $v_i = D(X_i)$ are governed by a multinomial distribution [2, Chap. 8]:

$$
\begin{aligned}
p(v_1, v_2, \ldots, v_n | \theta) &= p(n_1, n_2, \ldots, n_M | \theta) \\
&= n! \prod_{k=1}^{M} p_k(\theta)^{n_k} / n_k!
\end{aligned}
\tag{5.2}
$$

For signal detection, an input quantization summarizes input statistics by two sets ($m$ sets for $m$-ary detection) of discrete probabilities [3-9]. As a result, the detector enjoys a certain degree of nonparametricity, especially when the quantization is a coarse one. For parameter estimation, this is not quite the case. Because the multinomial probabilities $p_k$ are functions of the unknown parameter $\theta$, the functional form of $p_k(\theta)$ is the key to determine whether a digital estimator is parametric or nonparametric. We will call a digital estimator nonparametric if its design requires only a finite number of parameters from the input statistics and parametric, otherwise. Section 5.3 is a brief view of the parametric case, while Section 5.4 is a discussion of recent developments in nonparametric estimation based on input quantization.

One important advantage associated with the digital approach is the capability of solving non-Gaussian problems by treating Gaussian and non-Gaussian situations "equally". Since non-Gaussian problems have become increasingly important in many practical communication systems and since the performance of optimum estimation algorithms for the Gaussian case may be unacceptably poor under a non-Gaussian environment, this advantage is quite significant.

Technically, the design of a digital estimator does not require a laborious curve fitting for establishing an analytical statistical model for the noisy channel. As will be explained later, it is possible to develop estimation algorithms which require from signal and noise statistics simply the measurement of some discrete probabilities. Unlike Gaussian theory which has been well developed, non-Gaussian estimation problems are in general much more complicated and intractable. As a result, current techniques frequently lead to optimum or robust estimators which involve some continuous nonlinearities whose realizations are difficult. For the digital method, it is an objective that the resulting estimators are suitable for implementation by modern digital circuit technology.

Since any physical equipment has limited precision, the input digitization represents a *natural* approximation to the reality. In principle, the number of bits $b$ used for each digital sample determines the amount of information lost in A/D conversion. On the other hand, the complexity of the resulting detectors and estimators increases rapidly with $b$ (see Section 5.5). Fortunately, it has been indicated in many references (e.g., [1,3,12]) concerning statistical decisions based on quantized measurements that a "rough" quantization is usually adequate for a nearly optimum performance. For a theoretical support for using a short digital word, a relationship between input digitization and sampling input statistics is discussed in Section 5.2. After all, we are not concerned with the exact signal waveform itself but only with certain of its parameters. Under some regularity conditions, little of this required statistical information is lost by a rough quantization, even though the exact signal itself may be quite distorted.

## 5.2 Input Digitization and the Nyquist Sampling Theorem

Assume that the input samples follow a continuous distribution with density function $f(x)$ prior to digitization. The step size "$q$" of the digitization is determined by the digital word length $b$. For example, if the input samples are appropriately scaled to the dynamic range $[-1,1]$ in advance, then

$$q = 2 \cdot 2^{-b}.$$

When the samples are digitized, the density function $f(x)$ is "sampled" with a rate $1/q$, as shown in Figure 5.1.

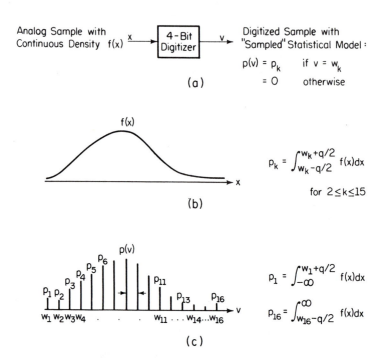

*Figure 5.1 Input digitization results in a sampling of underlying statistical model.*

Strictly speaking, this sampling is nonuniform since the digitized samples are not governed by $f(v_k)$ but, rather, by multinomial probabilities

$$p_k = \int_{a_{k-1}}^{a_k} f(x) \, dx$$

and since $p_k \neq f(v_k)q$ in general. However, by the Mean Value Theorem for definite integrals [13], there must exist a $v_k' \in (v_k - q/2, v_k + q/2)$ such that $p_k = f(v_k')q$. Therfore, the multinomial probabilities are equivalent to sample points $\{f(v_k')\}$ of $f(x)$. Although these sample points are not uniformly spaced, they satisfy $\max_k (v_k' - v_{k-1}') < 2q$ and can be treated by a nonuniform sampling theorem [14,15].

The density function $f(x)$ has a characteristic function $C(ju)$ which can be regarded as the "spectrum" of $f(x)$. From $C(ju)$, we can define the "bandwidth" of $f(x)$. Just as a strictly bandlimited time signal is rare, a precisely bandlimited density function scarcely exists [1]. However, it is possible to define $3-db$ bandwidth, $10-db$ bandwidth, etc., depending on the desired degree of accuracy. The bandwidth determines the Nyquist rate, which then gives the maximum step size $q_{max}$ or, equivalently, the minimum digital word length $b_{min}$. When $b \geq b_{min}$, the Sampling Theorem guarantees that the sample points $\{f(v_k')\}$ *uniquely determine* the continuous function $f(x)$.

The Gaussian density function, for example, has a Gaussian "spectrum" whose "bandwidth" should be small since $\exp(-u^2)$ declines rapidly. Therefore, it can be expected that a rough digitization (or uniform quantization) will not distort input statistics much. Indeed, as indicated in [1] and as shown by results in [3,7,16], a four-level uniform quantization (corresponding to 2-bit digitization) retains approximately 90% of the statistical information required for statistical inferences.

## 5.3 Asymptotically Efficient Estimation Algorithms Based on Quantized Samples

Based on quantized samples $v_1, v_2, \ldots, v_n$, the likelihood equation for estimating $\theta$ is given by

$$\frac{\partial \log p(v_1, v_2, \ldots, v_n | \theta)}{\partial \theta} = 0. \tag{5.3}$$

It follows from (5.2) that

$$\sum_{k=1}^{M} n_k \frac{p_k'(\theta)}{p_k(\theta)} = 0. \qquad (5.4)$$

Also, it is easy to derive the Cramer-Rao lower variance bound for unbiased estimates of $\theta$:

$$\text{CRB}(\theta) = \frac{1}{n} \left[ \sum_{k=1}^{M} \frac{p_k'(\theta)^2}{p_k(\theta)} \right]^{-1}. \qquad (5.5)$$

In general, no estimate can satisfy this bound because (5.4) can not be put into the form of $(\hat{\theta} - \theta)k(\theta) = 0$ with some statistic $\hat{\theta}$ and some function $k$ of $\theta$ [17]. The well-known maximum likelihood estimate (MLE) which is the solution of (5.4) can achieve the lower bound only in an asymptotic manner:

$$\lim_{n \to \infty} \frac{\text{CRB}(\theta)}{\text{var [MLE]}} = 1. \qquad (5.6)$$

In fact, all the optimum properties of the MLE are asymptotic ones [18]: namely, consistency, normality, and efficiency. The class of best asymptotically normal (BAN) estimates, introduced by Neyman [19], includes the MLE as a member and possesses all of these asymptotically optimal properties. Based on quantized observations $v_1, v_2, \ldots, v_n$, besides the MLE, there are two other BAN estimates. The minimum chi-square estimate (MCSE) is the solution of the equation

$$\sum_{k=1}^{M} \frac{n_k^2 p_k'(\theta)}{p_k(\theta)^2} = 0 \qquad (5.7)$$

which results from minimizing the functional

$$\chi^2 = \sum_{k=1}^{M} \frac{[n_k - np_k(\theta)]^2}{np_k(\theta)}. \qquad (5.8)$$

The modified minimum chi-square estimate (MMCSE) is the solution of the equation

$$\sum_{k=1}^{M} \frac{p_k(\theta)p_k'(\theta)}{n_k} = 0 \qquad (5.9)$$

which results from minimizing

$$\chi'^2 = \sum_{k=1}^{M} \frac{[n_k - np_k(\theta)]^2}{n_k}. \qquad (5.10)$$

Each of the MLE, the MCSE and the MMCSE is related to a minimization problem and is called an $M$-estimate [20]. In principle, an estimate can be obtained, at least numerically, if the functional form of $p_k(\theta)$ is given. This case will be referred to as "parametric estimation" since the functional form of $p_k(\theta)$ depends on that of $f(x|\theta)$. Normally, an analytical solution for any $M$-estimate mentioned above is not achievable. For numerical solutions, Newton's method can be found in Isaacson and Keller [21] and Fisher's method was employed by Rao [22].

## 5.4 Nonparametric Estimation Based on Quantized Samples

Although nonparametric statistical methods have been employed extensively in signal detection problems and density estimation, their applications to parameter estimation have not been notably explored. In this section the parameter estimation problem will be studied based on the assumption that the available input statistics include only two sets of parameters: namely, $\{p_k(\theta_0)\}$ and $\{p_k'(\theta_0)\}$, $k=1,2,...,M$, where $\theta_0$ is a fixed value. It is very easy to obtain $\{p_k(\theta_0)\}$ and $\{p_k'(\theta_0)\}$ from input statistics: the maximum likelihood estimate of $p_k(\theta_0)$ is [2, Chap. 8] the frequency of occurrence of the associated quantum $w_k$ when the true parameter is $\theta_0$, and $p_k'(\theta_0)$ can be obtained similarly by using the relation

$$p_k'(\theta_0) \approx [p_k(\theta_0 + h) - p_k(\theta_0)]/h,$$

where $h$ is a sufficiently small quantity. We will first develop a "locally efficient" parameter estimator which performs satisfactorily when the true parameter lies in the neighborhood of $\theta_0$. Based on this locally efficient estimator, three estimation algorithms are developed.

Assume that the parameter space is a small interval including a point $\theta_0$. Consider the likelihood equation (5.4). The Taylor series expansion for $p'_k(\theta)/p_k(\theta)$ about $\theta = \theta_0$ can be written as

$$[p'_k(\theta_0)/p_k(\theta)] = [p'_k(\theta_0)/p_k(\theta_0)]$$

$$+ (\theta - \theta_0)[p_k(\theta_0)p''_k(\theta_0) - p'_k(\theta_0)^2]p_k(\theta_0)^2 + o(\theta - \theta_0). \qquad (5.11)$$

For $\theta$ in the neighborhood of $\theta_0$, the higher-order terms can be neglected. Then, substituting (5.11) into (5.4) and solving for $\theta$ yields

$$\hat{\theta} \approx \frac{\displaystyle\sum_{k=1}^{M} n_k p'_k(\theta_0)/p_k(\theta_0)}{\displaystyle\sum_{k=1}^{M} n_k[-p_k(\theta_0)p''_k(\theta_0) + p'_k(\theta_0)^2]/p_k(\theta_0)^2} \qquad (5.12)$$

which should be an approximation to the MLE. To simplify further, we substitute $n_k$ by $np_k(\theta_0)$ in the denominator and use the fact that $\displaystyle\sum_{k=1}^{M} p''_k(\theta_0) = 0$ [this is because $\displaystyle\sum_{k=1}^{M} p_k(\theta) = 1$ for any $\theta$] to arrive at the following "locally optimum estimate" (LOE) of $\theta$:

$$\hat{\theta}_L = \sum_{k=1}^{M} b_k n_k + \theta_0 \qquad (5.13)$$

where the weighting coefficients

$$b_k = \frac{[p'_k(\theta_0)/p_k(\theta_0)]}{\left[\displaystyle\sum_{k=1}^{M} p'_k(\theta_0)^2/p_k(\theta_0)\right]} \qquad (5.13a)$$

depend on $p_k(\theta_0)$ and $p'_k(\theta_0)$, which are the only information assumed available from the statistical environment.

A special case happens when $\theta_0 = 0$ and $m = 2$. Then $p_2(0) = 1 - p_1(0)$, $p'_2(0) = -p'_1(0)$, and $n_2 = n - n_1$. As a result, the LOE is given by

$$\hat{\theta}_L = [(n_1/n) - p_1(0)]/p_1'(0). \tag{5.14}$$

If 0 is the quantization threshold so that $n_1$ represents the number of positive samples, this estimator is analogous to the sign test statistic in signal detection [23]. Depending on only two parameters $p_1(0)$ and $p_1'(0)$ which can be easily measured, this simple estimator features simplicity as well as a nonparametric nature.

Before the LOE is analyzed, we show a desirable structure for its implementation. Define

$$M_1 = n - N_1 = \text{no. of samples } X_i \text{ that exceed } a_1$$

$$M_2 = n - N_1 - N_2 = \text{no. of samples } X_i \text{ that exceed } a_2$$

$$\begin{array}{c} . \\ . \\ . \end{array}$$

$$M_{M-1} = n - N_1 - \cdots - N_{M-1}$$

$$= \text{no. of samples } X_i \text{ that exceed } a_{M-1}$$

$$M_M = 0.$$

Note that $N_k = M_{k-1} - M_k$ for $k = 2,3,...,M$. Then it is straightforward to prove that

$$\sum_{k=1}^{M} N_k b_k = nb_1 + \sum_{k=1}^{M-1} r_k M_k \tag{5.15}$$

where $r_k = b_{k+1} - b_k$, $k=1,2,...,M-1$. We thus obtain the block diagram of Figure 5.2, which shows that the input quantization as well as the computation of the LOE can be performed by employing an array of *identical* comparators and binary counters. The output of a comparator is either 0 or 1, depending on the relative magnitude of its inputs.

Now, let us define some local optimality properties here. An estimate $\hat{\theta}$ will be called *locally unbiased* about $\theta_0$ if

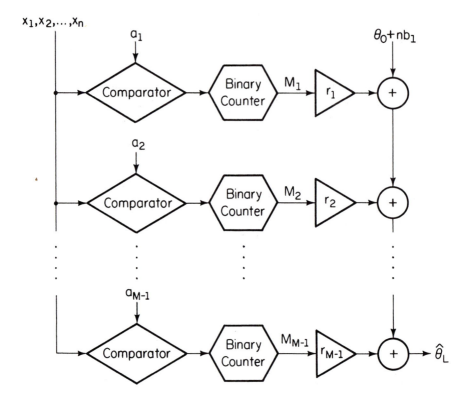

*Figure 5.2. Realization of the locally optimum estimator by a parallel connection of many identical elements.*

$$\lim_{\theta \to \theta_0} E(\hat{\theta}|\theta) = \theta_0 \tag{5.16}$$

and *locally consistent* at $\theta_0$ if, when $\theta = \theta_0$,

$$\lim_{n \to \infty} \hat{\theta} = \theta_0 \quad \text{in probability.} \tag{5.17}$$

An estimate $\hat{\theta}$ locally unbiased at $\theta_0$ will be called *locally efficient* at $\theta_0$ if

$$\lim_{\theta \to \theta_0} \text{CRB}(\theta)/\text{var}(\hat{\theta}|\theta) = 1 \tag{5.18}$$

where CRB represents the related Cramer-Rao variance lower bound for unbiased estimates. Note particularly that the definition of local efficiency does not involve the sample size. According to these definitions, an unbiased estimate must be locally unbiased, a consistent estimate must be locally consistent, and an efficient estimate must be locally efficient. However, an asymptotically efficient estimate, such as the MLE, is *not* necessarily locally efficient since such an efficiency refers to the limit $n \to \infty$.

It is not difficult to prove that the LOE of (5.13) is locally unbiased, locally consistent, and locally efficient at $\theta = \theta_0$. Detailed proofs can be found in [12] or [24]. This means that the LOE is nearly optimum if the parameter space is as assumed.

Define the efficiency of $\hat{\theta}_L$ as

$$\text{eff}(\hat{\theta}_L|\theta) = \text{CRB}(\theta)/E[(\hat{\theta}_L - \theta)^2|\theta]$$

$$= \text{CRB}(\theta)/\text{MSE}(\hat{\theta}_L|\theta) \tag{5.19}$$

where CRB is defined in (5.6) and $\text{MSE}(\hat{\theta}_L|\theta)$ denotes the mean-squared error of $\hat{\theta}_L$ given the true parameter $\theta$. Note that it is not impossible that $\text{eff}(\hat{\theta}_L|\theta)$ exceeds unity since CRB is a lower bound for the mean-squared error of the unbiased estimate while $\hat{\theta}_L$ is biased unless $\theta = \theta_0$ [24]. Indeed, with a tolerable bias, it is seen in Figure 5.3 that $\text{eff}(\hat{\theta}_L|\theta)$ is sometimes greater than unity in the generalized Gaussian case. It is clear that when the true parameter gets further from the point of local optimality ($\theta_0$), the bias and thus the mean-squared error become larger and the efficiency becomes smaller. The exact size of the parameter space within which the LOE performs satisfactorily depends on desired accuracy. For convenience, a parameter region within which $\text{eff}(\hat{\theta}_L|\theta)$ is no less than a specified value will be called a "confidence zone". Although an estimation problem with a parameter space restricted to a small interval may appear to be impractical, it is presented next that three estimation algorithms extend the advantage of LOE to a large parameter space.

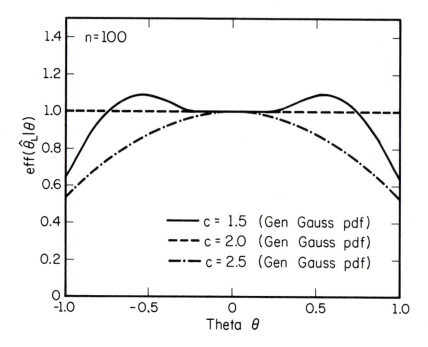

*Figure 5.3. Performance of the LOE in estimating the mean of a unit variance generalized Gaussian distribution (with c=1.5, 2, 2.5, respectively) using 100 samples. A uniform and symmetric (about 0) input quantization with step size 0.5 is used.*

*Algorithm 1: Feedback*

This algorithm is illustrated in Figure 5.4. Whenever the output estimate $\theta_p$ lies outside the reliable region $R_0$ of the locally optimum estimator, it is fed back to adjust the true parameter. For example, if $\theta$ is a location parameter, the adjuster will subtract $(\theta' - \theta_0)$ from each input sample; if $\theta$ is a scaling parameter, the adjuster will scale each sample by $(\theta'/\theta_0)$. The procedure will continue until $\theta'$ belongs to $R_0$. The final estimate is then obtained by "attaching" this $\theta_p$ to the last adjusting value. Before this algorithm is implemented for a specific parameter estimation problem, the problem of convergence (i.e., the possibility of an infinite loop) should be studied.

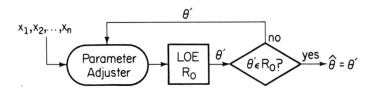

*Figure 5.4. Implementation of algorithm #1.*

*Algorithm 2: Parallel Processing*

For the feedback approach mentioned above, unless the parameter space is within the confidence zone of the LOE, it requires, on the average, more than one run to achieve the final decision. This would be a drawback when time is an important factor. Also, it must be studied carefully the possibility of generating an infinite loop (i.e., the situation where the estimate will never fall inside $R_0$). Assume that the parameter space is large but bounded and is partitioned into many (say, $L$) small regions. Then, it seems reasonable to pursue the possibility of employing $L$ LOEs each of which sufficiently and uniquely covers a small parameter region. If this idea can be realized, then, no feedback link is required and, with all $L$ LOEs functioning simultaneously on the same sample set, a reliable estimate should be obtained in one run. However, the difficulty resides in the objective that any estimation algorithm requires no more than $2M$ parameters $p_k(\theta_0)$ and $p_k'(\theta_0)$ from input statistics. Apparently, a sufficient condition is that all LOEs used are identical. An estimation algorithm satisfying this condition is described in Figure 5.5. The input samples $(X_1, X_2, \ldots, X_n)$ are fed simultaneously into L parallel "parameter adjusters".

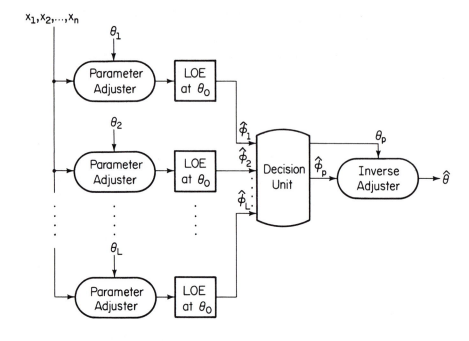

*Figure 5.5. Implementation of algorithm 2.*

Every adjuster tries to convert the samples so that the true parameter will be
pushed into the confidence zone of the LOE so that the LOE can handle it
well. Certainly one and only one of those $L$ paths achieves this end. In other
words, exactly one of those $L$ identical LOEs produces a "confident" estimate.
A decision unit thus follows the LOE's to determine which. Once the confident
one (say, the $p$-th) is extracted, an inverse parameter adjustment is performed
to bring the estimate back to its "original zone". The decision unit is obviously
an essential part of the whole scheme and is dependent on parameter type. As
a specific example, consider the estimation of a location parameter. For convenience, assume that each LOE is optimal at $\theta_0 = 0$ and let $R_0$ denote the
confidence zone of LOE. Then, the work of each parameter adjuster is sub-
tracting from each input sample $X_i$ a constant intended to shift the parameter

into $R_0$ which is a neighborhood of 0. Apparently, the successful adjuster will produce an adjusted parameter closest to zero. Therefore, selecting among $M$ estimates the one closest to 0 is a reasonable algorithm for the decision unit.

*Algorithm 3: Multiple-Decision + LOE*

Once again, assume that the parameter space is partitioned into $L$ small regions centered at $\theta_1, \theta_2, \ldots, \theta_L$, respectively. Now, instead of using $L$ units of LOE's simultaneously, a single LOE is used to follow an $L$-hypothesis testing:

$$H_1: \theta = \theta_1$$
$$H_2: \theta = \theta_2$$

$$\vdots$$

$$H_l: \theta = \theta_L$$

The idea is illustrated in Figure 5.6.

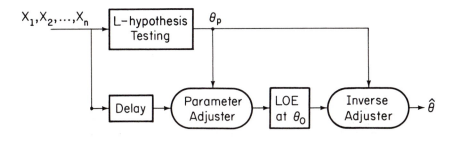

*Figure 5.6. Implementation of algorithm 3.*

The $L$-hypothesis testing is intended to locate the small region in which the true parameter falls. Assume that $H_p$ is the outcome of the $L$-hypothesis testing. Then, it is projected that the true parameter lies in the neighborhood of

$\theta_p$. Therefore, the parameter adjuster will convert the input data so that the true parameter is pushed into the confidence zone of the LOE. The output of the LOE is then inversely adjusted to where it was supposed to be.

The idea of the LOE can be extended to the case of simultaneously estimating several parameters. Assume that there are $m$ parameters to be estimated. Then each multinomial probability is a function of $m$ variables:

$$p_k = p_k(\lambda_1, \lambda_2, \ldots, \lambda_m) = \int_{a_{k-1}}^{a_k} f(x \mid \lambda_1, \lambda_2, \ldots, \lambda_m) \, dx.$$

Therefore, differentiating the multinomial model with respect to each unknown parameter will result in m simultaneous likelihood equations. Now, if the parameter space is a small region centered at some reference point $(\lambda_{10}, \lambda_{20}, \ldots, \lambda_{m0})$, each function of the unknown parameters can be approximated by the zero-order term and the first-order terms of its Taylor series expansion [13] about this reference point. Based on this approximation method, the likelihood equations can be simplified to simultaneous linear equations of $(\lambda_1, \lambda_2, \ldots, \lambda_m)$ which can then be solved by performing a simple matrix multiplication. All the coefficients of those linear equations are determined by $\{p_k(\lambda_{10}, \lambda_{20}, \ldots, \lambda_{m0})\}$ and

$$\frac{\partial p_k}{\partial \lambda_j}(\lambda_{10}, \lambda_{20}, \ldots, \lambda_{m0})$$

where $k = 1, 2, \ldots, M$, and $j = 1, 2, \ldots, m$.

These $(m+1)$ sets of numbers are all the resulting locally optimal estimator requires from input statistics and, again, can be obtained by measuring some frequencies of occurrence.


## 5.5 Estimator Performance Versus Computational Complexity

Since input statistics are to be summarized by two sets of probability parameters, these quantities must be stored in the memory. Assume that each input sample is coded into a $b$-bit binary word; then the memory space requirement is of order $2^b$ and is thus exponentially increasing with $b$.

Therefore, the choice of $b$ should depend on desired accuracy and available hardware support. Whenever the presented digital estimation algorithm is used to solve a specific problem, the trade-off between the performance and the number of bits used for each sample should be studied.

A conventional performance measure of parameter estimators is the asymptotic sample efficiency. In situations where the computation time of the estimate is linearly proportional to the sample size $n$, asymptotic sample efficiency and asymptotic time efficiency are synonomous. In other situations, an estimator may be asymptotically sample efficient but not asymptotically time efficient. For example, when a ranking of input samples is required, on-line computation time is at least proportional to $(n\log_2 n)$, which is known [25] as the time complexity of the most efficient sorting algorithm. As far as nonasymptotic performance is concerned, the conventional complexity is less important. However, whenever the computation speed of the estimate is lower than the sampling speed, a bottleneck situation develops. In this case, not only temporary storage is necessary but time efficiency is an important issue in performance comparison. This undesirable situation can happen even if the computation time is linearly proportional to the sample size, due to requiring too much computation per sample or using an ultrahigh sampling rate, for example. Since time is an important factor in many practical applications, the time efficiency of each digital estimator developed should be used as a performance measure whenever time efficiency and sample efficiency do not imply each other. In some situations, it is possible to improve time efficiency by means of parallel processing (i.e., simultaneous computation) [25]. In addition, the use of parallel architecture is highly desirable for the fast-growing VLSI implementation technology. Algorithm 2 presented above was designed for this purpose. In addition, it has been shown in [24] that this algorithm is very efficient in estimating the location parameter of a continuous, unimodal, and symmetric distribution.

## 5.6 Adaptive and Learning Procedures and Unified Implementation Techniques

Based on the digital approach, it is not difficult to design adaptive signal parameter estimators for situations where the statistical environments are non-stationary and/or where signal and noise are correlated. In some applications, it may be advantageous to develop efficient algorithms in the form of computer program packages each of which is capable of handling a class of estimation problems. The digital estimation algorithms presented are suitable for this purpose too. Indeed, with all signal and noise statistics (including their correlation if it exists) summarized by some easy-to-measure quantities, it is convenient to update efficiently the statistical environment from time to time. In particular, consider the implementation of the LOE shown in Figure 5.2. Those integers at the output of the binary counters can be sent to a central processing unit where the computation of the required frequencies is performed, say, every one hour, or, say every 24 hours, depending on the degree of nonstationarity of the statistical environment. Based on this, adaptive estimation algorithms can be accomplished.

### References

[1] B. Widrow, Statistical analysis of amplitude-quantized sampled-data systems, *AIEE Trans.-Appl. Indust.*, Vol. 81, pp. 555-568, 1961.

[2] P.J. Bickel and K.A. Doksum, *Mathematical Statistics: Basic Ideas and Selected Topics,* San Francisco, CA: Holden-Day, 1977.

[3] S.A. Kassam and J.B. Thomas, Generalizations of the sign detector based on conditional tests, *IEEE Trans. Commun.*, Vol. COM-24, pp. 481-487, 1976.

[4] L. Kurz, Nonparametric detectors based on partition tests, in *Nonparametric Methods in Communications,* New York, NY: Marcel Dekker, 1977.

[5] S.A. Kassam, Optimum quantization for signal detection, *IEEE Trans. Commun.*, Vol. COM-25, pp. 479-484, 1977.

[6] S.A. Kassam and J.B. Thomas, Dead-zone limiter: An application of

conditional tests in nonparametric detection, *J. Acoust. Soc. Amer.*, Vol. 60, pp. 857-862, 1976.

[7]   C. C. Lee and J.B. Thomas, Detectors for multinomial input, *IEEE Trans. Aero. Elec. Sys.*, Vol. AES-19, pp. 288-297, 1983.

[8]   C. C. Lee, Envelope digitization for detection of multiple pulses with incoherent phase, *Proc. 17th Conf. Inform. Sci. and Sys.*, Johns Hopkins University, March, 1983.

[9]   H.V. Poor and J.B. Thomas, Optimum quantization for local decisions based on independent samples, *J. Franklin Inst.*, Vol. 303, pp. 549-561, 1977.

[10]  R.E. Curry, *Estimation and Control with Quantized Measurements*, Cambridge, MA: MIT Press, 1970.

[11]  W. Kellog, Information rate in sampling and quantization, *IEEE Trans. Inform. Theory*, Vol. IT-13, pp. 546-551, 1967.

[12]  C. Lee, Estimation of signal parameters using quantized observations, *Proc. 1982 Conf. Inform. Sci. Sys.*, Princeton University, pp. 546-551, 1982.

[13]  W. Fulks, *Advanced Calculus - An Introduction to Analysis*, 2nd ed., New York, NY: Wiley, 1969.

[14]  J.L. Yen, On the nonuniform sampling of band width limited signals, *IRE Trans. Cir. Th.*, Vol. CT-3, pp. 251-257, 1956.

[15]  A.J. Jerri, The Shannon sampling theorem - its various extensions and applications: a tutorial review, *Proc. IEEE*, Vol. 65, pp. 1565-1596, 1977.

[16]  C.C. Lee and J.B. Thomas, Sequential detection based on simple quantization, *J. Franklin Inst.*, Vol. 312, pp. 119-135, 1981.

[17]  H.L. Van Trees, *Detection, Estimation and Modulation Theory, Part 1*. New York, NY: Wiley, 1968.

[18]  M.G. Kendall and A. Stuart, *The Advanced Theory of Statistics*, Vol. 2, New York, NY: Hafner, 1964.

[19]  J. Neyman, Contributions to the theory of the $\chi^2$ test, in *Proc. First*

*Berkeley Symp. Math. Stat. and Prob.,* Berkeley, CA: University of California Press, pp. 239-273, 1949.

[20]   R.J. Serfling, *Approximation Theorems of Mathematical Statistics,* New York, NY: Wiley, 1980.

[21]   E. Isaacson and H.B. Keller, *Analysis of Numerical Methods,* New York, NY: Wiley, 1966.

[22]   C.R. Rao, *Linear Statistical Inference and Its Applications,* 2nd ed., New York, NY: Wiley, 1968.

[23]   J.B. Thomas, Nonparametric detection, *Proc. IEEE,* Vol. 58, pp. 623-631, 1970.

[24]   C.C. Lee and Y.M. Lin, A unified approach to parameter estimation, *Proc. 22nd IEEE Conf. Dec. Contr.,* pp. 703-708, December 1983.

[25]   D.E. Knuth, *Sorting and Searching: The Art of Computer Programming,* Vol. 3, Reading, MA: Addison-Wesley, 1973.

# 6

# Robustness in Signal Detection

**H. Vincent Poor**

*Department of Electrical and Computer Engineering*
*University of Illinois at Urbana-Champaign*
*Urbana, Illinois*

## 6.1 Introduction

Signal detection systems frequently must operate in environments that are difficult to characterize with precise statistical models, and thus it is of interest to develop signal detection procedures that are robust against (i.e., insensitive to) deviations in the statistical behavior of signals and noise. During the past two decades there has been considerable work on the problem of designing such procedures, and in this chapter we present a survey of some of

This work was prepared under the support of the U.S. Office of Naval Research under Contract N00014-81-K-0014.

the principal developments in this area.

   We begin in Section 6.2 by discussing briefly the related problems of robust hypothesis testing and location estimation. Then, in Section 6.3 application of the methods developed for these problems to the problem of robust detection of signals in noise whose probability distribution is uncertain. The procedures considered in Section 6.3 are derived by optimization of risk-based performance criteria (e.g., probability of error). In Section 6.4 we consider an alternative formulation of robustness based on the optimization of signal-to-noise ratio criteria. We consider principally the problem of robust matched filtering in which signals and noise are modeled via their second-order statistics. Thus robustness here implies robustness with respect to deviations in second-order properties such as power spectra. We also consider briefly the problem of quadratic detection and a more general decision problem in the context of signal-to-noise ratio robustness.

## 6.2 Robust Hypothesis Testing and Location Estimation

### 6.2.1 Robust Hypothesis Testing

   The problem of robust hypothesis testing was introduced by Huber [1] in 1965. He considered the problem

$$H_0: \ X_i \sim P_0, \quad i = 1,\ldots,n$$

$$\text{versus} \tag{6.1}$$

$$H_1: \ X_i \sim P_1, \quad i = 1,\ldots,n$$

where $\underline{X} = (X_1,\ldots,X_n)^T$ is a vector of independent and identically distributed (i.i.d.) random vaiables taking values in a measurable space $(\hat{X},\hat{A})$ and where $P_0$ and $P_1$ are probability measures on $(\hat{X},\hat{A})$. For a test $\phi$ [with $\phi(x)$ equaling the probability of choosing $H_1$ given $\underline{X} = \underline{x}$ is observed] the conditional risks under $H_0$ and $H_1$ are given by $R_0(\phi) = E_0\{\phi(\underline{X})\}$ and $R_1(\phi) = 1 - E_1\{\phi(\underline{X})\}$, where, for simplicity, we have assumed a uniform cost structure. The three basic hypothesis testing design philosophies for (6.1) are the Bayesian, $\min_{\phi} [\pi_0 R_0(\phi) + \pi_1 R_1(\phi)]$ with $\pi_j$ being the prior probability of $Hj$ occurring; the minimax prior, $\min_{\phi} \max \{R_0(\phi), R_1(\phi)\}$; and the Neyman-Pearson, $\min_{\phi} R_1(\phi)$ subject to $R_0(\phi) \le \alpha$. The solution to each of these problems is given by the likelihood-ratio test

$$\phi(\underline{x}) = \begin{cases} 1 \\ \gamma \\ 0 \end{cases} \quad \text{if} \quad \prod_{i=1}^{n} \frac{dP_1}{dP_0}(x_i) \quad \begin{matrix} > \\ = \\ < \end{matrix} \quad \tau \qquad (6.2)$$

where $dP_1/dP_0$ denotes the (generalized) Radon-Nikodym derivative between $P_0$ and $P_1$, and where $\tau$ and $\gamma$ are chosen depending on which type of optimality is desired.

Since $P_0$ and $P_1$ are rarely known exactly, a more realistic hypothesis-tesing problem than (6.1) is the composite problem

$$H_0 : X_i \sim P_0 \in \hat{P}_0; \quad i = 1,2,\ldots,n$$

$$\text{versus} \qquad\qquad\qquad\qquad (6.3)$$

$$H_1 : X_i \sim P_1 \in \hat{P}_1; \quad i = 1,2,\ldots,n$$

where $\hat{P}_0$ and $\hat{P}_1$ are classes of probability measures on $(\hat{X}, \hat{A})$ representing uncertainty models for the data distribution under $H_0$ and $H_1$, respectively. For example, $\hat{P}_j$ might be of the so-called $\varepsilon$-contaminated mixture form,

$$\hat{P}_j = \{P \mid P = (1 - \varepsilon)P_j + \varepsilon U_j, \ U_j \in \hat{M}\} \qquad (6.4)$$

where $P_0$ and $P_1$ represent a known nominal model, $U_0$ and $U_1$ are unknown "contaminating" distributions, $\hat{M}$ is the class of all probability measures on $(\hat{X}, \hat{A})$, and $\varepsilon \in [0,1]$ is a degree of uncertainty placed on the nominal model by the designer.

To measure performance in the model of (6.3) we can replace the risks $R_0(\phi)$ and $R_1(\phi)$ with their suprema over $\hat{P}_0$ and $\hat{P}_1$, respectively, and thus the three classical design problems (Bayes, minimax prior, and Neyman-

Pearson) become (minimax) robust design problems. For many uncertainty classes of interest, the solutions to these problems are given by the solutions to the corresponding classical problems when the known distributions $P_0$ and $P_1$ are replaced with least-favorable distributions $Q_0 \in \hat{P}_0$ and $Q_1 \in \hat{P}_1$ satisfying

$$Q_0(\{\frac{dQ_1}{dQ_0} > \tau\}) \geq P(\{\frac{dQ_1}{dQ_0} > \tau\}) \quad \text{for all } P \in \hat{P}_0 \text{ and } \tau \geq 0 \quad (6.5a)$$

and

$$Q_1(\{\frac{dQ_1}{dQ_0} \leq \tau\}) \geq P(\{\frac{dQ_1}{dQ_0} \leq \tau\}) \quad \text{for all } P \in \hat{P}_1 \text{ and } \tau \geq 0 \quad (6.5b)$$

For example, for the classes of (6.4), the robust test is based on the likelihood ratio (see [1])

$$\prod_{i=1}^{n} \frac{dQ_1}{dQ_0}(x_i) = \prod_{i=1}^{n} \min \left\{ c'', \max \left\{ \frac{dP_1}{dP_0}(x_i), c' \right\} \right\} \quad (6.6)$$

where $c'$ and $c''$ depend on $\varepsilon$. Thus, in this case the robust test is based on a desensitized version of the nominal single-sample likelihood ratio, $\frac{dP_1}{dP_0}$. (Note that if $\varepsilon$ is too large, then $c' = c'' = 1$ implying that the classes $\hat{P}_0$ and $\hat{P}_1$ overlap, and the minimax robust test is trivial.)

Least-favorable pairs of distributions satisfying (6.5) have been found for many types of uncertainty models including *variational neighborhoods* [1],

$$\hat{P}_j = \{P \mid \sup_{A \in A} |P(A) - P_j(A)| \leq \varepsilon\}$$

where $P_j$ and $\varepsilon$ are interpreted as in (6.4); *band models* [2],

$$\hat{P}_j = \{P \mid P_{j,L}(A) \leq P(A) \leq P_{j,U}(A), \forall A \in \hat{A}\},$$

where $P_{j,L}$ and $P_{j,U}$ are fixed with $P_{j,L}(\hat{X}) \leq 1 \leq P_{j,U}(\hat{X})$; *Prohorov neighborhoods* [3],

$$\hat{P}_j = \{P \mid \rho(P,P_j) \leq \varepsilon\},$$

where $\rho$ denotes Prohorov distance and where $P_j$ and $\varepsilon$ are as in (6.4); *p-point classes* [4],

$$\hat{P}_j = \{P \mid P(A_k) = p_{j,k}, k = 1,\ldots,m\},$$

where $A_1,\ldots,A_m$ is a partition of $\hat{X}$ and the $p_{j,k}$'s are fixed with $\sum_{k=1}^{m} p_{j,k} = 1$; and combinations of these [5]. Moreover, the existence of least favorable distributions has been established for general uncertainty classes that are weakly compact and whose upper measures (or *capacities*) $v_j(A) \triangleq \sup_{P \in P_j} P(A)$, $A \in \hat{A}$, satisfy the 2-alternating property

$$v_j(A \cup B) + v_j(A \cap B) \leq v_j(A) + v_j(B) \tag{6.7}$$

for all $A, B \in \hat{A}$ (see [6]). For the latter situation, robust tests for (6.3) are based on the statistic

$$\prod_{i=1}^{n} \frac{dv_1}{dv_0}(x_i) \tag{6.8}$$

where $dv_1/dv_0$ is a Radon-Nikodym derivative defined for 2-alternating capacities.

Related results on robust hypothesis testing can be found in [7-9].

### 6.2.2 Robust Estimation of Location

Another statistical problem that is related to signal detection is that of location estimation, for which a robustness formulation was introduced by Huber [10] in 1964. Consider the observation model

$$X_i = \theta + \varepsilon_i, \quad i = 1,\ldots,n \tag{6.9}$$

in which $\varepsilon_1, \varepsilon_2, \ldots, \varepsilon_n$ is an i.i.d. sequence of errors with symmetric probability density $f$, and $\theta$ is an unknown location parameter to be estimated from an observation of $\underline{X}$. A useful class of estimates for $\theta$ is the class of M-estimates $\hat{\theta}_n$ defined via the relationship

$$\hat{\theta}_n(\underline{x}) = \arg \left\{ \min_\theta \sum_{i=1}^n \rho(x_i - \theta) \right\} \tag{6.10}$$

where $\rho$ is a function that defines the estimate. Examples of $M$-estimates are the sample mean $[\rho(x) = x^2]$, the sample median $[\rho(x) = |x|]$, and the maximum likelihood estimate $[\rho(x) = -\log f(x)]$. Note that within regularity $\hat{\theta}_n$ will be the solution to

$$\sum_{i=1}^n \psi(x_i - \theta)\Big|_{\theta = \hat{\theta}_n(\underline{x})} = 0 \tag{6.11}$$

where $\psi = \rho'$.

Within regularity conditions on the function $\rho$ (e.g., convexity), $M$-estimates are asymptotically normal with mean $\theta$ and variance $V(\psi, f)/n$, where

$$V(\psi, f) = \frac{\int \psi^2 f}{(\int \psi' f)^2} \tag{6.12}$$

with $\psi$ as above (see [10]). For fixed $f$ the Schwarz inequality implies that the asymptotic variance (6.12) is minimized by $\psi = -f'/f$ (or equivalently by $\rho = -\log f$), which leads to the maximum-likelihood estimate. The corresponding minimum value of (6.12) is

$$V(-f'/f, f) = 1/I(f) \tag{6.13}$$

where $I(f) = \int (f')^2/f$ is Fisher's information for location, so that this estimate is asymptotically efficient.

If $f$ is not known exactly but rather is known to lie in some class $\hat{F}$ of symmetric probability densities, then the minimization of (6.12) can be replaced with the minimax problem

$$\min_\psi \{ \sup_{f \in F} V(\psi, f) \} \tag{6.14}$$

which may lead to a robust choice for $\psi$. Within regularity on $\hat{F}$, the problem of (6.14) is solved by $\psi_R = -f'_L/f_L$ (assuming that the function $-\log f_L$ is convex), where $f_L$ is a least favorable member of $\hat{F}$ given by

$$f_L = \arg \left\{ \min_{f \in F} I(f) \right\} \tag{6.15}$$

(see [11]). Moreover, $(\psi_R, f_L)$ forms a saddlepoint for (6.14), i.e.,

$$V(\psi_R, f) \leq V(\psi_R, f_L) \leq V(\psi, f_L) \tag{6.16}$$

for all acceptable $\psi$ and all $f \in \hat{F}$. For example, if $\hat{F}$ is given by

$$\hat{F} = \{ f \mid f = (1 - \varepsilon)f_0 + \varepsilon h, \ h \in \hat{H} \} \tag{6.17}$$

where $f_0$ is a known nominal probability density with $-\log f_0$ convex, $\hat{H}$ is the class of all bounded symmetric densities, and $\varepsilon \in [0,1]$, then

$$\psi_L(x) = \max \ \{ -k, \min \ \{ \psi_0(x), k \} \} \tag{6.18}$$

where $\psi_0 = -f'_0/f_0$ and $k$ depends on $\varepsilon$.

Further details of this and related methods of robust parameter estimation can be found in [11].

## 6.3 Robustness in Signal Detection with Risk Criteria

### 6.3.1 Basic Methods for Robust and Locally Robust Detection

To model the problem of detecting a coherent signal in additive noise, we consider the hypothesis-testing problem:

$$H_0: X_i = N_i, \quad i = 1,\ldots,n$$

versus $\tag{6.19}$

$$H_1: X_i = N_i + \theta s_i, \quad i = 1,\ldots,n$$

where $\underline{X} = (X_1,\ldots,X_n)^T$ is a vector of real observations, $N_1,\ldots,N_n$ is an i.i.d. noise sequence with marginal probability distribution $F$, $\underline{s} = (s_1,\ldots,s_n)^T$ is a known signal sequence, and $\theta > 0$ is a signal-to-noise ratio (SNR) parameter.

If the noise distribution $F$ has a density $f$, then optimum tests for (6.19) are based on the likelihood ratio or equivalently on the log-likelihood ratio, which is given here by

$$\sum_{i=1}^{n} \log f(x_i - \theta s_i)/f(x_i). \tag{6.20}$$

For example, if $F$ is a $\hat{N}(0,1)$ distribution, then (6.20) becomes

$$\theta \sum_{i=1}^{n} s_i(x_i - \theta s_i/2) \tag{6.21}$$

which corresponds to a correlation detector. Note that the structure of (6.21) is very sensitive to large-magnitude observations. Thus, if the noise sequence is not exactly Gaussian but rather has a larger fraction of large observations than a Gaussian sample would have, then the intended (optimum) action of the tests based on (6.21) will be disturbed. In fact, one very large observation could completely dominate (6.21). The latter type of noise behavior is frequently encountered in detection systems due to impulsive phenomena.

The robustification of (6.21) was first considered by Martin and Schwartz in [12]. In particular, they considered the situation in which the nominal model of (6.19) with Gaussian noise is replaced by the composite problem

$$H_0: X_i \sim F \in \hat{F}_0, \quad i = 1,\ldots,n$$

versus $\hspace{5cm}$ (6.22)

$$H_1: X_i \sim F \in \hat{F}_1^i, \quad i = 1,\ldots,n$$

where $\hat{F}_0$ and $\hat{F}_1^i$ are classes of distribution functions on $\mathbb{R}$ (the real line) given by

$$\hat{F}_0 = \{F \mid F(x) = (1 - \varepsilon)\Phi(x) + \varepsilon U_0(x), \ U_0 \in \hat{H}'\} \tag{6.23}$$

and

$$\hat{F}_1^i = \{F \mid F(x) = (1 - \varepsilon)\Phi(x - \theta s_i) + \varepsilon U_1^i(x), \ U_1^i \in \hat{H}'\} \ (6.24)$$

where $\Phi$ denotes the $N(0,1)$ distribution function and where $\hat{H}'$ is the class of all distribution functions on $\mathbb{R}$. Note that the model of (6.22)-(6.24) does not preserve the additive-noise channel of (6.19) [i.e., $U_1^i(x)$ is not necessarily

$U_0(x - \theta s_i)$], and thus allows for inaccuracies in this assumption as well as in the assumption of Gaussian noise. To derive a robust alternative to (6.21) Martin and Schwartz applied the minimax robustness formulation of Huber [1], which is easily extended to the situation of independent but not identically distributed observations. As in the i.i.d. case the minimax robust tests for (6.22)-(6.24) are given by the optimum tests for time-varying least-favorable distributions, for which the log-likelihood ratio turns out to be

$$\sum_{i=1}^{n} \min \ \{k_i^{''}, \ \max \ \{k_i^{'}, \ \theta s_i(x_i - \theta s_i/2)\}\} \qquad (6.25)$$

where $k_i^{''} = -k_i^{'} \geq 0$ depends on $\varepsilon$, $\theta$, and $s_i$. Note that (6.25) processes the $x_i$'s as in (6.21) except that the accumulator ($\sum\limits_{i=1}^{n}$) is preceded by a time-varying soft-limiter

$$l_i(x) = \begin{cases} k_i^{'} & \text{if } x < k_i^{'} \\ x & \text{if } k_i^{'} \leq x \leq k_i^{''} \\ k_i^{''} & \text{if } x > k_i^{''} \end{cases} \qquad (6.26)$$

The resulting structure is termed a *correlator-limiter*. This structure thus gains robustness by limiting the effects of large observations and is a practical alternative to the linear detector of (6.21).

Note that if $k_i^{''} = 0$, then the $i$th sample is ignored in (6.25). This happens when $\varepsilon$ is large enough so that $\hat{F}_0$ and $\hat{F}_1^{i}$ overlap, or equivalently when the instantaneous signal-to-noise ratio (SNR) $\theta|s_i|$ is too small relative to the degree of uncertainty, $\varepsilon$. Thus for the commonly-occurring problem of detection with small SNR, an alternative robustness formulation to (6.22)-(6.24) is necessary.

For small-SNR detection in the model of (6.19) with known noise statistics, a useful design criterion is that of local optimality, which has as an objective the maximization of the derivative (with respect to $\theta$) of the power function $E_1\{\phi(\underline{X})\}$ at $\theta = 0$ subject to the false-alarm constraint $E_0\{\phi(\underline{X})\} \leq \alpha$. Within regularity, the locally optimum detector for (6.19) is given by a threshold test based on comparison of the statistic

$$\sum_{i=1}^{n} s_i \psi_{lo}(x_i) \tag{6.27}$$

with a threshold, where $\psi_{lo} = -f'/f$. For the unit Gaussian noise case $(F = \Phi)$, we have $\psi_{lo}(x) = x$, which makes (6.27) equivalent to (6.21) (since constants can be incorporated into the threshold). Thus, the locally optimum detector for (6.19) with Gaussian noise suffers from the same undesirable sensitivity as do the optimum detectors based on (6.21), and a robust alternative is desirable.

A robust version of the locally optimum detector can be sought by allowing the noise density $f$ to range over a class $\hat{F}$ of symmetric (about zero) densities and then considering the problem

$$\max_{\phi} \left\{ \inf_{f \in \hat{F}} \frac{\partial}{\partial \theta} E_1\{\theta(\underline{X})\} \Big|_{\theta=0} \right\} \quad \text{subject to} \quad E_0\{\theta(\underline{X})\} \leq \alpha. \tag{6.28}$$

Note that this formulation avoids the problem of overlapping hypotheses for small $\theta$ by preserving the additive-noise channel assumption and by requiring that the noise density be symmetric. The problem of (6.28) was considered by Martin and Schwartz [12] for the $\varepsilon$-contaminated model of (6.17) with nominal Gaussian noise and by Kassam and Thomas [13] for (6.17) with an abitrary nominal density. In these papers it is demonstrated that, for $\alpha$ sufficiently large, an asymptotic $(n \rightarrow \infty)$ solution to (6.28) is given by a threshold test based on the statistic

$$\sum_{i=1}^{n} s_i \psi_L(x_i) \tag{6.29}$$

where $\psi_L$ is from (6.18). Note that, for the nominally Gaussian case we thus have

$$\psi_L(x) = \begin{cases} -k & \text{if } x < -k \\ x & \text{if } -k \leq x \leq k \\ +k & \text{if } x > k \end{cases} \tag{6.30}$$

so that (6.29) applies soft limiting to the observations and then correlates the result with the signal. This structure is termed a *limiter-correlator*. In the general case, $\psi_0$ of (6.18) is the locally optimum nonlinearity for the nominal model, and so (6.27) is robustified against $\varepsilon$-contamination by adding soft limiting between the nonlinear operation $\psi_0$ and the correlation. As with the detector of (6.25), this intuitively produces robustness. It should be noted that this solution yields a saddlepoint for (6.28) only when $\alpha \geq \alpha_\varepsilon$, where $\alpha_\varepsilon$ is a lower bound depending on $\varepsilon$ and the nominal density. Unfortunately $\alpha_\varepsilon$ can be undesirably large for many applications. (A method for relaxing this restriction is discussed in [14].) However, even for $\alpha < \alpha_\varepsilon$, the structure of (6.29) still controls false-alarm probability over $\hat{F}$ and is robust in terms of maximin processing gain (defined below).

### 6.3.2 Robust Detectors Based on M-Estimates

Another method for deriving robust detection systems for the model of (5.19) was proposed by El-Sawy and VandeLinde in [15]. Their method consists of comparing a robust estimate of the SNR parameter $\theta$ to a threshold. In particular El-Sawy and VandeLinde proposed the class of *M-detectors*, which consists of those detectors which make a decision by comparing an $M$-estimate $\hat{\theta}_n$ of $\theta$ to a threshold, where $\hat{\theta}_n$ is given by

$$\hat{\theta}_n = \arg \left\{ \min_\theta \sum_{i=1}^{n} \rho(x_i - \theta s_i) \right\} \qquad (6.31)$$

where $\rho$ is a symmetric convex function that determines the test. In order to analyze the performance of $M$-detectors analytically in the model of (6.19), it is necessary to consider an asymptotic ($n \rightarrow \infty$) formulation and (to avoid singularity) to consider a sequence of alternative hypotheses (i.e., $H_1$'s) in which $\theta$ decreases with $n$. In particular, if we take $\theta_n = \nu/\sqrt{n}$ for some $\nu > 0$, then within regularity an $M$-detector based on a given function $\rho$ and threshold $\tau$ has asymptotic risks given by [15]

$$\lim_{n \to \infty} R_0(\phi) = 1 - \Phi\left(\frac{(\overline{s^2})^{1/2}\tau}{[V(\psi,f)]^{1/2}}\right), \qquad (6.32)$$

and

$$\lim_{n \to \infty} R_1(\phi) = 1 - \Phi\left(\frac{(\overline{s^2})^{1/2}(\tau - \nu)}{[V(\psi,f)]^{1/2}}\right),$$ (6.33)

where $\overline{s^2} \triangleq \lim_{n \to \infty} \frac{1}{n} \sum_{i=1}^{n} s_i^2$, $V(\psi,f)$ is as in (6.12), and where it is assumed that the noise density $f$ is symmetric about zero.

From (6.32) and (6.33) it is clear that, if $\tau < \nu$, the problem of designing good $M$-detectors is the same as the problem of designing good $M$-estimators; i.e., $V(\psi,f)$ is the pertinent design criterion. In particular, if $f$ is known only to lie in a class $\hat{F}$, then a saddlepoint $(\psi_R, f_L)$ for (6.14) will also yield a solution to the asymptotic robust detection problem

$$\min_{\rho} \sup_{f \in \hat{F}} \lim_{n \to \infty} R_1(\phi) \quad \text{subject to} \quad \sup_{f \in \hat{F}} \lim_{n \to \infty} R_0(\phi) \le \alpha.$$ (6.34)

Specifically, the $M$-detector based on $\rho_R$ with $(\psi_R = \rho_R')$ with threshold

$$\tau = [V(\psi_R, f_L)]^{1/2} \Phi^{-1}(1 - \alpha)$$ (6.35)

will be a saddlepoint for the constrained game in (6.34) if $\tau < \nu$ and will satisfy

$$\sup_{f \in \hat{F}} R_0(\phi) = R_0(\phi)\Big|_{f=f_L} = \alpha.$$ (6.36)

On the other hand, if $\tau > \nu$, then there is no saddlepoint for (6.34), although (6.36) will still be satisfied. Note that the condition $\tau < \nu$ is equivalent to the condition

$$\theta_n > \Phi^{-1}(1 - \alpha)/[nI(f_L)]^{1/2}$$ (6.37)

where $I$ is Fisher's information [as in (6.13)], so for fixed $n$ the SNR is constrained away from zero by this condition.

The $M$-estimate used for threshold comparison in the robust $M$-detector will be given by

$$\sum_{i=1}^{n} s_i \psi_R(x_i - \theta s_i)\Bigg|_{\theta = \hat{\theta}_n} = 0. \tag{6.38}$$

By assumption the function $\psi_R$ is nondecreasing (i.e., $-\log f_L$ is convex). So, comparison of $\hat{\theta}_n$ to a threshold is equivalent to comparing

$$\sum_{i=1}^{n} s_i \psi_R(x_i - T_n s_i) \tag{6.39}$$

to zero for some $T_n$. Thus the $M$-detector does not actually require solution of (6.38) for implementation. Note also that, unlike the correlator limiter of (6.25), the value of $\theta$ under $H_1$ need not be known for implementation of the robust $M$-detector.

The $M$-detection principle has been applied in several other robust signal detection problems. One of these is the problem of robust sequential detection in the model of (6.19) with a constant signal ($s_i = 1$, $i = 1,\ldots,n$) and with $\theta$ known under $H_1$. This problem has been treated by El-Sawy and VandeLinde in [16], wherein it is shown that robust sequential detection in this model can be accomplished by comparing at each sampling instant the robust $M$-estimate to two thresholds. In particular, the robust sequential detection scheme becomes for each $n$

$$\text{choose } H_0 \text{ if } \sum_{i=1}^{n} \psi_R(x_i - A_n) \leq 0$$

$$\text{choose } H_1 \text{ if } \sum_{i=1}^{n} \psi_R(x_i - B_n) \geq 0 \tag{6.40}$$

take another sample otherwise

Since the thresholds $A_n$ and $B_n$ are time varying, the implementation of (6.40) requires linear memory; however, a recursive (stochastic approximation) scheme with the same asymptotic properties as (6.40) is also developed in [16].

Another application of the $M$-detection idea is to the problem of detecting signals with unknown parmeters. This problem has been considered recently by Kelly [17], in which the following detection model is used:

$$H_0: \quad X_i = N_i, \quad i = 1,\ldots,n$$

versus $\hspace{5cm}$ (6.41)

$$H_1: \quad X_i = N_i + \theta s_i(\beta), \quad i = 1,\ldots,n$$

when $\beta$ is a vector of unknown signal parameters, $\theta$ is completely unknown (e.g., it may be negative) and the $N_i$ are i.i.d. with a symmetric density. Within appropriate conditions, a robust detector for (6.41) is obtained by comparing $|\hat{\theta}_n|$ to a threshold, where $(\hat{\theta}_n,\hat{\beta}_n)$ are joint robust $M$-estimates of $\theta$ and $\beta$ developed in [17]. (Note that the particular case of this problem in which $\{s_i(\beta), i = 1,\ldots,n\}$ is a sinusoid of unknown phase was considered earlier by El-Sawy in [18].)

### 6.3.3 Robust Detection in Dependent Noise

In all the methods discussed above, there is an underlying assumption that the noise is independent from sample to sample. In practice, however, samples are often taken at a high rate and so this independence assumption is frequently violated. For this reason it is of interest to consider the design of robust detection systems with dependent samples, and there have been several recent studies treating various aspects of this problem. In [19], the author has considered the problem of (6.19) (with constant signal) in which there is a weak moving -average type of dependence in the noise sequence. In particular, it is demonstrated the robust $M$-detector for noise sequences of the type

$$N_i = rY_{i-1} + Y_i + rY_{i+1}, \quad i = 1,2,\ldots,n \hspace{2cm} (6.42)$$

where $r$ is a dependence parameter and where the $Y_i$'s are i.i.d. with uncertain marginal density, is determined by a linearly corrected version of the robust $M$-detector for $r = 0$. (The linear correction term depends on $r$ and properties of the marginal distribution of the $Y_i$'s.) For the $\varepsilon$-contaminated $N(0,1)$ case with $r > 0$, this corresponds to a $\psi$ function that is similar to (6.30), but that redescends slightly for $|x| > k$.

Robust detection for (6.19) with a less structured dependence assumption has been considered by Moustakides and Thomas in [20]. In particular, Moustakides and Thomas consider the class of noise sequences $N_1,N_2,\ldots$ that have marginal densities in a mixture class (6.17) and that satisfy the mixing condition

$$|P(A \cap B) - P(A)P(B)| \leq \gamma_j P(A)P(B) \tag{6.43}$$

for all $A \in \hat{M}_{1,k}$ and $B \in \hat{M}_{k+j,\infty}$ and for all $j=1,2,\ldots,$ where $\hat{M}_{1,k}$ and $\hat{M}_{k+j,\infty}$ are the $\sigma$-fields generated by $\{N_1,\ldots,N_k\}$ and $\{N_{k+j},\ldots\}$, respectively, and where $\gamma_1,\gamma_2,\ldots$ is a fixed sequence. Moustakides and Thomas formulate the robustness problem by considering detectors that use statistics of the form

$$\sum_{i=1}^{n} s_i \psi(x_i) \tag{6.44}$$

and by defining robustness in terms of maximin *processing gain* (or *efficacy*), a quantity defined for the detector of (6.44) by

$$\lim_{n \to \infty} \frac{\left( \frac{\partial}{\partial \theta} E_i \left\{ \sum_{i=1}^{n} s_i \psi(X_i) \Big|_{\theta=0} \right\} \right)^2}{n \, \text{Var}_0 \left( \sum_{i=1}^{n} s_i \psi(X_i) \right)} \tag{6.45}$$

with false-alarm constraint. (This robustness formulation was introduced by Kassam, *et al.* in [21] to treat the problem of noise asymmetry.) Within regularity assumptions the solution to this problem is given by the nonlinearity

$$\psi_R(x) = \begin{cases} 0, & |x| < c \\ \psi_0(x) - \psi_0(c) & c \leq |x| \leq k \\ \psi_0(k) - \psi_0(c) & |x| > k \end{cases} \tag{6.46}$$

where $\psi_0$ and $k$ are from (6.30), and where $c$ is determined by the $\gamma_j$'s and $s_j$'s. Note that (6.46) is like (6.30) modified to have a null zone around the origin.

Another aspect of robust detection in dependent noise has been considered recently by Martin in [22]. Unlike [19], which considers weak but known dependence, and [20], which considers unknown but constrained dependence,

Martin considers autoregressive dependence in which the regression model is known and is driven by an i.i.d. sequence of uncertain distribution and in which the signal is of the form $\underline{s} = \underline{B}^T \underline{c}$ with $\underline{B}$ known and $\underline{c}$ possibly unknown. Martin's paper suggests that, in this situation, robust $M$-detection is best accomplished by first prewhitening the noise, and then applying an $M$-estimate to obtain an estimate of $\theta$ which can then be compared to a threshold for detection.

## 6.4 Robustness in Terms of Signal-to-Noise Ratio

### 6.4.1 Introduction

The results discussed in the preceding section were derived primarily by considering minimax robustness formulations with performance defined in terms of risks or related criteria. However, for improved tractability or for gaining intuition, it may be of interest to consider robustness in terms of alternate criteria. In particular, the use of performance measures such as signal-to-noise ratios is widespread in signal detection design formulations, and thus the consideration of robustness in terms of these criteria is of interest.

To consider this problem, let us return to the model of (6.3), in which we have i.i.d. observations in a measurable space $(\hat{X}, \hat{A})$ and marginal probability measure lying in one of the classes $\hat{P}_0$ or $\hat{P}_1$. Consider detection tests of the form

$$\phi_t(\underline{x}) = \begin{cases} 1 & \text{if } t(\underline{x}) \geq \tau \\ 0 & \text{if } t(\underline{x}) < \tau \end{cases} \tag{6.47}$$

where $t: (\hat{X}^n, \hat{A}^n) \rightarrow (\mathbb{R}, \hat{B})$ ($\hat{B}$ denotes the class of Borel sets in $\mathbb{R}$). One way of formulating the robust design problem for (6.3) is to consider the problem

$$\max_{t \in \hat{T}} \inf_{(P_0, P_1) \in \hat{P}_0 \times \hat{P}_1} D(t; P_0, P_1) \tag{6.48}$$

where $D(t; P_0, P_1)$ is some measure of signal-to-noise ratio at the output of the detection statistic $t$ when $P_0$ and $P_1$ are the true distributions under $H_0$ and

$H_1$, and where $\hat{T}$ is a class of detection statistics of interest. Note that a detection statistic solving (6.48) will yield the maximum possible worst-case signal-to-noise ratio for the uncertainty classes under $H_0$ and $H_1$, and thus will be robust from an intuitive viewpoint. This idea is closely related to Root's notion of stability in signal detection [23] and to Hampel's formulation of robust estimation (see, e.g., [24]).

A useful measure of signal-to-noise ratio for detection problems is the *deflection* or generalized signal-to-noise ratio (GSNR) defined by

$$D(t; P_0, P_1) \triangleq \frac{(E_{P_1}\{t(\underline{X})\} - E_{P_0}\{t(\underline{X})\})^2}{\mathrm{Var}_{P_0}\{t(\underline{X})\}} \qquad (6.49)$$

which, for fixed $P_0$ and $P_1$, is maximized over all $t$ by the likelihood ratio

$$t(\underline{x}) = \prod_{i=1}^{n} \frac{dP_1}{dP_0}(x_i)$$

(this follows straightforwardly from the Schwarz Inequality). The deflection is widely used for measuring detection system performance because of its tractability, its intuitive appeal, and its close relationship to error probability for some problems of practical interest (see, e.g., Gardner [25]). In the following we discuss solutions to (6.48) with $D$ from (6.49) for several special cases of interest.

### 6.4.2 Robust Matched Filtering

Consider the case in which $n=1$ is a separable Hilbert space (e.g., $\mathbb{R}^k$ or $L_2$) with product $\langle \cdot, \cdot \rangle$, and the model of interest is

$$H_0: \quad X = N$$

versus $\qquad (6.50)$

$$H_1: \quad X = N + s$$

where $N$ is a random element of $\hat{X}$ (representing noise) with covariance operator $\Sigma$ and where $s$ is a known element of $\hat{X}$ (representing a known signal)*.

---

* Note that $\Sigma$ can be any second-order noise quantity including the usual covariance matrix (in $\mathbb{R}^k$), the autocorrelation function (in $L_2$), or the

Consider the class of detection statistics

$$\hat{T} = \{\text{bounded linear functionals on } \hat{X}\} \qquad (6.51)$$

This corresponds in the case of $\mathbb{R}^k$ or $L_2$ observations to the class of detectors that consist of a linear filter followed by a threshold comparator. For this case we have straightforwardly that

$$D(t;P_0,P_1) = \frac{|\langle h,s \rangle|^2}{\langle h,\Sigma h \rangle}, \quad t \in \hat{T} \qquad (6.52)$$

where $h$ is the element of $\hat{X}$ satisfying $t(x) = \langle h,x \rangle$ for $x \in \hat{X}$.

The maximization of (6.52) over $h$ for fixed $s$ and $\Sigma$ is the classical linear matched filtering problem, and any solution to the equation $\Sigma h = s$ yields a maximum. On the other hand, if $s$ and $\Sigma$ are not known precisely but rather are known only to lie in some uncertainty classes $\hat{S}$ and $\hat{N}$, respectively, then (6.50) becomes a minimax *robust matched filtering* problem. Special cases of this problem have been considered by a number of authors, including an early study by Zetterberg [26] and more recent treatment by Kuznetsov [27,28], Kassam *et al.* [29,30], Aleyner [31], Burnashev [32], and by Verdú and the author [33,34]. General treatments of the problem in Hilbert space have been considered recently by the author in [35] and by Verdú and the author in [36]. For example, it follows from [35,36] that if $\hat{S}$ and $\hat{N}$ are convex sets, then saddlepoints $(h_R;s_L,\Sigma_L)$ for this problem are characterized by the necessary and sufficient conditions

$$\Sigma_L h_R = s_L$$

$$|\langle s_L,h_R \rangle| \leq |\langle s,h_R \rangle|, \quad \forall s \in \hat{S} \qquad (6.53)$$

and

$$\langle h_R,\Sigma_L h_R \rangle \leq \langle h_R,\Sigma h_R \rangle, \quad \forall \Sigma \in \hat{N}.$$

Several solutions to the equations (6.53) can be found in the works discussed above. As an example of the application of these conditions, suppose

power spectrum (in $L_2$ or $l_2$). (See [35] for examples.)

that $\Sigma$ is known precisely but $s$ is known only to lie in the class

$$\hat{S} = \{s \in \hat{X} \mid \|s - s_0\| \le \Delta\} \tag{6.54}$$

where $s_0$ is a known nominal signal and $\Delta$ is a degree of uncertainty in the actual signal $s$. Note that this uncertainty class can be used to model the situation in which a transmitted signal $s_0$ is possibly distorted in some unknown but bounded way by the channel so that the received signal $s$ is known only to be in $\hat{S}$ of (6.54). This model is also consistent with Slepian's notion of indistinguishable signals [37].

For this model, a robust matched filter $h_R$ is given by the (unique) solution to (see [35]) the equation

$$(\Sigma + \sigma_0 I)h_R = s_0 \tag{6.55}$$

where $I$ is the identity operator and where $\sigma_0$ is a positive scalar depending on $\Delta$ (of course, any scalar multiple of $h_R$ also solves (6.53)). Note that the solution to (6.55) is the filter matched to the nominal signal $s_0$ and the noise covariance $(\Sigma + \sigma_0 I)$. Since covariance $I$ corresponds to "white noise" in $\hat{X}$, we see that the effect on design of uncertainty of the form of (6.54) is the same as that of adding white noise of spectral height $\sigma_0$ to the channel. It is interesting to note that for the case in which the nominal noise is white (i.e., $\Sigma = N_0 I$ for scalar $N_0$) the solution to (6.55) is simply a scalar times $s_0$, which is equivalent to the nominal filter. This implies that in a white noise channel, the nominal matched filter is robust against signal distortion of the type (6.54).

Solutions to the robust matched filtering problem for other types of signal-distortion models and for several noise uncertainty models are given in [25-35]. An interesting related problem is that of designing the nominal signal to counteract possible signal distortion. This problem can be formulated as follows:

$$\max_{s_0 \in \hat{S}_0} \left\{ \max_{h \in \hat{X}} \min_{s \in \hat{S}} \frac{|\langle h, s \rangle|^2}{\langle h, \Sigma h \rangle} \right\} \tag{6.56}$$

where $\hat{S}$ is the signal uncertainty class and $\hat{S}_0$ is a class of allowable nominal signals. Note that a nominal signal solving (6.56) will be the best possible signal to use in conjunction with a matched filter designed to be robust against signal distortion in $\hat{S}$. This problem has been studied by Verdú and the author in [34], and solutions have been obtained for several distortion models of interest. For example, in the case $\hat{X} = \mathbb{R}^k$, if

$$\hat{S}_0 = \{s_0 \mid \|s_0\|^2 \leq P\} \tag{6.57}$$

where $P$ is a positive constant and if $\hat{S}$ is from (6.54), then the best nominal signal is any eigenvector of $\Sigma$ (with norm $\sqrt{P}$) corresponding to the minimum eigenvalue of $\Sigma$. It is interesting to note that this in fact is the best signal in $\hat{S}_0$ even in the absence of signal distortion. Moreover, because this $s_0$ is an eigenvector of $\Sigma$, the solution to (6.55) for this case will be a scalar multiple of $s_0$ which, similarly to the white noise case, is equivalent to the nominal filter. Thus, in the case of optimally designed signals within the models of (6.54) and (6.57), the nominal filter is robust against channel distortion. Unfortunately, this property does not carry over to other problems of practical interest, for which filters other than the nominal ones must be used to acheive minimax robustness.

### 6.4.3 Robustness in Terms of GSNR for Other Detection Problems

The matched filtering problem is the best developed in the context of robustness with respect to the GSNR criterion. However, several other problems have been considered in this context, and the following two brief examples are indicative of such problems.

*Example 1 (Robust Quadratic Receivers):* Suppose as in the matched filtering problem that $n=1$ and $\hat{X}$ is a Hilbert space. Consider the detection model

$$H_0 : \ X = N$$

$$\text{versus} \tag{6.58}$$

$$H_1 : \ X = N + S$$

where $N$ and $S$ are zero-mean, orthogonal random elements of $\hat{X}$ with covariance operators $\Sigma$ and $\Lambda$, respectively. For this problem, it is of interest to consider the class of detection statistics given by

$$\hat{T} = \{\text{bounded quadratic forms on } \hat{X}\} \qquad (6.59)$$

This class corresponds to the class of quadratic detectors (e.g., radiometers) that are commonly used for detecting stochastic signals.

Assuming that $N$ is Gaussian, we have for this class that

$$D(t;P_0,P_1) = \frac{(\text{tr } \{H\Lambda\})^2}{\text{tr } \{H\Sigma H\Sigma\}} \qquad (6.60)$$

where $H$ is a linear operator such that $t(x) = \langle x, Hx \rangle$ and where tr $\{A\}$ denotes the trace of $A$.

Maximization of (6.60) over $H$ for fixed $\Sigma$ and $\Lambda$ is the classical quadratic receiver design problem (see Baker [38]), and an optimum $H$ is given by any solution to the operator equation $\Lambda = \Sigma H\Sigma$. On the other hand, for $\Lambda$ and $\Sigma$ ranging over uncertainty classes $\hat{L}$ and $\hat{N}$, (6.48) becomes the robust quadratic receiver problem. The solutions to this problem are characterized by equations similar to those for the robust matched filter (6.53). Further details of this problem can be found in [36].

*Example 2 (Robust DSNR in a General Setting):* Consider the case in which $n$ and $\hat{X}$ are general with $\hat{P}_0$ and $\hat{P}_1$ convex, and

$$\hat{T} = \{\text{all measurable mappings from } (\hat{X}^n, \hat{A}^n) \text{ to } (\mathbb{R}, \hat{B})\} \qquad (6.61)$$

The problem of (6.49) was treated in this context by the author in [39].

Subject to mild conditions, solutions to (6.49) in this situation are given by

$$t(\underline{x}) = \prod_{i=1}^{n} \frac{dQ_1}{dQ_0}(x_i) \qquad (6.62)$$

where

$$(Q_0, Q_1) = \arg\left\{ \min_{(P_0, P_1) \in \hat{P}_0 \times \hat{P}_1} \int \left(\frac{dP_1}{dP_0}\right)^2 dP_0 \right\}. \qquad (6.63)$$

Note that for fixed $(P_0, P_1)$ we have

$$\max_{t \in T} D(t; P_0, P_1) = \left[ \int \left(\frac{dP_1}{dP_0}\right)^2 dP_0 \right]^n \qquad (6.64)$$

so that the pair from (6.63) is least favorable for maximum output deflection.

A pair of distributions in $\hat{P}_0 \times \hat{P}_1$ that is least favorable in Huber's sense and satisfies (6.5) will automatically be least favorable in the sense of (6.63) (see [39]); however, the converse of this fact is not true. In fact, the quantity $\int (dP_1/dP_0)^2 \, dP_0$ is only one of a large class of divergences all of which must be minimized by a pair $(Q_0, Q_1)$ in order for $(Q_0, Q_1)$ to be least favorable in the sense of (6.5).

## 6.5 Conclusion

In this chapter we have surveyed briefly some of the principal methods that have been developed for designing robust signal detection systems. These methods include techniques for dealing with uncertainty in the noise distribution as discussed in Section 6.3 and techniques for dealing with uncertainty in the second-order statistics of signal and noise as discussed in Section 6.4. The methods discussed here are all based on minimax design; the detection techniques developed thereby are intuitively robust and their performance robustness has been verified numerically throughout the works referenced in this chapter.

Similar methods have been developed for other statistical signal processing functions, such as signal estimation (see, e.g., [40-42]), and there are many interesting analogies among these and the robust signal detection problems. An extensive survey of this methodology can be found in a forthcoming paper by Kassam and the author [43].

## References

[1] P.J. Huber, A robust version of the probability ratio test, *Ann. Math. Statist.*, Vol. 36, pp. 1753-1758, 1965.

[2] S.A. Kassam, Robust hypothesis testing for bounded classes of probability densities, *IEEE Trans. Inform. Theory,* Vol IT-27, pp. 242-247, 1981.

[3] P.J. Huber, Robust confidence limits, *Z. Wahr. verw. Geb.,* Vol. 10, pp. 269-278, 1968.

[4] K.S. Vastola and H.V. Poor, On the p-point uncertainty class, *IEEE Trans. Inform. Theory,* Vol. IT-29, pp. 316-327, 1984.

[5] H. Rieder, Least favorable pairs for special capacities, *Ann. Statist.,* Vol. 5, pp. 909-921, 1977.

[6] P.J. Huber and V. Strassen, Minimax tests and the Neyman-Pearson lemma for capacities, *Ann. Statist.,* Vol. 1, pp. 251-263, 1973.

[7] N.M. Khalfina and L.A. Khalfin, On a robust version of the likelihood ratio test, *SIAM Th. Prob. Appl.,* Vol. 20, pp. 199-202, 1975.

[8] T. Bednarski, On solutions of minimax test problems for special capacities, *Z. Wahr. verw. Geb.,* Vol. 58, pp. 397-405, 1981.

[9] V.P. Kuznetsov, Stable rules for discriminating hypotheses, *Prob. Inform. Trans.,* Vol. 18, pp. 41-51, 1982.

[10] P.J. Huber, Robust estimation of a location parameter, *Ann. Math. Statist.,* Vol. 35, pp. 73-101, 1964.

[11] P.J. Huber, *Robust Statistics,* New York, NY: Wiley, 1981.

[12] R.D. Martin and S.C. Schwartz, Robust detection of a known signal in nearly Gaussian noise, *IEEE Trans. Inform. Theory,* Vol. IT-17, pp. 50-56, 1971.

[13] S.A. Kassam and J.B. Thomas, Asymptotically robust quantization for detection, *IEEE Trans. Inform. Theory,* Vol. IT-22, pp. 22-26, 1976.

[14] H.V. Poor and J.B. Thomas, Asymptotically robust quantization for detection, *IEEE Trans. Inform. Theory,* Vol. IT-24, pp. 222-229, 1978.

[15] A.H. El-Sawy and V.D. VandeLinde, Robust detection of known signals,

*IEEE Trans. Inform. Theory,* Vol. IT-23, pp. 722-727, 1977.

[16]   A.H. El-Sawy and V.D. VandeLinde, Robust sequential detection of signals in noise, *IEEE Trans. Inform. Theory,* Vol. IT-25, pp. 346-353, 1979.

[17]   P.A. Kelly, Robust estimation and detection of signals with arbitrary parameters, *Proc. 21st Annual Allerton Conf. Comm., Contr., Comp.,* pp. 602-609, 1983.

[18]   A.H. El-Sawy, Detection of signals with unknown phase, *Proc. 17th Annual Allerton Conf. Comm., Contr., and Comp.,* pp. 152-165, 1979.

[19]   H.V. Poor, Signal detection in weakly dependent noise - Part II: Robust detection, *IEEE Trans. Inform. Theory,* Vol. IT-28, pp. 744-752, 1982.

[20]   G.V. Moustakides and J.B. Thomas, Min-max detection of weak signals in $\phi$-mixing noise, *IEEE Trans. Inform. Theory,* Vol. IT-30, pp. 529-537, 1984.

[21]   S.A. Kassam, G. Moustakides and J.G. Shin, Robust detection of known signals in asymmetric noise, *IEEE Trans. Inform. Theory,* Vol. IT-28, pp. 84-91, 1982.

[22]   R.D. Martin, Robust estimation of signal parameters with dependent data, *Proc. 21st IEEE Conf. Dec. Contr.,* pp. 433-436, 1982.

[23]   W.L. Root, Stability in signal detection problems, in *Proc. Symp. Appl. Math.,* Vol. 16, Providence, RI: American Math. Society, 1964.

[24]   F.R. Hampel, A general qualitative definition of robustness, *Ann. Math. Statist.,* Vol. 42, pp. 1887-1896, 1971.

[25]   W.A. Gardner, A unifying view of second-order measures of quality for signal classification, *IEEE Trans. Comm.,* Vol. COM-28, pp. 807-815, 1980.

[26]   L.H. Zetterberg, Signal detection under noise interference in a game situation, *IEEE Trans. Inform. Theory,* Vol. IT-8, pp. 47-57, 1962.

[27]   V.P. Kutznetsov, Synthesis of linear detectors when the signal is inexactly given and the properties of the normal noise are incompletely known, *Radio Eng. Electron. Phys.,* (English Transl.), Vol. 19, pp. 65-

73, 1974.

[28]  V.P. Kuznetsov, Stable detection when the signal and spectrum of normal noise are inaccurately known, *Telecomm. Radio Eng.,* (English Transl.), Vol. 30-31, pp. 58-64, 1976.

[29]  S.A. Kassam, T.L. Lim and L.J. Cimini, Two dimensional filters for signal processing under modeling uncertainty, *IEEE Trans. Geosci. Elec.,* Vol. GE-18, pp. 331-336, 1980.

[30]  C.T. Chen and S.A. Kassam, Robust multi-input matched filters, *Proc. 19th Annual Allerton Conf. on Comm., Contr., Comp.,* pp. 586-595, 1981.

[31]  R.Sh. Aleyner, Synthesis of stable linear dectectors for an inaccurately known signal, *Radio Eng. Electron. Phys.* (English Transl.), Vol. 22, pp. 142-145, 1977

[32]  M.V. Burnashev, On the minimax detection of an inaccurately known signal in a white Gaussian noise background, *Theor. Prob. Appl.,* Vol. 24, pp. 107-119, 1979.

[33]  S. Verdú and H.V. Poor, Minimax robust discrete-time matched filters, *IEEE Trans. Comm.,* Vol. COM-31, pp. 208-215, 1983.

[34]  S. Verdú and H.V. Poor, Signal selection for robust matched filtering, *IEEE Trans. Comm.,* Vol. COM-31, pp. 667-670, 1983.

[35]  H.V. Poor, Robust matched filters, *IEEE Trans. Inform. Theory,* Vol. IT-29, pp. 677-687, 1983.

[36]  S. Verdú and H.V. Poor, On minimax robustness: A general approach and applications, *IEEE Trans. Inform. Theory,* Vol. IT-30, pp. 328-340, 1984.

[37]  D. Slepian, Indistinguishable signals, *Proc. IEEE,* Vol. 64, pp. 292-300, 1976.

[38]  C.R. Baker, Optimum quadratic detection of a random vector in Gaussian noise, *IEEE Trans. Comm.,* Vol. COM-14, pp. 802-805, 1966.

[39]  H.V. Poor, Robust decision design using a distance criterion, *IEEE Trans. Inform. Theory,* Vol. IT-26, pp. 575-587, 1980.

[40]   C.J. Masreliez and R.D. Martin, Robust Bayesian estimation for the linear model and robustifying the Kalman filter, *IEEE Trans. Auto. Contr.*, Vol. AC-22, pp. 361-371, 1977.

[41]   S.A. Kassam and T.L. Lim, Robust Wiener filters, *J. Franklin Inst.*, Vol. 304, pp. 171-185, 1977.

[42]   K.S. Vastola and H.V. Poor, Robust Wiener-Kolmogorov theory, *IEEE Trans. Inform. Theory*, Vol. IT-30, pp. 316-327, 1984.

[43]   S.A. Kassam and H.V. Poor, Robust techniques for signal processing: A survey, *Proc. IEEE* , Vol. 73, March 1985.

# 7

# Sequential Detection of a Positive Signal

**Sawasd Tantaratana**

*AT&T Bell Laboratories*
*Middletown, New Jersey*

## 7.1 Introduction

In this chapter we consider the problem of detecting a positive signal in additive noise. The observations are assumed to be discrete-time. Denote the observation random variables by $Y_1, Y_2, \ldots$, the noise random variables by $X_1, X_2, \ldots$, and the signal by $\theta_1$. We have to make a decision, based on the observations, whether the signal is absent or present. This is equivalent to testing an hypothesis $H_0$ versus $H_1$, where

$$H_0: \ Y_i = X_i, \quad i = 1, 2, \ldots \qquad (7.1)$$

$$H_1: \ Y_i = X_i + \theta_1, \quad i = 1, 2, \ldots$$

Throughout this chapter we denote a realization of a random variable by a lowercase letter. For example, $y_i$ is a realization of $Y_i$.

If a detector gathers $M$ (a number fixed prior to the experiment) observations and a decision (to accept $H_0$ or accept $H_1$) is based on these $M$ observations (also called samples), such a detector (or a test) is called a fixed-sample-size (FSS) detector. Therefore, an FSS detector is of the form

$$\phi(y_1, y_2, \ldots, y_M) \begin{cases} > \tau & \rightarrow & \text{say } H_1 \\ = \tau & \rightarrow & \begin{array}{l} \text{say } H_1 \text{ with prob. } \gamma \\ \text{and } H_0 \text{ with prob. } 1-\gamma \end{array} \\ < \tau & \rightarrow & \text{say } H_0 \end{cases} \qquad (7.2)$$

where $\phi(\cdot, \cdot, \ldots, \cdot)$ is a function of the variables. The values of $M$ and $\tau$ are such that the detector has a given false-alarm probability [Prob (say $H_1 | H_0$ is true)] and a given detection probability [Prob (say $H_1 | H_1$ is true )]. FSS detectors are discussed elsewhere in this book. Here, we consider sequential tests, the sample sizes (ie., the number of samples at which a decision is made) of which depend on the realizations of $Y_1, Y_2, \ldots$ We shall use $N$ to denote the sample size of a sequential test. Therefore, $N$ is a function of $Y_1, Y_2, \ldots$ and it becomes a random variable.

In this chapter, various sequential detection procedures are reviewed. Attention is given to results reported since 1970, since results prior to this date have been reviewed elsewhere; see Helstrom [1], Bussgang [2], and Ghosh [3], for example. In Section 7.2, Wald's sequential probability ratio test (SPRT) is defined and some of its properties are discussed. In Section 7.3, the asymptotic relative efficiency (ARE) of the SPRT and other sequential tests are studied. In Section 7.4, we turn our attention to nonparametric and robust sequential detectors. Various detectors are explained and their performances are discussed. Then, in Section 7.5, we discuss some types of sequential detectors which are designed to reduce the maximum expected value of the sample size. Finally, in Section 7.6, the detection problem with dependent observations is investigated.

## 7.2 The Sequential Probability Ratio Test

We now describe the SPRT discovered by Wald [4]. Assume that $X_1, X_2, \ldots$ are independent and identically distributed (iid) random variables with a known probability density function (pdf) $f(x)$ and that $\theta_1$ is a known signal. The likelihood ratio (probability ratio) up to $n$ observations for (7.1) is

$$\Lambda_n(\underline{y}) = \prod_{i=1}^{n} \frac{f(y_i - \theta_1)}{f(y_i)} \tag{7.3}$$

where $\underline{y} = (y_1, \ldots, y_n)$. The SPRT compares the probability ratio (7.3) to two constant thresholds, $A$ and $B$ (normally $0 < B < 1 < A < \infty$), for $n = 1, 2, \ldots$. The test stops if $\Lambda_n(\underline{y})$ is $\geq A$ with an acceptance of $H_1$ or if $\Lambda_n(\underline{y})$ is $\leq B$ with an acceptance of $H_0$. Equivalently, we may test the log of the probability ratio against $a = \ln(A)$ and $b = \ln(B)$ so that the SPRT becomes

$$\sum_{i=1}^{n} z_i \begin{cases} \geq a & \rightarrow \text{ accept } H_1 \\ \leq b & \rightarrow \text{ accept } H_0 \\ \text{otherwise} & \rightarrow \text{ take another sample and repeat} \end{cases} \tag{7.4}$$

where $z_i$ is a realization of $Z_i = \ln[f(Y_i - \theta_1)/f(Y_i)]$. The boundaries, decision regions, and a sample path for (7.4) are shown in Figure 7.1. The sample size $N$ is the value of $n$ at which a decision is made, i.e.,

$$N = \inf \{n : \sum_{i=1}^{n} Z_i \notin (b, a)\}. \tag{7.5}$$

Wald showed that the SPRT terminates with probability 1, i.e., $\text{Prob}(N < \infty) = 1$. Let us denote the Type I error, which is $\text{Prob}(\text{say } H_1 | H_0 \text{ true})$, by $\alpha$ and denote the Type II error, which is $\text{Prob}(\text{say } H_0 | H_1 \text{ is true})$ by $1 - \beta$. Note that $\beta$ equals the detection probability. It can be shown [4] that $\alpha$ and $\beta$ satisfy

$$\frac{\alpha}{\beta} \leq A^{-1} = e^{-a} \tag{7.6a}$$

and

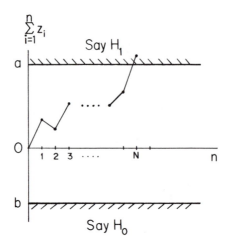

*Figure 7.1 Thresholds, decision regions, and a sample path of an SPRT.*

$$\frac{1-\beta}{1-\alpha} \leq B = e^b. \tag{7.6b}$$

Since $0 < \beta \leq 1$ and $0 < 1-\alpha \leq 1$, these inequalities imply

$$\alpha \leq e^{-a} \tag{7.7a}$$

and

$$\beta \geq 1 - e^b. \tag{7.7b}$$

The proof for (7.6a) and (7.6b) does not require the iid assumption, so that they are also valid for dependent and/or nonidentical observations, provided that $\Lambda_n(\underline{y})$ is the ratio of the joint pdf of $Y_1,...,Y_n$ under $H_1$ and the joint pdf of $Y_1,...,Y_n$ under $H_0$.

The inequalities in (7.6a) and (7.6b) arise from the overshoot across threshold $a$ or $b$ when the test terminates. If the mean and variance of the log-likelihood ratio are small compared to $a$ and $|b|$, the sample size is large and the overshoot is small on the average. In this case, we may neglect the overshoot and replace (7.6a) and (7.6b) with equalities, yielding approximations for $a$ and $b$ in terms of $\alpha$ and $\beta$:

$$a \approx \ln\frac{\beta}{\alpha} \tag{7.8a}$$

and

$$b \approx \ln\frac{1-\beta}{1-\alpha}. \tag{7.8b}$$

Therefore, the thresholds $a$ and $b$ can be computed easily from (7.8a) and (7.8b), once the values of $\alpha$ and $\beta$ are decided. This simplicity is one attractive feature of the SPRT.

We shall call the expected value of $n$ by the term *average sample number* (ASN), which is denoted by $E(N|0)$ when $H_0$ is true and by $E(N|\theta_1)$ when $H_1$ is true. Note that for an FSS (nonsequential) detector we have ASN = M = constant. It has been shown (Wald and Wolfowitz [5]) that, with iid observations, the SPRT possesses an optimum property in the sense that it minimizes $E(N|0)$ and $E(N|\theta_1)$ among all tests, sequential or nonsequential, with finite ASN and with error probabilities no larger than $\alpha$ and $1-\beta$ under $H_0$ and $H_1$, respectively. In other words, let the SPRT have errors $\alpha$ and $1-\beta$ (with proper choices of $a$ and $b$) and have ASN of $E(N|0)$ and $E(N|\theta_1)$. Also, let a competing test $T_p$ have error $\alpha'$ under $H_0$, error $1-\beta'$ under $H_1$, ASN of $E(N'|0) < \infty$ under $H_0$, and $E(N'|\theta_1) < \infty$ under $H_1$. The optimality of the SPRT states that the conditions

$$\alpha' \leq \alpha \quad \text{and} \quad 1-\beta' \leq 1-\beta \tag{7.9}$$

imply

$$E(N|0) \leq E(N'|0) \quad \text{and} \quad E(N|\theta_1) \leq E(N'|\theta_1). \tag{7.10}$$

The region for $\alpha'$ and $1-\beta'$ given by (7.9) is shown in Figure 7.2(a). Simons [6] extends the region for $\alpha'$ and $1-\beta'$ to

$$\frac{\alpha'}{\beta'} \leq \frac{\alpha}{\beta} \quad \text{and} \quad \frac{1-\beta'}{1-\alpha'} \leq \frac{1-\beta}{1-\alpha} \tag{7.11}$$

which is depicted in Figure 7.2(b). Note that (7.11) allows $\alpha'$ to be larger than $\alpha$ or $1-\beta'$ to be larger than $1-\beta$, but not both at the same time [i.e., (7.11) implies that $\alpha' + (1-\beta') \leq \alpha + (1-\beta)$]. Therefore, the region given by (7.11) includes the region given by (7.9), which is depicted in Figure 7.2(b). Recently, Krylov and Miroshnichenko [7] further extended the region for $\alpha'$ and $1-\beta'$ to

$$\omega(\alpha',1-\beta') \geq \omega(\alpha,1-\beta) \quad \text{and} \quad \omega(1-\beta',\alpha') \geq \omega(1-\beta,\alpha) \tag{7.12}$$

where

$$\omega(u,v) = (1-u)\ln\frac{1-u}{v} + u\ln\frac{u}{1-v}. \tag{7.13}$$

The region given by (7.12) is shown in Figure 7.2(c). It can be shown that this region includes the region given by (7.11). In fact, it is shown [7] that (7.12) is the largest region for which the SPRT is optimum.

There are some drawbacks associated with the SPRT, however. One of them is that the sample size $N$ in a particular experiment can be very large even though the ASN is moderate or small. This situation may be improved by terminating the test after a reasonably large value of n is reached. However, such a truncation alters the performance (i.e., error probabilities and ASN) of the detector. To keep the performance relatively unchanged, the truncation point should be such that the probability that $N$ is larger than this value is small. The second drawback associated with the SPRT is that the value of $\theta_1$ is required in carrying out the test. However, the actual value of the signal in practical situations may not be known and an estimated value is used in the design stage. Let us denote the actual value of the signal by $\theta$. If $0 < \theta < \theta_1$, then the detection probability is reduced and the ASN is increased. To see how they are affected, we evaluate the operating characteristic (OC) function and the ASN function, which are defined in the next paragraph. There are schemes to reduce the ASN when $0 < \theta < \theta_1$.

We shall consider some of them in Section 7.5. Another problem arising

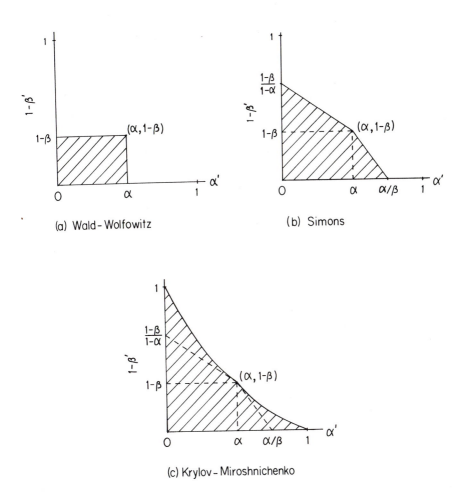

(a) Wald - Wolfowitz

(b) Simons

(c) Krylov - Miroshnichenko

*Figure 7.2 Regions of the errors for which the SPRT is optimum.*

for the SPRT is that the error probablities $\alpha$ and $1-\beta$ are related to the thresholds by two inequalities (7.6a) and (7.6b) or by approximations (7.8a) and (7.8b). No simple exact equality exists. For small ASN, the approximations (7.8a) and (7.8b) can be poor. We shall discuss some methods for computing the exact error probabilities, given $a$ and $b$, later in this section.

The OC function is defined as the probability of saying $H_0$ given that the exact signal is $\theta$ and the ASN function is the expected value of N given that the actual signal is $\theta$. Both of these are functions of $\theta$. Let $L(\theta)$ denote the OC function and $E(N|\theta)$ denote the ASN function. Note that $1-\alpha = L(0)$, $1-\beta = L(\theta_1)$, $E(N|0) =$ ASN under $H_0$ and $E(N|\theta_1) =$ ASN under $H_1$. Wald [4] derived the following appoximations (by neglecting the overshoot) for these functions:

$$
L(\theta) \approx
\begin{cases}
\dfrac{\exp(ah(\theta)) - 1}{\exp(ah(\theta)) - \exp(bh(\theta))}, & h(\theta) \neq 0 \\[2ex]
\dfrac{a}{(a - b)}, & h(\theta) = 0
\end{cases}
\tag{7.14}
$$

$$
E(N|\theta) \approx
\begin{cases}
\dfrac{bL(\theta) + a(1 - L(\theta))}{E(Z|\theta)}, & E(Z|\theta) \neq 0 \\[2ex]
\dfrac{-ab}{E(Z^2|\theta)}, & E(Z|\theta) = 0
\end{cases}
\tag{7.15}
$$

where $h(\theta)$ is the nontrivial solution of

$$
\int_{-\infty}^{\infty} [f(x - \theta_1)/f(x)]^{h(\theta)} f(x - \theta)\, dx = 1
\tag{7.16}
$$

if a nontrivial solution exists and it is zero otherwise, and where

$$
E(Z^k|\theta) = \int_{-\infty}^{\infty} \{\ln [f(x - \theta_1)/f(x)]\}^k f(x - \theta)\, dx.
\tag{7.17}
$$

If $\theta = 0$ ($H_0$ is true), then $h(\theta = 0) = 1$, and if $\theta = \theta_1$ ($H_1$ is true), then $h(\theta = \theta_1) = -1$, and (7.14) reduces to

$$
L(0) \approx \frac{e^a - 1}{e^a - e^b} \quad \text{and} \quad L(\theta_1) \approx \frac{e^b(1 - e^a)}{e^a - e^b}.
\tag{7.18}
$$

Typical shapes of OC and ASN functions are shown in Figure 7.3. Note that $E(N|\theta)$ attains a maximum value at $\theta = \theta^*$ between 0 and $\theta_1$. If $f(x)$ is a

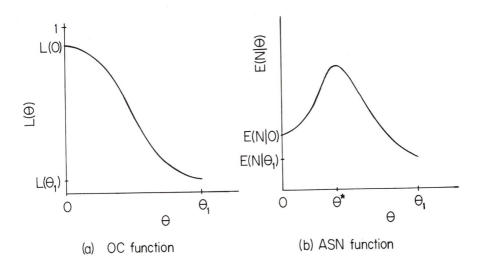

*Figure 7.3 Typical shapes of OC and ASN functions of a SPRT.*

symmetric pdf and if $a = -b$, then $E(N|\theta)$ is symmetric about $\theta^* = \theta_1/2$. We can see that if the actual signal $\theta$ is not $\theta_1$ (the value thought to be in the design stage of the detector), then the ASN may be very large.

The results above, [(7.14) and (7.15)], are approximate OC and ASN functions. They become asymptotically correct as $a$ and $|b|$ approach infinity [8]. They yield very accurate results when $a$ and $|b|$ are large compared to $E(Z|\theta)$. As indicated by (7.8), this is the case if the desired error probabilities $\alpha$ and $1-\beta$ are small, which is true in most applications of signal detection. In this case, the resulting ASN function is large. However, in some specific situations, the ASN is fairly small, which renders the approximations (7.14) and (7.15) inaccurate. In general there are no exact expressions for OC and ASN functions in closed form (with an exception when the log-likelihood ratio is a discrete random variable). We have to use numerical methods to compute exact values of the OC and ASN functions. One method is to compute, given $\theta$, the pdf of the test statistic, step by step, and evaluate the probabilities of accepting $H_0$ and of accepting $H_1$ for each $n$, $n = 1,2,\ldots$.

Summing up the appropriate probabilities, we obtain $L(\theta)$ and the probability of $N = n$, $n = 1,2,\ldots$. The ASN value $E(N|\theta)$ is then the summation $\sum_{n=1}^{\infty} n\ \text{Prob}(N = n|\theta)$. To compute the pdf of the test statistic at step $n$, we let

$$F_n(t,\theta) = \text{Prob}(\sum_{i=1}^{n} Z_i \leq t,\ N \geq n \mid \text{actual signal is } \theta),\quad n = 1,2,\ldots,$$

and let $f_n(t,\theta) = \partial F_n(t,\theta)/\partial t$. Therefore, $f_1(t,\theta)$ is the pdf of $Z_1$. Note that

$$\int_{-\infty}^{\infty} f_n(t,\theta)\ dt = \text{Prob}(\text{the test reaches } n \mid \theta) = \int_{b}^{a} f_{n-1}(t,\theta)\ dt.$$

For brevity, we drop $\theta$ so that $f_n(t) = f_n(t,\theta)$. Since $Z_n$ is independent of $Z_1 + \cdots + Z_{n-1}$, we can compute $f_n(t)$ by convolution:

$$f_n(t) = \int_{b}^{a} f_Z(t-\tau)f_{n-1}(\tau)\ d\tau,\quad n \geq 2 \tag{7.19}$$

where $f_Z(t)$ is the pdf of $Z_i$ given that the signal is $\theta$ and $f_1(t) = f_Z(t)$. The integral (7.19) can be computed recursively using numerical algorithms. See [9-10] for details and some numerical results.

A second method [11] involves numerical solutions of Fredholm integral equations. Let $L^*(t,\theta)$ be the probability of accepting $H_0$ and $\text{ASN}^*(t,\theta)$, be the ASN, given that the test has an initial value of $t$ and the signal is $\theta$. Note that $L(\theta) = L^*(0,\theta)$ and $E(N|\theta) = \text{ASN}^*(0,\theta)$. Observe that if the SPRT reaches step $n$ with a value $Z_1 + \cdots + Z_n = \tau$, we can treat the rest of the test as a new SPRT starting at $n$ with an initial value of $\tau$. This new SPRT must have $L(\tau,\theta)$ as the probability of accepting $H_0$ and $\text{ASN}(\tau,\theta)$ as its ASN function. Letting $n = 1$, we have

$$L^*(t,\theta) = \int_{-\infty}^{b} f_Z(\tau - t)\ d\tau$$

$$+ \int_b^a \text{Prob(say } H_0 \mid \text{ start at } n = 1 \text{ with } Z_1 = \tau) f_Z(\tau - t) \, d\tau$$

$$= \int_{-\infty}^b f_Z(\tau - t) \, d\tau + \int_b^a L^*(\tau, \theta) f_Z(\tau - t) \, d\tau \qquad (7.20)$$

where $f_Z(t)$ is defined above. Similarly, we have

$$ASN^*(t, \theta) = 1 + \int_b^a ASN^*(\tau, \theta) f_Z(\tau - t) \, d\tau. \qquad (7.21)$$

Equations (7.20) and (7.21) can be solved numerically. With $t = 0$, we have $L(\theta) = L^*(0, \theta)$ and $E(N \mid \theta) = ASN^*(0, \theta)$.

Recently, another method for computing $L(0)$, $L(\theta_1)$, $E(N \mid 0)$, and $E(N \mid \theta_1)$ has been proposed [12]. The derivation is lengthy but the results are

$$L(0) = \frac{r''(1) - r'(1)}{C_1 - C_2}, \quad L(\theta_1) = \frac{r'(0) - r''(0)}{C_1 - C_2} \qquad (7.22)$$

$$E(N \mid 0) = r'(1) - C_2 L(0), \quad E(N \mid \theta_1) = r'(0) - C_1 L(\theta_1) \qquad (7.23)$$

where $C_1$ and $C_2$ are some arbitrary constants and where $r'(t)$ and $r''(t)$ are functions (depending on the choices of $C_1$ and $C_2$) which can be computed by a recursive algorithm (see [12]). However, this method does not provide $L(\theta)$ and $E(N \mid \theta)$ for $\theta \neq 0$ and $\theta \neq \theta_1$. For a comparison of various methods, see [13].

If the random variable $Z_i$ is discrete and it can take only a finite number of possible values, each of which is an integral multiple of a constant, then exact OC and ASN functions can be derived (see [4, App. A.5.2, 14,15]). This situation arises when $Z_i$ is quantized into a finite number of levels. In particular, for a two-level quantization, the SPRT of the quantized data becomes a simple random walk and exact OC and ASN functions are readily available from results of random walk [14].

Let us briefly address the problem of truncating the SPRT. As mentioned earlier, to avoid the occasional long test, truncating the test at $n = n_T$ may be employed. However, truncation also changes the error probabilities. To avoid any significant change of the error probabilities, we choose $n_T$ which is large enough that Prob $(N > n_T | \theta = 0$ or $\theta = \theta_1)$ is small. To ensure this, we may compute Prob $(N < n_T | \theta = 0$ or $\theta = \theta_1)$ and choose an appropriate $n_T$ or we compute the mean and variance of $N$ at $\theta = 0$ and $\theta = \theta_1$ then we pick $n_T$ which is larger than the mean plus two or three times the standard deviation. We can use the result of (7.19) to compute the probability or use (7.21) for the mean and an equation similar to (7.21) for the second moment [11]. If the ASN at $\theta = 0$ and $\theta = \theta_1$ is large, we may use an asymptotic distribution of $N$ to estimate the required probability, mean, and variance. For the asymptotic behavior of $N$, see [16-19]. We note one interesting property of the distribution of $N$ is that it is exponentially bounded [20] in the sense that there exist constants $C > 0$ and $0 < \rho < 1$ such that

$$\text{Prob}(N > n) < C\rho^n. \qquad (7.24)$$

If $Z_i$ is quantized into two levels, the exact error probabilities and exact distribution of $N$ can be computed. For details, see [14,21,22].


## 7.3 Asymptotic Relative Efficiency

In this section we discuss the ARE of some sequential detectors. The ARE is a small-signal large-sample measure of one detector's efficiency relative to another's. We shall compare the SPRT with the FSS likelihood ratio detector. We also compare asymptotic efficiencies of asymptotic Wald detectors (to be defined later). The major result is that the ARE of an asymptotic Wald detector with respect to another is given by the ratio of their efficacies, which is the same result as the ARE of two corresponding FSS detectors.

To compare the SPRT with the FSS likelihood ratio test, let $M(\alpha,\beta)$ be the sample size of FSS likelihood ratio detector, i.e., detector (7.1) when $\phi(y_1,\ldots,y_M) = \prod_{i=1}^{M} [f(y_i - \theta_1)/f(y_i)]$, with error probabilities $\alpha$ under $H_0$ and $\beta$ under $H_1$. Likewise, let $E(N | \alpha,\beta,0)$ and $E(N | \alpha,\beta,\theta_1)$ be the ASN values under $H_0$ and $H_1$ of detector (7.4) such that it has error probabilities $\alpha$ under $H_0$ and $1-\beta$ under $H_1$. The ARE of the SPRT detector (7.4) with respect to the FSS likelihood-ratio detector is

$$ARE_{SPRT,FSS} = \lim_{\theta_1 \to 0} \frac{M(\alpha,\beta)}{E(N|\alpha,\beta,0)} \tag{7.25a}$$

under $H_0$ and

$$ARE_{SPRT,FSS} = \lim_{\theta_1 \to 0} \frac{M(\alpha,\beta)}{E(N|\alpha,\beta,\theta_1)} \tag{7.25b}$$

under $H_1$, where the limits are taken as $\theta_1 \to 0$ with $\alpha$ and $1-\beta$ remaining constant. With some mild regularity conditions on the pdf $f(x)$ (see [23-26]), we obtain the following approximations, for small $\theta_1$,

$$M(\alpha,\beta) \approx \left[ \frac{\sigma_0(\theta_1)\Phi^{-1}(\alpha) + \sigma_1(\theta_1)\Phi^{-1}(1-\beta)}{\mu_1(\theta_1) - \mu_0(\theta_1)} \right]^2 \tag{7.26}$$

$$E(N|\alpha,\beta,0) \approx \frac{\alpha \ln(\beta/\alpha) + (1-\alpha) \ln[(1-\beta)/(1-\alpha)]}{\mu_0(\theta_1)} \tag{7.27a}$$

$$E(N|\alpha,\beta,\theta_1) \approx \frac{\beta \ln(\beta/\alpha) + (1-\beta) \ln[(1-\beta)/(1-\alpha)]}{\mu_1(\theta_1)} \tag{7.27b}$$

where $\mu_j(\theta_1) = E(Z_i|H_j)$, $\sigma_j^2(\theta_1) =$ variance of $Z_i$ under $H_j$, and $\Phi^{-1}(\cdot)$ is the inverse of the standard normal distribution function $\Phi(\cdot)$ with

$$\lim_{\theta_1 \to 0} [(\mu_1(\theta_1) - \mu_0(\theta_1))^2/(\mu_0(\theta_1)\sigma_j(\theta_1))] = -2, \quad j = 0,1,$$

and with

$$\lim_{\theta_1 \to 0} [(\mu_1(\theta_1) - \mu_0(\theta_1))^2/(\mu_1(\theta_1)\sigma_j(\theta_1))] = 2, \quad j = 0,1,$$

(see [26] for conditions such that these limits hold), the ARE of (7.25a) and (7.25b) become

$$ARE_{SPRT,FSS} = -0.5 \frac{[\Phi^{-1}(\alpha) + \Phi^{-1}(1-\beta)]^2}{\alpha \ln(\beta/\alpha) + (1-\alpha) \ln[(1-\beta)/(1-\alpha)]} \qquad (7.28a)$$

under $H_0$ and

$$ARE_{SPRT,FSS} = 0.5 \frac{[\Phi^{-1}(\alpha) + \Phi^{-1}(1-\beta)]^2}{\beta \ln(\beta/\alpha) + (1-\beta)\ln[(1-\beta)/(1-\alpha)]} \qquad (7.28b)$$

under $H_1$. Note that these expressions depend on particular choices of $\alpha$ and $\beta$. Their values range from 1.61 to 9.52 for $\alpha \in (10^{-12}, 10^{-2})$ and $(1-\beta) \in (10^{-12}, 10^{-2})$.

The results (7.28a) and (7.28b) also hold when $Y_i$ is a discrete random variable with a finite number of possible values [26], for example, when $Y_i$ is the output of a quantizer.

Next, we consider the comparison of two sequential tests with constant thresholds. To obtain the ARE in the sense that $\theta_1 \to 0$ with $\alpha$ and $\beta$ remaining constant, the rate at which the ASN approaches infinity must not be too fast or too slow with respect to the rate at which $\theta_1$ approaches zero (otherwise, we have $\beta \to 1$ or $\beta \to \alpha$). To control these rates, it is convenient to use an index $r$ which approaches infinity and let $\theta_1 = 1/\sqrt{r}$ so that $\theta_1 \to 0$ as $r \to \infty$. Now, let $T_n$ be a statistic based on $Y_1, Y_2, \dots, Y_n$, i.e., $T_n$ is some function of $Y_1, \dots, Y_n$. With $\theta_1 = 1/\sqrt{r}$, define the following means and variances of $T_n$:

$$\psi_{0,n} = E(T_n | H_0), \qquad \psi_{1,n} = E(T_n | H_1) \qquad (7.29)$$

$$\sigma_{0,n}^2 = \mathrm{Var}(T_n | H_0), \quad \sigma_{1,n}^2 = \mathrm{Var}(T_n | H_1). \qquad (7.30)$$

In addition, we let

$$s_r = 1/2(\psi_{1,r} + \psi_{0,r}) \qquad (7.31)$$

and

$$d = \lim_{r \to \infty} [(\psi_{1,r} - \psi_{0,r})/\sigma_{0,r}]. \qquad (7.32)$$

Consider the following test: For each $r$, continue the test as long as

$$\frac{1}{d} \ln \left(\frac{1-\beta}{1-\alpha}\right) < \left(T_n - \frac{ns_r}{r}\right)\frac{1}{\sigma_{0,r}} < \frac{1}{d}\ln\frac{\beta}{\alpha}. \tag{7.33}$$

If the upper inequality is violated, $H_1$ is accepted, and if the lower inequality is violated, $H_0$ is accepted. Let the sample size be denoted by $N_r$, i.e.,

$$N_r = \inf \left\{n\colon (T_n - ns_r/r)\frac{d}{\sigma_{0,r}} \notin (\ln\frac{1-\beta}{1-\alpha}, \ln\frac{\beta}{\alpha}) \right\}. \tag{7.34}$$

Within some regularity conditions (see Lai [27]) on $\psi_{i,r}$ and $\sigma_{i,r}$ (including an assumption that $d$ exists), the asymptotic error probabilities of (7.33) are $\alpha$ and $1-\beta$; i.e.,

$$\lim_{r\to\infty} \text{Prob}(\text{say } H_1|H_0) = \alpha$$

and

$$\lim_{r\to\infty} \text{Prob}(\text{say} H_0|H_1) = 1-\beta.$$

The detector (7.33) is called an asymptotic Wald detector. In addition, we have the following approximations of ASN values, for large r,

$$E(N_r|H_0) \approx (-2r/d^2)\left[(1-\alpha) \ln \left(\frac{1-\beta}{1-\alpha}\right) + \alpha \ln \left(\frac{\beta}{\alpha}\right)\right] \tag{7.35}$$

and

$$E(N_r|H_1) \approx (2r/d^2)\left[(1-\beta) \ln\frac{1-\beta}{1-\alpha} + \beta \ln\left(\frac{\beta}{\alpha}\right)\right]. \tag{7.36}$$

To compare two asymptotic Wald detectors, let $T_n^*$ be another statistic based on $Y_1,\ldots,Y_n$ and let $\psi_{i,r}^*$, $\sigma_{i,r}^*$, $s_r^*$, $d^*$, and $N_r^*$ be defined similarly as above. The ARE of the asymptotic Wald detector using $T_n$ with respect to the asymptotic Wald detector using $T_n^*$ is

$$ARE_{T_n, T_n^*} = \begin{cases} \lim_{r \to \infty} E(N_r^* | H_0)/E(N_r | H_0) & \text{under } H_0 \\ \lim_{r \to \infty} E(N_r^* | H_1)/E(N_r | H_1) & \text{under } H_1 \end{cases} \qquad (7.37)$$

With (7.35) and (7.36), we obtain

$$ARE_{T_n, T_n^*} = \left(\frac{d}{d^*}\right)^2 = \lim_{r \to \infty} \left[\frac{(\psi_{1,r} - \psi_{0,r})/\sigma_{0,r}}{(\psi_{0,r}^* - \phi_{0,r}^*)/\sigma_{0,r}^*}\right]^2 \qquad (7.38)$$

under both $H_0$ and $H_1$. Within some mild conditions on $\psi_{1,r}$ and $\psi_{1,r}^*$, the ratio in (7.38) can be put into the form

$$ARE_{T_n, T_n^*} = \frac{\lim_{r \to \infty} [\{\partial \psi_{1,r}/\partial \theta_1 |_{\theta_1 = 0}\}/(\sqrt{r}\, \sigma_{0,r})]^2}{\lim_{r \to \infty} [\{\partial \psi_{1,r}^*/\partial \theta_1 |_{\theta_1 = 0}\}(\sqrt{r}\, \sigma_{0,r}^*)]^2} \qquad (7.39)$$

which is the ratio of the efficacies of $T_n$ and $T_n^*$. Note that this is the same result as the ARE of an FSS detector using statistic $T_n$ with respect to an FSS detector using statistic $T_n^*$ [28]. Therefore, the ARE of an asymptotic Wald detector using $T_n$ with respect to the SPRT is the same as the ARE of an FSS detector using $T_n$ with respect to an FSS likelihood ratio detector. In addition, it follows that the ARE of an asymptotic Wald detector using $T_n$ with respect to an FSS detector using $T_n$ is given by (7.28a) under $H_0$ and (7.28b) under $H_1$. For example, if $T_n$ is the Wilcoxon statistic, the ARE of (7.33) with respect to the SPRT is $12\sigma^2 \left(\int_{-\infty}^{\infty} f^2(x)\, dx\right)^2$, where $\sigma^2 =$ variance of $X_i$ [29], and the ARE of (7.33) with respect to the FSS Wilcoxon detector is given by (7.28a) and (7.28b).

Note that for the asymptotic Wald detector (7.33), the error probabilities are asymptotically $\alpha$ and $1 - \beta$. The error probabilities for small r may be quite different from $\alpha$ and $1 - \beta$.

The derivation of the results (7.35) and (7.36) relies on the weak convergence of a continuous-time random process $T_r(t)$, constructed from $T_n$, to a Wiener process. The random process $T_r(t)$ is defined, for each $r$, as

$$T_r(t) = \frac{T_{[rt]} - (t/2)(\psi_{1,r} + \psi_{0,r})}{\sigma_{0,r}} + \frac{(rt - [rt])(T_{[rt]+1} - T_{[rt]})}{\sigma_{0,r}} \quad (7.40)$$

where $[rt]$ is the largest integer less than or equal to $rt$, and where $T_0 = 0$. The latter term in (7.40) is added to make $T_r(t)$ continuous. Under some regularity conditions, $T_r(t)$ converges weakly, as $r \to \infty$, to a Wiener process with drift $-dt/2$ under $H_0$, with drift $dt/2$ under $H_1$, and with variance $t$. In this case, the detector (7.33) behaves approximately the same as a sequential test of drift of a Wiener process when $r$ is large (i.e., $\theta_1$ is small).

Let us digress briefly to state results of a sequential test of a Wiener process. Denote by $W_{\mu,\sigma}(t)$ the Wiener process with drift $\mu t$ and variance $\sigma^2 t$, i.e., $E(W(t)) = \mu t$ and $E(W(t) - \mu t)^2 = \sigma^2 t$. Consider testing $W_{\mu,\sigma}(t)$ against $a^*$ and $b^*$: Continue as long as

$$b^* < W_{\mu,\sigma}(t) < a^*. \quad (7.41)$$

Then the probability of reaching $b^*$ before $a^*$ is (see [30])

$$P_{b^*}(\mu) = \begin{cases} \dfrac{1 - \exp(-2a^*\mu/\sigma^2)}{\exp(-2b^*\mu/\sigma^2) - \exp(-2a^*\mu/\sigma^2)}, & \mu \neq 0 \\[3mm] \dfrac{a^*}{(a^* - b^* a^*)}, & \mu = 0 \end{cases} \quad (7.42)$$

and the expected value of the stopping time $T$, where $T = \inf \{t: W_{\mu,\sigma}(t) \notin (b^*, a^*)\}$, is

$$E(T|\mu) = \begin{cases} [b^* P_{b^*}(\mu) + a^*(1 - P_{b^*}(\mu))]/\mu, & \mu \neq 0 \\[2mm] -a^* b^*/\sigma^2, & \mu = 0. \end{cases} \quad (7.43)$$

Note that these are similar to (7.14) and (7.15). However, (7.42) and (7.43) are exact equalities since a continuous-time random process has no overshoot over the boundary when the test stops.

Let us get back to approximating the test (7.33) by (7.41). In this case $\mu = -d/2$ under $H_0$, $\mu = d/2$ under $H_1$, $\sigma = 1$, $a^* = d^{-1} \ln(\alpha/\beta)$, and $b^* = d^{-1}\ln[(1-\beta)/(1-\alpha)]$. Under (7.42), the error probabilities of (7.33) are

$$\text{Prob (say } H_1|H_0) \approx \frac{1 - [1 - \exp(da^*)]}{[\exp(db^*) - \exp(da^*)]} = \alpha$$

and

$$\text{Prob (say } H_0|H_1) \approx \frac{[1 - \exp(-da^*)]}{[\exp(-db^*) - \exp(-da^*)]} = 1-\beta.$$

With $n \approx rt$, we use (7.43) to obtain the ASN values:

$$E(N_r|H_0) \approx rE(T|H_0) = r\frac{(1-\alpha)b^* + \alpha a^*}{-d/2}$$

$$= \frac{-2r}{d^2}\left[(1-\alpha)\ln\left(\frac{1-\beta}{1-\alpha}\right) + \alpha \ln\left(\frac{\beta}{\alpha}\right)\right] \qquad (7.44a)$$

and

$$E(N_r|H_1) \approx rE(T|H_1) = r\frac{(1-\beta)b^* + \beta a^*}{d/2}$$

$$= \frac{2r}{d^2}\left[(1-\beta)\ln\left(\frac{1-\beta}{1-\alpha}\right) + \beta \ln\left(\frac{\beta}{\alpha}\right)\right]. \qquad (7.44b)$$

For the particular case of the SPRT, we have

$$(Tn - ns_r/r)d/\sigma_{0,r} = \ln \Lambda_n(\underline{y})$$

and the weak convergence to a Wiener process, as $r \to \infty$, has been shown to hold if the pdf $f(x)$ has a finite Fisher information $I(f) = \int (f'(x)/f(x))^2 f(x) \, dx$ [31], where $f'(x)$ is $df(x)/dx$.

The results (7.28) and (7.39) are termed Pitman-type asymptotic efficiencies, referring to ones that are obtained by letting $H_1$ approach $H_0$ while keeping $\alpha$ and $1-\beta$ constant. Another type of asymptotic relative efficiency has been investigated by Berk [32,33], in which he lets the thresholds $a$ and $|b|$ approach infinity. The efficacy is defined as the limiting value of the ratio of the log-error and expected sample size. The results obtained do not depend on $\alpha$ and $\beta$ and they are different from results of Pitman efficiency.

For details, see [32,33].

### 7.4 Nonparametric and Robust Sequential Detectors

It is well known that the performance of parametric detectors (FSS likelihood ratio and SPRT detectors) is sensitive to deviations of the actual noise pdf from the assumed pdf. Therefore, if $f(x)$ is only partially known, nonparametric or robust detectors should be used. Many results have been reported on nonparametric and robust sequential detectors based on quantized detectors since 1970. We discuss in this section nonparametric sequential detectors based on quantized data, and robust sequential detectors.

Suppose that $Y_1, Y_2, \ldots$ are quantized into discrete levels and that we know (or we can estimate) the probability (under $H_0$ or $H_1$) of $Y_i$ falling on each level, then we can set up an SPRT for the quantized data. Wald's approximations for the OC and ASN functions, as given in Section 7.2, are applicable in this case. Results have been reported in various works [14,34-37]. The ARE of such a sequential detector with respect to an FSS likelihood ratio detector using the same set of quantized data is given by (7.28). We can also obtain the ARE of a sequential detector using the quantized data with respect to the FSS likelihood ratio detector using unquantized data. The result is the product of (7.28) and the ARE of the FSS detector using quantized data with respect to the FSS detector using unquantized data. For example, consider the particular case of a two-level quantizer; in which case we have a sequential sign detector. If the noise $X_i$ is a Gaussian random variable, then the optimum FSS detector is a linear detector. Since the ARE of an FSS sign detector with respect to the FSS linear detector is $2/\pi = 0.64$ for Gaussian noise [29], the ARE of a sequential sign detector with respect to an FSS linear detector is the product of (7.28) and 0.64. If $\alpha = 10^{-12}$ and $\beta = 10^{-2}$, the result is $9.52 \cdot 0.64 = 6.06$ under $H_0$ and $1.61 \cdot 0.64 = 1.03$ under $H_1$. Therefore, even a sequential sign detector, based simply on the signs of the observations, is better, asymptotically, than the optimum FSS detector. The sequential sign detector still retains a better finite-sample-size efficiency for a wide range of $\alpha$ and $1-\beta$, as demonstrated in [14]. For quantizers with more than two levels, further improvement of the performance is observed [34].

Suppose now that $\theta_1$ is known and the pdf $f(x)$ is symmetric about $x = 0$ but otherwise unknown. If $\theta_1$ is small (so the average sample size is large), then we may use a consistent estimate of the mean of $Y_i$ (which is 0 under $H_0$ and is $\theta_1$ under $H_1$) and a consistent estimate of the variance of $Y_i$ (or $X_i$) to set up a sequential test. Let $\hat{\theta}_n$ and $\hat{\sigma}_n^2$ be estimates of $E(Y_i)$ and var$(Y_i)$, based on $n$ observations $y_1,\ldots,y_n$. Suppose that $\hat{\theta}_n \to 0$ under $H_0$, $\hat{\theta}_n \to \theta_1$ under $H_1$, and $\hat{\sigma}_n^2 \to \sigma^2 = $ var$(Y_i)$. Consider the following test: Continue testing as long as

$$b\hat{\sigma}_n^2/\theta_1 < n(\hat{\theta}_n - \theta_1/2) \triangleq U_n < a\hat{\sigma}_n^2/\theta_1. \tag{7.45}$$

Accept $H_1$ (or $H_0$) if the upper (or lower) inequality is violated. Assume that $\hat{\theta}_n$ and $\hat{\sigma}_n$ are such that a continuous-time random process constructed from $U_n$, $U^n(t) \triangleq U_{[nt]} + (nt - [nt])(U_{[nt]+1} - U_{[nt]})$ converges weakly to a Wiener process $W_{\mu,\sigma}(t)$, where $\mu = (2\theta - \theta_1)/2$ (which equals $-\theta_1/2$ under $H_0$ and $\theta_1/2$ under $H_1$). Then, for large sample size, (7.45) behaves approximately the same as testing $W_{\mu,\sigma}(t)$ against $b\sigma^2/\theta_1$ and $a\sigma^2/\theta_1$. With (7.42) and (7.43), we obtain OC and ASN functions for (7.45) as

$$L(\theta) \approx \begin{cases} \dfrac{1 - \exp[-a(2\theta/\theta_1 - 1)]}{\exp[-b(2\theta/\theta_1 - 1)] - \exp[-a(2\theta/\theta_1 - 1)]}, & \theta \neq \theta_1/2 \\[4mm] \dfrac{a}{a - b}, & \theta = \theta_1/2 \end{cases} \tag{7.46}$$

$$E(N|\theta) \approx \begin{cases} \dfrac{[bL(\theta) + a(1 - L(\theta))]\sigma^2}{(\theta - \theta_1/2)\theta_1}, & \theta \neq \theta_1/2 \\[4mm] \dfrac{-ab\sigma^2}{\theta_1}, & \theta = \theta_1/2 \end{cases} \tag{7.47}$$

If we let $a = \ln(\beta/\alpha)$ and $b = \ln[(1-\beta)/(1-\alpha)]$, then $L(0) \approx 1-\alpha$ and $L(\theta_1) \approx 1-\beta$.

An intuitive approach to estimating the mean and the variance is to take the sample mean and sample variance, as in the Student-$t$ test [38], i.e.,

$$\hat{\theta}_n = (y_1 + \cdots + y_n)/n$$

and

$$\hat{\sigma}_n{}^2 = [(y_1 - \hat{\theta}_n)^2 + \cdots + (y_n - \hat{\theta}_n)^2]/(n - 1)$$

The test statistic is a special case of the $U$-statistic, which has been shown to converge weakly to the Wiener process [39]. This sequential-$t$ test works particularly well when the noise is Gaussian (the ARE of the Student-$t$ detector with respect to the linear detector is 1 for Gaussian noise, i.e., it is asymptotically optimum). Therefore, if we have reason to believe that $X_i$ is Gaussian or near Gaussian, then the sequential-$t$ test is a good candidate. Otherwise, tests based on the ranks of data usually perform better, at least in terms of the ARE. Sen and Ghosh [40-42] have studied weak convergence of rank statistics and evaluate the ARE of sequential rank tests with constant boundaries. Let $R_{ni}(d)$ be the rank of $|y_i - d|$ among $|y_1 - d|, |y_2 - d|, \ldots, |y_n - d|$ and let $J(u)$ be a score function which is increasing in $u$, $0 \leq u < 1$. Consider the following test: Continue the test as long as

$$b < C_n^* \, \theta_1 T_n(\theta_1/2)/v^2 < a \tag{7.48}$$

where

$$T_n(d) = \sum_{i=1}^{n} J[R_{ni}(d)/(n+1)]\mathrm{sgn}(X_i - d) \tag{7.49a}$$

$$\mathrm{sgn}(u) = \begin{cases} 1, & u > 0 \\ 0, & u = 0 \\ -1, & u < 0 \end{cases} \tag{7.49b}$$

$$v^2 = \int_0^1 J^2(u) \, du \tag{7.49c}$$

and $C_n^*$ is an estimate (based on $y_1, \ldots, y_n$) of

$$C(F) = \int_{-\infty}^{\infty} \frac{d}{dx} J(F(x) - F(-x)) \, dF(x) \qquad (7.49d)$$

where $F(x) = \int_{-\infty}^{x} f(t) \, dt$. See [41] for an expression for $C_n^*$. Weak convergence of a continuous-time process constructed from the test statistic $T_n(\theta_1/2)$ has been established [41]. Therefore, approximations for the OC function can be obtained using (7.42), yielding the same expression as (7.46). If we set

$$a = \ln(\beta/\alpha) \text{ and } b = \ln\left(\frac{1-\beta}{1-\alpha}\right)$$

then the asymptotic error probabilities are $\alpha$ and $1-\beta$. Using (7.43), the ASN can be approximated by

$$E(N|\theta) \approx \begin{cases} \dfrac{[bL(\theta) + a(1 - L(\theta))]}{(\theta - \theta_1/2)\theta_1} (v/C(F))^2, & \theta \neq \theta_1/2 \\[3mm] \dfrac{-ab(v/C(F))^2}{\theta_1^2}, & \theta = \theta_1/2. \end{cases} \qquad (7.50)$$

Therefore, the ARE of the sequential rank test (7.48) with respect to the sequential-$t$ test is the ratio of (7.47) and (7.50), yielding

$$ARE_{rank,t} = \sigma^2 C^2(F)/v^2. \qquad (7.51)$$

If $J(u) = u$, then $T_n(\theta_1|2)$ is the Wilcoxon signed rank statistic and $v^2 = 1/3$, $C(F) = 2\int f^2(x) \, dx$, so that (7.51) becomes

$$12\sigma^2 \left( \int_{-\infty}^{\infty} f^2(x) \, dx \right)^2,$$

which is the ARE of an FSS Wilcoxon detector with respect to the FSS linear detector. Its value is lower bounded by 0.864 [43, p. 239]. It is $3/\pi = 0.95$ if $f(x)$ is Gaussian and it is 1.5 if $f(x)$ is a Laplacian.

The detectors (7.45) and (7.48) assume that $\theta_1$ is known. The value $\theta_1/2$ in both (7.45) and (7.48) is used to adjust the test statistic so that the approximating Wiener process has a positive drift of $\mu_1$ under $H_1$ and negative drift of $-\mu_1$ under $H_0$. Therefore, the Wiener process drifts toward the upper threshold $a$, most of the time, under $H_1$ and it drifts toward the lower threshold $b$, most of the time, under $H_0$. Now, consider $H_0$: $Y_i = X_i$ and $H_1$: $Y_i = X_i + \theta_1$, where $\theta_1 > 0$ and $f(x)$ is known only in that it is symmetric. In this case, the value of $\theta_1$ is assumed unknown so we cannot use $\theta_1/2$ to make adjustment on the drift of a Wiener process, as we did in (7.45) and (7.48). Instead, we use a test statistic such that the approximating Wiener process has zero drift under $H_0$ and positive drift under $H_1$. A sequential test can be constructed by testing the test statistic against a threshold. Stop and accept $H_1$ if the threshold is crossed. Otherwise, if a predetermined number of sample (say $n_T$) is reached, $H_0$ is accepted. The threshold and $n_T$ are chosen (using Wiener process approximations or simulation) such that the Type I error is $\alpha$ and the probability of detection is at an acceptable level at some signal-to-noise ratio. The threshold and decision regions are shown in Figure 7.4.

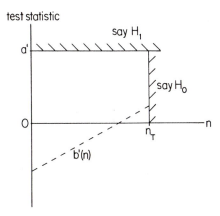

*Figure 7.4. Threshold and decision regions of a nonparametric detector.*

Miller [44,45] studies such a nonparametric sequential test using the Wilcoxon signed rank statistic, i.e., continue testing as long as $n < n_T$ and

$$\frac{1}{n} \sum_{i=1}^{n} R_{ni} \, \text{sgn}(y_i) < a'$$  (7.52)

with an acceptance of $H_1$ if (7.52) is violated for $n \leq n_T$, where $R_{ni}$ is the rank of $|y_i|$ among $|y_1|,\ldots,|y_n|$, $\text{sgn}(\cdot)$ is defined in (7.49b), and $a'$ is a constant depending on the required value of Type I error $\alpha$ and the maximum sample size $n_T$. With fixed $n_T$, increasing $a'$ decreases the Type I error as well as the detection probability. If $a'$ is fixed, a larger $n_T$ increases the Type I error and the detection probability. The choice of $a'$ is obtained from approximation using the Wiener process or from results of simulation. Again, the weak convergence of a continuous-time random process, constructed from the test statistic, can be established [42,46]. Therefore, with reasonably large $n_T$ and $a'$, we have [45]

$$\text{Prob}(\text{say } H_1 | H_0) \approx 2[1 - \Phi(a'\sqrt{3}/\sqrt{n_T})]$$  (7.53)

or

$$a' \approx (n_T/3)^{1/2} \, \Phi^{-1}(1-\alpha/2) \, .$$  (7.54)

The power function (probability of saying $H_1$) of the test is approximated by [45]

$$\text{Prob}(\text{say } H_1) \approx \exp(2a'\mu'/(\sigma')^2)\Phi\left[\frac{-\mu'\sqrt{n_T}}{\sigma'} - \frac{a'}{\sigma'\sqrt{n_T}}\right]$$

$$+ \Phi\left[\frac{\mu'\sqrt{n_T}}{\sigma'} - \frac{a'}{\sigma'\sqrt{n_T}}\right]$$  (7.55)

where

$$\mu' \approx E[\text{sgn}(Y_i + Y_j)]$$

and

$$(\sigma')^2 \approx \text{Covariance(sgn } (Y_i + Y_j), \text{sgn}(Y_k + Y_j)),$$

both of which depend on $\theta_1$ and $f(x)$.

Note that the test statistic in (7.52) is finite for a finite $n$. Therefore, it is possible to add a lower threshold $b'(n)$, as shown in Figure 7.4, for early acceptance of $H_0$ without altering the Type I error and the power function. The threshold $b'(n)$ is such that when it is added to the maximum possible value of the test statistic from $n + 1$ to $n_T$, the result is less than $a'$.

If the sample size is large, the Wilcoxon signed rank statistic requires lengthy ranking. The ranking can be reduced with slight modification, at a cost of reduced power. Observe that the rank of $|y_i|$ may change everytime an additional observation is obtained, i.e., $R_{ni}$ and $R_{(n+1)i}$ are usually different. In other words, all the samples have to be reranked in each step. To avoid reranking of all the data from step $n$ to step $n + 1$, Reynolds [47] proposed using $R_{ii}$ instead of $R_{ni}$ and using $\sum_{i=1}^{n} R_{ii} \text{ sgn}(y_i)/(i+1)$ as the test statistic. Note that $R_{ii}$ is the rank of $|y_i|$ among $|y_1|, \ldots, |y_i|$. When a new sample, $y_{n+1}$ is obtained, only the rank of $|y_{n+1}|$ among $|y_1|, |y_2|, \ldots, |y_{n+1}|$ is needed to update the test statistic. Again, the Wiener process is used to derive the approximate power function. As a result, the ranking time is reduced, but a slight loss of power is observed. Further modification has been studied by Tantaratana and Thomas [48], in which the ranking is done among the most recent $m$ observations, where $m$ is a fixed number. Numerical results showed that a reasonably small $m$, 5 to 10, is sufficient to obtain a power function close to that of a test with ranking among all the data.

Let us return to the hypothesis that $\theta_1$ is known and we know that $f(x)$ belongs to some class $\hat{F}$ of pdf's. In this situation, we wish to design a robust sequential detector such that for all members of $\hat{F}$, the error probabilities are no larger than $\alpha$ and $1-\beta$. Huber [49] seemed to be the first one to describe a robust sequential test based on a contamination model. Let $f_Y(y|H_0)$ and $f_Y(y|H_1)$ be the pdf of $Y_i$ under $H_0$ and $H_1$, which can be described by the model

$$f_Y(y \mid H_0) = (1-\varepsilon)f(y) + \varepsilon h_0(y) \tag{7.56a}$$

$$f_Y(y \mid H_1) = (1-\varepsilon)f(y-\theta_1) + \varepsilon h_1(y) \tag{7.56b}$$

where $h_i(y)$ is a pdf belonging to the class of all pdf's $\hat{H}$. Values of the contamination factor $\varepsilon$ must be small enough that (7.56a) and (7.56b) have no common member. Consider the following test: Continue testing as long as

$$b < \sum_{i=1}^{n} \ln[q_1(y_i)/q_0(y_i)] < a \tag{7.57}$$

where

$$q_0(y) = \begin{cases} (1-\varepsilon)f(y), & \text{if } f(y-\theta_1)/f(y) < C_0 \\ [(1-\varepsilon)/C_0]f(y-\theta_1), & \text{if } f(y-\theta_1)/f(y) \geq C_0 \end{cases}$$

$$q_1(y) = \begin{cases} (1-\varepsilon)f(y-\theta_1), & \text{if } f(y-\theta_1)/f(y) > C_1 \\ C_1(1-\varepsilon)f(y), & \text{if } f(y-\theta_1)/f(y) \leq C_1 \end{cases}$$

where $C_1$ and $C_0$ are constants that make $q_1(y)$ and $q_0(y)$ valid pdf's. Huber has shown that if $Y_i$ has a pdf given by (7.56a), where $h_0(y)$ is any member of $\hat{H}$, then the Type I error of (7.57) is no larger than the Type I error when $Y_i$ has pdf $q_0(y)$. A similar statement holds for Type II error. In other words, if $a = \ln(\beta/\alpha)$ and $b = \ln[(1-\beta)/(1-\alpha)]$, the detector (7.57) produces Type I error $\leq \alpha$ when $f_Y(y \mid H_0)$ is given by (7.56a) and Type II error $\leq 1-\beta$ when $f_Y(y \mid H_1)$ is given by (7.56b), for all $h_0(y)$ and $h_1(y)$ in $\hat{H}$. Therefore, detector (7.57) is most robust in the sense that the error probabilities are guaranteed. Further properties of (7.57) were studied by Schultheiss and Wolcin [50].

With similar assumptions as above that $f(x)$ is known to be a member of the class $\hat{F}$ and that $\theta_1$ is known, El-Sawy and VandeLinde [51] proposed two asymptotically robust detectors, one using an $M$-estimator to estimate the parameter $\theta$ and the other using stochastic approximation. They are in the form given by (7.45), except that the variance $\sigma_n^2$ is replaced with a variance which is the saddle-point solution of an equation. Specifically, the $M$-estimator sequential detector uses as an estimate $\hat{\theta}_n$ the value of $\theta$ which minimizes the function

$$\sum_{i=1}^{n} \Psi(y_i - \theta) \tag{7.58}$$

where $\Psi(t)$ is a convex and symmetric function and is strictly increasing for positive $t$. In addition, $\Psi(t)$ satisfies some mild regularity conditions given in [51]. Let $\hat{C}$ be the class of functions satisfying these conditions and $\Psi'(t)$ be the derivative of $\Psi(t)$. Suppose that there exists an $f_0 \in \hat{F}$ and $\phi_0 = -\ln f_0 \in \hat{C}$ such that

$$\sup_{f \in \hat{F}} V^2(\Psi_0, f) = V^2(\Psi_0, f_0) \triangleq V_0^2 = \inf_{\Psi \in \hat{C}} (\Psi, f_0) \tag{7.59}$$

where

$$V^2(\Psi, f) = \frac{\int\limits_{-\infty}^{\infty} (\Psi'(x))^2 f(x) \, dx}{\left[ \left( \frac{\partial}{\partial \theta} \int\limits_{-\infty}^{\infty} \Psi'(x - \theta) f(x) \, dx \right) \Big|_{\theta=0} \right]^2}.$$

Consider the following test:

$$\ln \frac{1-\beta}{1-\alpha} = b < \frac{n \theta_1 (\hat{\theta}_n - \theta_1/2)}{V_0^2} = \ln \frac{\beta}{\alpha}. \tag{7.60}$$

It has been shown [51] that (7.60) guarantees, asymptotically as $\theta_1 \to 0$, that the error probabilities are no larger than $\alpha$ and $1-\beta$ for any member $f \in \hat{F}$. For the second detector proposed in (7.51), the estimate $\hat{\theta}_n$ is replaced with the location estimate obtained by stochastic approximation. The error probabilities are guaranteed in an asymptotic sense. However, the convergence rate of a stochastic approximation is generally slower than that of $M$-estimation.

## 7.5 Sequential Tests Which Reduce the Maximum ASN

It was mentioned in Section 7.2 that a disadvantage of the SPRT is larger $E(N|\theta)$ when $\theta$ is between 0 and $\theta_1$. If $f(x)$ is symmetric and $\alpha = 1 - \beta$, then $\max\limits_{\theta} E(N|\theta)$ occurs at $\theta^* = \theta_1/2$. This maximum ASN value is normally larger than the sample size $M$ of a corresponding FSS likelihood ratio detector with the same $\alpha$ and $\beta$. The ratio $E(N|\theta^*)/M$, where $E(N|\theta^*) = \max\limits_{\theta} E(N|\theta)$, grows as $\alpha$ and $1 - \beta$ become smaller. Therefore, at small error probabilities the mismatch between the actual signal strength $\theta$ and the design value $\theta_1$ may cause the SPRT to be less efficient than a corresponding FSS detector. There are various schemes that can correct this situation and we discuss three of them: a truncation of the SPRT, boundary modifications of the SPRT, and multistage detectors.

In Section 7.2 we discussed briefly the truncation of an SPRT. There, the purpose was to avoid an occasional long test and the truncation point was chosen such that it has negligble effect on the performance of the SPRT. However, $\max\limits_{\theta} E(N|\theta)$ may still be large. Here, we wish to truncate the SPRT with a purpose to alter the performance [i.e., to reduce $(E(N|\theta^*)]$. If we simply truncate the SPRT (without changing the thresholds) so that $E(N|\theta^*)$ is reduced to an acceptable level, then the error probabilities are altered. To bring the error probabilities back to $\alpha$ and $1 - \beta$, we need to readjust the thresholds. Tantaratana and Poor [52,53] studied the behavior of a truncated SPRT and proposed design techniques to compute the truncation point and the thresholds so that the error probabilities are approximately $\alpha$ and $1 - \beta$. The studied detector is in the form: Continue the test as long as $n < n_T$ and

$$b' < \sum_{i=1}^{n} z_i < a',$$ (7.61a)

with an acceptance of $H_0$ (or $H_1$) if the lower (or upper) inequality is violated. If n reaches $n_T$, test

$$\sum_{i=1}^{n} z_i \begin{cases} > c' & \to H_1 \\ = c' & \to H_1 \text{ with prob. } \gamma' \\ \text{otherwise} & \to H_0 \end{cases} \qquad (7.61b)$$

where $z_i = \ln[f(y_i - \theta_1)/f(y_i)]$. The decision regions are depicted in Figure 7.5.

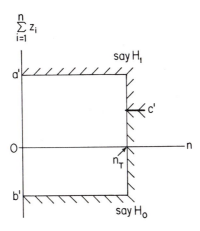

*Figure 7.5. Decision regions of a truncated SPRT.*

Normally, $a' > \ln(\beta/\alpha)$ and $b' < \ln[(1-\beta)/(1-\alpha)]$ to keep the errors down to $\alpha$ and $1-\beta$. The truncated detector (7.61) can be viewed as a mixture of the SPRT and the FSS likelihood ratio detector. It may behave more like the untruncated SPRT or more like the FSS detector or between them, depending on the mixture degree. With a proper choice of mixture, the detector (7.61) can be designed to have $E(N|\theta^*)$ near (but slightly smaller than) the sample size $M$ of the FSS detector while it retains $E(N|0)$ and $E(N|\theta_1)$ near (but slightly larger than) those of the untruncated SPRT. Hence, the truncated detector (7.61) is better than the untruncated SPRT when $\theta$ is near $\theta^*$ while it is almost as good as the untruncated SPRT for $\theta = 0$ and $\theta = \theta_1$. With respect to the FSS detector, the resulting ASN is always smaller than the sample size M of the FSS likelihood ratio detector.

Anderson [54] was the first to modify the constant boundaries of the SPRT to triangular boundaries. He considered linearly converging boundaries, as shown in Figure 7.6a. The test statistic is still $Z_1 + Z_2 + \cdots + Z_n$. Using the Wiener process approximation, he derived expressions for the OC and ASN functions. With proper choice of boundaries, his results showed considerable reduction of $E(N|\theta^*)$ while $E(N|0)$ and $E(N|\theta_1)$ were only slightly larger than those of the SPRT. However, no method was given regarding the design of the boundaries. Later, Fabian [55] obtained some simple expressions for the error probabilities.

Other modifications of the SPRT to reduce $E(N|\theta^*)$ were proposed by Read [56] and Baruah and Bhattacharjee [57]. In [56], a minimum, say $n_0$ samples are obtained first and the SPRT starts from $n = n_0$. The boundaries are as shown in Figure 7.6b. In [57], two triangular boundaries were suggested for $n < n_0$ (see Figure 7.6c). Both of these modifications showed reduction of the maximum value of ASN. In [58], Lai has proved that a sequential test, with $\alpha = 1 - \beta$, which minimizes the maximum ASN has two converging boundaries $b(n)$ and $a(n) = -b(n)$ with the property that $a(n)$ is nonincreasing. Expression for $a(n)$ was not available but upper and lower bounds for $a(n)$ were given. Lorden [59] studied the so-called 2-SPRTs, which consists of 2 SPRTs, one for testing 0 versus $\theta_0$ and the other for testing $\theta_0$ versus $\theta_1$, where $\theta_0 \in (0, \theta_1)$. It was shown that such a test approximately minimizes $E(N|\theta_0)$.

We now discuss multistage detectors, in which samples are taken in groups, each of which may consist of a different number of samples from those of other groups. The maximum number of groups is predetermined. At the end of each stage (i.e., each group), the test statistic is compared to a threshold. If it is less than the threshold, $H_0$ is accepted; otherwise, we continue to the next stage. A decision (accept $H_0$ or accept $H_1$) must be made at the last stage, however. Therefore, $H_1$ can be accepted only in the last stage. To be more specific, let us describe a two-stage detector [60,61] as follows:

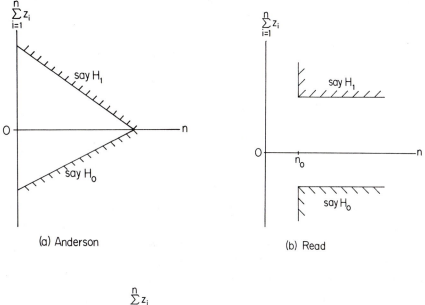

(a) Anderson

(b) Read

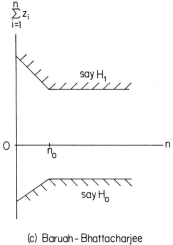

(c) Baruah-Bhattacharjee

*Figure 7.6. Some boundary modifications of the SPRT.*

*Stage 1*: Take $M_1$ samples, compute the test statistic $T_1(y_1,...,y_{M_1})$, and test

$$T_1(y_1,...,y_{M_1}) \begin{cases} < b_1 & \to H_0 \\ = b_1 & \to H_0 \text{ with prob. } \gamma_1 \\ \text{otherwise} & \to \text{go to stage 2} \end{cases} \qquad (7.62a)$$

*Stage 2*: Take another $M_2$ samples and test

$$T_2(y_1,...,y_{M_1 + M_2}) \begin{cases} > b_2 & \to H_1 \\ = b_2 & \to H_1 \text{ with prob. } \gamma_2 \\ \text{otherwise} & \to H_0 \end{cases} \qquad (7.62b)$$

where $M_i$, $b_i$, and $\gamma_i$ are predetermined constants. If $f(x)$ is known, $T_i(\cdot)$ is the likelihood ratio; otherwise, $T_i(\cdot)$ is a nonparametric or a robust statistic. One advantage of this type of detector, compared to those discussed above, is that nonparametric two-stage detectors can be easily designed and exact performance can be calculated. The asymptotic performance of detector (7.62) has a smaller $E(N|0)$ but larger $E(N|\theta_1)$ than the sample size $M$ of an FSS detector that has the same error probabilities and uses the same type of test statistic. However, with respect to the SPRT, $E(N|0)$ and $E(N|\theta_1)$ are larger than those of the SPRT, but $E(N|\theta)$ is smaller than that of the SPRT if $\theta$ is in the neighborhood of $\theta^*$. Let $\alpha_{12}$ be the probability of going to the second stage under $H_0$. The ARE of detector (7.62) with respect to a corresponding (i.e., using the same type of test statistic) FSS detector is

$$ARE_{2,FSS} = \begin{cases} [\Phi^{-1}(1-\alpha) - \Phi^{-1}(1-\beta)]^2/(1+\alpha_{12}k)R^2, & \text{under } H_0 \\ [\Phi^{-1}(1-\alpha) - \Phi^{-1}(1-\beta)]^2/(1+\beta_{12}k)R^2, & \text{under } H_1 \end{cases} \qquad (7.63)$$

where $k = M_1/M_2$, $\beta_{12} = \Phi(R - \Phi^{-1}(1 - \alpha_{12}))$. $R$ is the solution of

$$\beta = \Phi[R - \Phi^{-1}(1-\alpha_{12})] - \Phi[d - R(1+k)^{1/2}]$$
$$+ F[\Phi^{-1}(1-\alpha_{12}) - R, \; d - R(1+k)^{1/2}, \; (1+k)^{1/2}]$$

where $F(\cdot,\cdot,\rho)$ is the standard bivariate normal distribution function with correlation coefficient $\rho$ and $d$ satisfies

$$\alpha_{12} - \alpha = \Phi(d) - F[\Phi^{-1}(1-\alpha_{12}), d, (1+k)^{1/2}].$$

Note that (7.63) depends on $\alpha_{12}$ and $k$. If we tabulate (7.63) for various values of $\alpha_{12}$ and $k$, we can use the results to pick $\alpha_{12}$ and $k$ that give high $ARE$. An $ARE$ of 2 under $H_0$ is possible with proper choices of $\alpha_{12}$ and $k$.

Extension of two-stage detectors to multistage detectors is possible. However, the thresholds $b_1, b_2, \ldots$ become more difficult to design, unless the test is simplified (e.g., only the samples in the $i$th group are used to compute the test statistic in the $i$th stage). Another modification of (7.62) is to add an upper threshold $a_1, a_2, \ldots$ in each stage so that early acceptance of $H_1$ is possible. Multistage detectors have been demonstrated to work well for nonparametric statistics [60-62]. Similar methods have been applied to clinical tests with an assumption of normal pdf [63-65].

## 7.6 Sequential Detection with Dependent Observations

So far we have discussed only the case with iid observations $Y_1, Y_2, \cdots$ Suppose now that they are dependent. The optimum property of the SPRT with thresholds $a$ and $b$ has been proved under the iid assumption, so it may not be optimum in this case. In fact, only the results (7.6) and (7.7) are valid for dependent observations. We now summarize some results that have been reported on sequential detection with dependent observations.

Cochlar and Vrana [66] showed that if $X_1, X_2, \ldots$ are dependent Gaussian random variables, then the optimum (in the Bayes sense which implies optimum in the sense of minimizing errors) detector has the form

$$\frac{f_n(y_1, \ldots, y_n | H_1)}{f_n(y_1, \ldots, y_n | H_0)} \begin{cases} \geq a(n) & \rightarrow H_1 \\ \leq b(n) & \rightarrow H_0 \\ \text{otherwise} & \rightarrow \text{continue} \end{cases} \tag{7.64}$$

where $f_n(y_1, \ldots, y_n | H_i)$ is the $n$-variate pdf of $Y_1, \ldots, Y_n$ under $H_i$, and $a(n)$ and $b(n)$ are variable thresholds. However, the design of $a(n)$ and $b(n)$ is still an open problem. The detector (7.64) was shown to be optimal only for Gaussian noise. For non-Gaussian noise, no such result has been proved.

A sequential test of the probability ratio against two variable thresholds, as in (7.64), is called a generalized sequential probability ratio test (GSPRT). There has been some study ([67], for example) of the properties of the GSPRT. However, the problem of an optimum detector for dependent observations with general pdf has not yet been solved.

There are relatively few results reported on sequential detection with dependent observations, most of them use constant thresholds $a$ and $b$. Lai [68] has shown that an SPRT with constant thresholds $a$ and $b$ is asymptotically, as $\alpha + (1-\beta) \to 0$, optimum in certain cases. Phatafod [69] derived approximate OC and ASN functions for an SPRT with constant thresholds when the noise is a Markov chain, the results of which were used for sequential detection of quantized data in [70]. In [71], some simulation results are reported for detection of a signal with random phase when the thresholds are constant and the observations are dependent Gaussian random variables. In [72], the effect of dependence on the SPRT, designed under the independence asumption, is investigated for a moving average noise. Results show that the error probabilities can be larger or smaller than the designed values of $\alpha$ and $1-\beta$, depending on whether the parameter of the moving average is positive or negative.

## 7.7 Conclusion

In this chapter we have reviewed various results on sequential detection of a constant signal, with emphasis on results reported since 1970. We began with some refinement on the optimality of the SPRT and techniques for the calculation of exact OC and ASN functions. Then, the AREs of the SPRT and various sequential detectors were discussed. In Section 7.4, various non-parametric and robust seqential detectors were reviewed. Most of the results are approximations, obtained from results of sequential test of a Wiener process. In Section 7.5, various modified schemes which reduce the maximum ASN were considered. Finally, results on sequential tests with dependent observations were discussed briefly .

# References

[1]   C.W. Helstrom, Sequential Detection, in *Communication Theory*, A.V. Balakrishnan, Ed., New York, NY: McGraw-Hill, pp. 272-292, 1968.

[2]   J.J. Bussgang, Sequential methods in radar detections, *Proc. IEEE*, Vol. 58, pp. 731-743, 1970.

[3]   B.K. Ghosh, *Sequential Tests of Statistical Hypotheses*, Reading, MA: Addison-Wesley, 1970.

[4]   A. Wald, *Sequential Analysis*, New York, NY: Wiley, 1947.

[5]   A. Wald and J. Wolfowitz, Optimum character of the sequential probability ratio test, *Ann. Math. Statist.*, Vol. 19, pp. 326-339, 1948.

[6]   G. Simons, An improved statement of optimality for sequential probability ratio tests, *Ann. Statist*, Vol. 4, pp. 1240-1243, 1976.

[7]   N.V. Krylov and T.P. Miroschnichenko, On extending the optimality region of Wald's test, *Theory Prob. Appl.*, Vol. 25, pp. 165-169, 1980.

[8]   R.H. Berk, Some asymptotic aspects of sequential analysis, *Ann. Statist*, Vol. 1, pp. 1126-1138, 1973.

[9]   L.A. Aroian and D.E. Robison, Direct methods for exact truncated tests of the mean of a normal distribution, *Technometrics*, Vol. 11, pp. 661-675, 1969.

[10]  B.A. Rozanov, Distribution of accumulated value of decision statistics in sequential analysis, *Radio Eng. and Electron. Physics*, Vol. 17, pp. 1667-1672, 1972.

[11]  G.E. Albert, On the computation of the sampling characteristics of a general class of a sequential decision problem, *Ann. Math. Statist.*, Vol. 25, pp. 340-356, 1954.

[12]  I. Vrana, On direct method of analysis and synthesis of the SPRT, *IEEE Trans. Inform. Theory*, Vol. IT-28, pp. 905-911, 1982.

[13]  E. Dalle Mese, G. Marchetti and L. Verrazzani and G. Corsini, Comments on "On a direct method of analysis and synthesis of the SPRT", *IEEE Trans. Inform. Theory*, Vol. IT-30, pp. 573-575, 1984.

[14]  S. Tantaratana and J.B. Thomas, On sequential sign detection of a

constant signal, *IEEE Trans. Inform. Theory,* Vol. IT-23, pp. 304-314, 1977.

[15]    B.V. Ustinov, Exact design of sequential detector of quantized binary signals, *Radio Eng. and Electron. Physics,* Vol. 17, pp. 396-400, 1972.

[16]    K.C. Chanda, Asymptotic distribution of the sample size for a sequential probability ratio test, *J. Amer. Stat. Assoc.,* Vol. 66, pp. 178-183, 1971.

[17]    A.T. Martinsek, A note on the variance and higher central moments of the stopping time of an SPRT, *J. Amer. Stat. Assoc.,* Vol. 76, pp.701-703, 1981.

[18]    T.L. Lai and D. Siegmund, A nonlinear renewal theory with applications to sequential analysis I, *Ann. Statist.,* Vol. 5, pp. 946-954, 1977.

[19]    T.L. Lai and D. Siegmund, A nonlinear renewal theory with applications to sequential analysis II, *Ann. Statist.,* Vol. 7, pp. 60-76, 1979.

[20]    R.H. Berk, Stopping times of SPRT's based on exchangeable models, *Ann. Math. Statist.,* Vol. 41, pp. 979-990, 1970.

[21]    Yu. A. Kutznetsov, Determination of the probabilies of errors of the first and second kinds in truncated sequential analysis, *Telecom. and Radio Eng.,* pp. 67-70, 1972.

[22]    S. Tantaratana, Distribution of a random walk with an application to a truncated nonparametric sequential test, *Proc. IEEE,* Vol. 69, pp. 1582-1584, 1981.

[23]    E. Paulson, A note on the efficiency of the Wald sequential test, *Ann. Math. Statist.,* Vol. 18, pp. 447-450, 1947.

[24]    S.A. Aivazian, Comparison of the optimal properties of the Wald and Neyman-Pearson criteria, *Theory Prob. Appl.,* Vol. 4, pp. 83-89, 1959.

[25]    R.E. Bechhofer, A note on the limiting relative efficiency of the Wald sequential probability ratio test , *J. Amer. Stat. Assoc.,* Vol. 55, pp. 660-663, 1960.

[26]    S. Tantaratana and J.B. Thomas, Relative efficiency of the sequential probability ratio test in signal detection, *IEEE Trans. Inform. Theory,*

Vol. IT-24, pp. 22-31, 1978.

[27]   T.L. Lai, Pitman efficiencies of sequential tests and uniform limit theorem in nonparametric statistics, *Ann. Statist.*, Vol. 6, pp. 1027-1047, 1978.

[28]   G.E. Noether, On a theorem of Pitman, *Ann. Math. Statist.*, Vol. 26, pp. 64-68, 1955.

[29]   J.B. Thomas, Nonparametric detection, *Proc. IEEE*, Vol. 58, pp. 623-631, 1970.

[30]   D.A. Darling and A.J.F. Siegert, The first passage problem for a continuous Markov process, *Ann. Math. Statist.*, Vol. 24, pp. 624-639, 1953.

[31]   W.J. Hall and R.M. Loynes, Weak convergence of processes related to the likelihood ratio, *Ann. Statist.*, Vol. 5, pp. 330-341, 1977.

[32]   R.H. Berk, Asymptotic efficiencies of sequential tests, *Ann. Statist.*, Vol. 4, pp. 891-911, 1976.

[33]   R.H. Berk, Asymptotic efficiencies of sequential tests II, *Ann. Statist.*, Vol. 6, pp. 813-819, 1978.

[34]   S. Tantaratana and J.B. Thomas, Quantization for sequential signal detection, *IEEE Trans. Comm.*, Vol. COM-25, pp. 696-703, 1977.

[35]   J.G. Shin and S.A. Kassam, Sequential detection based on quantization and conditional testing, *Proc. 1979 Conf. Inform. Sci. Sys.*, Johns Hopkins Univ., pp. 487-492, 1979.

[36]   C.C. Lee and J.B. Thomas, Generalizations of the sequential sign detector, *Proc. 17th Allerton Conf. Commun., Contr. Comp.*, Univ. of Illinois, pp. 848-857, 1979.

[37]   R.F. Dwyer, Sequential partition detectors with applications, Ph.D. Dissertation, Dept. of Elec. Eng. and Electrophysics, Polytechnic Institute of New York, 1976.

[38]   D.R. Cox, Large sample sequential tests of composite hypotheses, *Sankhya Ser. A*, Vol. 25, pp. 5-12, 1963.

[39]   R.G. Miller, Jr., and P.K. Sen, Weak convergence of *U*-statistics and

Von Mises differentiable statistical functions, *Ann. Math. Statist.*, Vol. 43, pp. 31-41, 1972.

[40]   P.K. Sen, The invariance principle for one sample rank order statistic, *Ann. Statist.*, Vol. 2, pp. 49-62, 1974.

[41]   P.K. Sen and M. Ghosh, Sequential rank tests for location, *Ann. Statist.*, Vol. 2, pp. 540-552, 1974.

[42]   P.K. Sen, *Sequential Nonparametrics: Invariance Principles and Statistical Inference*, New York, NY: Wiley, 1981.

[43]   E.L. Lehmann, *Testing Statistical Hypotheses*, New York, NY: Wiley, 1959.

[44]   R.G. Miller, Jr., Sequential signed-rank test, *J. Amer. Stat. Assoc.*, Vol. 65, pp. 1554-1561, 1970.

[45]   R.G. Miller, Jr., Sequential rank tests - one sample case, *Proc. Sixth Berkeley Symp. Math. Stat. and Prob.*, Vol. 1, Berkeley, CA: Univ. of California Press, pp. 97-108, 1972.

[46]   H.I. Braun, Weak convergence of sequential linear rank statistics, *Ann. Statist.*, Vol. 4, pp. 554-575, 1976.

[47]   M.R. Reynolds, Jr., A sequential signed-rank test for symmetry, *Ann. Statist.*, Vol. 3, pp. 382-400, 1975.

[48]   S. Tantaratana and J.B. Thomas, A class of nonparametric sequential tests, *IEEE Trans. Inform. Theory*, Vol. IT-27, pp. 596-606, 1981.

[49]   P.J. Huber, A robust version of the probability ratio test, *Ann. Math. Statist.*, Vol. 36, pp. 1753-1758, 1965.

[50]   P.M. Schultheiss and J.J. Wolcin, Robust sequential probability ratio detectors, *EASCON '75*, pp. 36A-36H, 1975.

[51]   A.H. El-Sawy and V.D. VandeLinde, Robust sequential detection of signals in noise, *IEEE Trans. Inform. Theory.* Vol. IT-25, pp. 346-353, 1979.

[52]   S. Tantaratana, A truncated sequential test: Performance and design with prescribed error probabilities, *Proc. 15th Annual Conf. on Inform. Sci. and Sys.*, Johns Hopkins Univ., pp. 333-338, 1981.

[53]   S. Tantaratana and H.V. Poor, Asymptotic efficiencies of truncated sequential tests, *IEEE Trans. Inform. Theory*, Vol. IT-28, pp. 911-923, 1982.

[54]   T.W. Anderson, A modification of the sequential probability ratio test to reduce the sample size, *Ann. Math. Statist.*, Vol. 31, pp. 165-197, 1960.

[55]   V. Fabian, Note on Anderson's sequential procedures with triangular boundary, *Ann. Statist.*, Vol. 2, pp. 170-176, 1974.

[56]   C.B. Read, The partial sequential probability ratio test, *J. Amer. Stat. Assoc.*, Vol. 66, pp. 646-650, 1971.

[57]   H.K. Baruah and G.P. Bhattacharjee, A modification of the sequential probability ratio test for testing a normal mean, *Australian J. Statist.*, Vol. 22, pp. 178-187, 1980.

[58]   T.L. Lai, Optimal stopping and sequential tests which minimize the maximum expected sample size, *Ann. Statist.*, Vol. 1, pp. 659-673, 1973.

[59]   G. Lorden, 2 SPRT's and the modified Kiefer-Weiss problem of minimizing an expected sample size, *Ann. Statist.*, Vol. 4, pp. 281-291, 1976.

[60]   S. Tantaratana and H.V. Poor, A two stage version of the Kassam-Thomas nonparametric dead-zone limiter detection system, *J. Acoust. Soc. Amer.*, Vol. 71, pp. 110-115, 1982.

[61]   S. Tantaratana, Performance of a two-stage nonparametric conditional detector for Rician density, *Proc. IEE, Part F,* Vol. 130, pp. 331-336, 1983.

[62]   S. Tantaratana, $M$-stage nonparametric rank detectors which reduce the average sample size and ranking time, *Proc. 20th Allerton Conf. Comm., Contr. Comp.,* Univ. of Illinois, pp. 723-732, 1982.

[63]   S.J. Pocock, Group sequential methods in the design and analysis of clinical trials, *Biometrika,* Vol. 64, pp. 191-199, 1977.

[64]   D.L. Demets and J.H. Ware, Grouped sequential methods for clinical trials with one-sided hypothesis, *Biometrika,* Vol. 67, pp. 651-660, 1980.

[65]    A.L. Gould and A.J. Pecore, Group sequential methods for clinical tri-
        als allowing early acceptance of $H_0$ and incorporating costs, *Biome-
        trika*, Vol. 69, pp. 75-80, 1982.

[66]    J. Cochlar and I. Vrana, On the optimum sequential test of two
        hypotheses for statistically dependent observations, *Kybernetika*, Vol. 14,
        pp. 57-69, 1978.

[67]    B. Eisenberg, B.K. Ghsoh and G. Simons, Properties of generalized
        sequential probability ratio tests, *Ann. Statist.*, Vol. 4, pp. 237-252,
        1976.

[68]    T.L. Lai, Asymptotic optimality of invariant sequential probability ratio
        tests, *Ann. Statist.*, Vol. 9, pp. 318-333, 1981.

[69]    R.M. Phatafod, Sequential analysis of dependent observations I, *Biome-
        trika*, Vol. 52, pp. 157-165, 1965.

[70]    B. Dimitriadis and D. Kazakos, A nonparametric sequential test for
        data with Markov dependence, *IEEE Trans. Aero. Elec. Sys.*, Vol.
        AES-19, pp. 338-347, 1983.

[71]    I. Vrana and M.M. El-Hefnawi, On the evaluation of properties of the
        sequential probability ratio test for statistically dependent observations,
        *Kybernetika*, Vol. 14, pp. 189-205, 1978.

[72]    S. Tantaratana, Performance of a sequential linear detector with depen-
        dent noise, *Proc. 17th Ann. Conf. on Inform. Sci. Sys.*, Johns Hopkins
        Univ., pp. 530-533, 1983.

# 8

# Recent Developments in Nonlinear Time-Series Modeling

**Dag Tjøstheim**

*Department of Mathematics*
*University of Bergen*
*Bergen, Norway*

## 8.1 Introduction

Parametric analysis and modeling of signals using linear stationary time series models has found application in a variety of contexts, including speech and seismic signal processing, spectral estimation, process control, and others. The statistical theory of such models is well established and quite complete, and efficient computational algorithms exist in a number of cases.

In comparison the results on nonlinear time-series models are very sparse and at a varying level of rigor. However, a major research effort has been

Supported in part by the AFOSR Contract No. F49620 82 C 0009 made in these areas in the last decade or so. Some of the new models proposed have strong connections to dynamical system models like the Kalman filtering scheme. Others have been motivated by nonlinear random vibration theory and control theory.

In this chapter we survey some of these recent developments. To fix notations let $\{X_t\}$ be the stochastic process representing the observed time series. Unless otherwise is indicated, $\{X_t\}$ will be assumed to be scalar. The process $\{X_t, \ t = 0, \pm 1, ... \}$ is said to be *strictly stationary* if $\{X_{t_1}, ..., X_{t_n}\}$ and $\{X_{t_1+k}, ..., X_{t_n+k}\}$ have the same distribution for $n = 1, 2, ...$ and for all integers $k$ and $t_1, ..., t_n$. The process is *second-order stationary* if $E(X_t)$ and $\text{cov}(X_t, X_s)$ exist and if

$$E(X_t) = E(X_{t+k}) \text{ and } \text{cov}(X_t, X_s) = \text{cov}(X_{t+k}, X_{s+k})$$

for all integers $s, t$, and $k$. In linear stationary modeling the process $\{X_t\}$ is usually assumed to be generated from an ARMA $(p, q)$ model; i.e., it can be written as

$$(X_t - \mu) - \sum_{i=1}^{p} a_i(X_{t-i} - \mu) = e_t + \sum_{i=1}^{q} b_i e_{t-i}. \tag{8.1}$$

Here $\mu$, $a_1, ..., a_p$ and $b_1, ..., b_q$ are real constants, while $\{e_t\}$ is a white noise process such that $E(e_t) = 0$ and $\text{cov}\ (e_t, e_s) = \sigma^2 \delta_{ts}$. In statistical inference applications one employs the stronger assumption that the $e_t$'s are identically and independently distributed (iid), or that they constitute a martingale difference sequence. The parameter $\mu$ is the mean of the series and is often assumed to be zero.

We will denote by $F^X_t$ and $F^e_t$ the $\sigma$-algebras generated by $\{X_s, \ s \leq t\}$ and $\{e_s, s \leq t\}$, respectively. It is customary to make the assumption that $e_{t+s}$ is independent of $F^X_t$ for $s > 0$. The process $\{X_t\}$ will be said to be *stable* if the characteristic polynomial $A(z) = z^p - \sum_{i=1}^{p} a_i z^{p-i}$ has its zeros inside the unit circle. In this case, if the $e_t$'s are iid, it is well known that a strictly stationary solution $\{X_t\}$ to (8.1) exists so that $X_t$ depends only on $\{e_s, s \leq t\}$. In this situation consistent and asymptotically normal estimates of the parameters can be found as was proven already in the classical papers by Mann and Wald (1943 a,b). The process is said to be invertible if the polynomial $B(z) = z^q + \sum_{i=1}^{q} b_i z^{q-i}$ has its zeros inside the unit circle. In this case $F^X_t = F^e_t$, and the process $\{e_t\}$ can be used in forming forecasts of $\{X_t\}$.

In a majority of applications to signal processing, pure autoregressive (AR) models have been used; i.e., $b_1 = \cdots = b_q = 0$ in (8.1), and in most of this chapter we consider nonlinear generalizations of the AR process. In Section 8.2 we will illustrate what can be gained using nonlinear models by studying a simple example. Attempts of setting up a general framework for nonlinear models are reviewed in Section 8.3, and in Section 8.4 we survey some special classes of models which have attracted considerable attention lately and describe how they can be fitted to data. Finally, in Section 8.5 we look at the above mentioned properties of stability/stationarity, invertibility/forecasting, and also discuss briefly consistency/asymptotic normality in the context of these models.

Needless to say, this review is far from complete, and it is to a high degree colored by the author's special background and interests. From the outset we will stay almost exclusively in the time domain, and we will limit ourselves to models without trends and seasonalities. For other recent reviews (mainly on linear and stationary models) we refer to Cox (1981) and Newbold (1981). Spectral properties have been treated in the September 1982 issue of the *Proceedings of the IEEE*.

## 8.2 A Motivating Example

For linear models one essentially is concerned only with second-order or correlation structure, and predictors and pattern recognition procedures are based on this. Nonlinear models give a more complete probabilistic description. This means that predictions may be improved, and better characterization of the data may be obtained in a pattern recognition context, since more of the structure is taken into account. We illustrate this difference on a simple example (Granger and Andersen 1978, Chap.5).

Consider the process $\{X_t\}$ defined by

$$X_t = be_{t-1}X_{t-2} + e_t \qquad (8.2)$$

where $\{e_t\}$ is a process consisting of iid variables with zero mean and finite variance $E(e_t^2) = \sigma^2$. It can be shown (cf. Granger and Andersen 1978, Chap. 5, and techniques of Section 8.5.1 of this chapter) that there exists a solution $\{X_t\}$ to (8.2) such that $\{X_t\}$ is both second order and strictly stationary if $b^2\sigma^2 < 1$. We have $E(X_t) = 0$ and using (8.2) it follows that

$$E(X_t X_{t-h}) = b^2 E(e_{t-1}X_{t-2}e_{t-h-1}X_{t-h-2})$$

$$+ bE(e_{t-1}X_{t-2}e_{t-h}) + bE(e_t e_{t-h-1}X_{t-h-2}) + E(e_t e_{t-h}). \qquad (8.3)$$

Using the iid property of $\{e_t\}$ it is easily seen that cov $(X_t, X_{t-h}) = 0$ for $h \neq 0$. Thus if we look at the correlation structure only, then $\{X_t\}$ is white noise, and the optimal one-step linear predictor from this point of view is $\hat{X}_{t|t-1} = E(X_t) = 0$. Moreover, for pattern recognition purposes $\{X_t\}$ is described by a single parameter, namely var $(X_t)$.

However, if we assume that $X_t$ is invertible, then the optimal nonlinear one-step least-squares predictor is given by

$$\tilde{X}_{t|t-1} = E(X_t | F^X_{t-1}) = be_{t-1}X_{t-2}, \qquad (8.4)$$

where a recursive algorithm for expressing $e_{t-1}$ in terms of $\{X_s, s \leq t-1\}$ can be found from (8.2) by replacing $t$ with $t-1$. We refer to Granger and Andersen (1978, Chap. 8) for a discussion of this point and for a discussion of invertibility conditions on $\{X_t\}$. The prediction error for the nonlinear forecast is clearly $\sigma^2$, whereas the prediction error for the linear predictor is var $\{X_t\} = \sigma^2/(1 - b^2\sigma^2)$, and depending on the values of $b$ and $\sigma^2$ a substantial improvement in prediction performance could be obtained by taking the nonlinear structure into account. It should be noted, however, that the invertibility requirements put some restrictions on the range of possible values for $b^2\sigma^2$.

Also, further information for pattern recognition purposes can be extracted if the nonlinear structure of $\{X_t\}$ is taken into account. For example it can be shown (Granger and Andersen 1978, p. 44) that $Y_t = X_t^2$ has the autocorrelation structure of an ARMA (2,1) model and the parameters of that ARMA model could be used as a means of characterizing $\{X_t\}$.


## 8.3 A General Framework for Nonlinear Models

Special examples like the one just considered are of somewhat limited interest if they cannot be put in a larger context of a general theoretical framework for nonlinear time-series models. The main purpose of this section is to review some attempts in this direction.

### 8.3.1 Volterra Expansion and State-Dependent Models.

The linear time-series models in a sense are based on the fact that for a second-order stationary, purely nondeterministic process it is possible to express $\{X_t\}$ by means of a linear moving-average representation

$$X_t = \sum_{i=0}^{\infty} h_i e_{t-i} \qquad (8.5)$$

in terms of uncorrelated random variables $\{e_t\}$, and where this representation is causally invertible (see, e.g., Andersen 1970, Chap. 7). The second-order stationary and invertible ARMA model is a special case of this representation. Wiener (1958) in a pioneering effort in the nonlinear case was looking for conditions which would guarantee the existence of a representation

$$X_t = h(e_t, e_{t-1}, \ldots) \qquad (8.6)$$

which is invertible so that

$$e_t = \phi(X_t, X_{t-1}, \ldots) \qquad (8.7)$$

and where the $e_t$'s are iid (and in fact uniformly distributed). His early investigation of this problem contains mathematical gaps (Kallianpur 1981) and at present there still does not seem to exist a complete solution. However, conditions do exist in the Markov chain case (Rosenblatt 1959, Hanson 1963).

Assuming that a representation of the form (8.6) exists and that $h$ is analytic, for some fixed time point $t_0$ we can expand (following Priestley 1980) $h$ about $\{e_{t_0}, e_{t_0-1}, \ldots\}$ and are then led to a Volterra expansion of the type used by Wiener (1958), namely

$$X_t = h(e_{t_0}, e_{t_0-1}, \ldots) + \sum_{i=0}^{\infty} \left[ \frac{\partial h}{\partial e_{t-i}} \right]_{t=t_0} (e_{t-i} - e_{t_0-i})$$

$$+ \frac{1}{2} \sum_{i=0}^{\infty} \sum_{j=0}^{\infty} \left[ \frac{\partial^2 h}{\partial e_{t-i} \, \partial e_{t-j}} \right]_{t=t_0} (e_{t-i} - e_{t_0-i})(e_{t-j} - e_{t_0-j}) + \cdots (8.8)$$

which may be written as

$$X_t = \mu + \sum_{i=0}^{\infty} g_i e_{t-i} + \sum_{i=0}^{\infty} \sum_{j=0}^{\infty} g_{ij} e_{t-i} e_{t-j} + \cdots . \qquad (8.9)$$

If the model is invertible as in (8.7), we can also write

$$e_t = \mu' + \sum_{i=0}^{\infty} g_i' X_{t-i} + \sum_{i=0}^{\infty} \sum_{j=0}^{\infty} g_{ij}' X_{t-i} X_{t-j} + \cdots \qquad (8.10)$$

where we look at these as formal expansions without specifying the mode of convergence.

To be able to work with models of this type in practice, only a finite number of lags should be involved, and Priestley uses the above to motivate models of the form

$$X_t = h'(X_{t-1}, \ldots, X_{t-p}; e_t, e_{t-1}, \ldots, e_{t-q}) \qquad (8.11)$$

which he assumes can be rewritten as

$$X_t - \mu(x_{t-1}) - \sum_{i=1}^{p} a_i(x_{t-1}) X_{t-i} = e_t + \sum_{i=1}^{q} b_i(x_{t-1}) e_{t-i} \qquad (8.12)$$

where he considers $x_{t-1} = (X_{t-1}, \ldots, X_{t-p}; e_{t-1}, \ldots, e_{t-q})$ as a "state vector", and where the model itself is called a *state-dependent* model of order $(p, q)$. In a way this model can be interpreted as a locally linear ARMA model. Many of the proposed special nonlinear models in Section 8.4 fit into the framework described by (8.12).

Priestley also indicates some general recursive properties of these models and suggests ways of model fitting and estimation. However, these should really be taken as indicative of the general problems involved. At present it seems difficult to fit data directly to a general model of the type (8.12).

In Priestley (1981, Chap. 11.5.1) Volterra models are coupled with the concept of polyspectra. The $k$th-order polyspectrum for a strictly stationary $\{X_t\}$ is defined by

$$h_k(\omega_1,\ldots,\omega_{k-1}) =$$

$$(2\pi)^{-k+1} \sum_{s_1=-\infty}^{\infty} \cdots \sum_{s_{k-1}=-\infty}^{\infty} C(s_1,\ldots,s_{k-1}) \exp\left(-i \sum_{j=1}^{k-1} \omega_j s_j\right) \quad (8.13)$$

where $C(s_1,\ldots,s_{k-1})$ denotes the joint cumulant of order $k$ of the set of random variables $\{X_t, X_{t+s_1},\ldots,X_{t+s_{k-1}}\}$, and where it is assumed that

$$\sum_{s_1=-\infty}^{\infty} \cdots \sum_{s_{k-1}=-\infty}^{\infty} |C(s_1,\ldots,s_{k-1})| < \infty. \quad (8.14)$$

Polyspectra have been used to give a general frequency-domain approach to nonlinear systems. Basic properties and estimation procedures have been discussed by Brillinger (1965) and Brillinger and Rosenblatt (1967). Subba Rao and Gabr (1980) have constructed a test of linearity based on the bispectrum ($k = 3$ in (8.13)).

### 8.3.2 An Alternative Approach

A somewhat different approach to nonlinear modeling has been taken in Harrison and Stevens (1976), Ledolter (1981), and Tjøstheim (1983). It can be partly motivated from a desire to obtain effective recursive forecasting schemes analogous to those used in Kalman filtering, but it is also motivated in part by the difficulties encountered in employing AR models with deterministic time-varying coefficients. Such models are given by

$$X_t - \sum_{i=1}^{p} a_{ti} X_{t-i} = e_t \quad (8.15)$$

and have been used in speech recognition (Makhoul 1975, Markel and Gray

1977, Hall *et al.* 1983). They are in general nonstationary, and it appears difficult to develop a satisfactory statistical theory for them, although some progress has been made on the so-called spectral factorization problem for such models (Hallin and Ingenbleek 1983, Hallin 1984).

In an attempt to make these models more amenable to analysis, one may try to replace the coefficients $(a_{t1},...,a_{tp})$ by a stochastic process $\{\theta_t(p)\} = \{(\theta_{t1},...,\theta_{tp})\}$, resulting in a doubly stochastic model

$$X_t - \sum_{i=1}^{p} \theta_{ti} X_{t-i} = e_t. \qquad (8.16)$$

As will be seen in Section 8.5.2, in special cases it is possible to find conditions which ensure stationarity of $\{X_t\}$. More important, perhaps, is the fact that it is possible to specify models for $\{\theta_t(p)\}$ so that explicit recursive forecasting algorithms may be constructed for $\{X_t\}$.

The process $\{\theta_t(p)\}$ may be interpreted as a state process, but in general it is different from the concept of state introduced in connection with the model (8.12), since $\{\theta_t(p)\}$ will not be described solely in terms of $\{X_t\}$ and $\{e_t\}$, but rather it will be assumed to be generated by a separate mechanism. To include the possibility of direct dependence in the AR coefficients on past values of $\{X_t\}$, we introduced in Tjøstheim (1983) the general doubly stochastic model

$$X_t - A_0(t-1,X) - \sum_{i=1}^{p} A_i(t-1,X)\theta_{ti} X_{t-i} = B(t-1,X)e_t \qquad (8.17)$$

where $\{X_t\}$ is now a general $d$-dimensional process, $A_0(t-1,X)$ is a $d$-dimensional vector function, $A_i(t-1,X)$, $i = 1,...,p$, and $B(t-1,X)$ are $d \times d$ matrix functions all measurable with respect to $F^X_{t-1}$, and $\{\theta_t(p)\} = \{(\theta_{t1},...,\theta_{tp})\}$ is a $pd \times d$ matrix process. The product type interaction between $A_i(t-1,X)$, $\theta_{ti}$ and $X_{t-i}$ has been chosen mainly for mathematical convenience. Here we will assume that the processes $\{\theta_t(p)\}$ and $\{e_t\}$ are independent, that $\{e_t\}$ consists of zero-mean and finite variance iid variables such that for $s > 0$, $e_{t+s}$ is independent of $F^X_t \vee F^\theta_t$, although, at least for some problems, it is possible to use somewhat weaker assumptions.

As is the case for the model described by (8.12), the model (8.17) should be considered as giving a convenient theoretical framework for nonlinear modeling. We will see in the next section that most of the nonlinear models proposed in the recent literature come out as special cases of (8.17). The model needs further specification in order to fit it to real data.

In practice the functions $A_i(t-1,X)$, $i=0,\ldots,p$, and $B(t-1,X)$ must be assumed known except possibly for a few parameters. We also need to postulate a model for the parameter process $\{\theta_t(p)\}$. One could of course take the point of view that $\{\theta_t(p)\}$ is known or partially known from external knowledge of the system described by the time series $\{X_t\}$, but, in general, there will at most be a mathematical model available for $\{\theta_t(p)\}$, and the values of $\{\theta_t(p)\}$ will have to be inferred from this model and the observational data $\{X_t\}$. This means that the problem of evaluating $\{\theta_t(p)\}$ is a (nonlinear) filtering problem with $\{\theta_t(p)\}$ taking the place of the state process. Some examples of specification of $\{\theta_t(p)\}$ are given in Sections 8.4.3 and 8.5.2.

### 8.3.3 Nonlinear Models in Continuous Time

Much of the recent mathematical theory on nonlinear filtering has been developed in continuous time with strong emphasis on stochastic differential equations. Some of the most important developments have their roots in the recursive Kalman-Bucy (1961) linear filtering algorithms. Nonlinear generalizations of these have been obtained using the so-called innovations approach (see, e.g., Fujisaki et al. 1972, Davis and Marcus 1981). In this setup, both the observational process $\{X_t\}$ and the state process $\{\theta_t(p)\}$ are generated by nonlinear mechanisms, and in addition a feedback coupling between the two processes is postulated. The resulting nonlinear recursive algorithms for the optimal filter are typically formulated in terms of conditional probability distributions and requires an infinite number of operations. They are therefore not usually possible to implement in practice, and much research has been directed towards the problem of finding cases where the recursive equations are finite dimensional. Benes (1981) is the recipient of the 1982 IEEE Information Theory Group Award Paper for his fundamental contribution to this problem.

The continuous-time innovations approach is heavily based on martingale theory and in particular on characterization results for square-integrable martingales. Due to lack of smoothness such characterization results are largely missing in discrete time, and apart from the quasi-linear conditional Gaussian case (Liptser and Shiryayev 1978, Chaps. 13 and 14), which will be discussed in Section 8.5.2, we are not aware of a discrete analog to the innovations approach to nonlinear filtering theory.

## 8.4 Some Special Classes of Nonlinear Models

Several special classes of nonlinear time series have been studied recently. We have found it convenient to subdivide these into three main categories.

### 8.4.1 Models Motivated by Nonlinear Differential Equations

Many dynamical systems in engineering require nonlinear differential equations for an adequate description of their behavior. One example is nonlinear vibrations. Typically, these are described by deterministic second-order differential equations of the form

$$\ddot{x}(t) + f[\dot{x}(t)] + g[x(t)] = h(t) \tag{8.18}$$

where $f$ and $g$ are nonlinear functions representing, respectively, the damping force and the restoring force, and where $h(t)$ is a deterministic input which could be zero or could be, for example, a sinusoid. Two well-known examples are Duffing's equation

$$\ddot{x}(t) + c\dot{x}(t) + ax(t) + b[x(t)]^3 = h(t) \tag{8.19}$$

and Van der Pol's equation

$$\ddot{x}(t) + f[\dot{x}(t)] + ax(t) = h(t). \tag{8.20}$$

The solution of nonlinear differential equations of the above type has some characteristic features which are absent in the linear case. Prime among these are phenomena such as amplitude-dependent frequency, jump resonances, and limit cycles (cf. Struble 1962). Time-series analysts have been particularly intrigued by the concept of a limit cycle, which somewhat loosely can be described as the phenomenon that the output (i.e., the solution of the differential equation) of a stable nonlinear system may contain sustained oscillations which persist in the absence of input, whereas for a stable linear system the output dies away when the input is switched off. Furthermore, these nonlinear oscillations may have a distinctive asymmetrical appearance (e.g., sawtooth pattern), and it is therefore difficult to model them using harmonic analysis of linear time-series models.

Sometimes it seems unrealistic to assume that the input of (8.18) is deterministic and consists, for example, of a cosine with a specified frequency. In such situations it may be appropriate to replace $h(t)$ with a stochastic input force with a continuous spectrum. In discrete time this results in a nonlinear time series model which in the first-order case will be given by

$$X_t - f(X_{t-1}) = e_t \tag{8.21}$$

where we now make the additional assumption that the input $\{e_t\}$ constitutes a white noise process with the $e_t$'s being iid. Such models have been analyzed by Jones (1978) (see also Aase 1983) using recursions and formal power series expansions. Jones' effort was not mainly motivated by constructing models exhibiting the typical nonlinear features mentioned above, and it seems to be difficult to pinpoint such behavior unless one makes special assumptions on the function $f$, and, to obtain larger flexibility, increases the order. We will now describe two functional forms that have been used for $f$.

*Threshold Autoregressive Models*

These models were originally introduced by Tong (1977) in connection with the analysis of river flow data. The underlying idea is a piecewise linearization of the model by introduction of a local threshold dependence on the amplitude $X_t$. Thus a first-order threshold autoregressive TAR(1) model is described by

$$X_t = \begin{cases} a^1 X_{t-1} + e_t^1, & \text{if } X_{t-1} < d \\ a^2 X_{t-1} + e_t^2, & \text{if } X_{t-1} \geq d \end{cases} \tag{8.22}$$

Higher order models with several thresholds may be similarly defined. In the nomenclature of Tong and Lim (1980) a SETAR$(m,p,\ldots,p)$ model is given by

$$X_t - \sum_{i=1}^{p} a_i^{\,j} X_{t-i} = e_t^{\,j} \tag{8.23}$$

if $[X_{t-1},\ldots,X_{t-p}]^T \in F_j$ for $j = 1,\ldots,m$, where $F_1,\ldots,F_m$ are disjoint regions of the $p$-dimensional Euclidean space $R^p$, such that $\bigcup_{j=1}^{m} F_j = R^p$. Moreover, $\{e_t^{\,j}\}$, $j = 1,\ldots,m$, are independent white noise series consisting of iid variables.

It is interesting to note that this model essentially comes out as a special case of both (8.12) and (8.17). For example, in (8.17) let $A_0$ and $\{\theta_t(p)\}$ be constant and $A_i(t-1,X) = a_i^{\,j}$ and $B(t-1,X) = d^j$, say, for $[X_{t-1},\ldots,X_{t-p}]^T \in F_j$. Multivariate and more general-type threshold models have been defined in Tong and Lim (1980).

It has been shown by simulation that the class of threshold AR models is rich enough to contain models with realizations having behavior resembling limit cycles. This is not unexpected in view of the chosen model specifications. Consider, for example (Tong and Lim 1980), equation (8.23) with $p = 1$ and $m = 3$, and let $F_1 = (-\infty, r_1)$, $F_2 = [r_1, r_2]$ and $F_3 = (r_2, \infty)$, where $r_1$ and $r_2$ are real numbers such that $r_1 < 0 < r_2$. Moreover, assume that $|a^1| < 1$, $|a^2| > 1$ and $|a^3| < 1$. Then for small values of $|X_{t-1}|$ the system tends to explode, since $X_{t-1} \in F_2$ and $|a^2| > 1$, whereas for large values of $|X_{t-1}|$, the system damps down since then $X_{t-1} \in F_1 \cup F_3$ and $|a^1|$ and $|a^3| < 1$, and the end result is oscillatory behavior.

To be able to fit threshold models to data one must be able to determine the order, the regions $F_1,\ldots,F_m$ and the corresponding quantities $a_i^{\,j}$. This can be done by an iterative search technique using least squares. For a given order, a given number of threshold variables describing the threshold regions, the parameters $a_i{}^j$ are first determined. The resulting residuals can be computed from (8.23) and $\sum_t (e_t^j)^2$ evaluated. Individual orders $p_j$ can be determined for each threshold region using an AIC-type criterion (cf. Akaike 1973, Schwarz 1978, Hannan and Quinn 1979), and the AIC criterion can next be applied to the overall model to determine the appropriate number of thresholds and the associated regions. In practice one would usually start by considering a set of threshold regions defined by just a single past observation $X_{t-d}$, where the AIC criterion can be applied to determine the most appropriate value of d. We refer to Tong and Lim (1980) and Lim and Tong (1983) for details, where this procedure is applied to both simulated and real data. For the selected data sets the threshold models have a smaller residual variance than the competing linear models, but at a considerable cost, it appears, in model and computational complexity.

*Exponential Autoregressive Models*

These models were introduced and studied in Ozaki (1980) and Haggan and Ozaki (1981). The point of departure is an ordinary AR($p$) model, where the AR coefficient $a_i$ is replaced by $\phi_i + \pi_i \exp(-\gamma X_{t-1}^2)$ with $\phi_i$, $\pi_i$ and $\gamma$ being real constants such that $\gamma \geq 0$. This results in a model

$$X_t - \sum_{i=1}^{p} [\phi_i + \pi_i \exp(-\gamma X_{t-1}^2)]X_{t-i} = e_t. \tag{8.24}$$

Again it is clear that this model is a special case of (8.12) and (8.17); taking $A_0(t-1,X)$, $\{\theta_t(p)\}$ and $B(t-1,X)$ to be constants and

$$A_i(t-1,X) = \phi_i + \pi_i \exp(-\gamma X_{t-1}^2).$$

The crucial point of the chosen functional form is that for large values of $|X_{t-1}|$ we have $A_i(t-1,X) \approx \phi_i$, while for small values of $|X_{t-1}|$ we have $A_i(t-1,X) \approx \phi_i + \pi_i$. Hence, in this respect the model behaves rather like a threshold AR model except that the AR coefficients now change smoothly between two extreme values.

In view of this it is not surprising that exponential autoregressive models are capable of producing oscillations resembling limit cycles. Actually for a first-order model,

$$X_t - [\phi + \pi \exp(-\gamma X_{t-1}^2)]X_{t-1} = e_t, \qquad (8.25)$$

an example of limit cycle behavior can be constructed as in the first-order threshold case, namely by requiring $|\phi| < 1$ and $|\phi + \pi| > 1$. The mechanism is the same as before; for small $X_{t-1}$ the system tends to explode since $|\phi + \pi| > 1$, while for large $X_{t-1}$ the system damps down due to $|\phi| < 1$.

The determination of model and parameters from data appears computationally simpler than in the threshold case. Haggan and Ozaki (1981) propose the following procedure for estimating the parameters: First fix the value of $\gamma$; then $\phi_1, \pi_1, \ldots, \phi_p, \pi_p$ may be estimated by standard least-squares regression analysis of $X_t$ on $X_{t-1}$, $[\exp(-\gamma X_{t-1}^2)]X_{t-1}, \ldots, X_{t-p}$, $[\exp(-\gamma X_{t-1}^2)]X_{t-p}$. The order $p$ of the model is decided by using an AIC type criterion. Finally, the analysis above is repeated using a range of values of $\gamma$, and the AIC criterion is used to select the most suitable value.

For examples where this is applied to simulated and real data we refer to Haggan and Ozaki (1981). A combined threshold/exponential autoregressive model is discussed in Ozaki (1981).

### 8.4.2 Bilinear Models

In a time-series context the bilinear models have been introduced by Granger and Andersen (1978) and Subba Rao (1981). A scalar bilinear time series $\{X_t\}$ of type $BL(p,q,m,k)$ is defined by the difference equation

$$X_t - a_0 - \sum_{i=1}^{p} a_i X_{t-i} = e_t + \sum_{i=1}^{q} c_i e_{t-i} + \sum_{i=1}^{m} \sum_{j=1}^{k} b_{ij} X_{t-i} e_{t-j} \quad (8.26)$$

where $\{e_t\}$ is zero-mean iid white noise. A special case of this model has already been discussed in Section 8.2. The model (8.26) clearly is a special case of (8.12). If it is invertible, so that it is possible to express $e_t$ as a measurable function of $\{X_s, \ s \leq t\}$, it is also a special case of (8.17), since

then $a_0 + \sum_{j=1}^{q} c_j e_{t-j}$ may be identified with $A_0(t-1, X)$, whereas

$a_i + \sum_{j=1}^{k} b_{ij} e_{t-j}$ may be identified with $A_i(t-1, X)$. In the noninvertible case it is of course formally possible to include bilinear models in the general framework of Section 8.3.2 by adding an MA part in (8.17), but this seems to lead to genuine complications in the theory of these models.

We are not aware of a full multivariate generalization of bilinear processes, and the theory in the scalar case is far from complete. Nevertheless, it is perhaps the class of models that has attracted most attention lately (Subba Rao and Gabr 1980, Guegan 1983, Pham and Tran 1981, Quinn 1982a and b, Tong 1983, Bhaskara Rao *et al.* 1983). This seems to be because it is relatively simple in structure and yet flexible enough to be adapted to a large number of various types of data sets.

Bilinear models have their origin in bilinear differential equations used to describe input-output relations in deterministic control theory (see, e.g., Mohler 1973). It has been shown in the *deterministic* case that, although bilinear models contain a finite number of parameters, over a finite interval they approximate any "reasonable" nonlinear relationship of Volterra series type (Brockett 1976). Thus there is some justification for taking the model introduced in (8.26) as a finite-parameter approximation to the general nonlinear model (8.9), although it is not known at present how accurate this approximation is in the stochastic case.

Since bilinear models are close to linear models it is possible to obtain (Subba Rao 1981) the covariance structure in some special cases. We will return to other theoretical properties in a more general setting in the next section. Here we only indicate how bilinear models can be fitted to data.

We follow Subba Rao (1981) and look at a model $BL(p,0,p,k)$, i.e., the model given by

$$X_t - a_0 - \sum_{i=1}^{p} a_i X_{t-i} = e_t + \sum_{i=1}^{p} \sum_{j=1}^{k} b_{ij} X_{t-i} e_{t-j}. \qquad (8.27)$$

First consider $p$ and $k$ given and let $\beta^T = [-a_0, -a_1, \ldots, -a_p, b_{11}, \ldots, b_{pk}]$ be the parameter vector. Then we obtain an estimate of $\beta$ by minimizing the residual sum of squares $Q(\beta) = \sum_t e_t^2$, where $e_t$ is obtained recursively from (8.27), once initial conditions $e_0, \ldots, e_{m-1}$ are chosen. Here $m = \max(p,k) + 1$. This estimate coincides with the maximum likelihood estimate in the case of Gaussian $e_t$'s, since the Jacobian of the transformation from $\{e_m,\ldots,e_n\}$ to $\{X_m,\ldots,X_n\}$ is unity. The quantity $Q(\beta)$ can be minimized by an iterative Newton-Raphson procedure

$$\beta^{(k+1)} = \beta^{(k)} - H^{-1}(\beta^{(k)})G(\beta^{(k)}) \tag{8.28}$$

where the vector $G(\beta)$ and the matrix $H(\beta)$ are determined from

$$G(\beta) = \left[\frac{\partial Q(\beta)}{\partial \beta_i}\right] \quad \text{and} \quad H(\beta) = \left[\frac{\partial^2 Q(\beta)}{\partial \beta_i \partial \beta_j}\right] \tag{8.29}$$

respectively. The elements of $G(\beta)$ and $H(\beta)$ contain first- and second-order derivatives $\partial e_t/\partial \beta_i$ and $\partial^2 e_t/\partial \beta_i \partial \beta_j$. These can be found recursively from (8.27) after differentiating this equation once and twice with respect to $\beta$. Subsequently, an AIC-type criterion is used to determine the values of $p$ and $k$. To avoid too many parameters, one may use best subset bilinear models (as can be done for the other nonlinear models as well), where only a fixed number of the parameters are allowed to be nonzero.

The estimation procedure described here is illustrated on real and simulated data in Subba Rao (1981), and for the studied data sets better fit is obtained than for the linear models.

### 8.4.3 Doubly Stochastic Models

By a doubly stochastic model we will here understand models defined as in (8.16). Such models fall outside the general framework provided by (8.12), but it is of course a trivial special case of (8.17), and in Tjøstheim (1983) the term "doubly stochastic" was used for the more general model (8.17).

In a sense the doubly stochastic models go back to early attempts to develop adaptive methods for business forecasting of time series whose parameters change in time (cf. Trigg and Leach 1967, Makridakis and Wheelwright 1977). Forecasting by adaptive filtering was first introduced heuristically and without reference to a model for the changes in structure over time. A stochastic model for the parameters was suggested by Harrison and Stevens (1976). They also realized the fundamental importance of Kalman type filtering schemes in this context, although they reasoned from Bayesian arguments. The close connection between Kalman filtering and Bayesian theory was noted by Ho and Lee (1964). Ledolter (1981) considers (8.16) in conjunction with an autoregressive model for the parameter process $\{\theta_t(p)\} = \{(\theta_{t1},...,\theta_{tp})\}$, resulting in a model

$$X_t = \theta_t^T(p)Y_{t-1} + e_t$$

$$\theta_t(p) = C\theta_{t-1}(p) + \varepsilon_t \qquad (8.30)$$

where $Y_{t-1} = [X_{t-1},...,X_{t-p}]^T$ and $\{e_t\}$ and $\{\varepsilon_t\}$ are zero-mean independent Gaussian processes. He also discusses processes with moving-average terms and extended Kalman filtering. Tjøstheim (1983) allows more general parameter processes, where for example $\{\theta_t(p)\}$ may be a Markov chain. The Markov chain model can be considered as a stochastic version of the deterministic step function model of the AR coefficients which have been used in speech processing (cf. Makhoul 1975, Markel and Gray 1977).

The fact that the model (8.16) contains product terms $\theta_{ti}X_{t-i}$ makes it nonlinear and also implies that the model (8.30) is conceptually different from ordinary Kalman state-space models, where $Y_{t-1}$ is replaced by a known deterministic function independent of the observational process $\{X_t\}$. (See also regression-type Kalman models; Ledolter 1979). This distinction leads to a difference in character of the recursive forecasting equations for these models, as will be seen in Section 8.5.2. If a Markov chain model is used for $\{\theta_t(p)\}$, both the observational and state-space equations are nonlinear, and this further complicates the problem of finding recursive forecasting algorithms.

A somewhat singular case of a doubly stochastic process results if $\{\theta_t(p)\}$ is without dependence structure, i.e., $\theta_{ti} = a_i + \beta_{ti}$, where $\{\beta_t(p)\} = \{(\beta_{t1},...,\beta_{tp})\}$ is a process of iid variables and the $a_i$'s are constants. These processes have been labelled random coefficient autoregressive (RCA) processes. The iid assumption is restrictive, but it has the advantage that it makes it possible to develop a fairly complete theory of statistical inference. This has been done in a series of papers by Nicholl's and Quinn. Most of their results have been collected in a recent monograph (Nicholls and Quinn 1982).

To fit doubly stochastic models to data one must be able to determine the parameters entering the observational and state equation from the data. In this respect the situation is different from ordinary Kalman filtering schemes, where the coefficients of the system are often assumed to be known.

Procedures for determining the parameters in special cases with applications to data are given in Harrison and Stevens (1976) and Ledolter (1981), and in Nicholls and Quinn (1982) for the RCA case. These will be outlined only briefly here. It should be noted at the outset that, unlike linear models and the nonlinear models treated in Sections 8.4.1 and 8.4.2, the introduction of the additional process $\{\theta_t(p)\}$ in general implies that least-squares and maximum likelihood estimates do not coincide asymptotically for a Gaussian residual process $\{e_t\}$.

We will illustrate maximum likelihood estimation (Ledolter 1981) on the special model (8.30). The unknown parameters in this case are $\sigma^2 = E(e_t^2)$, the matrix $C$ and the covariance matrix $\Omega$ of $\{\varepsilon_t\}$. The log likelihood is given by

$$L(\sigma^2,\Omega,C\,|\,X_1,\ldots,X_n) = n\log\sigma - 1/2\,\log f_t$$

$$- \frac{1}{2\sigma^2}\sum_{t=1}^{n}(X_t - Y_{t-1}^T\tilde{\theta}_{t\,|\,t-1}(p))^2\,/f_t \qquad (8.31)$$

where $\tilde{\theta}_{t\,|\,t-1} = E(\theta_t(p)|F^X_{t-1})$, where $f_t = 1 + Y_{t-1}{}^T\tilde{P}_{t\,|\,t-1}Y_{t-1}$, with $\sigma^2\tilde{P}_{t\,|\,t-1}$ being the conditional covariance matrix of $\theta_t(p)$ given $F^X_{t-1}$, and where recursive algorithms exist for the computation of these quantities (cf. Ledolter 1981 and Section 8.5.2).

The maximum likelihood estimate of $\sigma^2$ is given by

$$\hat{\sigma}^2 = \frac{1}{n}\sum_{t=1}^{n}(X_t - Y_{t-1}{}^T\tilde{\theta}_{t\,|\,t-1}(p))^2\,/f_t, \qquad (8.32)$$

and the concentrated log-likelihood function is

$$L_c(\Omega,C\,|\,X_1,\ldots,X_n) = -n\,\log\hat{\sigma} - 1/2\sum_{t=1}^{n}\log f_t. \qquad (8.33)$$

Estimates of $C$ and $\Omega$ (subject to the constraint that the symmetric matrix $\Omega$

be positive definite) are found by numerical maximization in (8.33), and these estimates are subsequently substituted in (8.32) to obtain an estimate of $\sigma^2$.

In the non-Gaussian case and for more general parameter processes an alternative to maximum likelihood estimates is obtained by minimization of the conditional sum of squares given by $\sum_t [X_t - E(X_t|F^X_{t-1})]^2$.

## 8.5 Some General Properties and Problems

We will look at three types of problems which are fundamental to the theory of time series and for which extensive results exist in the linear case. The main emphasis will be on problems of stationarity and invertibility/forecasting, with only a short discussion of estimation.

### 8.5.1 Stationarity

In general from a mathematical point of view we would like our processes to be both strictly and second-order stationary. Strict stationarity makes it easier to prove asymptotic results in estimation theory, and the additional requirement of existence of second moments makes it possible to use least squares as an optimality principle in forecasting. For the ARMA model (8.1) with a zero-mean finite variance residual process $\{e_t\}$ consisting of iid variables, the properties of strict and second-order stationarity coincide. If $\{X_t\}$ is required to be $F^e_t$-measurable, then a necessary and sufficient condition for both is that the polynomial $A(z) = z^p - \sum_{i=1}^{p} a_i z^{p-i}$ has its zeros inside the unit circle. This equivalence ceases to be true for nonlinear systems, where, in general, extra conditions have to be imposed to secure the existence of second moments of $\{X_t\}$.

The assumption of both strict and second-order stationarity may appear overly restrictive from a practical point of view, and in some cases it certainly is. However, it should be realized that a strictly stationary nonlinear model is capable of producing realizations with a distinctive nonstationary outlook. As an example consider the first order doubly stochastic process

$$X_t - \theta_t X_{t-1} = e_t \tag{8.34}$$

where $\{\theta_t\}$ is a strictly stationary Markov chain with a finite set of states $m_1,...,m_k$. Suppose that $E(e_t) = 0$ and $E(e_t^2) = \sigma^2 < \infty$, and that $\{e_t\}$ and $\{\theta_t\}$ are independent. Then there exists a solution to (8.34) which is both strictly and second-order stationary if $|m_i| < 1$ for $i = 1,2,...,k$. But a single realization of this process could, depending on the properties of the transition probability matrix of $\{\theta_t\}$, be difficult to distinguish from the realizations of a nonstationary AR(1) process with a deterministic time-varying coefficient.

The techniques used to approach the problem of stationarity depend on the particular nonlinear class considered. The processes considered in Section 8.4.1 are Markov processes (or possibly Markov vector processes) under the iid assumption on $\{e_t\}$. Since it is usual to consider a Markov process for $t \geq 0$, we will consider $\{X_t\}$ to be defined for $t \geq 0$. The process $\{X_t, \ t = 0,1,...\}$ is said to be strictly stationary if $\{X_{t_1},...,X_{t_n}\}$ and $\{X_{t_1+k},...,X_{t_n+k}\}$ have the same distribution for $n = 1,2,...$ and for all *non-negative* integers $k$ and $t_1,...,t_n$. One sided second-order stationarity is defined likewise. For a Markov process $\{X_t, \ t = 0,1,...\}$ with a time-invariant transitional probability function it is well known (cf. Stout 1974, p. 191) that $\{X_t\}$ is strictly stationary if and only if $X_0$ and $X_1$ have the same distribution; i.e., if there exists an invariant initial distribution.

A general sufficient condition for the existence of such distributions is the so-called Doeblin condition (Stout 1974, p.193), but this condition seems difficult to apply to our case. However, Tweedie (1975) gives some alternative conditions which are directly applicable to our situation. Tweedie gives sufficient conditions for ergodicity, which in his terminology includes the existence of a stationary initial distribution. For the process defined in (8.21) Tweedie's conditions imply strict stationarity if (these are not the weakest possible conditions) $e_t$ has a density with infinite support (e.g., Gaussian), the function $f$ is continuous and there exist constants $\alpha,\beta > 0$ such that

$$E(|f(x) + e_t| - |x|) \leq -\beta \qquad \text{for } |x| > \alpha. \tag{8.35}$$

As an example of the application of this result consider the exponential autoregressive process

$$X_t - [\phi + \pi \exp(-\gamma X_{t-1}^2)]X_{t-1} = e_t. \tag{8.36}$$

Here $f(x) = [\phi + \pi \exp(-\gamma x^2)]x$ and $f$ is continuous. Moreover,

$$E\{|[\phi + \pi \exp(-\gamma x^2)]x + e_t| - |x|\}$$

$$\leq (|\phi| + |\pi| - 1)|x| + E(|e_t|), \tag{8.37}$$

and if $|\phi| + |\pi| < 1$, the condition (8.35) is fulfilled by taking $\alpha = E(|e_t|)/(1 - |\phi| - |\pi|)$. This means that if $|\phi| + |\pi| < 1$, it is possible to find an initial distribution for $X_0$ such that $\{X_t, t \geq 0\}$ is strictly stationary and ergodic. As is easily checked, $|\phi| + |\pi| < 1$ implies the existence of second moments as well, so that the process is also second order stationary. The condition reduces to the familiar condition $|\phi| < 1$ in the ordinary AR(1) case. These results can easily be extended to higher-order processes. For some related results we refer to Jones (1978) and Aase (1983).

Some bilinear processes of type (8.26) can be transformed to a Markov process model and the approach above can be used (cf. Guegan 1983). However, in this case it is possible in general to express $\{X_t, t = 0,\pm 1,...\}$ explicitly in terms of a nonlinear moving average of past $e_t$'s.

As an example consider the bilinear process

$$X_t - \sum_{j=1}^{p} a_j X_{t-j} = e_t + \left(\sum_{j=1}^{p} b_j X_{t-j}\right) e_{t-1} \tag{8.38}$$

and let $Y_t = [X_t,...,X_{t-p+1}]^T$, $C = [1,0,...,0]^T$, $A_p = [a_1,...,a_p]$, and $B_p = [b_1,...,b_p]$. Moreover, let

$$A = \begin{bmatrix} A_{p-1} & a_p \\ I_{p-1} & 0 \end{bmatrix} \quad \text{and} \quad B = \begin{bmatrix} B_p \\ 0 \end{bmatrix} \tag{8.39}$$

where $I_{p-1}$ is the identity matrix of dimension $p-1$. Then (8.38) can be written

$$Y_t - AY_{t-1} = Ce_t + BY_{t-1}e_{t-1}, \tag{8.40}$$

and it is easily verified that if it exists,

$$Y_t = Ce_t + \sum_{i=1}^{\infty} \prod_{j=1}^{i} (A + Be_{t-j})Ce_{t-i} \tag{8.41}$$

represents a solution of (8.40). To show that the expression on the right-hand side of (8.41) defines a strictly stationary process, it is, due to the time invariance of the coefficients and the fact that the $e_t$'s are iid, enough to show that the infinite series in (8.41) converges in absolute mean (cf. Bhaskara Rao *et al.* 1983). It is not difficult to show that a sufficient condition for this is that $\rho(A \otimes A + \sigma^2 B \otimes B) < 1$, where $\otimes$ is used to denote tensor product, $\sigma^2 = E(e_t^2)$ and $\rho$ is the spectral radius of the resulting matrix. For $p = 1$ this reduces to $a_1^2 + b_1^2\sigma^2 < 1$ and to $|a_1| < 1$ in the ordinary AR(1) case with $b_1 = 0$. If we assume that $E(e_t^4) < \infty$, the same condition implies convergence in quadratic mean and $\{X_t\}$ is both strictly and second-order stationary. The approach outlined here has been extended to a larger class of bilinear models in Bhaskara Rao *et al.* (1983). The question of existence of strictly stationary solutions to bilinear equations has also been considered by other authors (Granger and Andersen 1978, Pham and Tran 1981, Quinn 1982a).

The problem seems more complicated in the doubly stochastic case. We will illustrate this for the AR(1) model

$$X_t - \theta_t X_{t-1} = e_t \tag{8.42}$$

where $\{\theta_t\}$ is assumed to be a strict-sense stationary process independent of $\{e_t\}$ which consists of iid random variables with $E(e_t^2) = \sigma^2 < \infty$. Using (8.42) recursively, we have

$$X_t = \sum_{j=0}^{r-1} \left(\prod_{i=0}^{j-1} \theta_{t-i}\right) e_{t-j} + \left(\prod_{i=0}^{r-1} \theta_{t-i}\right) X_{t_0} \tag{8.43}$$

where $r = t - t_0$, and where by convention $\prod_{i=0}^{j-1} \theta_{t-i} = 1$ for $j = 0$. Thus if the process is defined on $(-\infty, \infty)$, it is reasonable to consider

$$X_t = \sum_{j=0}^{\infty} \left(\prod_{i=0}^{j-1} \theta_{t-i}\right) e_{t-j} \tag{8.44}$$

as a candidate for a solution of (8.42), and formally it is not difficult to verify that $\{X_t\}$ defined by (8.44) satisfies (8.42). The problem is to find appropriate conditions for the convergence of the infinite sum on the right-hand side of (8.44). The problem is similar to the corresponding problem for the bilinear model; but in that case it simplifies since it essentially reduces to a problem where we get a sum of products of independent random variables. For the same reason the RCA case, where $\{\theta_t\}$ is iid, is comparatively easy to treat, and conditions have been stated for these processes in a general multivariate setting (Nicholls and Quinn 1982, Chap. 2).

For a dependent sequence $\{\theta_t\}$, to our knowledge very few results exist. This case was treated in Tjøstheim (1983). Sufficient conditions for strict-sense stationarity [almost sure convergence in (8.44)] seems easier to obtain than for second-order stationarity. The reason for this is that when considering almost sure convergence, we can take the logarithm of the product term $\prod_{i=0}^{j-1} \theta_{t-i}$ and consider a sum of dependent variables instead. This technique was used by Quinn (1982b), although not explicitly for the doubly stochastic case, and it can be shown that $E(\log|\theta_t|) < 0$ will imply that $\{X_t\}$ is well defined as a strictly stationary process.

As for the bilinear model (8.38), quadratic mean convergence in (8.44), under the stated conditions on $\{\theta_t\}$ and $\{e_t\}$, implies both second-order and strict stationarity (cf. Nicholls and Quinn 1982, p. 37, for the analogous RCA case). To prove quadratic mean convergence two techniques were used in Tjøstheim (1983). One technique was based on recursions on the characteristic function of $(\theta_t, \theta_{t-1}, \ldots, \theta_{t-j+1})$, which in turn is used to obtain recursions for moments of type $E(\theta_t^2 \theta_{t-1}^2 \cdots \theta_{t-j+1}^2)$. Another method was to try to use conditioning in evaluating these moments.

In the special case of a zero-mean MA(1) process for $\{\theta_t\}$ the first technique was used to show that a necessary and sufficient condition for strict and second order stationarity of $\{X_t\}$ is

$$\text{var}(\theta_t) + 2[\text{cov}(\theta_t, \theta_{t-1})]^2 < 1. \qquad (8.45)$$

The second method was used for the case where $\{\theta_t\}$ is a stationary Markov chain with two states $m_1$ and $m_2$ such that $P(\theta_{t+1} = m_j | \theta_t = m_j) = 1 - q$ and $P(\theta_t = m_j) = 1/2$ for $j = 1,2$. A sufficient condition for strict-sense stationarity is $|m_1 m_2| < 1$, whereas a sufficient condition for strict and second-order stationarity is that $m_1^2 + m_2^2 < (q + |1 - 2q|)^{-1}$. This inequality gives sharpest bounds for $q < 1/2$. Then $m_1^2 + m_2^2 < (1 - q)^{-1}$. In this range of $q$-values, as $q$ decreases, then the range of $m_1$ and $m_2$ specified by the inequality decreases. This is intuitively reasonable, since decreasing $q$ means that the $\{\theta_t\}$ process has a tendency to spend rather long visits at each of its two levels and this destabilizes the $\{X_t\}$ process if one of the levels is significantly larger than unity [cf. explosive processes in the ordinary AR(1) case].

A third technique for evaluating $E(\prod_{i=1}^{j-1} \theta_{t-i}^2)$ is given by Pourahmadi (1984) who treats the equivalent expression $E[\exp(\sum_{i=1}^{j-1} \log \theta_{t-i}^2)]$ and finds conditions for stationarity by studying the distribution of partial sums of the process $\{Y_t\}$ defined by $Y_t = \log \theta_t^2$.

### 8.5.2 Invertibility, Innovations Process, and Forecasting

The process $\{X_t\}$ is invertible if for each $e_t$ of its generating process, $e_t$ is $F^X{}_t$-measurable. If $\{X_t\}$ is invertible, we may use $\{e_t\}$ in forecasting formulas and subsequently replace each $e_t$ by an expression in terms of $\{X_s, s \le t\}$ to express the forecasts solely in terms of past observations. An especially important case arises when $e_t = X_t - E(X_t | F^X{}_{t-1})$, i.e., when $\{e_t\}$ can be identified with the innovations process and when in addition $F^X{}_t = F^e{}_t$.

For the nonlinear models of Markov type in Section 8.4.1 we have trivially that $\{e_t\}$ can be identified with the innovations process. The optimal least-squares one-step forecast for the model (8.21) is simply given by $\tilde{X}_{t|t-1} = E(X_t | F^X{}_{t-1}) = f(X_{t-1})$, while, for example, for the AR($p$)

threshold process defined by (8.23),

$$\tilde{X}_{t|t-1} = \sum_{i=1}^{p} \sum_{j=1}^{m} a_i^j I(Y_{t-1} \in F_j) X_{t-i} \qquad (8.46)$$

where $I$ is the indicator function, and where as before $Y_t = [X_t, X_{t-1}, \ldots, X_{t-p+1}]^T$.

For the bilinear model (8.26), if $\{X_t\}$ is invertible, we have that $e_{t-i}$ is $F^X_{t-1}$-measurable for $i \geq 1$, and thus $\{e_t\}$ can in this case be identified with the innovations process. The optimal least-squares forecast is then given by

$$\tilde{X}_{t|t-1} = a_0 + \sum_{j=1}^{p} a_j X_{t-j} + \sum_{j=1}^{q} c_j e_{t-j} + \sum_{i=1}^{m} \sum_{j=1}^{k} b_{ij} X_{t-i} e_{t-j} \qquad (8.47)$$

where the invertibility means that each $e_{t-j}$ can be expressed in terms of $\{X_s, s \leq t-j\}$. In practice this must be done recursively using (8.26), but invertibility is necessary to guarantee convergence of this procedure.

Unfortunately very little is known about conditions for invertibility for bilinear models. Some preliminary results are given in Quinn (1982b) (strict sense) and Granger and Andersen (1978, Chap. 8) and Subba Rao (1981), who require existence of second moments in addition. The problem is more difficult, at least when quadratic mean convergent expressions are required, than the corresponding stationarity problem treated in the preceding subsection, since $e_t$ has to be expressed in terms of $\{X_s, s \leq t\}$, which are *dependent* stochastic variables.

For doubly stochastic processes the invertibility problem is not immediately meaningful since an additional process $\{\theta_t\}$ is involved. Moreover, in general it is not possible to identify $\{e_t\}$ with the innovations process, not even in the RCA case. Nevertheless, doubly stochastic processes seem promising from a forecasting point of view, since explicit recursive algorithms can be constructed for important subclasses. This is due to the similarity in the definition of these processes to ordinary Kalman filtering models. An especially important subclass is the class of conditionally Gaussian processes treated in Tjøstheim (1983). Such processes were originally introduced in a nonlinear filtering context in Liptser and Shiryayev (1978, Chap. 13). To define them we go back to the expression (8.17) for the general doubly stochastic process. It is convenient to rewrite this slightly. Let $\psi_{ti} = \text{vec}(\theta_{ti})$, where $\text{vec}(\theta_{ti})$ is the $d^2$-dimensional column vector obtained by stacking the columns of $\theta_{ti}$ one on top of the other from left to right, and let $\psi_t^T = [\psi_{t1}^T,\ldots, \psi_{tp}^T]$. For any three matrices $a$, $b$ and $c$ for which the product $abc$ is well defined it is well known that $\text{vec}(abc) = (c^T \otimes a)\text{vec}(b)$. Using this when vectorizing (8.17), we obtain

$$X_t - A_0(t-1,X) - F(t-1,X)\psi_t = B(t-1,X)e_t \qquad (8.48)$$

where $F(t-1,X)$ is the $d \times pd^2$ matrix function given by

$$F(t-1,X) = [X_{t-1}^T \otimes A_1(t-1,X)\cdots X_{t-p}^T \otimes A_p(t-1,X)] \qquad (8.49)$$

We now introduce the conditionally Gaussian process by assuming that the parameter process $\{\psi_t\}$ is described by an ordinary multivariate AR(1) model

$$\psi_t - C_0 - C\psi_{t-1} = D\varepsilon_t \qquad (8.50)$$

where $\{e_t\}$ and $\{\varepsilon_t\}$ are independent processes each consisting of iid Gaussian vector variables with zero mean and identity covariance matrix. Moreover, we assume that $A_i(t-1,X)$, $i = 0,1,\ldots,p$, and $B(t-1,X)$ are uniformly bounded with probability 1, and that the process is started in $t_0$ in such a way that second moments of initial conditions exist, and the conditional distribution of $\psi_{t_0}$ given $X_s$ for $t_0-p+1 \leq s \leq t_0$ is Gaussian. In general these assumptions imply that $\{X_t\}$ is nonstationary.

The optimal one-step forecast is given by

$$\tilde{X}_{t|t-1} = A_0(t-1,X) + F(t-1,X)C_0 + F(t-1,X)CE(\psi_{t-1}|F^X_{t-1}) \qquad (8.51)$$

and the problem (nonlinear filtering) is to find $E(\psi_t|F^X_t)$. Using the theory of Liptser and Shiryayev (1978, Ch. 13) it was shown in Tjøstheim (1983) that we get a closed recursive algorithm for $m_t = E(\psi_t|F^X_t)$ and $\gamma_t = E[(\psi_t - m_t)(\psi_t - m_t)^T|F^X_t]$, namely

$$m_t = C_0 + Cm_{t-1} + K_1(t-1,X)K_2^{-1}(t-1,X)$$

$$[X_t - A_0(t-1,X) - F(t-1,X)C_0 - F(t-1,X)Cm_{t-1}] \qquad (8.52)$$

and

$$\gamma_t = C\gamma_{t-1}C^T + DD^T - K_1(t-1,X)K_2^{-1}(t-1,X)K_1^T(t-1,X) \qquad (8.53)$$

where

$$K_1(t-1,X) = DD^TF^T(t-1,X) + C\gamma_t - 1C^TF^T(t-1,X) \qquad (8.54)$$

and

$$K_2(t-1,X) = B(t-1,X)B^T(t-1,X) + F(t-1,X)DD^TF^T(t-1,X)$$
$$+ F(t-1,X)C\gamma_{t-1}C^TF^T(t-1,X). \qquad (8.55)$$

Here $A^{-1}$ denotes the pseudoinverse (Liptser and Shiryayev 1978, p. 51) of the matrix $A$.

It should be noted that in a time-series model context, even in the simple case where $A_i(t-1,X)$, $i = 0, 1,\ldots, p$, and $B(t-1,X)$ of (8.17) are replaced by constants, the recursive equation (8.53) for the conditional covariance matrix is conceptually different from that of the standard Kalman filtering situation. In the ordinary Kalman model, $\gamma_t$ is deterministic and (8.53) is replaced by a deterministic Ricatti-type equation, so that $\gamma_t$ can be precomputed from a knowledge of the parameters of the system prior to any observation being made. In the present case, however, $\gamma_t$ is genuinely stochastic and its value at time $t$ cannot be computed until the values of $F(t-1,X)$ and $B(t-1,X)$ are available, i.e., until we have observed $X_{t-1}$. It should be noted that in the conditional Gaussian case it is also possible to introduce an innovations process $\bar{e}_t$ so that $F^X_t = F^{(X_0,\bar{e})}_t$ under some mild conditions. We refer to Liptser and Shiryayev (1978, Th. 13.5).

For a more general parameter process $\{\psi_t\}$ the predictor equation (8.46) is still valid, but it is not in general possible to find a closed system of equations involving finite-order conditional moments of $\psi_t$. However, Bayesian arguments can be used to obtain algorithms for the conditional probability distribution of $\psi_t$ given $\{X_s, s \le t\}$, from which $E(\psi_t|F^X_t)$ can be found from a finite-dimensional algorithm in case $\psi_t$ has a finite range; e.g., $\psi_t$ is a finite state-space Markov chain. We refer to Tjøstheim (1983) for details.

### 8.5.3 Estimation and Identification

To be able to use nonlinear time-series models in practice, one must be able to fit the models to data. We have outlined computational procedures for determining parameters for various model classes in Section 8.4, and we have indicated how AIC-type criteria can be used to identify the orders once a model class has been selected. However, very little is known about the theoretical properties of these procedures. An exception is the class of RCA processes for which a fairly extensive theory of estimation (but not identification) exists (Nicholls and Quinn 1982). Sometimes properties like consistency and asymptotic normality appear to be taken for granted also for other model classes, but some of the simulation results performed indicate that there are reasons for being cautious.

Klimko and Nelson (1978) have given results on consistency and asymptotic normality of conditional least-squares estimation in a general discrete-time stochastic process context. Much of the theory is based on martingale results and can be used for both stationary and nonstationary processes under appropriate conditions. It has been shown in Tjøstheim (1984) that it is possible, at least partly, to base estimation theory of nonlinear time-series models on such results. For example, it is possible to generalize Nicholl's and Quinn's results for RCA processes, but it is also possible to obtain conditions for consistency and asymptotic normality for other classes of models such as exponential autoregressive processes.

The theory in Tjøstheim (1984) has been developed under fairly restrictive growth conditions on the moments of $\{X_t\}$. It would be an interesting task to try to extend the very recent results of Lai and Wei (1982, 1983) on linear nonstationary AR models to nonlinear classes of models. In their papers they remove the stationarity condition of the classical Mann-Wald (1943a,b) papers, and they obtain consistency of least-squares estimates of the AR coefficients $(a_1,...,a_p)$ without any stability conditions on the characteristic polynomial $A(z) = z^p - \sum_{i=1}^{p} a_i z^{p-i}$ and with a very general nonstationary residual process $\{e_t\}$, whereas much more restrictive conditions have to be imposed to obtain asymptotic normality.

# References

[1]   K.K. Aase, Recursive estimation in non-linear time series models of autoregressive type, *J. Roy. Stat. Soc. Ser. B,* Vol. 45, pp. 228-237, 1983.

[2]   H. Akaike, Information theory and an extension of the maximum likelihood principle, in *2nd International Symposium on Information Theory,* B.N. Petrov and F. Czaki, Eds., Akademiai Kiado, Budapest, pp. 276-281, 1973.

[3]   T.W. Anderson, *Statistical Analysis of Time Series,* New York, NY: Wiley, 1971

[4]   V.E. Benes, Exact finite dimensional filters for certain diffusions with nonlinear drift, *Stochastics,* Vol. 5, pp. 65-92, 1981.

[5]   M. Bhaskara Rao, T. Subba Rao and A.M. Walker, On the existence of strictly stationary solutions to bilinear equations, *J. Time Series Anal.,* Vol. 4, pp. 95-110, 1983.

[6]   D.R. Brillinger, An introduction to polyspectra, *Ann. Math. Statist.,* Vol. 36, pp. 1351-1374, 1965.

[7]   D.R. Brillinger and M. Rosenblatt, Asymptotic theory of $k$-th order spectra, in *Spectral Analysis of Time Series,* B. Harris, Ed., New York, NY: Wiley, pp. 153-188, 1967.

[8]   R.W. Brockett, Volterra series and geometric control theory, *Automatica,* Vol. 12, pp. 167-172, 1976.

[9]   D.R. Cox, Statistical analysis of time series: Some recent developments. *Scand. J. Statist.,* Vol. 8, pp. 93-115, 1981.

[10]  M.H.A. Davis and S.I. Marcus, An introduction to nonlinear filtering, in *Stochastic Systems: The Mathematics of Filtering and Identification and Applications,* M. Hazewinkel and J.C. Willems, Eds., Doordrecht, Holland: D. Reidel, pp. 53-76, 1981.

[11]  M. Fujisaki, G. Kallianpur and H. Kunita, Stochastic differential equations for the nonlinear filtering problem, *Osaka J. Math.* Vol. 1, pp. 19-40, 1972.

[12] C.W.J. Granger and A.P. Andersen, *An Introduction to Bilinear Time Series Models,* Göttingen, Germany: Vanderhoeck and Ruprecht, 1978.

[13] D. Guegan, Une condition d'ergodicité pour des modèles bilinéaires à temps discret, *C. R. Acad. Sci. Paris,* Vol.297, pp. 537-540, 1983.

[14] V. Haggan and T. Ozaki, Modelling nonlinear random vibrations using an amplitude dependent autoregressive time series model, *Biometrika,* Vol. 68, pp. 189-196, 1981.

[15] M.G. Hall, A.V. Oppenheim and A.S. Willsky, Time-varying parameter modelling of speech, *Signal Processing,* Vol. 5, pp. 267-285, 1983.

[16] M. Hallin, Spectral factorization of nonstationary moving average processes, *Ann. Statist.,* Vol. 12, pp. 172-192, 1984.

[17] M. Hallin and J. Fr. Ingenbleek, Nonstationary Yule-Walker equations, *Statist. and Probab. Letters,* Vol. 1, pp. 189-195, 1983.

[18] E.J. Hannan and B.G. Quinn, The determination of the order of an autoregression, *J. Roy. Stat. Soc. Ser. B,* Vol. 41, pp. 190-195, 1979.

[19] D.L. Hanson, A representation theorem for stationary Markov chains, *J. Math. Mech,,* Vol. 12, pp. 731-736, 1963.

[20] P.J. Harrison and C.F. Stevens, Bayesian forecasting (with discussion), *J. Roy. Stat. Soc. Ser. B,* Vol. 38, pp. 205-248, 1976.

[21] Y.C. Ho and R.C.K. Lee, A Bayesian approach to problems in stochastic estimation and control, *IEEE Trans. Auto. Contr.,* Vol. AC-9, pp. 333-339, 1964.

[22] D.A. Jones, Non-linear autoregressive processes, *Proc. Roy. Soc. London, A,* Vol. 360, pp. 71-95, 1978.

[23] G. Kallianpur, Some ramifications of Wiener's ideas on nonlinear prediction, in *Norbert Wiener Collected Works Volume III,* P. Masani, Ed., Cambridge, MA: MIT Press, pp. 402-424, 1981.

[24] R.E. Kalman, A new approach to linear filtering and prediction problems, *Trans. ASME J. Basic Eng.,* Vol. 82, pp. 35-45, 1960.

- 227 -

[25]    R.E. Kalman and R.S. Bucy, New results in linear filtering and prediction theory, *Trans. ASME J. Basic Eng.,* Vol. 83, pp. 95-108, 1961.

[26]    L.A. Klimko and P.I. Nelson, On conditional least squares estimation for stochastic processes, *Ann. Statist.,* Vol. 6, pp. 629-642, 1978.

[27]    T.L. Lai and C.Z. Wei, Least squares estimates in stochastic regression models with applications to identification and control of dynamic systems, *Ann. Statist.,* Vol. 10, pp. 154-166, 1982.

[28]    T.L. Lai and C.Z. Wei, Asymptotic properties of general autoregressive models and strong consistency of least squares estimates of their parameters, *J. Multivariate Anal.,* Vol. 13, pp. 1-23, 1983.

[29]    J. Ledolter, A recursive approach to parameter estimation in regression and time series models, *Comm. Stat.,* Vol. A8, pp. 1227-1245, 1979.

[30]    J. Ledolter, Recursive estimation and adaptive forecasting in ARIMA models with time varying coefficients, in *Adaptive Time Series Analysis II,* D.F. Findlay, Ed., New York, NY: Academic Press, pp. 449-471, 1981.

[31]    K.S. Lim and H. Tong, A statistical approach to difference-delay equation modelling in ecology - two case studies, *J. Time Series Anal.,* Vol. 4, pp. 239-268, 1983.

[32]    R.S. Liptser and A.N. Shiryayev, *Statistics of Random Processes, Vol. 2, Applications,* New York: Springer-Verlag, 1978.

[33]    J.I. Makhoul, Linear prediction: A tutorial review, *Proc. IEEE,* Vol. 32, pp. 561-581, 1975.

[34]    S. Makridakis and S.C. Wheelwright, Adaptive filtering: An integrated autoregressive/moving average filter for time series forecasting, *Op. Res.,* Vol. 28, pp. 425-437, 1977.

[35]    H.B. Mann and A. Wald, On the statistical treatment of linear stochastic difference equations, *Econometrica,* Vol. 11, pp.173-220, 1943a.

[36]    H.B. Mann and A. Wald, On stochastic limit and order relationships,

*Ann. Math. Statist.,* Vol. 14, pp. 217-226, 1943b.

[37]   J.D. Markel and A.H. Gray, Jr., *Linear Prediction of Speech,* New York, NY: Springer-Verlag, 1977.

[38]   R.R. Mohler, *Bilinear Control Processes,* New York, NY: Academic Press, 1973.

[39]   P. Newbold, Some recent developments in time series analysis, *International Statistical Review,* Vol. 49, pp. 53-66, 1981.

[40]   D.F. Nicholls and B.G. Quinn, *Random Coefficient Autoregressive Models. An Introduction,* Lecture Notes in Statistics Vol. 11, New York, NY: Springer-Verlag, 1982.

[41]   T.Ozaki, Non-linear time series models for non-linear random vibrations, *J. Appl. Prob.,* Vol. 17, pp. 84-93, 1980.

[42]   T. Ozaki, Non-linear threshold autoregressive models for non-linear vibrations, *J. Appl. Prob.,* Vol. 18, pp. 443-451, 1981.

[43]   D.P. Pham and L.T. Tran, On the first order bilinear time series model, *J. Appl. Prob.,* Vol. 18, pp. 617-627, 1981.

[44]   M. Pourahmadi, On the solution of a doubly stochastic model, Technical Report, Center for Stochastic Processes, Department of Statistics, University of North Carolina, Chapel Hill, N.C., 1984.

[45]   M.B. Priestley, State dependent models: A general approach to time series analysis, *J. Time Series Anal.,* Vol. 1, pp. 47-71, 1980.

[46]   M.B. Priestley, *Spectral Analysis and Time Series,* New York, NY: Academic Press, 1981.

[47]   B.G. Quinn, A note on the existence of strictly stationary solutions to bilinear equations, *J. Time Series Anal.,* Vol. 3, pp. 249-252, 1982a.

[48]   B.G. Quinn, Stationarity and invertibility of simple bilinear models, *Stoch. Proc. Appl.,* Vol. 12, pp. 225-230, 1982b.

[49]   M. Rosenblatt, Stationary processes as shifts of independent random variables, *J. Math. Mech.,* Vol. 8, pp. 665-681, 1959.

[50]   G. Schwarz, Estimating the dimension of a model, *Ann. Statist.,* Vol.

6, 1978.

[51] W. Shou-Ren, A. Hong-Zhi and H. Tong, On the distribution of a simple stationary bilinear process, *J. Time Series Anal.*, Vol. 4, pp. 209-216, 1983.

[52] W. Stout, *Almost Sure Convergence*, New York, NY: Academic Press, 1974.

[53] R.A. Struble, *Nonlinear Differential Equations*, New York, NY: McGraw-Hill, 1962.

[54] T. Subba Rao, On the theory of bilinear models, *J. Roy. Stat. Soc. Ser. B*, Vol. 43, pp. 244-255, 1981.

[55] T. Subba Rao and M.M. Gabr, A test for the linearity of stationary time series, *J. Time Series Anal.*, Vol. 1, pp. 145-158, 1980.

[56] D. Tjøstheim, Some doubly stochastic time series models, Technical Report, Center for Stochastic Processes, Department of Statistics, University of North Carolina, Chapel Hill, NC, 1983.

[57] D. Tjøstheim, Estimation in nonlinear time series models, Technical Report, Center for Stochastic Processes, Department of Statistics, University of North Carolina, Chapel Hill, NC, 1984.

[58] H. Tong, Discussion of a paper by A.J. Lawrance and T. Kottegoda, *J. Roy. Stat. Soc. Ser. A*, Vol. 140, pp. 34-35, 1977.

[59] H. Tong and K.S. Lim, Threshold autoregression, limit cycles and cyclical data (with discussion), *J. Roy. Stat. Soc. Ser. B*, Vol. 42, pp. 245-292, 1980.

[60] D.W. Trigg and A.G. Leach, Exponential smoothing with an adaptive response rate, *Op. Res. Q.*, Vol. 18, pp. 53-59, 1967.

[61] R.L. Tweedie, Sufficient conditions for ergodicity and recurrence of Markov chains on a general state space, *Stoch. Proc. Appl.*, Vol 3, pp. 385-403, 1975.

[62] N. Wiener, *Non-linear Problems in Random Theory*, Cambridge, MA: MIT Press, 1958.

# 9

# In Search of Multiparameter Markov Processes

Eugene Wong

*Department of Electrical Engineering
and Computer Science
University of California, Berkeley, California*

## 9.1 Introduction

One of the problems that John Thomas and I first tackled concerned the transition density of Markov processes. Through the Fokker-Planck equation we were able to show that the polynomial expansions first noted by Barrett and Lampard [1] could be interpreted in terms of the Sturm-Liouville problem to which the Fokker-Planck equation gives rise. My interest in Markov processess, kindled then, has never waned.

Over the years I have worked on a number of aspects of Markov processes, but one topic, above all, has continued to both challenge and frustrate me. This is the topic of multiparameter Markov processess, or Markovian random fields. Once again, I have returned to the topic, and thanks to an appointment as Miller Professor I am able to work on it full time this year. Though perhaps somewhat premature, I would like to pose the questions that have continually challenged me, my outline and approach, and present a few preliminary results. In the process it may also be interesting to briefly review the history of this topic.

## 9.2 Markovian Random Fields.

Let $\{X_t, \ t \in T\}$ be a family of random variables defined on a fixed probability space $(\Omega, \ F, \ P)$ and parameterized by elements of a set $T$. When $T$ is an interval of the real line, $\{X_t, \ t \in T\}$ is simply an ordinary process. When $T$ is a subset of a multidimensional space (say $\mathbb{R}^n$), then $\{X_t, \ t \in T\}$ is called a random field or multiparameter process, or a process with multidimensional time.

The way to extend the definition of "Markov process" was first suggested by Lévy [2]. A random field $\{X_t, \ t \in T\}$ is said to be Markovian if whenever $\partial D$ is a smooth surface separating $T$ into a bounded part $D^-$ and a possibly unbounded part $D^+$, then $t \in D^+$ and $t' \in D^-$ imply that $X_t$ and $X_{t'}$ are conditionally independent given the boundary data $\{X_s, \ s \in \partial D\}$. If we identify $D^-$ as the "past", $D^+$ as the "future", and $\partial D$ as the "present", then being Markovian means the conditional independence of "past" and "future" given the "present". This interpretation makes the Lévy definition consistent with the definition in the one-dimensional case.

My original interest in random fields was to find good models for images. From that point of view, Lévy's definition is attractive. It promises to delineate a class of processes that would represent both tractable and realistic models. Markovian independence gives one enough independence for computation to be possible, but not so much as to render the sample functions too ill behaved to be realistic.

## 9.3 Brownian Motion

For the one-parameter case, a Brownian motion can be defined as a Gaussian process $\{B_t, \ 0 \leq t < \infty\}$ with zero mean and a covariance function

$$EB_t B_s = \min(t,s). \tag{9.1}$$

The parameter space can be extended to the entire real line by modifying the covariance function to read

$$R(t,s) = EB_t B_s = (|t| + |s| - |t-s|)/2. \tag{9.2}$$

Lévy [2] defined a Brownian motion with $T = \mathbb{R}^n$ as a random field $\{B_t, \ t \in \mathbb{R}^n\}$ with zero mean and covariance function

$$R(t,s) = (|t| + |s| - |t-s|)/2 \tag{9.3}$$

where $|t|$ now denotes not the absolute value but the Euclidean norm

$$|t| = \left( \sum_i t_i^2 \right)^{1/2}.$$

Lévy conjectured that so defined, the Brownian motion had some kind of Markovian property if the dimension of $t$ was odd, but none if the dimension was even.

Lévy's conjecture was made precise and verified by McKean [3], who showed that for $n = 2k + 1$, $B_t$ has the following Markovian property: Given the value of $B_t$ and its $k+1$ "normal derivatives" on the boundary, $\partial D$, its "past" and "future" are indeed conditionally independent. Two points in McKean's proof are particularly important. First, the highest-order "normal derivative" needed on the boundary is always a generalized process so that the boundary data need to be defined with some care. Second, the source of the Markovian property for the Brownian motion with an odd-dimensional parameter appears to lie in the fact that for $n = 2k + 1$ the covariance function as given by (9.3) satisfies the equation

$$\triangle^k R(t,s) = A_k \delta(t-s) \tag{9.4}$$

where $\triangle$ is the Laplacian operator. Both the need to deal with generalized processes and the connection with the Laplacian operator are recurrent themes in Markovian random fields.

Gangoli [4] has considered generalizations of the Brownian motion for the cases where $T$ is a Riemannian manifold and the covariance function is defined by a modified version of (9.3) where $|t-s|$ is replaced by the Riemannian distance $d(t,s)$. A natural question is: Does the resulting Brownian motion have any Markovian property? The answer is almost certainly yes if the parameter space has a Laplace-Beltrami operator, as for example in the case of spaces with constant curvature [5].

### 9.4 Ornstein-Uhlenbeck Processes

A one-parameter Ornstein-Uhlenbeck process (suitably normalized) can be defined as a Gaussian process with zero mean and a covariance function

$$R(t,s) = e^{-|t-s|}, \quad -\infty < t,s < \infty. \tag{9.5}$$

What would be a natural generalization for $T = \mathbb{R}^n$? The answer is provided as a part of the answer to a little different question.

Consider a zero-mean random field $\{X_t,\ t \in \mathbb{R}^n\}$ such that

$$R(t,s) = EX_tX_s = EX_{\tau \cdot t}X_{\tau \cdot s} \tag{9.6}$$

for all Euclidean motions $\tau$ (rotations and translations). It is easy to show that in this case $R(t,s)$ must be a function of just $|t-s|$. Furthermore, if $X_t$ is quadratic mean continuous then $R(t,s)$ must have the form

$$R(t,s) = \int_0^\infty \frac{J_{(n-2)/2}(\lambda|t-s|)}{(\lambda|t-s|)^{(n-2)/2}} F(d\lambda) \tag{9.7}$$

where $F$ is a finite Borel measure known as the spectral distribution of the process. In the late 1960s I posed the question: What must $F(\cdot)$ be in order that the process $X_t$ be Markovian? It turned out that with a strict interpretation the question was not an interesting one. For $n \geq 2$ there is no finite, measure $F$ for which the corresponding process is Markovian. However, if we relax the condition that $F$ be finite then

$$F(d\lambda) = \frac{\lambda^{n-1} \, d\lambda}{\beta^2 + \lambda^2} \tag{9.8}$$

indeed yields a Markov process. However, (9.8) implies that

$$R(t,s) = A_n \frac{K_{(n-2)/2}(\beta \,|\, t - s \,|)}{(\beta \,|\, t - s \,|)^{(n-2)/2}} \tag{9.9}$$

and $X_t$ must be considered a generalized process for $n \geq 2$. What does it mean then to say that $X_t$ is Markovian? The answer is roughly as follows: Let $D$ be a smooth $(n-1)$ surface. Although $X_t$ is not well defined as a random variable at each point $t \in \partial D$, the surface integral of $X_t$ on any subset $A$ of $\partial D$ is well defined as a second-order random variable $X(A)$. $\{X(A), A \in \partial D\}$ then represents the boundary data. To make this argument precise, we need to define $X_t$ as a generalized process and define $X(A)$ by using an approximating sequence of testing functions [5].

In 1973, Nelson [6] independently proposed the Gaussian random field defined by (9.8) in the context of constructive quantum field theory, and called it the "Euclidean free field". One of the outstanding problems in a constructive quantum field theory is to construct non-Gaussian random fields that are isotropic and homogeneous (i.e., distributions are invariant under rotations and translations) and Markovian. To date, the success is limited.

## 9.5 Wiener Processes

In one dimension a Brownian motion or a Wiener process can be viewed as a zero-mean Gaussian process with a covariance function $\min(t,s)$ or as the indefinite integral of a Gaussian white noise. It is easy to define a Gaussian white noise $\eta_t$ for $t \in \mathbb{R}^n$, and using it, we can define a Wiener process $W$ by the integral

$$W_t = \int_{A_t} \eta_s \, ds \tag{9.10}$$

where $A_t$ is the $n$-dimensional rectangle with the origin and $t$ as two of its corners.

Of course, (9.10) is not properly an integral but merely a symbolic expression of the fact that $W$ is more appropriately defined as a set-parametered process $W(A)$ which is independent on disjoint sets. To be specific let $W(A)$ be a Gaussian process parameterized by Borel sets $A$ with $EW(A) = 0$ and $EW(A)W(B) = $ volume $(A \cap B)$. Now a Wiener process can be defined as $W(A_t)$.

For $t, s \in \mathbb{R}^n$ define the partial ordering $t > s$ by

$$t > s \quad \bullet \quad t_i \geq s_i \text{ for all } i.$$

Then $W_t$ is a martingale with respect to this partial ordering, and as such is the basis for a theory of stochastic integration that has been developed since 1974 [7,8]. Here we are less interested in the martingale property of $W$ than in any Markovian property it may possess. Thus we would be interested in stochastic integration only if it has something to do with Markovian random fields. As we shall see later, such a connection indeed exists.

Meanwhile, a natural question is: Is $W_t$ a Markov process? Surprisingly, the answer is "no". To see this, consider $\mathbb{R}^2$ and a triangular domain $D^-$ bounded by the 45-degree line $\partial D = \{(\alpha, 1-\alpha), 0 \leq \alpha \leq 1\}$ as shown in Figure 9.1.

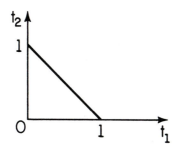

*Figure 9.1*

Now $W(1,1) = W(D^-) + W(A_{(1,1)} \cap D^+)$ and the second term is independent of $\{W_t, t \in D^-\}$. For $W$ to be Markovian (in the Lévy sense) we need

$$E[W(D^-) \mid W_t, \; t \in \partial D] = W(D^-).$$

By a simple projection computation, we can show that

$$E[W(D^-) \mid W_t, \; t \in \partial D] = 2 \int_0^1 W_{u,u-1} \, du$$

which is definitely not equal to $W(D^-)$ [9].

It is indeed surprising that the Wiener process $W_t$, as the indefinite integral of white noise, is not Markovian. However, once we have discovered that it is not, it is not too difficult to conjecture as to the reason. Intuitively, "Markov" should be one derivative away from "white." In $\mathbb{R}^n$, an integral of white noise is $n$ derivatives, not one, from it. Of course, this very vague intuitive notion needs clarification, but to do so needs mathematical machinery. To deal with differentiation in $\mathbb{R}^n$ requires a theory of differential forms, and in our case, stochastic differential forms. Put in another way: We need to be able to integrate on $r$-dimensional sets in $\mathbb{R}^n$ ($r \leq n$) and not merely on $n$-dimensional sets. Thus the theory of stochastic integration associated with martingales that has been developed in recent years is not irrelevant, but inadequate.

### 9.6 In Search of a White Noise Connection

Consider an Ornstein-Uhlenbeck process on $\mathbb{R}^3$ with a covariance function given by (9.9). The case of $\beta = 0$ is an acceptable case, and it gives

$$R(t,s) = A \frac{1}{|t-s|}. \tag{9.11}$$

Now consider a vector $Z_t = (Z_t{}^1, Z_t{}^2, Z_t{}^3)$ of independent and identically distributed Ornstein-Uhlenbeck processes each with a covariance function

$$R(t,s) = \frac{1}{|t-s|}. \tag{9.12}$$

Let $\eta_t = \nabla Z_t$ be the divergence of $Z_t$ (considered as a generalized process).

Then $\eta_t$ is a Gaussian white noise. This provides a way of whitening an Ornstein-Uhlenbeck process that is not available without embedding it in a vector of independent processes [10]. We shall reexpress this relationship in terms of differential forms later, and use it to demonstrate explicitly the Markovian nature of an Ornstein-Uhlenbeck process.

The vector process $Z_t$ is also related to Lévy's Brownian motion in a simple and geometrically suggestive way. Itô [11] has shown that a generalized random vector field such as $Z_t$ can be uniquely decomposed into irrotational (curl = 0) and solenoidal (gradient = 0) components. Denote the irrotational component of $Z_t$ by $Z_{it}$. Then

$$Z_{it} = \nabla B_t \qquad (9.13)$$

where $B_t$ is a Lévy's Brownian motion. Since the divergence of the solenoidal component is zero, we also have

$$\nabla \cdot \nabla B_t = \triangle B_t = \eta_t. \qquad (9.14)$$

That is, the Laplacian of $B_t$ is a white noise.

The connection among Gaussian white noise, the O-U process and Lévy's Brownian motion affirms our belief that Markovian random fields "come from" white noise fields and the connection is through geometric differentiation operations. It also points a possible way to the construction of non-Gaussian Markovian fields such as these needed in quantum field theory. But before such construction can be developed, we need a calculus of stochastic differential forms.

### 9.7 In Search of a Stochastic Calculus.

Let $W_t$ be a one-parameter Wiener process, and consider a stochastic differential equation of the Itô type

$$dX_t = m(X_t, t) \, dt + \sigma(X_t, t) \, dW_t. \qquad (9.15)$$

Under quite general conditions the solution $X_t$ is a sample continuous Markov process, and this provides a way of constructing a large class of Markov processes in the one-dimensional case. To generalize the technique requires several things. First of all, it is not clear which process should play the role of $W_t$. There are at least three candidates: Lévy's Brownian motion $B_t$ defined in Section 9.3, the Wiener process $W_t$ defined in Section 9.5, and the Ornstein-Uhlenbeck process defined in Section 9.4 or possibly the vector version defined in Section 9.6. Second, it is not clear how the differential operator $d$ is to be defined, and once defined how the term $\sigma\, dW$ is to be interpreted.

Intuitively, what I think we need is a definition for differential forms that would simultaneously deal with differentials of fields that are not strictly differentiable and with nonlinear operations that cannot be handled by the theory of generalized processes. This is exactly what the Itô calculus achieves in one dimension. We need its generalization to $\mathbb{R}^n$.

To give the basic ideas of what I think is needed, let us confine ourselves to the two-dimensional case $\mathbb{R}^2$. Define oriented $r$-rectangles ($r = 1,2$) as follows: A 1-rectangle is a line segment parallel to one of the two axes, and each 1-rectangle has one of two orientations. A 2-rectangle is just an ordinary rectangle with sides parallel to the two axes and has two possible orientations (pointing out and pointing in, say). Finally, a 0-rectangle is just a point and it too is given two possible orientations. If $A$ is an oriented rectangle, then $-A$ is the same rectangle with the opposite orientation.

For a number of reasons we need to consider linear combinations of the form

$$\sum_k \alpha_k A_k$$

where $\alpha_k$ are real numbers and $A_k$ are oriented rectangles of the same dimension. The linear combinations satisfy certain natural axioms [12] and are known as $r$-chains ($r = 0,1,2$). Observe that the boundary of an oriented $r$-rectangle is a sum of oriented $(r-1)$-rectangles. Hence the boundary of an $r$-chain is an $(r-1)$-chain.

A two-dimensional set in $\mathbb{R}^2$ can be approximated by a sequence of 2-chains (by subdivision, for example). A one-dimensional curve in $\mathbb{R}^2$ can also be approximated by a sequence of 1-chains (by staircase-like approximations, for example). Now suppose that $X$ is a linear map of the space of $r$-chains into a space of square-integrable random variables. With appropriate continuity conditions, $X$ can be extended to all sets that can be approximated by $r$-chains. Intuitively, $X(A)$ for an $r$-dimensional set $A$ can be thought of as an integral

$$X(A) = \int_A \xi$$

where $\xi$ is a random differential $r$-form, except that for many interesting cases $\xi$ is only a generalized $r$-form ($r$-current). We shall call $X$ a random $r$-cochain (or equivalently a random $r$-form).

The exterior differential of a random $r$-cochain is an $(r+1)$-cochain defined as follows:

$$(dX)(A) = X (\partial A) \tag{9.16}$$

when $\partial A$ is the boundary of $A$. This is nothing but the Stoke's theorem, used here as a definition rather than as a property. Now take a Wiener process $W_t$. It can be considered as a 0-form. Its exterior derivative $dW$ is a 1-form, so that $dW$ is parameterized by one-dimensional curves. If we define $d_1 W$ and $d_2 W$ by

$$d_1 W = dW \quad \text{on horizontal line segments}$$
$$= 0 \quad \text{on vertical line segments}$$

and

$$d_2 W = dW \quad \text{on vertical line segments} \tag{9.17}$$
$$= 0 \quad \text{on horizontal line segments}$$

then

$$dW = d_1 W + d_2 W$$

and $d_i W$ are both 1-forms. It is easy to show that

$$d(d_2W) = -d(d_1W) = \eta$$

is a white noise 2-form, and because of it both $d_1W$ and $d_2W$ are Markovian. We now see that although $W_t$ is not Markovian, its exterior derivative $dW$ is Markovian in the sense that its horizontal and vertical components $d_iW$ are both Markovian.

Thus far everything is linear. To proceed further, we need to introduce the exterior product $X \wedge Y$ (between $r$ and $p$ forms) which is a nonlinear operation. For example, $d_1W \wedge d_2W$ is a 2-form that takes the value

$$W(dt_1, t_2) \; W(t_1, dt_2)$$

on an incremental rectangle $dt_1 \wedge dt_2$ at $(t_1, t_2)$. It turns out that the exterior product is closely related to the type-2 stochastic integral introduced in [7] and the multiple Itô integral introduced in [13].

In the theory of stochastic integration developed for two parameter martingales, one source of difficulty has been the lack of a useful calculus. For example, the differentiation formula (expressed as a transformation of integrals into integrals) derived in [14] is difficult to use. With the introduction of stochastic differential forms, a much simpler calculus is beginning to emerge. For example, let $W$ be a two-parameter Wiener process. Let $f$ be a twice continuously differentiable function. Then $f(W)$ is a 0-form and its exterior derivative is a 1-form given by

$$df(W_t) = f'(W_t) \wedge dW_t + 1/2 f''(W_t) \wedge dv_t \tag{9.18}$$

where $v_t$ is just the area of $A_t$ (the rectangle bounded by the origin and $t$), $d$ denotes exterior differentiation and $\wedge$ denotes exterior product.

The introduction of differential forms also makes possible certain transformations that should preserve Markovian properties in a way analogous to the Itô differential equations. As an example, consider an equation

$$dX_t = X_t \wedge dt + dW_t. \tag{9.19}$$

As a global equation, it has no solution. We can see this by noting that $ddX_t = 0$ ($dd$ of any form is 0) but $d(X_t \wedge dt + dW_t) = dX_t \wedge dt \neq 0$.

However, the equation has a solution on any path if we require it to be satisfied only on that path. Now, suppose that we take a collection of paths
$\Gamma = \{\gamma\}$ such that no two paths in $\Gamma$ ever cross and collectively the paths
cover the entire space $\mathbb{R}^2$. Then solving the differential equation on each path
yields a 0-form $X_t$ on $\mathbb{R}^2$. For example, let $\Gamma$ be the set of radial paths, i.e.,

$$\gamma_\theta = \{(r\cos\theta, r\sin\theta), \ 0 \le r \le \infty\}, \ \ 0 \le \theta \le 2\pi$$

then, on $\gamma_\theta$ (9.19) becomes

$$X(dr,\theta) = X(r,\theta)dr + W(dr\cos\theta, dr \sin\theta)$$

and the solution is

$$X(r,\theta) = e^r X_0 + \int_0^r e^{-(r-u)} W(du \cos\theta, dr \sin\theta).$$

This solution can be written in a coordinate-free form as

$$X_t = e(t) \, [ \, X_0 + \int_{\gamma_t} e^{-1} \, dW \, ]$$

where $\rho$ is a 0-form defined by $e(t) = \exp|t|$ and $\gamma_t$ is the radial path from
the origin to $t$.

I believe that equations such as (9.19), solved locally on paths, provide a
way of transforming processes that preserves Markovian properties. The extent
to which this is true is under active investigation.

## 9.8 Conclusion

The development of a theory of Markovian random fields faces a number
of obstacles. On the one hand, in any dimension higher than 1 the Markovian
property appears to be incompatible with sample continuity, so that one has to
deal with generalized processes. At the same time, the very nature of the Markovian property is local, so that generalized processes per se are not a suitable
model. Furthermore, to construct non-Gaussian Markov processes requires nonlinear operations that cannot be handled by the existing theory of generalized
processes. I am convinced that what is needed is a stochastic calculus like the

one Itô developed for one dimension, but one that is necessarily differentio-geometric in higher dimensions.

## References

[1]    J.F. Barrett and D.G Lampard, An expansion for some second-order probability distributions and its applications to noise problems, *IRE Trans. on Inform. Theory,* Vol. IT-1, pp. 10-15, 1955.

[2]    P. Lévy, A special problem of Brownian motion, and a general theory of Gaussian random functions, *Proc. 3rd Berkeley Symp. Math. Stat. and Prob.,* Vol. 2, Berkeley, CA: Univ. of California Press, pp. 133-175. 1956.

[3]    H.P. McKean Jr., Brownian motion with a second dimensional term, *Theory Prob. Appl.,* Vol. 8, pp. 335-365, 1963.

[4]    R. Gangoli, Abstract harmonic analysis and Lévy's Brownian motion of several parameters, *Proc. 5th Berkeley Symp. Math. Stat. and Prob., Vol. II-1,* Berkeley, CA: Univ. of California Press, Vol. II-1, pp. 13-30, 1967.

[5]    E. Wong, Homogeneous Gauss-Markov random fields, *Ann. Math. Statist.,* Vol. 40, pp. 1625-1634, 1969.

[6]    E. Nelson, The free Markov field, *J. Functional Analysis,* Vol. 12, pp. 211-227, 1973.

[7]    E. Wong and M. Zakai, Martingales and stochastic integrals for processes with a multidimensional parameter, *Z. Wahr. verw. Geb.,* Vol. 29, pp. 109-122, 1974.

[8]    R. Cairoli and J. Walsh, Stochastic integrals in the plane, *Acta Math.* Vol. 134, pp. 111-183, 1975.

[9]    J. Walsh, Martingales with a multidimensional parameter and stochastic integrals in the plane, *Notes for cours de troisiéme cycle, University of Paris, VI,* 1977.

[10]   C. Belisle, Private communication, 1983.

[11]     K. Itô Isotropic random current, *Proc. 3rd Berkeley Symp. Math. Stat. and Prob., Vol. 2*, Berkeley, CA: Univ. of California Press, pp. 125-132, 1956.

[12]     H. Whitney, *Geometric Integration Theory*, Princeton, NJ: Princeton University Press, 1957.

[13]     B. Hajek and E. Wong, Set parametered martingales and multiple stochastic integration, *Lecture Notes in Mathematics, No. 851*, Berlin: Springer-Verlag, pp. 119-151, 1980.

[14]     E. Wong and M. Zakai, Differentiation formulas for stochastic integrals in the plane, *Stoch. Proc. Appl.*, Vol. 6, pp. 339-349, 1978.

# PART II

## CODING, NETWORKS,

## AND

## SIGNAL PROCESSING

# 10

# Coding for Interference Channels

Ian F. Blake

*Department of Electrical Engineering*
*University of Waterloo*
*Waterloo, Ontario*

## 10.1 Introduction

The understanding of the use and performance of coded communication systems on a variety of channels has increased considerably over the past twenty years. From a subject that was once regarded as too esoteric and too expensive to implement, it has developed into an integral and often crucial part of many systems. More recently there has been considerable interest in the situation where the channel contains an intelligent jammer. This assumption introduces new and interesting aspects to the problem and to the systems designer. In such a situation it is generally assumed that the jammer has complete knowledge of the transmitter/receiver operation except for the state of some pseudorandom generator which is used to randomly vary the transmitted signal in some manner. The jammer attempts to use the limited amount of power at his disposal to assure the maximum degradation of system peformance. Although the problem has an obvious military flavor, much work on it has appeared in the public domain and some of this literature will be considered here.

When the channel is modeled with a jammer, the communication problem takes on significant differences from the more usual situation involving stationary memoryless channels. Questions such as optimum signal design and receiver structure become more challenging, and although many of these remain unanswered certain approaches have been identified as significant. The purpose of this chapter is to introduce a few of these approaches in a restricted setting. Only one type of system will be considered in any detail, that of frequency hopped $M$-ary frequency shift keying (FH/MFSK), and the purpose is not to be encyclopedic but to give a brief introduction to the area.

The next section introduces the two types of spread-spectrum systems typically analyzed in the literature as well as the types of jamming strategies usually considered. The following two sections analyze the performance of the FH/MFSK system under the assumptions of partial band and tone jamming, respectively. The final section considers other approaches and some possible areas for future work.

## 10.2 System Model

The concept of spectrum spreading has been investigated for at least forty years [1] as a method for combating interference. Simply stated, one takes a baseband signal and modulates it in such a way that the bandwidth of the transmitted signal is several orders of magnitude greater than that of the baseband signal. The purpose of such a scheme is to attempt to defeat the efforts of an intelligent jammer who is assumed to have knowledge of the system operation and who is able to use the jamming power in such a way to do the most harm. The receiver despreads the received signal and this process usually spreads any narrowband noise. The ultimate aim of the design of a spread spectrum system is to make the strategy of the jammer the same as that which would be used in the absence of specific infomation. Thus if the optimal jamming strategy is broadband noise, the communicator has defeated any system knowledge the jammer might have.

There are two basic techniques to achieve the spectrum spreading and both involve the use of pseudorandom (PN) shift register sequences. In a direct sequence (DS) system the baseband signal is multiplied by a $\pm 1$ PN sequence. The width of an individual bit in the PN sequence, called a chip interval, is inversely proportional to the bandwidth of the product signal. The receiver has a sequence generator synchronized to that of the transmitter and recovers the baseband signal by multiplying the received signal by the PN sequence it generates. If the jamming signal is relatively narrowband, the multiplication of it by the sequence will expand its bandwidth and baseband filtering will then remove much of the jamming power.

In a frequency-hopped (FH) system the baseband signal is first modulated as an $M$-ary FSK (MFSK) signal which is then modulated onto a carrier whose frequency is pseudorandomly hopped over a predetermined set of frequencies, the hopping pattern being determined by the succession of states of a shift register. The bandwidth expansion of this system is largely determined the set of hopping frequencies. The effect of the pseudorandom carrier is removed at the receiver, which is able to generate the same frequency hopping pattern. The number of frequency hops per data symbol is an important parameter of the system. If the carrier remains constant over one or more data symbols it is referred to as a slow hopping system, whereas if it hops several times per data symbol it is a fast hopping system. Hybrid FH and DS systems can also be considered but are less popular in the literature.

The jammer has some fixed amount of power and his aim is to use it in such a way that, knowing the details of the transmitter/receiver, but not the state of the shift register, maximum degradation of the communicator's performance is achieved. Typical jamming strategies analyzed include partial band, partial time, and tone jamming. Other strategies, such as repeat playback, where the jammer transmits a delayed version of the communication in order to confuse the receiver, can apparently be very effective but are difficult to analyze. As a matter of convenience for the analysis, it is often assumed there is no background or thermal noise present, and this will be assumed here. It should be noted, however, that in some situations the presence of such background noise can have a dramatic effect on the results.

For partial band jamming the jammer spreads the available power uniformly across some fraction of the communicator's bandwidth where the fraction is chosen to maximize performance degradation. The effect of this strategy on an FH system is that the carrier will randomly hop into and out of a jammed portion of the spectrum. If the fraction of the communication band being jammed is $\rho$, it is often convenient to assume that the probability that any particular hop is jammed is $\rho$ and this event is independent from hop to hop. The equivalent situation for a DS system is partial time jamming where the jammer turns the full power on and off at random but with an average duty cycle of $\rho$. To achieve independence for the event that adjacent chips are jammed, it is necessary to interleave the DS signal before transmission on the channel and to deinterleave at the receiver.

For an FH/MFSK system a tone jamming strategy is often adopted where the jammer divides the available power into discrete tones of amplitudes slightly larger than those used by the communicator. If such a tone is placed into the communicator's slot, but not on the communicator's tone, the receiver will choose the incorrect tone. Of course, the jammer is only able to jam a fraction of the slots.

It will be shown later that the effects of either partial band, partial time or tone jamming can be catastrophic on system performance when optimized over the apppropriate parameter. The typical remedy for this situation is to introduce diversity and/or coding. In a fast frequency hopped system where the carrier hops $m$ times per data symbol, $m > 1$, there is a natural form of diversity. Assuming that the hops are independently jammed, the information from each hop can be combined to form a data symbol decision statistic. To achieve diversity with a DS system the code symbol is divided into $m$ subintervals before being multiplied by the PN sequence. These are interleaved over a sufficiently long period so that after deinterleaving at the receiver it can be assumed that the $m$ subintervals are jammed independently. The information from the $m$ subintervals is then combined in some manner to form a decision statistic. The situation is similar when both coding and diversity are used.

While channel information and soft decisions are always helpful, this is particularly so of the jamming channel. In an $m$ diversity situation, for example, if at least one of the $m$ diversity chips is received without being jammed, then under the assumption of negligible background noise, it will yield a correct decision. In a coded system there is the option of declaring an erasure if channel measurement information indicates a lack of confidence in the code symbol decision. Many other situations arise where it is useful to incorporate channel state information into receiver decisions, and a few of these will be commented upon in later sections.

Only one spread spectrum system will be considered here, that of FH/MFSK. Both slow hopping (1 hop per data symbol) and fast hopping ($m$ hops per data symbol) in partial band and tone jamming will be examined. The aim is to use this system to explore the analytical approaches taken for such systems and the type of results obtained.

For any type of spread-spectrum system we let $W$ be the spread-spectrum bandwidth, $R_b$ the data rate in bits per second, $S$ the received signal power, and $J$ the jammer power. The received energy per data bit, $E_b$, can be written as $ST_b = S/R_b$ where $T_b$ is the data interval and the equivalent wideband power spectral density of the noise can be written $N_0 = J/W$, and consequently

$$E_b/N_0 = (S/R_b)/(J/W) = (W/R_b)/(J/S)$$

The quantity $W/R_b$ is proportional to the bandwidth expansion of the system and is referred to as the processing gain. The quantity $J/S$ is called the jamming margin.

With this background material the performance of the FH/MFSK system in partial band and tone jamming is examined in the next two sections.

## 10.3 The Partial Band Jamming Case

The performance of BFSK ($M = 2$) in additive white Gaussian noise (AWGN) with two-sided power spectral density $N_0/2$ is considered first. For two orthogonal signals on such a channel the probability of error is given by

$$P_e = \frac{1}{2} \exp\,(-E_b/2N_0)$$

where each signal has energy $E_b$ and receiver detection is assumed, here and throughout the chapter, to be noncoherent. In a partial band jamming situation where a fraction $\rho$ of the bandwidth is jammed, we assume that the signal is jammed with probability $\rho$ and is noise free with probability $(1 - \rho)$ and that successive symbols are jammed independently. The probability of error in this case is given by

$$P_e(\rho) = \frac{\rho}{2} \exp(-\rho E_b/2N_0)$$

Assuming that the jammer knows the transmitted signal energy, this expression can be maximized over the duty cycle $\rho$, which gives the result

$$\max_{0<\rho<1} P_e(\rho) = e^{-1}/(E_b/N_0), \quad E_b/N_0 \geq 2$$

$$\geq e^{-1}/(E_b/N_0), \quad E_b/N_0 < 2$$

For the $M$-ary case [2], $M = 2^K$, the probability of bit error on the uniform channel is given by

$$P_b = \frac{1}{2(M-1)} \sum_{i=2}^{M} (-1)^i \binom{M}{i} \exp\left(-\frac{KE_b}{N_0}\left(i - \frac{1}{i}\right)\right)$$

$$\leq 2^{K-2}\exp\left(-\frac{KE_b}{2N_0}\right) \tag{10.1}$$

where the inequality is given by the union bound. For the partial band channel, for the worst case $\rho$, the probability of error can be expressed as

$$P_b = \alpha/(E_b/N_0), \quad \text{for} \quad E_b/N_0 \geq \gamma \tag{10.2}$$

and the worst case $\rho$ is given by

$$\rho_{WC} = \gamma/(E_b/N_0)$$

where $\alpha$ and $\gamma$ are decreasing functions of $K$. The performance loss which goes from an exponential dependence on signal-to-noise ratio to an inverse linear one is catastrophic.

The traditional solution to this problem is to introduce diversity. In the case of MFSK, each symbol interval is divided into $m$ subintervals and the same $M$-ary symbol transmitted on different carrier frequencies. If the channel characteristics are such that the $m$ transmissions result in independent statistics at the receiver, these statistics can be summed to yield a final decision statistic on the symbol. For the broadband case the optimal receiver involves passing the square of the output of a matched filter/envelope detector through a $\ln(I_0(\cdot)$ nonlinearity and the addition of bias terms before summing the outputs of the $m$ branches [3]. The nonlinearity is often replaced by a square-law device and the loss of performance is usually negligible. For partial band interference the question of optimal combining is more challenging and a variety of suboptimal schemes have been considered [3-6]. Although an exact expression for the error probability exists for the case of $M$ orthogonal signals using $m$th-order diversity with linear combining (i.e., where the sum of squares of the envelope detector output is used as the symbol decision statistic), it is more convenient to use a Chernoff bound technique [2,7] which gives

$$P_b \leq \max_{0 \leq \rho \leq 1} \min_{0 \leq \lambda \leq 1} 2^{K-2} \left( \rho \, \exp\left( -\frac{\lambda}{\lambda+1} \frac{KE_b}{mN_0} \rho \right) / (1 - \lambda)^2 \right)^m$$

where $\lambda$ is the Chernoff parameter. This gives

$$P_b \leq 2^{K-2} \left( \frac{4me^{-1}}{KE_b/N_0} \right)^m \tag{10.3}$$

for the worst-case duty factor of

$$\rho_{WC} = \frac{3m}{KE_b/N_0}$$

provided that $\rho_{WC} < 1$. For $E_b/N_0 < 3m/K$, $\rho_{WC} = 1$, implying that broadband jamming is the optimum. It should be noted that since this optimization is with respect to an upper bound, the results are approximate but nonetheless useful.

The upper bound of (10.3) can further be optimized over the order of diversity used to give

$$P_b \leq 2^{K-2}\exp\left(-\frac{KE_b}{4N_0}\right) \qquad (10.4)$$

which occurs at an optimum order of diversity of $m = KE_b/4N_0$ and $\rho_{WC} = 3/4$. Notice that the performance obtained by the introduction of optimum diversity comes to within 3 db of restoring the degradation due to partial band jamming–and in particular restores the exponential dependence of the bit error rate on the signal-to-noise ratio.

Coding can improve the situation further. To normalize the notation and to facilitate comparison of coded systems, we follow the notation of Levitt [8] and use $m$ for the order of diversity per $M$-ary symbol and $L$ for the order of diversity per bit. Since there are $L$ chips per bit we have $R_c = LR_b$. For all the results quoted the optimum order of diversity is assumed to be $E_b/4N_0$ and the worst-case duty factor is $\rho_{WC} = 3/4$. The results for three classes of convolutional codes are stated in [8], drawing on some results from [7,9]. For orthogonal convolutional codes the probability of bit error can be upper bounded by

$$P_b < \frac{1}{2}\exp\left(-\frac{KE_b}{4N_0}\right) \qquad (10.5)$$

For such codes, for each bit shifted into a $K$-bit shift register one of $M = 2^K$ orthogonal signals is transmitted. Comparing (10.5) to (10.4) it is seen that for $K \geq 2$ the performance is slightly better than for the uncoded case. The optimum diversity for such a system is given by $m_{Opt} = L_{Opt} = E_b/4N_0$ which is reduced by a factor of $K$ from the uncoded case. Thus there is a trade-off between the order of diversity required and the rate of the code.

The performance of the well-known constraint length 7 and rate 1/2 binary convolutional code (e.g., see [10, App. B]) in the worst-case partial band noise for optimal diversity is given by

$$P_b < 18 \exp(-5E_b/4N_0)$$

for which $m_{Opt} = 2$ and $L_{Opt} = 4$. The dual $K$ codes investigated by Viterbi and Jacobs [7] and Odenwalder [9] give the performance

$$P_b < 2^{K-2}\exp\left(\frac{-KE_b}{2N_0}\right)$$

which has the same asymptotic performance in worst-case partial band noise as that of the uncoded system without diversity in broadband noise.

The performance of coded systems for spread-spectrum applications can be evaluated or bounded for a particular code, but a more general approach is often called for. Such an approach has been pursued by a variety of authors using an information-theoretic approach. The computational cutoff ráte of a channel, $R_0$, with a discrete set of inputs $X$ and a continuous set of outputs $Y$, is

$$R_0 = \int_Y \left(\sum_X q(x)(p(y\,|\,x))^{1/2}\right)^2 dy$$

while for a discrete set of outputs it becomes

$$R_0 = \sum_Y \left(\sum_X q(x)(p(y\,|\,x))^{1/2}\right)^2 .$$

The random coding bound on the bit error for binary block codes of rate $r$ bits per symbol, $r < R_0$, is given by [11]

$$P_b < 2^{-(K\alpha-1)}$$

where $\alpha = R_0/r$. For convolutional codes of constraint length $K$ the upper bound can be written [11]

$$P_b < \frac{2^{-K\alpha}}{(1 - 2^{-(\alpha-1)})^2} \tag{10.6}$$

It has been suggested [12] that the parameter $R_0$ is a far more useful performance indicator of a coded digital modulation system than any other single parameter such as capacity since it directly relates to the probability of bit error and is easily computable.

For a binary input channel this parameter can be expressed as [13]

$$R_0 = 1 - \log_2(1 + Z)$$

where

$$Z = (4p(1 - p))^{1/2} \qquad \text{for the BSC}$$

$$= e^{-E_s/N_0} \qquad \text{for the AWGN channel.}$$

Because of the simple manner in which $R_0$ is defined, the effect of including soft decision information in the receiver is easily obtained. For example, for a binary input to the AWGN channel, if all information at the receiver is preserved, then

$$R_0 = 1 - \log_2(1 + e^{-E_s/N_0}) \tag{10.7}$$

while if the information is hard quantized, then

$$R_0 = 1 + \log_2(1 + (4p(1 - p))^{1/2})$$

Similar results are obtained for the $M$-ary orthogonal signal case [14].

From (10.7), with $E_s = E_b r$ we can write [11]

$$\frac{E_b}{N_0} = -\alpha \frac{\ln(2^{1-R_0} - 1)}{R_0}.$$

Using this relationship with a given code rate and dimension $K$, a value of $\alpha$ can be found to yield the required probability of error bound as given in (10.6). From the value of $\alpha$ can be found the required $E_b/N_0$. Thus the relatively straightforward approach using random coding upper bounds on the probability of error can yield useful results. Furthermore, it can carry over to the partial band jamming case, for which it can be shown [11] that

$$R_0 = 1 - \log_2(1 + \rho e^{-\rho E_s/N_0})$$

and hence

$$E_b/N_0 = -\frac{\alpha}{\rho R_0} \ln\left(\frac{2^{1-R_0} - 1}{\rho}\right)$$

for which

$$\max_{0 \leq \rho \leq 1} \frac{E_b}{N_0} = \frac{\alpha e^{-1}}{R_0(2^{1-R_0} - 1)}.$$

For smaller values of $R_0$ ($R_0 < .548$) the maximizing value for $\rho$ is 1 implying that for such values the broadband jammer is optimum.

The random coding approach is clearly a powerful technique for the evaluation of coding strategies to combat interference channels. Another approach pursued by Omura and Levitt [15,16] shows that the bit error probability for any specific code can be upper bounded by an expression of the form

$$P_b \leq B(R_0).$$

The function $B(\cdot)$ is unique to the code being used while the cutoff rate parameter $R_0$ is independent of the code and depends on the type of modulation, interference, and receiver structure. This decoupling of the effects of the coding from the rest of the system facilitates a comparison of a variety of coding/diversity options. Although the approach is a little too involved to consider in detail here, we nonetheless give a brief indication of it.

For receivers using no channel-state information, assuming an $M$-input symmetric channel, the cutoff rate can be expressed as

$$R_0 = \log_2(M) - \log_2(1 + (M-1)D)$$

where

$$D = \min_{\lambda \geq 0} D(\lambda)$$

and

$$D(x,\hat{x},\lambda) = E\left(e^{\lambda(m(y,\hat{x})-m(y,x))}\Big|_x\right)$$

where $m(y,x)$ is the decision metric of the receiver, $\lambda$ is the Chernoff bound parameter, and it is assumed that

$$D(x,\hat{x},\lambda) = D(\lambda) \quad \text{if } x \neq \hat{x} \text{ and } D(x,\hat{x},\lambda) = 1 \text{ otherwise.}$$

The probability of deciding that a codeword $\hat{x}$ was transmitted, when in fact $x$ was transmitted, can be upper bounded by using the Chernoff technique, as $D^{m(x,\hat{x})}$. Thus for a specific code the error probability can be upper bounded by

$$P_b \leq G(D)$$

and since $D$ can be expressed as a function of $R_0$, we have

$$P_b \leq B(R_0)$$

The analysis of receivers that use channel-state information is very similar. Here it is assumed that for each use of the channel the jammer state can be characterized by a random variable $Z$ where $Z$ takes on the value 1 with probability $\rho$ and 0 with probability $(1-\rho)$ and these values are independent with successive uses of the channel. If the receiver uses the decision metric $m(y,x|z)$, the analysis proceeds as before, with the results averaged over the jammer state variable. In the work of Omura and Levitt [15] the example of FH/MFSK on the partial band jamming channel for the four possible cases of hard and soft decisions with and without jamming state information is considered. The approach is powerful and useful for the class of problems it is intended for and will no doubt find further applications.

## 10.4 The Tone Jamming Case

A different jammer strategy, which is particularly effective against FH/MFSK, divides the total jammer power into $q$ tones of equal power. These tones are placed across the spread bandwidth in some fashion. The most effective strategy under most reasonable sets of assumptions is to place at most one jamming tone in each hopping band of $M$ frequencies. However, other strategies can also be considered. The analysis given here will follow that of Levitt [8], which is an extension of earlier work of Houston [17] on the problem.

If the symbol rate is $R_s$ symbols per second, then in order to achieve orthogonal frequency tones for noncoherent reception, they must have a frequency separation of $R_s$ hertz. Across the spread bandwidth there are $W/R_s$ possible transmitted tones which are assumed to be divided into frequency bands, each band containing $M$ frequencies with the transmitter pseudorandomly hopping among the bands.

If the total jammer power available is $J$, it will be divided into $q$ tones of equal power such that

$$\frac{J}{q} = \frac{S}{\alpha}, \quad \alpha < 1$$

so that if a jammer tone falls in a band containing a communicator's tone, it will have slightly greater power than the communicator's tone and perhaps cause an error. The jammer can choose $\alpha$ to optimize the degradation of the communicator's performance. The probability that any particular tone is jammed is

$$\rho = \frac{q}{W/R_s} = \frac{\alpha}{KE_b/N_0}.$$

If the jammer places $n$ tones in each band, then the probability that a band is jammed is

$$\mu = M\frac{\rho}{n}$$

and Levitt refers to this as a band multitone strategy with $n$ tones.

If the transmitted tone is jammed with a jammer tone with the same frequency but with a phase offset of $\phi$, the power in the energy detector will be

$$S\left(1 + \frac{2 \cos \phi}{\alpha^{1/2}} + \frac{1}{\alpha}\right)$$

If another tone in the band is also jammed an error may or may not be made depending on the phase offset.

The $n = 1$ and $M = 2^K$ case yields the result that [7,8,18]

$$P_b = \begin{cases} \dfrac{1}{2}, & \alpha_{WC} = \dfrac{KE_b}{MN_0}, & \dfrac{E_b}{N_0} < \dfrac{M}{K} \\[4mm] \dfrac{M}{2KE_b/N_0}, & \alpha_{WC} = 1, & \dfrac{E_b}{N_0} > \dfrac{M}{K} \end{cases}$$

As with the partial band case, the effect of the tone jamming is to convert an exponential dependence of error probability on the signal-to-noise ratio to an inverse linear one. Unlike the partial band case, however, performance degrades for the tone jamming case as $K$ increases.

The performance of a band multitone strategy for $n > 1$ can also be evaluated [8], taking into account the energy detector decision mechanism and the effect of the phase offset when the communicator's tone is jammed. However, performance improves as $n$ is increased making such a strategy inadvisable.

As with partial band jamming, the exponential dependence of error probability on signal-to-noise ratio can be restored with diversity. In this case each $M$-ary symbol is divided into $m$ subintervals or chips, each chip being transmitted on a different frequency. If it is assumed that the detector is able to determine when a chip is jammed, then if any of the chips are not jammed, a correct decision is made on the $M$-ary symbol. If all the chips are jammed the detector outputs are linearly combined. For $M \geq 4$ the performance of such a scheme with optimum diversity for an $n = 1$ tone jammer is upper bounded by

$$P_b \leq \frac{M}{2} e^{-\delta E_b/N_0}, \quad m_{0pt} = \delta E_b/N_0$$

where $\delta$ decreases with increasing $K$. Under the assumptions made the tone jammer is more effective compared to the case of optimum diversity used with partial band jamming.

The model of tone jamming of the previous work was extended by McEliece and Rodemich[19] in an interesting manner. The MFSK transmitted signal is modeled by an $M$-tuple $\underline{X} = (X_1, X_2, ..., X_M)$, where only one of the components is nonzero. The magnitude of the nonzero component is made a random variable according to some distribution. The information is contained entirely in the location of the nonzero component, while the variation in its magnitude is designed only to degrade jammer performance. The jamming noise is also an $M$-tuple $\underline{Z} = (Z_1, Z_2, ..., Z_M)$ of nonnegative random variables independent of $\underline{X}$. If $E(X^2) = \lambda$ and

$$\frac{1}{M} \sum_{i=1}^{M} E(Z_j^2) = 1$$

then $\lambda$ is the signal-to-noise ratio of the model. The receiver observes $\underline{R} = (R_1, R_2, ..., R_M)$, where

$$R_j = |X_j + e^{i\theta_j} Z_j|, \quad j = 1, 2, ..., M$$

where $\theta_1, \theta_2, ..., \theta_M$ are independent phase angles uniformly distributed over the interval $(0, 2\pi)$. The receiver chooses the index $j$ for which $R_j$ is the largest. If the nonzero component of $\underline{X}$ is constrained to be a constant, then the optimal jamming vector has exactly one nonzero component, which is the same as the optimal tone jammer of Houston [17] and Levitt [8], described under more general circumstances. If the transmitter chooses the amplitude of the nonzero component at random, it can be shown that [19] the minimax solution to the resulting game theoretic situation yields only one component of the jamming vector nonzero and the resulting symbol error performance is twofold improved over that of the constant-amplitude case. This model and game-theoretic approach to the MFSK/interference channel, while not providing dramatic new results, does provide a fresh approach and insight. Hopefully, such approaches can be exploited further.

The incorporation of channel-state information remains an important area for further investigation. The work of Omura and Levitt [15,16] already discussed has shown the importance of incorporating such information into receiver design. Another aspect of this work was recently investigated by Viterbi [18]. To adopt his notation, suppose that the communicator hops at $R_H$ hops per second and sends one $M$-ary symbol (tone) per hop, where the tones have a frequency spacing of $R_H$ hertz. The probability that the communicator's band is jammed is

$$P_H = \frac{J/S}{W/MR_H}$$

and if the band is jammed, there is a probability of $1/2$ that any particular bit is in error. The probability of bit error for this uncoded system can then be written as

$$P_b = \left( \frac{M}{2 \log_2 M} \right) \frac{1}{E_b/N_0}$$

For a BSC with crossover probability $P_s$, the computational cutoff rate $R_0$ is, as noted before,

$$R_0 = 1 - \log_2(1 + (4P_s(1 - P_s))^{1/2})$$

For coded FH/MFSK to transmit an $M$-ary symbol per hop requires $\log_2(M)$ binary symbols per hop, and if the code rate $r = R_0$, then each use of the channel transmits $R_0$ bits per binary symbol, yielding $R_0 \log_2(M)$ bits per hop. To ensure independence, the coded binary symbols must be interleaved and deinterleaved appropriately. Furthermore $P_b$ is now $P_s$, the binary symbol error probability. There results the equation

$$E_b/N_0 = \left( \frac{M}{2 \log_2 M} \right) \frac{1}{R_0 P_s}$$

where

$$P_s = (1 - (1 - \alpha^2)^{1/2})/2, \qquad \alpha = 2^{1-R_0} - 1$$

which gives the relationship between $E_b/N_0$ and $R_0$.

The following "ratio-threshold mitigation" technique is introduced for this channel [18]. Let the outputs of the $M$ receiver matched filters for the tones be ordered as $(Z_1, Z_2, ..., Z_M)$ in ascending order by magnitude, and the $\log_2(M)$ decision symbols are obtained from the index of the filter yielding the largest output. With each such decision symbol is now associated a quality bit, $Q$, which takes on the value 0, implying a good-quality decision, if $Z_M/Z_{M-1} \geq \theta$ and 1, a bad decision, otherwise. The parameter $\theta$ may be chosen by the communicator in order to minimize the degradation caused by the tone jammer. It is shown [18] that the minmax solution for $\theta$ is given by

$$\theta_0 = [1 + (1 - 2(2 - 1/P_s))^{1/2}]/2$$

for which the relationship between $E_b/N_0$ and $R_0$ is now given by

$$E_b/N_0 = \left(\frac{M}{\log_2 M}\right) \frac{1}{R_0 \theta_0 P_s}.$$

By examining the resulting curve it is shown that the minimum $E_b/N_0$ is obtained for a code rate (computational cutoff rate) of approximately 1/2. It is further noted that it is quite feasible for the communicator to vary the center frequency of the transmitted band continuously and that a reasonable penalty for the jammer to pay for the inaccuracy of the jamming tones is 3 dB. For a ratio threshold of $\theta = 3.7$ corresponding to the optimum choice for $R_0 = 1/2$, it is shown that for $M = 2$ or 4 there is little or no degradation for the tone jammer over the broadband jammer and only about 1.5-d$b$ degradation for $M = 8$. This approach of incorporating channel-state information into the receiver structure and its analysis, as well as the results obtained, are clearly a significant contribution to the literature and will no doubt be extended in future work.

## 10.5 Comments

As mentioned in the introduction, the interference channel introduces some new challenges and approaches to the classical communication situation. The two types of interference considered here, the partial band jammer and the tone jammer, are the most analyzed in the literature and have served to introduce the methods available.

The variety of coding techniques, modulation techniques, diversity combining techniques, and jamming situations make the development of more powerful general techniques, such as those Omura and Levitt [15,16], interesting. The more information-theoretic approaches of McEliece and Stark [20,21] are also interesting. Although the results of this approach are perhaps less directly indicative of error performance of the system, they are nonetheless important for the insight to the problem that they yield. They are formulated in game-theoretic terms with the mutual information between the coding channel input and the output, the payoff function. Jammer and coder strategies are discussed for the AWGN channel, both broadband and partial band, both with and without channel-state information. The interesting results obtained generally support the conclusions obtained by the more conventional analysis.

## References

[1]  R.A. Scholtz, The origins of spread spectrum communications, *IEEE Trans. Comm.,* Vol. COM-30, pp. 822-854, 1982.

[2]  B.K. Levitt and J.K. Omura, Coding tradeoffs for improved performance of FH/MFSK systems in partial band noise, *National Telecommunications Conference*, pp. D9.1.1-D9.1.5, 1981.

[3]  R.W. Boyd, Diversity transmission of $M$-ary orthogonal signals in a hostile environment, *MILCOM 83*, pp. 1.3.12-1.3.16, 1983.

[4]  J.S. Lee, L.E. Miller and Y.K. Kim, Error performance analysis of linear and nonlinear combining square-law receivers for $L$-hops per bit FH/BFSK waveforms in worst-case partial-band jamming, *MILCOM 83*, pp. 1.5.22-1.5.28, 1983.

[5]    Y.K. Kim, L.E. Miller and J.S. Lee, The exact performance analysis of two types of adaptive receivers for multi-hops per symbol FH/MFSK systems in partial-band noise jamming and system thermal noise, *MIL-COM 83*, pp. 38.2.1-38.2.6, 1983.

[6]    K.S. Gong, Performance of diversity combining techniques for FH/MFSK in worst case partial band noise and multi-tone jamming, *MILCOM 83*, pp. 1.4.17-1.4.21, 1983.

[7]    A.J. Viterbi and I.M. Jacobs, Advances in coding and modulation for noncoherent channels affected by fading, partial band and multiple-access interference, in *Advances in Communication Systems,* Vol. 4, A.V. Balakrishnan, Ed., New York, NY: Academic Press, pp. 279-308, 1975.

[8]    B.K. Levitt, Use of diversity to improve FH/MFSK performance in worst case partial band noise and multitone jamming, *MILCOM 82*, pp. 28.2.1-28.2.5, 1982.

[9]    J.P. Odenwalder, Dual-$k$ convolutional codes for noncoherently demodulated channels, *Proc. Int. Telemetering Conf.*, Vol. XII, pp. 165-174, 1976.

[10]   G.C. Clark, Jr., and J. B. Cain, *Error-Correction Coding for Digital Communications*, London, England: Plenum Press, 1981.

[11]   A.J. Viterbi, Spread spectrum communications - myths and realities, *IEEE Communications Magazine*, Vol. 17, pp. 11-18, 1979.

[12]   J.L. Massey, Coding and modulation in digital communications, *Proc. Int. Zurich Sem. Digital Commun.*, Zurich, Switzerland, 1974.

[13]   A.J. Viterbi and J.K. Omura, *Principles of Digital Communications and Coding*, New York, NY: McGraw-Hill, 1979.

[14]   E.A. Bucher, Coding options for efficient communication on non-stationary channels, *Nat. Telecomm. Conf. Rec.*, pp. 4.1.1-4.1.7, 1980.

[15]   J.K. Omura and B.K. Levitt, A general analysis of anti-jam communication systems, *Nat. Telecomm. Conf.*, pp. B7.1.1-B7.1.5, 1981.

[16]   J.K. Omura and B.K. Levitt, Coded error probability evaluation for anti-jam communication systems, *IEEE Trans. Comm.*, Vol. COM-30,

pp. 896-903, 1982.

[17]   S.W. Houston, Modulation techniques for communication, Part 1: Tone and noise jamming performance of spread spectrum $M$-ary FSK and 2-ary, 4-ary DPSK waveforms, *NAECON Convention Rec.*, pp. 51-58, 1975.

[18]   A.J. Viterbi, A robust ratio-threshold technique to mitigate tone and partial band jamming in coded MFSK systems, *MILCOM 82*, pp. 22.4.1-22.4.5, 1982.

[19]   R.J. McEliece and E.R. Rodemich, A study of optimal jamming strategies vs. noncoherent MFSK, *MILCOM 83*, pp. 1.1-1.6, 1983.

[20]   W.E. Stark and R.J. McEliece, Capacity and coding in the presence of fading and jamming, *Nat. Telecomm. Conf.*, pp. B7.4.1-B7.4.5, 1981

[21]   R.J. McEliece and W.E. Stark, An information-theoretic study of communication in the presence of jamming, *IEEE Int. Conf. on Comm.*, pp. 45.3.1-45.3.5.

# 11

# The Use of Gibbs Distributions
# In Image Processing

**Haluk Derin**

*Department of Electrical and Computer Engineering*
*University of Massachusetts*
*Amherst, Massachusetts*

## 11.1 Introduction

In this chapter, we discuss the potential of Gibbs distributions (GDs) as models in image processing applications. We briefly review the definitions and basic concepts of Markov random fields (MRFs) and GDs and present some realizations from these distributions. The use of statistical models and methods in image processing has increased considerably over the recent years. Most of these studies involve the use of MRF models and processing techniques based

This research was partially supported by ONR under Grant N00014-83-K-0059 and by the National Science Foundation under Grant ECS-8403685.

on these models. The pioneering work on MRFs due to Dobrushin [1], Wong [2], and Woods [3] involves extending the Markovian property in one dimension to higher dimensions. However, due to lack of causality in two dimensions the extension is not straightforward. Some properties in one dimension, for example, the equivalence of one-sided and two-sided Markovianity, do not carry over to two dimensions. The early work by Abend *et al.* [4] presents a causal characterization for a class of MRFs called Markov mesh random fields. This work also includes a formulation pointing out the Gibbsian property of a Markov chain without fully realizing the connection. Other attempts in extending the Markovian property to two dimensions include the autoregressive models: the "simultaneous autoregressive" (SAR) models and the "conditional Markov" models introduced by Chellappa and Kashyap [5].

Markov random fields and related two-dimensional autoregressive models have been used in numerous studies in image processing (Woods and Radewan [6], Hansen and Elliott [7], Derin *et al.* [8]). In some cases, the models used are adequate for the special processing desired; in others, simplifying approximations are done on the models to make them suitable for the desired processing. However, it is safe to say that until the MRF-GD equivalence was discovered recently, the full power of the MRF as a spatial interaction (correlation) model has not been exploited. The GD was introduced in 1925 by Ising [9], who used it to model molecular interaction in ferromagnetic materials. Since then it has received considerable attention in both the statistical mechanics and the statistics literature. In addition to models for ferromagnetic materials, lattice gas models [10], and binary alloys [11], GDs have found applications in a wide range of fields, such as agricultural studies reported by Besag [12], neural modeling of inference and learning, social and economic models, optimal VLSI design applications, and image-processing applications.

The equivalence of GDs and MRFs, proved in the 1970s independently by Averintzev [13] and Spitzer [14], opened up a whole new set of possibilities in image-processing applications. The inherent difficulties in the characterization and processing of MRFs are to a large extent alleviated by the MRF-GD equivalence. The difficulties involved in dealing with the conditional distributions in MRFs are eliminated, because the joint distribution is readily available with the GD characterization. The well-known work by Besag [12] laid the groundwork for the GD characterization of MRFs. Another detailed treatment on GD-MRF equivalence is presented by Kinderman and Snell [15].

The use of GDs in image processing is fairly recent and the examples are few, but the potential for their use as statistical image models is enormous. First, Hassner and Sklansky [16] proposed MRF-GD as models for texture. They considered the first-order binary MRF, the so-called Ising model, to characterize various binary textures and presented algorithms for generating realizations of these random fields and for estimating their parameters. Cross and Jain [17] also proposed GD characterization of MRFs to model multilevel textures. More specifically, they used autobinomial class of GDs as models, the Metropolis [18] exchange algorithm to generate realizations, and the so-called "coding method" (Besag [12]) to estimate model parameters from realizations. Other image-processing work using the GD models are due to Cohen and Cooper [19], Geman and Geman [20], and Elliott *et al.* [21,22]. Cohen and Cooper [19] presented a hierarchical GD model for textured images and a split-and-merge type of segmentation algorithm. Geman and Geman [20] gave an extensive exposition on the GD characterization of MRFs and presented a relaxation-type "spin-flip" algorithm which they called the "Gibbs sampler." They also presented a segmentation algorithm using the Gibbs sampler and an "annealing" process to obtain the MAP (maximum *a posteriori*) estimate of an image from a corrupted version. Their algorithm, however, requires a very large number of passes over the image data and is therefore computationally intense.

Finally, in [21] and [22] the author and coworkers presented GD model 3 for noisy or textured images. For the case of textured images, the model is hierarchical, the "high level" GD model describing the spatial correlation between different region types in the image and "low-level" GD models describing the different textures that make up the image. Based on these models, a MAP segmentation algorithm which uses a dynamic programming formulation is developed. The algorithm involves a single pass over the image data and yields very accurate segmentation results. Also in [22], a linear parameter estimation scheme, which compares favorably with the coding method, is proposed.

In this chapter, following a review of definitions of MRFs and GDs and results that relate the two, we present some results pertaining to a class of MRFs. We also propose a class of GDs which can appropriately be used in image processing applications and we present several realizations from the class of GDs being proposed.

The rest of the chapter is organized as follows. In Section 11.2, basic definitions on MRFs are presented. In Section 11.3, basic definitions on GDs and results on MRF-GD equivalence are presented. Various properties of certain classes of MRFs are discussed in Section 11.4. In Section 11.5, the newly proposed class of GDs and realizations from it are presented. Concluding remarks and a discussion on future research directions comprise Section 11.6.

## 11.2  Background on Markov Random Fields

In this section we present the basic definitions pertaining to MRFs and discuss the advantages and the limitations of MRFs as models in image processing. We focus our attention on discrete two-dimensional random fields defined over rectangular lattice structures. For our purposes it suffices to consider random fields defined over a finite lattice of points (corresponding to pixels in a digital image) defined as

$$L = \{(i,j) : 1 \le i \le N_1, \ 1 \le j \le N_2\} \tag{11.1}$$

We start out by defining a neighborhood system on this rectangular lattice $L$.

*Definition 1:* A collection of subsets of $L$ described as

$$\eta = \{\eta_{ij} : (i,j) \in L, \ \eta_{ij} \subset L\} \tag{11.2}$$

is a *neighborhood system* on $L$ if and only if $\eta_{ij}$, the *neighborhood* of pixel $(i,j)$, is such that

(a) $(i,j) \notin \eta_{ij}$, and $\qquad\qquad\qquad\qquad\qquad$ (11.3)

(b) If $(k,l) \in \eta_{ij}$, then $(i,j) \in \eta_{kl}$ $\qquad\qquad\qquad$ (11.4)

for any $(i,j) \in L$.

We can now define an MRF with respect to the neighborhood system $\eta$ defined over the lattice $L$.

*Definition 2:* Let $\eta$ be a neighborhood system defined over lattice $L$ given in (11.1). A random field $X = \{X_{ij}\}$ defined over lattice $L$ is a *Markov random field* (MRF) with respect to the neighborhood system $\eta$ if and only if

$$P(X = x) > 0 \quad \forall \; x \tag{11.5}$$

and

$$P(X_{ij} = x_{ij} | X_{k1} = x_{k1}, \; (k,l) \in L, \; (k,l) \neq (i,j))$$

$$= P(X_{ij} = x_{ij} | X_{k1} = x_{k1}, \; (k,1) \in \eta_{ij}) \tag{11.6}$$

for all $(i,j) \in L$.

Note that capital letters are used to represent random variables and random fields and lowercase letters to represent specific realizations. A hierarchically ordered sequence of neighborhood systems that are commonly used in the context of image modeling consists of $\eta^1$, $\eta^2$, $\eta^3$,... neighborhood systems. $\eta^1 = \{\eta^1_{ij}\}$ is such that for each $(i,j) \in L$ (except for pixels in the boundaries) $\eta^1_{ij}$ consists of the four pixels neighboring pixel $(i,j)$. $\eta^2 = \{\eta^2_{ij}\}$ is such that $\eta^2_{ij}$ consists of the eight pixels neighboring $(i,j)$. The neighborhood structure for $\eta^1$ and $\eta^2$ as well as for $\eta^3$, $\eta^4$, and $\eta^5$ are shown in Figure 11.1. The neighborhood system $\eta^1$ is often called the "four-neighbor" or "nearest-neighbor" or "first order" system; $\eta^2$ is called the "eight neighbor" system or "second order" system. In general, $\eta^m$ is called the $m$th-order neighborhood system.

Due to the finite lattice used, the neighborhood of pixels on the boundaries are necessarily smaller unless a toroidal (periodic) lattice structure is assumed. It should be pointed out that the neighborhood systems that can be defined over $L$ are not limited to the hierarchically ordered sequence of neighborhood systems described above, nor do they have to be isotropic or homogeneous. For a more extensive treatment of MRFs we refer the reader to Kinderman and Snell [15].

According to the definition above, an MRF is characterized by the

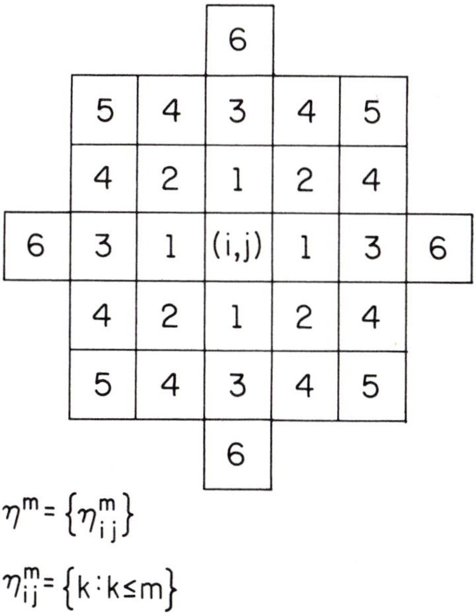

$$\eta^m = \left\{\eta^m_{ij}\right\}$$

$$\eta^m_{ij} = \left\{k : k \leq m\right\}$$

*Figure 11.1 - Hierarchially arranged neighborhood systems $\eta_m$.*

conditional distributions in (11.6) called the *local characteristics* of the random field. This characterization is intuitively appealing, because in most image processing applications, it is natural to expect that the image value at a pixel does not depend on the image data outside its neighborhood, when the image data on its neighborhood are given. It does not constitute a theoretical restriction either, because all random fields satisfy (11.6) with respect to a large enough neighborhood system, e.g., $\eta_{ij} = L$ for all $(i,j) \in L$. On the other hand, as it will be shown in the following sections, MRF models even with respect to small neighborhood systems such as $\eta^2$ prove to be very flexible and powerful. Moreover, the positivity condition (11.5) in the definition of an MRF does not pose a significant restriction.

Despite the intuitive appeal of the MRF definition there are inherent difficulties in dealing with the local characteristics (conditional distributions). Some of these difficulties are described below:

1. *Consistency difficulties.* The local characteristics may not uniquely and consistently define a random field (a joint distribution).

2. *Unavailability of the joint distribution.* The joint distribution is not readily obtainable from the local characteristics.

3. *Lack of causality.* There is no unique or preferred direction of causality in two-dimensional random processes.

4. *Processing difficulties.* The lack of causality and the inaccessibility of the joint distribution causes difficulties in processing the image data.

These difficulties, which do not exist in the case of one-dimensional Markov processes, impose severe limitations in the use of MRFs in two-dimensional signal processing. Fortunately, the newly discovered link between MRFs and GDs alleviates these difficulties and makes MRF models more accessible as a tool in image processing. In the next section we present the basic definition for GDs and the result that relates GDs to MRFs.

### 11.3 Gibbs Distributions

Consider the finite rectangular lattice-neighborhood system structure described in the preceding section. To define the GD, it is first necessary to define the "cliques" associated with $(L, \eta)$, a lattice-neighborhood system pair.

*Definition* 3. A "clique" of the pair $(L, \eta)$, denoted by $c$, is a subset of $L$ such that

(a) $c$ consists of a single pixel, or

(b) for $(i,j) \neq (k,l), (i,j) \in c$ and $(k,l) \in c$ implies that $(i,j) \in \eta_{kl}$.

The collection of all cliques of $(L, \eta)$ is denoted by $C(L, \eta)$. For convenience the arguments of $C(L, \eta)$ is dropped below.

The clique types associated with the first-order and the second order neighborhood systems $\eta^1$ and $\eta^2$ are shown in Figure 11.2.

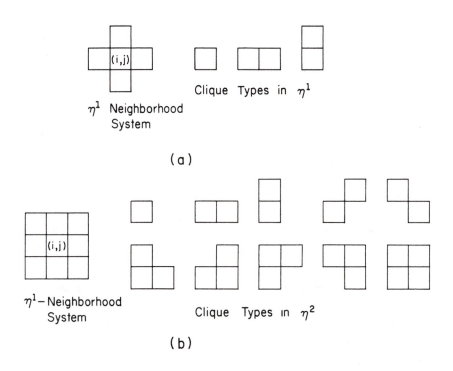

$\eta^1$ Neighborhood System

Clique Types in $\eta^1$

(a)

$\eta^1$-Neighborhood System

Clique Types in $\eta^2$

(b)

*Figure 11.2 Neighborhood systems $\eta^1$ and $\eta^2$, and their associated clique types.*

We now define GD or equivalently Gibbs random field (GRF).

*Definition* 4: Let $\eta$ be a neighborhood system defined over a finite lattice $L$. A random field $X = \{X_{ij}\}$ defined on $L$ is a *Gibbs random field* (GRF) (or a random field having a *Gibbs distribution*) with respect to the neighborhood system $\eta$ if and only if its joint distribution is of the form

$$P(X = x) = \frac{1}{Z} e^{-U(x)} \tag{11.7}$$

where

$$U(x) = \sum_{c \in C} V_c(x) \tag{11.8}$$

$\triangleq$ energy function

$$V_c(x) \triangleq \text{potential associated with clique } c \tag{11.9}$$

$$Z = \sum_x e^{-U(x)} \tag{11.10}$$

$\triangleq$ partition function

The partition function $Z$ is simply a normalizing constant so that the sum of the probabilities of all realizations is unity. The only condition on the otherwise totally arbitrary *clique potential* $V_c(x)$ is that it depends only on the pixel value in clique $c$.

As mentioned previously, the origins of GDs lie in the physics and statistical mechanics literature [9,10,18]. Ising [9], first, used a special GD for a binary, nearest-neighbor system, now known as the Ising model, to describe the magnetic properties of ferromagnets. GDs are also used in lattice gas models in statistical mechanics [10]. The fact that GDs originated in physical sciences is evident from the terminology used.

The joint distribution expression in (11.7) has the physical interpretation that the smaller $U(x)$, the energy of the realization $x$ is, the more likely that realization is [i.e., larger $P(X = x)$]. Frequently, a GD is defined such that the exponent in the joint distribution is expressed as $-(1/T) U'(x)$, where $T$ is called the "temperature" and $U'(x)$ is the energy function. The physical interpretation is that when $T$ is large, the distribution $P(X = x)$ is more widespread. In other words, when the system is "hot," a great many realizations are highly probable. In this chapter, we lump the temperature parameter $T$ together with the energy function $U'(x)$ and consider $U(x)$ as the energy function.

A separate temperature parameter $T$ is particularly useful when it is desired to reach to (or to determine) a low-energy state (or high-probability configuration) by a state-transition mechanism starting from an arbitrary initial state. During this process the temperature $T$ is slowly decreased, a procedure called "annealing," so that the distribution becomes more peaked and convergence to a low energy (or high probability) state is assured. If $T$ is decreased too fast, the system is locked into a local minimum energy (or maximum probability) state and the global minimum energy state is never reached. The rate at which temperature $T$ can be decreased is called the "annealing schedule" and it is an important and difficult problem in statistical physics. Geman and Geman [20] have presented an image segmentation and restoration algorithm based on some type of relaxation (a suitable state-transition mechanism) and an annealing schedule. With this relaxation-annealing procedure, starting from the noisy and degraded image they seek to reach a state (image estimate) that maximizes the *a posteriori* distribution of the uncorrupted image. But due to the fact that the theoretically allowed annealing schedule is extremely slow, the state reached in a reasonable length of computation time is an approximation of the maximum *a posteriori* estimate. A few alternatives for the state-transition mechanisms that takes a Gibbsian system to lower-energy states is discussed in the following sections.

The GD is basically an exponential distribution. However, by choosing the clique potential function, $V_c(x)$, properly, a wide variety of distributions both for discrete and continuous random fields can be formulated as GDs. We consider certain classes of GDs in the following sections. For a detailed account of various other types of GDs, we refer the reader to Besag [12].

The source of revived interest in GD, especially in the context of image modeling and processing, is an important result which establishes a one-to-one correspondence between MRFs and GDs. We now state this result. For a proof, see [12,15].

*Theorem* 1: Let $\eta$ be a neighborhood system defined on finite lattice $L$. A random field $X = \{X_{ij}\}$ is a Markov random field with respect to $\eta$ if and only if its joint distribution is a Gibbs distribution with cliques associated with $\eta$.

It follows from this theorem that the local characteristics of the MRF are readily obtained from the joint distribution in (11.7) as

$$P\left(X_{ij} = x_{ij} | X_{kl} = x_{kl}, (k,l) \neq (i,j)\right) = \frac{e^{-\sum\limits_{c \in C} V_c(x)}}{\sum\limits_{x_{ij}} e^{-\sum\limits_{c \in C} V_c(x)}}$$

$$= P(X_{ij} = x_{ij} | X_{kl} = x_{kl}, (k,l) \in \eta_{ij}) \qquad (11.11)$$

The summation in (11.11) is over the range space of the random variable $X_{ij}$. Due to cancellations, the local characteristics given in (11.11) reduce to a simple expression involving $x_{ij}$ and $x_{kl}$'s for $(k,l) \in \eta_{ij}$.

This significant result constitutes a breakthrough of a sort in making MRF models readily accessible in two- or higher-dimensional signal modeling. The difficulties inherent in the MRF formulation mentioned in the preceding section are mostly overcome by using the GD characterization of MRF's. More specifically, making use of the GD equivalence, the following are achieved:

1.  The joint distribution of the random field is readily expressed.

2.  Local characteristics are easily obtained from the joint distribution and concerns regarding consistency are eliminated.

3.  Besides the intuitive appeal of the MRF models, GD models allow for a physical interpretation.

4.  GD models are parsimonious; in most cases they are characterized by a few parameters only.

5.  Availability of the joint distribution in product form, one factor for each clique, allows for a causal processing of the image. Specifically, cliques and/or neighborhoods can be processed in any order.

### 11.4 Markov Mesh Random Fields

In this section we present some properties of MRFs that are relevant to image processing applications and discuss a special class of MRFs, called Markov mesh random fields (MMRF). The following is a result that follows from the MRF-GD equivalence.

*Theorem* 2: The joint distribution of a MRF on a finite rectangular lattice $L$ with neighborhood systems $\eta^1$ or $\eta^2$ can be expressed as

$$P(X=x) = \prod_{(i,j)\in L} \rho_{ij}(x_{ij}, x_{i-1,j}, x_{i-1,j-1}, x_{i,j-1}) \qquad (11.12)$$

with necessary adjustments for $i = 0$ or $j = 0$ or both. The $\rho_{ij}$'s in (11.12) are unspecified functions.

This result simply follows from rearranging (11.7) in such a way that for each $(i,j)$ certain cliques are grouped together to yield $\rho_{ij}(x_{ij}, x_{i-1,j}, x_{i-1,j-1}, x_{i,j-1})$. The partition function $Z$ is also factored and one factor combined with each $\rho_{ij}$. Note that $\rho_{ij}$'s in (11.12) are not uniquely specified. Different groupings of the set of all cliques will result in different $\rho_{ij}$'s. Actual calculation of a set of $\rho_{ij}$'s for which (11.12) will hold may be extremely difficult due to the necessary normalization. Fortunately, however, computation of $\rho_{ij}$'s is not necessary. The important point is that such a representation for $P(X = x)$ exists. For a special class of MRFs, however, $\rho_{ij}$'s in (11.12) are obtained in terms of causal conditional distributions.

The following results, which find applications in image processing, are implied by the product expansion in (12).

*Theorem* 3: For $X = \{X_{ij}\}$ an MRF on a finite rectangular lattice $L$ with neighborhood systems $\eta^1$ or $\eta^2$,

(a) $P(X_a = x_a, \ a \in A \,|\, X_b = x_b, \ b \in B)$

$$= P(X_a = x_a, \ a \in A \,|\, X_b = x_b, \ b \in \delta B) \qquad (11.13)$$

where $A$ and $B$ are any two disjoint subsets of $L$ and $\delta B$ is the subset of $B$ consisting of the pixels neighboring $B'$ (' denotes complement).

(b) The columns (and rows) of the random field $X$ constitute a vector Markov chain.

Proof for part (a) of Theorem 3 is obtained by forming the conditional distribution in the LHS of (11.13) and using the product expansion of (11.12) for the joint distribution. Part (b), on the other hand, is simply a special case of part (a), where $A$ is a column (or row), $B$ is all the previous columns (rows) and $\delta B$ is the column (row) closest to $A$. Both the general case and the special case are illustrated in Figure 11.3. It should be noted that Theorem 3 can be extended to the case of larger neighborhood systems, in which case $\delta B$

would be a thicker boundary of $B$ and the Markov chain would be a higher-order one.

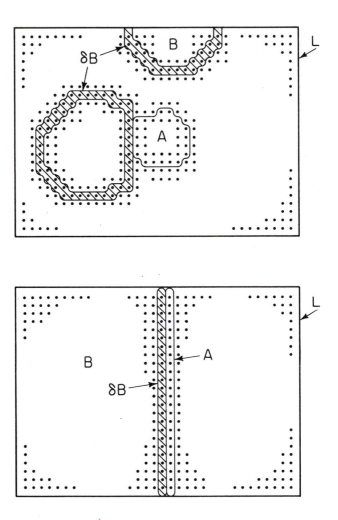

*Figure 11.3 Subsets of L that are used in Theorem 3.*

We now present the definition and some relevant properties of Markov mesh random fields (MMRF), a special class of MRFs first introduced by Abend *et al.* [4] and later by Kanal [23]. MMRF is a class of MRF which has a causal and unilateral characterization, and therefore is potentially useful in image processing (see Derin *et al.* [8]).

*Definition* 5:   A random field $X = \{X_{ij}\}$ defined over a finite rectangular lattice $L$ is a *Markov mesh random field* if for each $(i,j) \in L$ it satisfies

$$P(X_{ij} = x_{ij}|X_a = x_a, \ a \in A_{ij})$$
$$= P(X_{ij} = x_{ij}|X_a = x_a, \ a \in C_{ij}) \qquad (11.14)$$

where

$$A_{ij} = \{(k,l){\in}L : k < i \text{ or } l < j\} \qquad (11.15)$$

and $C_{ij}$ is a subset of $B_{ij}$ which is defined as

$$B_{ij} = \{(k,l) \in L : k \le i \text{ and } l \le j, \ (k,l) \ne (i,j)\} \qquad (11.16)$$

The sets $A_{ij}$ and $B_{ij}$ are shown in Figure 11.4a. The sets $C_{ij}$'s are totally arbitrary except for the condition that $C_{ij}$ has to be a subset of the corresponding $B_{ij}$. The type of $C_{ij}$ sets determines the particular type of MMRF.

The following are some properties of MMRF that are first reported in [4]. Their proof follows from the definition of MMRFs given in (11.14), (see [4]).

*Theorem* 4:   An MMRF defined as above satisfies the following properties:

(a) $P(X{=}x) = \displaystyle\prod_{(i,j){\in}L} P(X_{ij} = x_{ij}|X_a = x_a, \ a \in C_{ij}) \qquad (11.17)$

(b) Corresponding to any choice of $\{C_{ij}\}$, there is a family of subsets of $L$, $\{D_{ij}\}$ such that

$$P(X_{ij} = x_{ij}|X_a = x_a, \ a \in L, \ a \ne (i,j))$$
$$= P(X_{ij} = x_{ij}|X_a = x_a, \ a \in D_{ij}) \qquad (11.18)$$

Moreover, the $\{D_{ij}\}$ family constitutes a neighborhood system according to

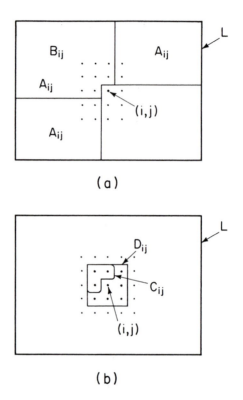

(a)

(b)

*Figure 11.4 Subsets of L describing a MMRF.*

Definition 1.

(c) MMRF $X$ is an MRF with respect to neighborhood system $\{D_{ij}\}$.

Proof for part (c) simply follows from part (b), which in turn is implied by part (a).

The neighborhood system $\{D_{ij}\}$ corresponding to a particular choice of $\{C_{ij}\}$ is determined using (11.17). Of particular interest is the case in which

$$C_{ij} = \{(i-1,j),(i-1,j-1),(i,j-1)\} \tag{11.19}$$

The corresponding $\{D_{ij}\}$ is the eight-neighbor system, $\eta^2$. For this choice of $\{C_{ij}\}$, the joint distribution expression in (11.17) for the MMRF is in the form of joint distribution expression in (11.12). So

$$P(X_{ij} = x_{ij} | X_{i-1,j} = x_{i-1,j}, \ X_{i-1,j-1} = x_{i-1,j-1}, \ X_{i,j-1} = x_{i,j-1}) \tag{11.20}$$

is one possible choice for $\rho_{ij}(x_{ij}, x_{i-1,j}, x_{i-1,j-1}, x_{i,j-1})$, for an MMRF with $\{C_{ij}\}$ given in (11.19). The $C_{ij}$ given in (11.19) and the corresponding neighborhood $D_{ij}$ are shown in Figure 11.4b. For other choices of $\{C_{ij}\}$'s and corresponding $\{D_{ij}\}$'s, we refer the reader to [4] and [23].

We finally point out the following interesting properties of MMRFs.

*Theorem 5:* For $X = \{X_{ij}\}$ an MRF on a finite rectangular lattice $L$ with neighborhood system $\eta^1$ or $\eta^2$,

(a) The expansion in (11.17) is also a sufficient condition for $X$ to be an MMRF.

(b) If the $\rho_{ij}(x_{ij}, x_{i-1,j}, x_{i-1,j-1}, x_{i,j-1})$'s in the expansion (11.12) are such that

$$\int \rho_{ij}(x_{ij}, x_{i-1,j}, x_{i-1,j-1}, x_{i,j-1}) \ dx_{ij} = 1 \tag{11.21}$$

for each $(i,j) \in L$, then

$$P(X_{ij} = x_{ij} | X_{i-1,j} = x_{i-1,j}, \ X_{i-1,j-1} = x_{i-1,j-1}, \ X_{i,j-1} = x_{i,j-1})$$
$$= \rho_{ij}(x_{ij}, x_{i-1,j}, x_{i-1,j-1}, x_{i,j-1}) \tag{11.22}$$

(c) It follows from (a) and (b) that if $\rho_{ij}$ in the expansion (11.12) satisfies (11.21), then $X$ is an MMRF.

Proofs of these results follow simply from the definitions and appropriate conditional distribution formulations. Statement and proof of (b) are due to Cristi (private communication).

The utility of the MMRF model stems from its causal characterization given in (11.14) and also in the expansion of (11.17). In addition, these models can be readily simulated and they constitute a wide subclass of MRFs.

On the other hand, due to the directional characterization, specifying the conditional distributions in (11.20) in accordance with certain image characteristics is not a simple task.

## 11.5 A Class of Gibbs Distribution

The class of Gibbs distributions as defined in Definition 4 is a very wide class of exponential distributions. Below, we briefly mention some special classes of GD which have found applications in image processing or have been cited in the relevant literature. We then present a new class of GDs, which we found to be very useful in image-processing applications. In our extensive experimentations, we saw that this class of GDs is suitable for modeling a wide variety of textures as well as blob-like regions in images, which we call "high-level" modeling. Finally, we present several realizations from this class of GDs and briefly discuss the known methods for obtaining realizations from MRFs or GDs.

In the hierarchical scheme of neighborhood systems discussed in Section 11.3, second order $\eta^2$ or larger neighborhood systems have cliques consisting of more than two pixels (see Figure 11.2 for cliques of $\eta^2$). But it is also possible that the potential functions $V_c(x)$ for certain clique types are specified to be 0, in which case these potential terms do not appear in the exponent of the joint distribution. A special class of GDs, called *auto-models*, are defined as GDs with only "single-pixel cliques" and "pair-cliques" (cliques with two pixels) being nonzero, irrespective of the order of the neighborhood system. The energy function for auto-model GDs have the form

$$U(x) = \sum_{a \in L} G_a(x_a) + \sum_{\substack{a,b \in L \\ a \in \eta_b}} G_{ab}(x_a, x_b) \tag{11.23}$$

where $G_a(\cdot)$ and $G_{ab}(\cdot, \cdot)$ are arbitrary functions. For a detailed exposition on auto-models, we refer the reader to Besag [12].

Depending on the choice for $G_a(\cdot)$ and $G_{ab}(\cdot, \cdot)$ functions, there are several known subclasses of auto-models [12]. Some of these are:

1. *Auto-logistic*: If the random field $X$ is also binary (each r.v. of the field is a $0-1$ r.v.), then the energy function in (11.23) takes the form

$$U(x) = \sum_{a \in L} \alpha_a x_a + \sum_{\substack{a,b \in L \\ a \in \eta_b}} \beta_{ab} x_a x_b \qquad (11.24)$$

Auto-logistic models have been used by Flinn [11], Hassner and Sklansky [16], and Cohen and Cooper [19] in statistical physics and image-processing applications.

2. *Auto-normal*: If the set of r.v.'s that constitute the random field $X$ is jointly Gaussian distributed, it is easily seen that the quadratic in the exponent of their joint distribution is indeed of the form given in (11.23). So *a Gaussian random field is necessarily an auto-Gibbs random field.* Auto-normal models have been investigated by Moran [24] and used by Cohen and Cooper [19] and by Chellappa and Chatterjee [25] for texture modeling. In using auto-normal models, the critical point, which is usually overlooked, is to make sure that the clique parameters are specified in such a way that the inverse of the matrix in the quadratic is positive definite, so that the joint distribution to be, is a valid multivariate Gaussian distribution.

3. *Auto-binomial*: First introduced by Besag [12], the auto-binomial distribution is defined such that each r.v. in the random field is conditionally binomially distributed with probability of success $\theta$ and number of tries $M-1$, where $\theta$ is a parameter determined by the neighbors of the r.v. in consideration and $M$ is the number of values each r.v. can take. Auto-binomial distributions are used by Cross and Jain [17] as texture models.

4. *Auto-Poisson*: The auto-Poisson distribution introduced by Besag [12] is defined such that each r.v. is conditionally Poisson distributed with parameters depending on the neighbors of that r.v.

5. *Auto-exponential*: The auto-exponential distribution is also defined by Besag [12] such that each r.v. is conditionally negative-exponential distributed with parameters depending on the neighbors of that r.v.

We now present another class of auto-model GDs which is suitable for image-processing applications. Our extensive experimentations indicate that this class of GDs is very versatile and powerful even with first- or second-order neighborhood systems. We specify this special class of GDs in terms of the potential function; therefore, we are not concerned with the consistency problems encountered in conditional distribution characterizations.

Although the model is valid for continuous valued random fields, for convenience, we focus our attention on discrete random fields. More specifically, we assume that each r.v. $X_a$ takes a finite number of values; without loss of generality, say, $\{0,1,\ldots,M-1\}$. We now specify the single-pixel and pair clique potentials [as in (11.23)] for this class as follows:

$$G_a(x_a) = \alpha_m \quad \text{if } x_a = m, \; \forall \; a \in L \tag{11.25}$$

$$G_{ab}(x_a,x_b) = \beta_{ab}|x_a - x_b|^r \quad \text{if } x_a = m, \; x_b = n \tag{11.26}$$

for all $a,b \in L$ such that $a \in \eta_b$. The parameter $r$ is a nonnegative number and it specifies a particular subclass of distributions. We have generated realizations of these distributions for values $r = 0$, $0.5$, $1.0$, and $2.0$. For $r = 0$ we assume that $|x_a - x_b|^r = 0$ if $x_a = x_b$.

The potential functions of (11.25) and (11.26) for the $r = 0$ case can be expressed equivalently in terms of a different but related set of parameters as

$$G_a(x_a) = \gamma_m \quad \text{if } x_a = m, \; \forall \; a \in L \tag{11.27}$$

$$G_{ab}(x_a,x_b) = \begin{cases} +\delta_{ab} & \text{if } x_a \neq x_b \\ -\delta_{ab} & \text{if } x_a = x_b \end{cases} \tag{11.28}$$

for all $a,b \in L$ such that $a \in \eta_b$. The parameters $\{\alpha_m\}$ and $\{\gamma_m\}$ serve as the "external field" for the spatial interaction system and they determine the relative numbers of values of $\{0,1,\ldots,M-1\}$ in the image. The controlling mechanism, however, is intricate and equal $\alpha_m$'s (or equal $\gamma_m$'s) do not necessarily imply uniform distribution of the $M$ gray levels.

The spatial interaction (bonding strength) parameters $\{\beta_{ab}\}$ or $\{\delta_{ab}\}$ serve as a measure of the reward (or the penalty) for the alikeness of $x_a$ and $x_b$. The larger the magnitude of these parameters are, the more severe the rewards (or the penalties) become. The sign of the parameters determine whether it is a reward or a penalty. The parameter $r$ in (11.26) is another variable that controls the relative magnitude of the reward (or the penalty) with respect to $|x_a - x_b|$, the separation between the two pixel values $x_a$ and $x_b$. The $r = 0$ case corresponds to a "color-blind" situation, where the reward (or the penalty) is independent of the magnitude of $|x_a - x_b|$ as long as $|x_a - x_b| \neq 0$. This characteristic is easily observed in realizations obtained for the $r = 0$ case. For large values of $r$, even for $r = 2$, the rewards (or the penalties) become more severe as $|x_a - x_b|$ increases. Therefore, in realizations for $r \geq 2$, when the parameter are such that alikeness is favored, the image data are formed in such a way that transitions between gray levels are smooth. For the most part, gray-level transitions occur between adjacent gray levels. This effect, too, can be observed in realizations obtained for the $r = 2$ case.

A simplifying assumption on this class of GDs would be to assume that the random field is homogeneous. This would imply that the bonding-strength parameters $\beta_{ab}$'s depend only on the clique type pixels $a$ and $b$ form, but not on the absolute positions of $a$ and $b$ in the lattice. Thus, if there are $K$ types of pair cliques associated with the neighborhood system (e.g., $K = 2$ for $\eta^1$ and $K = 4$ for $\eta^2$), we can denote the bonding-strength parameters as $\{\beta_1, \beta_2, \ldots, \beta_K\}$ and replace each $\beta_{ab}$ in (11.26) by the corresponding $\beta_k$. A similar argument holds for the parameters $\{\delta_{ab}\}$ for the $r = 0$ subclass of GDs. Note that while setting the external field parameters $\{\alpha_m\}$ and $\{\gamma_m\}$ as in (11.25) and (11.27), we have already assumed homogeneity. Under more general assumptions, it is possible that these parameters, too, can depend on the position of pixel $a$ in the image.

We generated realizations of this class of GD for different parameter values. We assumed four gray levels $\{0, 1, 2, 3\}$, i.e., $M = 4$, and $\eta^2$, the eight-neighbor, as the neighborhood system. For the neighborhood system $\eta^2$, there are four types of pair cliques: horizontal, vertical, diagonal-45°, and diagonal-135° and the corresponding bonding strength parameters being $\beta_1$, $\beta_2$, $\beta_3$, $\beta_4$, respectively. Diagonal-45° is the diagonal that makes 45° with the horizontal axis, and diagonal-135° makes 135° with the horizontal axis. There is also the external field parameters $\alpha_0$, $\alpha_1$, $\alpha_2$, $\alpha_3$ corresponding to the four gray levels $\{0, 1, 2, 3\}$ to be specified. So $r$ determines the subclass and the parameters $\{\alpha_0, \alpha_1, \alpha_2, \alpha_3, \beta_1, \beta_2, \beta_3, \beta_4\}$ determine the particular distribution. For the case of $r = 0$, equivalently the parameters $\{\gamma_0, \gamma_1, \gamma_2, \gamma_3, \delta_1, \delta_2, \delta_3, \delta_4\}$ need to be specified, where $\delta_i$'s correspond to the same pair-clique types described above.

We present here several realizations from the subclass $r = 0$ (Figures 11.5 to 11.10) and from the subclass $r = 2$ (Figures 11.11 to 11.14). We specified the parameters to create various visual effects and different textural features. Each figure consists of four different $64\times64$ realizations: $a,b,c,d$, arranged in clockwise manner with $a$ being the upper left quadrant. In each figure we focused on one feature (e.g., blobby, stripes, diagonal, maze-like, and blocks) and by strengthening the parameters we caused the feature under consideration to be more pronounced. In most cases, we observe that the realization and hence the distribution is very sensitive to the parameters. In some cases, we had to introduce unequal $\alpha_i$ or $\gamma_i$ parameters to obtain relatively uniform distribution of the gray levels. The parameter values corresponding to the figures presented are given in Tables 11.1 and 11.2, corresponding to the $r = 0$ and $r = 2$ realizations, respectively.

What is presented here are only a few representative realizations. In our opinion, many other visual effects or textural features can be modeled or generated by this class of GDs. However, even the few realizations presented here indicate that the model used is extremely flexible and powerful to be used in image processing, even with the relatively small neighborhood system $\eta^2$.

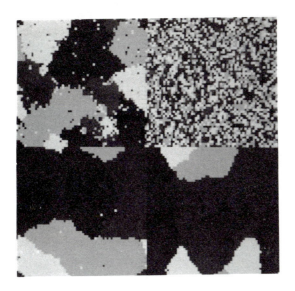

*Figure 11.5 Realizations from a GD (r = 0,64×64,50 iterations; for parameters see Table 11.1).*

*Figure 11.6 Realizations from a GD (r = 0,64×64,50 iterations; for parameters see Table 11.1).*

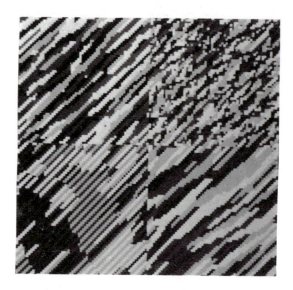

*Figure 11.7 Realizations from a GD* ($r$ = $0,64\times64,50$ iterations; for parameters see Table 11.1).

*Figure 11.8 Realizations from a GD* ($r$ = $0,64\times64,50$ iterations; for parameters see Table 11.1).

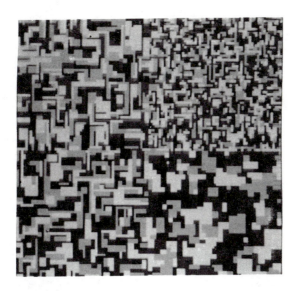

*Figure 11.9 Realizations from a GD ($r$ = 0,64×64,50 iterations; for parameters see Table 11.1).*

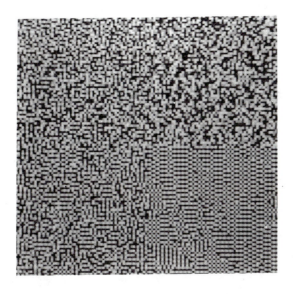

*Figure 11.10 Realizations from a GD ($r$ = 0,64×64,50 iterations; for parameters see Table 11.1).*

*Figure 11.11 Realizations from a GD (r = 2,64×64,50 iterations; for parameters see Table 11.2).*

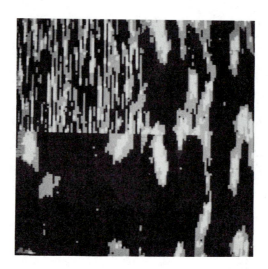

*Figure 11.12 Realizations from a GD (r = 2,64×64,50 iterations; for parameters see Table 11.2).*

- 291 -

*Figure 11.13 Realizations from a GD* ($r = 2,64\times64,50$ iterations; for parameters see Table 11.2).

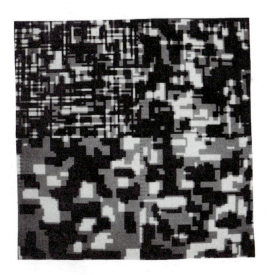

*Figure 11.14 Realizations from a GD* ($r = 2,64\times64,50$ iterations; for parameters see Table 11.2).

Table 11.1

*Parameters For Realizations From GDs With r = 0*

$(\gamma_i = 1.0, i = 0,1,2,3)$

| Figure | Part | $\delta_1$ | $\delta_2$ | $\delta_3$ | $\delta_4$ |
|--------|------|------|------|------|------|
| 5 | a | 0.1 | 0.1 | 0.1 | 0.1 |
|   | b | 0.3 | 0.3 | 0.3 | 0.3 |
|   | c | 0.5 | 0.5 | 0.5 | 0.5 |
|   | d | 0.7 | 0.7 | 0.7 | 0.7 |
| 6 | a | 0.2 | -0.2 | -0.2 | -0.2 |
|   | b | 0.5 | -0.5 | -0.5 | -0.5 |
|   | c | 1.0 | -1.0 | -1.0 | -1.0 |
|   | d | 5.0 | -5.0 | -5.0 | -5.0 |
| 7 | a | 0.5 | 0.5 | 0.5 | -0.5 |
|   | b | 1.0 | 1.0 | 1.0 | -1.0 |
|   | c | 1.0 | 1.0 | 5.0 | -5.0 |
|   | d | 5.0 | 5.0 | 5.0 | -5.0 |
| 8 | a | 0.5 | 0.5 | -0.5 | -0.5 |
|   | b | 1.0 | 1.0 | -1.0 | -1.0 |
|   | c | 5.0 | 5.0 | -5.0 | -5.0 |
|   | d | 5.0 | 5.0 | -10.0 | -10.0 |
| 9 | a | 1.0 | 1.0 | -0.5 | -0.5 |
|   | b | 2.0 | 2.0 | -1.0 | -1.0 |
|   | c | 4.0 | 4.0 | -2.0 | -2.0 |
|   | d | 5.0 | 5.0 | -1.0 | -1.0 |
| 10 | a | -0.1 | -0.1 | -0.1 | -0.1 |
|    | b | -0.5 | -0.5 | -0.5 | -0.5 |
|    | c | -1.0 | -1.0 | -1.0 | -1.0 |
|    | d | -5.0 | -5.0 | -5.0 | -5.0 |

- 293 -

Table 11.2

*Parameters For Realizations From GDs With* $r = 2$

| Figure | Part | $\alpha_0$ | $\alpha_1$ | $\alpha_2$ | $\alpha_3$ | $\beta_1$ | $\beta_2$ | $\beta_3$ | $\beta_4$ |
|--------|------|-----|-----|-----|------|-----|-----|------|------|
| 11 | a | 0 | 0 | 0 | 0 | 0.5 | 0.5 | 0.5 | 0.5 |
| | b | 0.4 | 0 | 0 | 0.4 | 0.5 | 0.5 | 0.5 | 0.5 |
| | c | 0.45 | 0 | 0 | 0.45 | 0.5 | 0.5 | 0.5 | 0.5 |
| | d | 0.5 | 0 | 0 | 0.5 | 0.5 | 0.5 | 0.5 | 0.5 |
| 12 | a | 0 | 0 | 0 | 0 | 0 | 2.0 | 0 | 0 |
| | b | 0.3 | 0 | 0 | 0.4 | 0.1 | 2.0 | 0.1 | 0.1 |
| | c | 0.4 | 0 | 0 | 0.4 | 0.1 | 2.0 | 0.1 | 0.1 |
| | d | 0.6 | 0 | 0 | 0.6 | 0.5 | 2.0 | 0.1 | 0.1 |
| 13 | a | 0 | 0 | 0 | 0 | 0.3 | 0.3 | 0.3 | -0.3 |
| | b | 0 | 0 | 0 | 0 | 0.5 | 0.5 | 0.5 | -0.5 |
| | c | 0 | 0 | 0 | 0 | 0.8 | 0.8 | 0.5 | -0.5 |
| | d | 0.2 | 0 | 0 | 0.2 | 1.0 | 1.0 | 0.7 | -0.7 |
| 14 | a | 0.48 | 0 | 0 | 0.24 | 4.0 | 4.0 | -2 | -2 |
| | b | 0.8 | 0 | 0 | 0.6 | 4.0 | 4.0 | -1.9 | -1.9 |
| | c | 1.1 | 0 | 0 | 0.9 | 4.0 | 4.0 | -1.8 | -1.8 |
| | d | 2.0 | 0 | 0 | 1.7 | 4.0 | 4.0 | -1.5 | -1.5 |

So far, we have not discussed how these realizations from this class of GDs are generated. Basically there are two well-known methods of generating realizations from MRFs or GDs. They are the "exchange"-type and the "spin-flip"-type algorithms. In the exchange-type algorithm, also known as the Metropolis algorithm [18], two pixels are chosen at random. Their values are exchanged if they are different and if the exchange will take the system to a more probable (lower-energy) configuration. If the new configuration is less probable, the exchange will or will not take place depending on the comparison of the ratio of the probabilities of the new and the old configurations with a random number uniform on [0,1]. The randomization is necessary to ensure that the system does not get stuck in a local high probability configuration.

The ratio of the probabilities of the new and the old configurations are calculated easily due to the GD formulation, without actually determining either of the probabilities, which would be extremely difficult.

It is well known that this algorithm will converge to a configuration that maximizes the joint probability, but the rate of convergence is a difficult problem of statistical physics and a completely satisfactory solution to this problem does not exist. As would be expected, the initial configuration does not influence the convergence properties of the algorithm. It might only take a few more iterations to converge for certain initial configurations as compared to others. The Metropolis algorithm has been used by Cross and Jain [17] in generating textures using MRF models. A major drawback of the Metropolis algorithm is that the number of pixels in each gray level does not change during iterations of the algorithm, due to the fact that new configurations are generated simply by exchanging two pixel values. This, in our opinion, is a severe limitation because it implies that an effective external field control cannot be exercised in the Metropolis algorithm. We, therefore, chose to use the second method for generating realizations from a MRF (or GD).

The second set of algorithms for generating realizations from an MRF (or GD) are known as "spin-flip" algorithms. Recently a version of this algorithm is presented by Geman and Geman [20] in an image-processing context. This algorithm, which they called the "Gibbs sampler," works as follows. A pixel is chosen at random or in a deterministic manner. The value of the pixel is renewed by disregarding its present value, noting the values in its neighborhood $\eta_{ij}$ and replacing the pixel value by a random number generated according to the conditional distribution $P(x_{ij}|x_{kl}, (k,l) \in \eta_{ij})$ specified by the MRF (or GD). The pixel visiting mechanism can be random or deterministic, such as raster scan, the important point being that each pixel should be visited infinitely often as the algorithm proceeds *ad infinitum*. This algorithm has the characteristics of a relaxation algorithm in image processing; therefore, it is also called *stochastic relaxation* [20]. The rate of convergence, in this algorithm also, is an important and difficult problem. For a treatment of the convergence issues we refer the reader to [20].

In obtaining realizations for the class of GDs proposed in this paper we used the Gibbs sampler spin-flip algorithm in a raster scan fashion. One complete scan of the image is considered as one iteration. In each realization we ran the algorithm for 50 iterations. We did not carry out a sophisticated convergence test. We observed the realization after 20, 30, 50, and 100 iterations and saw that beyond 50 iterations the visual features of the image did not change appreciably. So we carried out the algorithm for 50 iterations in all the other realizations. In obtaining the realizations presented in this paper, we used the Computer Vision facilities of the Department of Computer and Information Sciences at the University of Massachusetts, Amherst, MA. Each $64 \times 64$ realization of 50 iterations took on the order of 3 to 6 minutes of CPU time on a network of VAX-780's and VAX-750's.

## 11.6 Conclusion

In this chapter, we have presented a brief expose on definitions and essential concepts of Markov random fields (MRF) and Gibbs distribution (GD) and also on the equivalence of the two random field models. Our main objective was to review the use of GDs in image processing applications and to make GD models more widely known in the signal processing community. We think, over the coming years, we will witness a dramatic increase in the application of GDs to a wide range of problems.

We have also presented some properties of a subclass of MRFs called Markov mesh random fields, that are pertinent in image processing applications. We have also proposed a new subclass of GDs and demonstrated by several realizations that the class of distributions proposed can be very useful in image modeling. In different realizations we have seen that the class of GD being proposed can be used to model regions in an image that are blob-like or block-like, as well as to model a wide variety of textures. The realizations presented are merely representative and they do not fully demonstrate the power and the potential of GD models or of the particular subclass of GD that is proposed.

Despite the enormous potential of GDs as random field models, there are still some very important and difficult issues related to GD models. One such issue is the problem of parameter estimation in these models. This problem can be described as follows. Assuming a particular distribution which is Gibb-sian and given a realization from that distribution, we would like to estimate the parameters of the distribution. In this chapter, we have not touched on this problem at all. The most commonly known parameter estimation tech-nique is the "coding method" which was first introduced by Besag [12] and used by others [17]. The coding method is basically a maximum likelihood estimation technique that yields estimates that maximize the conditional joint distribution of a subset of the random field conditioned on the rest of the field. It requires the solution of a set of nonlinear equations. Therefore, it is cumbersome and difficult to use reliably.

Many researchers, including the author and co-workers, are studying the parameter estimation problem for GDs. Results on alternative parameter esti-mation methods are just beginning to emerge [26,27]. In [26], Elliott and Derin propose a linear estimation method based on histogramming the image which involves a least-squares solution of a set of linear equations. Early results are promising. Some of the other problems related to GD that require attention are properly choosing the neighborhood systems and the cliques to be considered and properly choosing the particular GD to be used as the model.

## Acknowledgments

I would like to thank Mr. Jinyu Kuang, who diligently prepared the simu-lations used in this chapter and to my colleague Professor Howard Elliott, for his cooperation during the time we carried out this research.

## References

[1]   R. L. Dobrushin, The description of a random field by means of condi-tional probabilities and conditions of its regularity, *Theory Prob. Appl.*, Vol. 13, pp. 197-224, 1968.

[2]   E. Wong, Recursive causal linear filtering for two-dimensional random fields, *IEEE Trans. Inform. Theory*, Vol. IT-24, pp. 50-59, January 1978.

[3]   J. W. Woods, Two-dimensional discrete Markovian fields, *IEEE Trans.*

*Inform. Theory,* Vol. IT-18, pp. 232-240, March 1972.

[4]   K. Abend, T. J. Harley and L. N. Kanal, Classification of binary random patterns, *IEEE Trans. Inform. Theory,* Vol. IT-11, pp. 538-544, October 1965.

[5]   R. Chellappa and R. L. Kashyap, Digital image restoration using spatial interaction models, *IEEE Trans. Acoust. Speech Sig. Proc.,* Vol. ASSP-30, pp. 461-472, June 1982.

[6]   J. W. Woods and C. H. Radewan, Kalman filtering in two-dimensions, *IEEE Trans. Inform. Theory,* Vol. IT-23, pp. 473-482, July 1977.

[7]   F. R. Hansen and H. Elliott, Image segmentation using simple Markov field models, *Comp. Graph. Im. Proc.,* Vol. 20, pp. 101-132, 1982.

[8]   H. Derin, H. Elliott, R. Cristi and D. Geman, Bayes smoothing algorithms for segmentation of images modelled by Markov random fields, *IEEE Trans. Pat. Analy. Mach. Intel.,* Vol. PAMI-6, pp. 707-720, November 1984.

[9]   E. Ising, *Zeitschrift Physik,* Vol. 31, p. 253, 1925.

[10]   D. Ruelle, *Statistical Mechanics,* Benjamin, New York, 1977.

[11]   P. A. Flinn, Monte Carlo calculation of phase separation in a two-dimensional Ising system, *Journ. Statist. Phys.,* Vol. 10, pp. 89-97, 1974.

[12]   J. Besag, Spatial interaction and the statistical analysis of lattice systems, *Journ. Roy. Statist. Soc.,* series B., Vol. 36, pp. 192-226, 1974.

[13]   M. B. Averintzev, On a method of describing discrete parameter random fields, *Problemy Peredacci Informacii,* Vol. 6, pp. 100-109, 1970.

[14]   F. Spitzer, Markov random fields and Gibbs ensembles, *Amer. Math. Mon.,* Vol. 78, pp. 142-154, February 1971.

[15]   R. Kinderman and J. L. Snell, *Markov Random Fields and Their Applications,* Providence, R.I.: American Mathematical Society, 1980.

[16]   M. Hassner and J. Sklansky, The use of Markov random fields as models of texture, *Comput. Graph. Im. Proc.,* Vol. 12, pp. 357-370, 1980.

[17]   G. R. Cross and A. K. Jain, Markov random field texture models,

*IEEE Trans. Pat. Analy. Mach. Intel.*, Vol. PAMI-5, pp. 25-39, January 1983.

[18]  N. Metropolis, A. W. Rosenbluth, M. N. Rosenbluth, A. H. Teller and E. Teller, Equation of state calculations by fast computing machines, *Journ. Chem. Phys., Vol. 21, pp. 1087-1092, June 1953.*

[19]  F. S. Cohen and D. B. Cooper, Real-time textured image segmentation based on non-causal Markovian random field models, *Proc. of SPIE Conf. Intel. Robot.*, Cambridge, MA., November 1983.

[20]  S. Geman and D. Geman, Stochastic relaxation, Gibbs distributions and the Bayesian restoration of images, submitted to *IEEE Trans. Pat. Analy. Mach. Intel.,* September 1983.

[21]  H. Elliott, H. Derin, R. Cristi and D. Geman, Application of the Gibbs distribution to image segmentation, *Proc. 1984 IEEE Int. Conf. on ASSP,* San Diego, CA, March 1984.

[22]  H. Elliott, H. Derin and R. Soucy, Modelling and segmentation of noisy and textured images using Gibbs random field models, Univ. Mass. Tech. Rep., Univerisity of Massachusetts, Amherst, MA, September 1984.

[23]  L. N. Kanal, Markov mesh models, in *Image Modeling,* New York, Academic Press, 1980.

[24]  P. A. P. Moran, A Gaussian Markovian process on a square lattice, *J. Appl. Prob.,* Vol. 10, pp. 54-62, 1973.

[25]  R. Chellappa and S. Chatterjee, Classification of textures using Gaussian Markov random fields, submitted to *IEEE Trans. Acoust. Speech Sig. Proc.*

[26]  H. Elliott and H. Derin, A new approach to parameter estimation for Gibbs random fields, submitted to 1985 Int. Conf. on Acoust. Speech Sig. Proc., August 1984.

[27]  R. Cristi, Analysis of some statistical properties for a class of spatial distributions: The Ising model with random parameters, Tech. Rep. Dept. Elect. Eng., The University of Michigan, Dearborn, May 1984.

# 12

# The Routing Problem in Computer Networks

Anthony Ephremides

*Department of Electrical Engineering*
*University of Maryland*
*College Park, Maryland*

## 12.1 Introduction

Few problems in the field of computer communication networks have received as early and extensive attention as the routing problem. The reason for this is twofold. First there have been numerous studies of flow problems in network theory that provide a basis for modeling the routing problem in a mathematically tractable way and, second, routing has proved to be a necessary and fundamental design choice for the operation of message- or packet-switched networks. In its simplest form the statement of the routing problem is as follows. Consider, as in Figure 12.1, a node that receives messages from an incoming link and has a choice of forwarding them via one of two outgoing links.

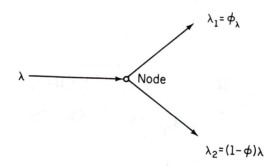

*Figure 12.1 Routing in terms of a simple diagram.*

Let $\lambda$ be the average rate of the arrival message stream. By implementing a specific routing decision the node produces two outgoing streams the average rates of which are $\lambda_1$ and $\lambda_2$. Of course in order to maintain equilibrium and finite delays it is necessary that

$$\lambda_1 + \lambda_2 = \lambda$$

and thus $\lambda_1$ and $\lambda_2$ can be represented as

$$\lambda_1 = \phi\lambda, \qquad \lambda_2 = (1-\phi)\lambda$$

where $0 \le \phi \le 1$. The routing problem consists of choosing $\phi$ to maximize a given performance measure which is usually related to the average delay per message in the network. A variety of constraints usually accompany this optimization problem. A more detailed formulation will follow later. Now we provide an early view of the classification of routing algorithms according to various solution philosophies. These philosophies emerge according to the answers chosen for the following questions:

1.   *How* is $\phi$ chosen (i.e. *by* whom and on the basis of *what* information?)

2.   *How often* is $\phi$ updated?

3.   Are there any limitations in the *range of values* $\phi$ can take?

The first question leads to a distinction between *centralized* and *distributed* routing algorithms. A centralized algorithm defers the choice of the $\phi$-variables across the entire network to a single controller. The controller bases his decisions on global information about conditions everywhere in the network. On the other hand, a fully distributed algorithm requires that each individual node decide the values of his $\phi$-variables without coordinating his decisions with those of other nodes. These decisions are taken on the basis of local information only, that is, on the traffic conditions that are locally measurable by each node or are easily obtainable by means of a few control message exchanges between neighboring nodes. There are of course intermediate approaches that mix centralized and distributed decision making. Such approaches lead to algorithms that are called *hierarchial*. The properties of distributed routing algorithms that are responsible for their popularity include relatively low communication overhead for control message exchanges and superior network survivability in the presence of component failures. On the other hand, distributed algorithms are prone to oscillatory, unstable behavior and to sluggishness of network response when traffic conditions change.

The second question distinguishes *static* from *dynamic* algorithms. A static algorithm implies that the values of the $\phi$-variables are chosen once and for all and stay constant throughout the life cycle of the network's operation. A dynamic algorithm, at the other extreme, chooses for each and every individual message (or packet) the outgoing link. It is clear that for a truly dynamic algorithm it is difficult to define $\phi$ meaningfully. There are again intermediate situations that entail more or less frequent updating of the values of $\phi$. Such algorithms ara called *quasi-static*. They allow the network to operate with constant $\phi$-values for a finite period of time $T$ (small with respect to the network's life cycle) and then proceed to revise these values. It is evident that a purely static algorithm is inappropriate for any real network that anticipates load variations and/or topological changes. On the other hand, purely dynamic routing is difficult to implement without substantially increasing the processing time (and, therefore, total delay) of each message at every node.

Finally, the third question separates *fixed* from *alternate* routing algorithms. It must be pointed out there is some confusion in the literature concerning these terms. Some authors use them to characterize virtual circuit operation and to distinguish that from datagram service or permanent virtual circuits mode. Here we mean something entirely different. A fixed routing algorithm constrains the values of $\phi$ to be either zero or 1 while an alternate routing algorithm allows $\phi$ to take any value in the closed interval [0,1]. The implication is that under a fixed routing regime *all* of the traffic received by a node between two update instants is assigned the same outgoing link, while with an alternate algorithm the message stream is allowed to be *split* between alternate routes. The only reason for considering fixed algorithms is the low implementation cost and the reduction of the message processing time at the node. However, a fixed algorithm permits periodic updating of the values of $\phi$ if it is also a quasi-static algorithm. In fact, for each of the three categories of algortihms described so far an independent choice of algorithm characteristics can be made. Thus we can have static, alternate, centralized algorithms, or quasi-static, fixed, distributed ones, or any other combination from these classes.

In the remainder of this exposé we will keep the foregoing distinctions in mind as we review the various formulations of, and solutions to, the routing problem.

## 12.2 Early Analytical Approaches

Unlike other communication network design problems, such as topological design or error and flow control, the routing problem is amenable to analytical formulation, if certain assumptions are made. We will describe here a few of the most notable analytical approaches.

In [1] the first mathematical model was proposed to accomplish centralized, static, alternate routing. To appreciate the degree of difficulty associated with the analytical treatment of the routing problem, we must emphasize that even though the centralized, static, alternate problem is the least complex of the routing problems, the model proposed in [1] falls short of obtaining a true solution even in the presence of strong, idealized assumptions.

Consider a network of $N$ nodes and $M$ links. Let $r_i(j)$ represent the average rate of exogenous message traffic entering the network at node $i$ and destined for node $j$ for $i,j = 1,2,...,N$. These quantities represent the traffic load matrix. Each entry represents the value of one commodity[1]; that is, each source-destination pair corresponds to a separate commodity. Let $C_i$ represent the capacity of link $i$, $i = 1,2,...,M$ in bits/s.

Assume that the average length of each messsage is $1/\mu$ bits. Suppose that the routing variables are chosen so as to induce traffic of average rate $\lambda_i$ on link $i$, $i = 1,2,...,M$. Obviously, the value of $\lambda_i$ is determined by the $r_i(j)$'s and by the routing variables. If the assumption is made that the link $i$ behaves like an $M|M|1$ queueing system, independently of all other links and with customer arrival rate $\lambda_i$ and service rate $\mu C_i$, then it is possible to express the average delay per message for traversing that link as

$$T_i = \frac{1}{\mu C_i - \lambda_i}$$

for $\lambda_i < \mu C_i$. The preceding assumption is a very strong one and requires some discussion. It was observed early by Kleinrock [2] that packet-switched or, more generally, store-and-forward communication networks can be modeled as queueing networks. Each link can be thought of as an autonomous service system with service time composed of three components: propagation time (which is independent of message length and is negligible for short distances), transmission time (which depends on link capacity and message length), and processing time (often quite small and partly dependent on message length). Messages arriving at a node are stored in a buffer of sufficiently large capacity, so that overflows are rare. Thus each link has all the attributes of a queueing system. Unfortunately, only a very specialized class of interconnected queueing systems is amenable to analysis. This is the class of Jacksonian networks, so termed because of the pioneering study of them by Jackson [3]. Recently, a great deal of attention has been paid to non-Jacksonian networks for the purpose of extending to them the analytical treatment techniques that were successful in the case of Jacksonian networks. A Jacksonian network

---

[1] This is why routing problems are sometimes related to multi-commodity flow problems.

consists of *independent* exponential servers that are interconnected so that a customer may visit several of them in succession. The exogenous customer arrival streams are assumed to be Poisson processes. In order for a communication network to be usefully modeled by a Jacksonian network it is therefore necessary to assume the following:

1. The exogenous message arrival streams are Poisson processes (obviously an inaccurate assumption, but not the real source of error).

2. The service time for each message on each link is exponentially distributed with rate $\mu C_i$ (again, an inaccurate assumption that neglects propagation and the message-length-independent component of processing time, but one that we can tolerate if we fit the statistics of the real service time to those of an exponentially distributed one).

3. The service times at different links for the *same* message are independent.

The last assumption is the truly problematic one since each message retains its length as it traverses successive links. Thus the "service" times it encounters on different links are strongly correlated. Making the crucial *independence* assumption permits the use of Jacksonian models for communication networks. In the brief history of the development of the field of multiuser systems and networks the independence assumption ranks alongside Abramson's Poisson assumption for the ALOHA channel [4] as the most celebrated "poetic-license" type of liberty taken by scientists in the modeling process. For certain types of, so-called "large and balanced" networks, experimental results have shown that the independence assumption can be tolerable if used with care and applied judiciously [5]. In any event, with the independence assumption the routing problem becomes

$$\min_{\{\lambda_i\}} T$$

where

$$T = \sum_{i=1}^{M} \lambda_i \ \frac{1}{\mu C_i - \lambda_i}$$

that is, minimize the weighted total average delay, subject to the constraints $0 \leq \lambda_i < \mu C_i$. The optimization can be carried out by a variety of classical methods since $T$ is a convex function of the $\lambda_i$'s. The flow deviation method (a form of steepest descent algorithm) was used in [1] to produce a set of optimizing link flow rate values. For this reason the approach was called the flow assignment procedure. Note that just by obtaining a set of optimal flows we have not yet solved the routing problem. The next step is to find the values of the routing variables (the $\phi$'s) which, when applied to the given input variables [the $r_i(j)$'s], will produce the desired link flows (the $\lambda_i$'s). It is clear that for certain topologies of the network and for certain regions of values of the input variables it is not possible to realize the $\lambda$-values obtained by solving the minimization problem. In those cases the already complicated mathematical programming problem of matching the inputs to the induced flows by means of the appropriate splitting fractions "$\phi$" becomes an approximation problem in which the objective function becomes not to find exactly, but simply to come "close" to the desired value.

In view of the disheartening results obtained from this first attempt to analyze the routing problem, it can be understood why Gallager's algorithm [6], which appeared in the literature in 1977, was hailed as a major break-through. In that algorithm a solution was obtained for a distributed, alternate, quasi-static routing problem that minimized weighted average delay, which guaranteed the absence of loops and did not explicitly require the independence assumption. Using the notation introduced above and defining the following additional quantities we can briefly state the nature of the algorithm's result. Let

$r_i(j)$ = average rate of exogenous traffic entering at $i$ for $j$ (as before)

$t_i(j)$ = average rate of total traffic entering $i$ for $j$

$\lambda_{ik}$ = average rate of combined traffic of all commodities on link $(i,k)$, i.e., on the link that connects nodes $i$ and $k$ (replacing what was called $\lambda_i$ before); this quantity is zero if there is no link $(i,k)$, and

$\phi_{ik}(j)$ = routing variable of node $i$ for link $(i,k)$ and for commodity (destination) $j$; equivalently, the percentage of the commodity $j$ that node $i$ routes to neighbor $k$ [if there is no link (i,k), then $\phi_{ik} = 0$]

Clearly, the following are true:

$$t_i(j) = r_i(j) + \sum_{k=1}^{N} \phi_{ki}(j)t_k(j), \quad \forall \; i,j$$

$$\lambda_{ik} = \sum_{j=1}^{N} t_i(j)\phi_{ik}(j), \quad \forall \; i,k$$

$$\phi_{ik}(j) \geq 0, \quad \forall \; i,k,j$$

$$\sum_{k=1}^{N} \phi_{ik}(j) = 1, \quad \forall \; i,j$$

Instead of assuming that the average delay $T_{ik}$ per mesage on link $(i,k)$ is given by the $M|M|1$ formula used before, which would be tantamount to making the independence assumption, it is simply assumed that the delay is an increasing, convex function of the link flow $f_{ik}$ only.[2] Then the routing problem becomes

$$\min_{\{\phi's\}} \; T$$

where

$$T = \sum_{i} \sum_{k} f_{ik} T_{ik}$$

that is, minimizing the average weighted total delay as before. So the problem looks like the earlier one except that it attempts minimization directly with respect to the routing variables rather than indirectly by means of the link flows, and that it does not make the independence assumption; that is, it still looks like *static centralized, alternate* routing problem, but in a less restricted framework. It is during the attempt to solve this problem that it became clear that a *distributed quasi-static* implementation of the solution was feasible, thus transforming the algorithm into a distributed, quasi-static, alternate routing

---

[2] It can be argued that this assumption is equivalent to assuming independence because only for a network of interconnected *exponential* servers is it true that the average delay in each stage depends on the average flow in that stage only (and not on the average flows in the other stages). However, Gallager's algorithm has been generalized to allow arbitrary convex increasing dependence of link delay on all the flows [7].

scheme. Convergence of that implementation was shown and a scheme to avoid loops at all stages of the algorithm was incorporated into the solution. A major difficulty that had to be resolved was the nonconvex dependence of the objective function on the routing variables. Another nontrivial complication associated with this algorithm is the need to find an initial feasible and loop-free set of flows by other means. There exist algorithms and methods to achieve this goal, however, and thus it is possible to establish the initial conditions the algorithm needs. The nature of the algorithm is briefly the following. Each node, between periodic updates, measures a local "distance measure" to his neighbors.[3] It then passes to, and receives from, his neighbors information about those measurements. This exchange of information must follow specific rules of order to avoid loops and to guarantee convergence. Then each node alters the previous values of the $\phi_{ik}$'s by appropriate step sizes so that more traffic is sent toward those neighbors that promise less delay, and less traffic is routed via the neighbors that exhibit tardiness. If the rate of change of the input variables is less than the convergence rate of the algorithm, it becomes possible to "track" the "shifting" optimum set of values of the routing variables.

An important drawback of this algorithm is that it cannot be implemented in its pure form because of the difficulty in obtaining well-behaved estimates of the quantities that each node must measure and because of the problems associated with its convergence. Its chief value lies in the fact that it showed how analytical treatment can "drive" the choices of practical routing algorithms, thus making total reliance on heuristics unnecessary. It also inspired subsequent work on routing that eventually led to very practical and robust schemes that can be, and have been, implemented.

It was later shown by Bertsekas [8,9] that Gallager's algorithm can be viewed as as special case of a much more general class of optimization techniques known as projected Newton methods and Goldstein-Levitin-Poljak gradient projection methods. These methods have been adequately described in the

---

[3] This measure was originally the derivative of the link delay with respect to the flow on the link (called the incremental delay); it was subsequently generalized to be an almost arbitrary measure of some sort of delay.

literature but have failed so far to be translated into useful routing algorithms. It is noteworthy that the end-to-end flow control problem which was previously unanalyzed and unmodeled, was reduced to a routing problem in the context of the Gallager-Bertsekas class of models by a simple ingeneous observation explained in [10].

Gallager's work inspired two major contributions to the routing problem that produced usable and useful results. We examine those in detail in the next section.

### 12.3 Fail-Safety and Stability of Distributed Algorithms

As mentioned earlier, from a practical standpoint it is the class of distributed, quasi-static, and fixed algorithms that are preferable for implementation. The reasons are that a *distributed* algorithm involves less overhead due to control traffic and is less vulnerable to failures, a *quasi-static* algorithm has the chance to respond to slow trends and changing conditions in the network, and a *fixed* algorithm is simple to implement and reduces processing time. It was by using such algorithms in the ARPANET[4] in its early stages of development (early and mid-1970s) that the deficiencies of these algorithms were first discovered. Heuristic improvements failed to fully eliminate these deficiencies. It was through an elegant analysis and demonstration by Bertsekas [11] that a solid explanation of the behavior of these algorithms was obtained. Furthermore, some techniques that stemmed from that analysis succeeded in correcting the undesirable features of the algorithm's behavior. The principal potential defect of a routing algorithm which is distributed and quasi-static and which performs all-or-none (fixed) routing is its propensity for instability and oscillation. Oscillation, as such, is not necessarily a defect. It is oscillation between the poorest-performing routing regimes that is undesirable and this is exactly the kind of behavior that such algorithms often displayed. They tended to degenerate toward an oscillation between two or more sets of routing variables, each corresponding to a very poor level of performance.

A graphic illustration of this phenomenon due to Bertsekas is briefly the

---

[4] The first and largest packet switched network in the United States and the world.

following. Consider a simple network as in Figure 12.2.

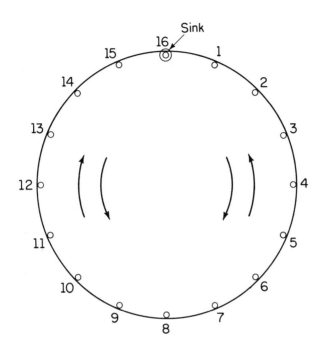

*Figure 12.2 Simple ring network on which fixed, quasi-static, distributed routing induces instability.*

Each link is full duplex with sufficient capacity. The only destination node is node 16. Every other node except the SINK's antipodal one, node 8, receives one unit of flow of exogenous traffic. Average total delay is the performance measure and distributed, quasi-static, fixed routing is to be performed. Each node at every update instant must select either the clockwise or the counter-clockwise route. It can be seen that the optimum solution is the one according to which nodes 1 through 7 route counterclockwise and nodes 9 through 15 route clockwise. If, between updates, node 8 starts receiving an infinitesmal amount of traffic from the outside, regardless of which way he will route it, the following will happen. Within a maximum of three updates all the nodes will be oscillating between all-clockwise and all-counterclockwise routing. It is quite evident that when all nodes route in the same direction, performance is worst.[5]

One method of altering this behavior consists of changing the fundamental characteristics of the algorithm, such as converting it to a centralized one or to an alternate routing algorithm. If, however, these basic features of the routing scheme must be preserved, other cures must be discovered. One of them is called *biasing* and was invented on the basis of heuristic considerations; it was implemented with limited success. Common engineering sense suggests that in every oscillation a sufficient increase of the "friction" or "damping" coefficient will eliminate the periodic response. Thus, if the delay cost in each link is "biased" so that, even if the amount of flow carried by the link is zero, the delay penalty is greater than zero, then a tendency to retard the onset of oscillation is observed. In fact, the larger the bias is, the less likely the occurrence of oscillations becomes. But it is only a matter of degree. Bertsekas showed that for any finite amount of bias,[6] a sufficiently large perturbation of the inputs will again throw the system into an unstable mode.

A method that did prove successful was based on the analysis which was just described and which predicted the oscillatory behavior. Instead of requiring that all nodes perform the updating of their routing variables simultaneously every $T$ seconds, this method interleaves the update instants of the different nodes in a manner that preserves all of the desirable properties of the routing algorithm [namely, its distributed, quasi-static, and all-or-none (fixed) nature] while at the same time avoiding the violent responses that are caused when all nodes update simultaneously. Thus node 1 updates at instants $t_1$, $t_1 + T$, $t_1 + 2T$, etc., node 2 updates at $t_2 = t_1 + T/N$, $t_2 + T$, $t_2 + 2T$, and

---

[5] The same result was verified analytically for arbitrary topologies and for an arbitrary number of destination nodes.

[6] An infinite amount of bias is uniteresting because it will trivially lock the system into stability by making any solution acceptable; obviously, the introduction of an infinite bias (or a finite bias for that matter) results in the minimization of a cost function different from the original one.

so on. This multiplexing of the updating instants allows the effects of each individual node's actions to be taken into account by the other nodes.

A very important consideration in automatic routing is fail-safety. Nodes and, especially, links in real networks are known to fail. In order to implement automatic routing procedures it is necessary to establish provisions for recovery from failure. If the topological design of a network has provided it with some degree of connectivity, then it is possible for the message traffic that was assigned to follow a particular path which includes a broken link to be rerouted to the destination via an alternate path. It is desirable to achieve the discovery of alternate paths in a smooth way that will be transparent to the nodes that are not in the immediate vicinity of the failure. Such a goal had been considered too ambitious and almost unrealizable until Merlin and Segall [12] proposed a very simple distributed protocol that ensures reliability in the presence of failures or other topological changes. The protocol is actually very simple to describe and, like most protocols in computer networks, difficult to prove. Each node is required to maintain a list of two entities associated with each destination of the network. These are the identity of one of his neighboring nodes, which he selects according to some criteria (not necessary to be specified here), and an estimate of the "distance" to the destination node according to a chosen metric. These two entities are supposed to be updated periodically whether there are topological changes or not. To ensure proper distributed updating without loops and deadlocks, the destination node, initiates each update period by communicating a special message to his immediate neighbors. According to a carefully specified set of simple ordering rules that must be adhered to, each node participates in the process of propagating the message (and the updating function that it triggers) through the network. A key, built-in feature of this process is that, after spreading to the peripheral nodes of the network, it bounces back and revisits each node until it returns ultimately to the destination node, thereby completing the update cycle. When there are no topological changes this updating process resembles very much Gallager's routing algorithm and can be used to simply implement a routing scheme that optimizes a performance measure. If failures occur, however, a simple modification of the protocol permits the automatic discovery of alternate paths. The modification consists of requiring the nodes that sense the failure to generate a special message that is sent to the destination and that requests the initiation of an out-of-order update cycle. The destination is then required to initiate such a cycle and to *number* it. By so doing, it ensures that the nodes will not be confused if a new failure occurs while the reaction cycle to an earlier one is still on progress. A simple change in the actions of the nodes during an update cycle ensures the successful discovery of an alternate path.

The Merlin-Segall protocol proved to be a useful idea that motivated many subsequent routing algorithms [13-16] for store-and-forward, as well as for radio, networks. In fact some of the algorithms that will be described in the next section bear a strong similarity to that protocol. In turn, it is clear that the Merlin-Segall algorithm bears a strong resemblence to the loop-free version of Gallager's algorithm, thus showing the continuity that almost always characterizes research.

## 12.4 Practical Algorithms

In Section 12.2 emphasis was placed on the mathematical abstraction of the routing problem. In Section 12.3 some practical considerations were incorporated into the mathematical models showing how an already complex analytical problem becomes more complicated in the transition from the idealized environment to the real world. In this section a brief account is given of the types of approaches to routing that are taken in the actual network design process.

The key to the design of a network is the specification of its architecture. For a large, integrated, self-sufficient, multiuser communication system the term "architecture" is taken to mean the collection of the *functions,* the *structure,* the *links* and the *protocols* that describe the operation of the system. In other words, it must be decided what the network, which will interconnect a given set of users and computers, will do (functions), how these functions will be performed (structure), what direct exchanges of information will be necessary or permitted (links), and what rules of order will be obeyed (protocols). Even for a simple system this task is overwhelming in its scope and complexity. However, it must be done. Networks have been designed and operated without waiting for the theoretical formulation and/or solution of the design problem. In fact, the field of networking stands unique[7] among engineering fields in that practice and application has lead and outpaced theoretical development and support by a wide margin.

The main concerns that have characterized the building of networks have centered around the establishment of a common language to describe the problem areas and to characterize the issues, as well as of technical standards for the interfacing of components and operating systems. Routing, therefore, has been addressed as a small part of the overall architecture. Simplicity was favored over optimality in order to save on overhead of implementation even at the expense of performance.

As various network architectures emerged, a tendency was observed to choose routing algorithms that were fixed, quasi-static, and distributed (as mentioned in the preceding sections) but which selected the entire paths at the originating node rather than allowing the choice of the next neighbor to be visited at every step. For example, *explicit routing,* used in IBM's SNA architecture, requires the specification of the path number in the header of the message to be routed toward a given destination. A fixed total number of paths is prespecified and thus intermediate nodes can infer which is the next node to be visited by reading the message header. The development of the Open System Interconnection (OSI) architecture proposed by the International Standards Organization (ISO) over several years of heated discussions (which often centered on economic and political, rather than technical, considerations) reveals the tendency to assign explicit routes by strongly favoring virtual circuit operation under which, again, entire routes are specified.

At the other extreme there have been cases where, for a variety of reasons, the method of flooding was chosen to implement routing. Flooding is very simple to implement: every node sends a given message to every one of his neighbors regardless of the desired destination. The message will necessarily reach its destination in this manner. It is of course clear that flooding causes many unnecessary transmissions. The question is how to trade-off cost of implementation versus cost of operation and performance. In general this question

---

[7] In the possible company of optical communications

remains unanswered. Over the years, as the theoretical study of the routing problem progressed, its conclusions have been gradually translated to "design wisdom" that has guided the actual design of routing algorithms. Most networks, including the ARPANET, have modified their routing algorithms several times and are still searching for the optimum choice.

## 12.5 The Radio-Network Case

The discussion so far has assumed implicitly that the networks considered are of the store-and-forward type with land-line links. An equally important class of networks consists of the so-called radio networks. The links in these networks are radio-based. The key difference in this case is that a radio link is a multiple access and broadcast channel; that is, an individual node's transmission is subject to interference from the transmissions of other nodes and it can be also received by nodes other than the destination node. These properties of the radio links give new dimensions to the routing problem. Furthermore, in a radio network a node is not necessarily stationary. Mobility of the nodes may induce frequent topological changes that make the routing problem much more difficult and challenging.

In this section we describe two routing algorithms that are designed for a special type of a radio network and we compare several attributes of their performance to those of their chief competitor, flooding. The work reported here is original, although a brief presentation of the results has been made at the Johns Hopkins conference on Information Sciences and Systems [17]. Consider the case of $N$ mobile nodes that wish to remain interconnected via radio links. Suppose that the communication range is variable and cannot cover the entire geographical area of node dispersion. Many factors may account for such circumstances: limited power, interference, variable antenna orientation, node motion, physical objects, etc. In such an environment the first question is how these nodes can organize themselves into a reliable network by means of a distributed algorithm. This question corresponds to the physical layer design according to the OSI architecture model. The second question is how the discovered links can be activated by each node, again in a distributed way, and without interference. This question addresses the multiple access aspect of the radio environment and corresponds to the link layer of the OSI model. These questions can be handled in a variety of ways. In [18-21] some solutions and algorithms are described that can take care of these fundamental issues.

Next comes the question of routing that resides naturally in the third (or network) layer of the OSI architecture. How should a node send a message to a remote destination? Clearly, due to the assumed volatility of the connectivities in the network, it is not possible to employ any of the existing methods of routing. In other words, we cannot assume that a node may know the location of the destination node or his distance from that node. The only exception is flooding which can still be used. It must be noted, however, that in a radio environment flooding has additional disadvantages since it generates unnecessary interfering and bandwidth-consuming traffic. Nevertheless, flooding will ensure the delivery of the message to its destination. The question is at what cost relative to that of other candidate algorithms. Let us consider one alternative.

Suppose that node $i$ wishes to send a message to node $j$. There is no prior knowledge about the location of $j$ nor of his distance from $i$ in terms of any specific distance measure. A natural thing to do is to send a short query to all neighbors of $i$. Instead of uncontrollably flooding this query message farther out, $i$'s neighbors perform the steps of a structured process that is inspired by the Merlin and Segall protocol described in the preceding section. Each neighbor of $i$ passes on the received query to every neighbor of his except to those from which he has already received the query. Furthermore, he does not pass on that query to anyone if he had originated a query about the same destination node himself (and to which query he has not yet received a response). In this manner the query will start propagating in all directions away from the originating node. The first node, who on receipt of the query, finds that he has knowledge of the whereabouts of the destination node currently under search, either because that node is a direct neighbor or because he has already found out by means of a response to an earlier query, immediately generates a response which he transmits to all nodes from which he has received a query about that destination node. Each node who receives a response to a query passes it on to all those neighbors from which he has received queries. In this manner the response propagates back toward the inquiring node in a controlled fashion without unnecessary flooding. Clearly, care must be taken in specifying the precise rules of order in such a process of propagation in order to avoid cycles and deadlocks for any possible relative ordering of the steps of this basically asynchronous process of transmissions and retransmissions of the same query. As in the case of the Merlin-Segall protocol, the procedure described above does avoid cycles and deadlocks and does terminate with the response to the query received by the originating node. It is possible, however, that there will be redundant responses since the response message may propagate along different parallel paths back to the origin.

The reason that a query, rather than the main message itself, is forwarded in this manner to the destination is twofold. First, it is a much shorter message since it consists merely of a flag and of the source-destination identity. Second, and most important, all nodes that participate in this search process gain knowledge of the whereabouts of that particular destination node, thus eliminating the need for future queries of their own should they later desire to send a message to that node themselves. The path actually selected for routing the message after receipt of the response to the query is not important here. It could simply be the one via the neighbor through whom the response was received first, or a selection process can be implemented that is based on some distance measure. It is assumed that an acknowledgment message mechanism exists so that a node can detect a change of connectivities that destroys the previously sought and established path and can reinitiate a query. It is clear that the number of steps involved in a second search will be in general less than in the original one, since nodes with valid existing paths to the destination are likely to be encountered in the close vicinity of the inquiring node.

A simple modification of the algorithm just described may generate additional knowledge about the connectivities in the network at a rather negligible additional overhead cost that may eventually save in total overhead. It was assumed that the query message consisted only of a flag and of the identity of the destination node. Suppose that it is enlarged to include the identity of the inquiring node as well. Furthermore, as an additional option, it may include a field for updating a "distance" value that could be simply the number of "hops". Each intermediate node augments the distance field entry before passing it on (if the distance measure is simply the number of hops, the entry is augmented by one). In this manner, as the query propagates outward, several nodes gain knowledge of the whereabouts of the *source* node, plus that of its distance from them. This information can be stored at each intermediate node for future use. Thus many future queries become unnecessary. As far as the response message is concerned, it, too, may be enlarged to include an entry for distance. Thus, as it propagates back toward the source node, the distance entry is appropriately augmented to provide to all nodes knowledge that can be used to choose among alternate paths. In all other respects the algorithm remains unchanged.

In order to evaluate the performance of these algorithms it was necessary to utilize simulation techniques. It is impossible to analyze mathematically the performance, no matter what idealized assumptions are made, simply because there is strong dependence on topological layouts and on mobility scenarios neither of which can be analytically modeled.

The following performance measures were chosen:

1.  Average delay $=$ (total time for delivery of $n$ packets)/$n$

2.  Overhead $=$ (total number of extra transmissions for delivery of $n$ packets)/$n$ for the flooding algorithm, and $(A_1X_1(n) + A_2X_2(n))/nA$ for the proposed algorithms, where

    $X_1(n) =$ number of query transmissions for delivery of n packets

    $X_2(n) =$ number of reply transmissions for delivery of n packets

    $A_1 =$ number of bits in a query $\Big\rbrace = \Big\lbrace$ 6,   original algorithm
    $A_2 =$ number of bits in a reply $\quad\quad\quad$ 14,   modified algorithm

    $A =$ number of bits in a packet $= 1000$

3.  Maximum memory $=$ the maximum number of items waiting to be processed by any node at any time.

These measures were further parameterized by network topology and by input traffic characteristics. Specifically, networks of $N = 15$ nodes were simulated with either a "path", or a "ring", or a "fully connected", or an "arbitrary" topology. Furthermore, the average rate of originating traffic was varied as a parameter. Finally, the duration of the active period of network operation was also considered as a parameter since the proposed algorithms "learn" the whereabouts of the destination nodes over a period of time, and then, assuming that no topological changes take place, operate without the need of overhead query traffic. Of course, in order to make a fair assessment of the capabilities of the algorithms, it is necessary to consider topological changes or, equivalently, consider the overhead traffic associated with them for a relatively short active period.

In the simulation it was assumed that there were no transmission errors of any sort. Also, queueing delays at the nodes were neglected. Thus the simulated performance study represents, at best, a pilot attempt to assess the potential promise of the proposed algorithms. As the selected curves presented in Figures 12.3a-12.3c show, there is a uniform superiority of the proposed algorithms to the flooding algorithm. Certainly, flooding would probably be the only feasible solution if the rate of topological changes were so high that the responses to the query messages were obsolete. By the same token, an algorithm that learns the full topology of the network once and for all and then proceeds to operate in a manner appropriate for land-line, store-and-forward networks that are not subject to topological changes, would be the best choice for a radio network without rapid node mobility or fluctuation of propagation conditions. It is in the intermediate situations of relatively common, but not overwhelmingly fast, changes that a probing sort of algorithm, such as the ones proposed, might be preferable. Still, it is not known whether other algorithms are better suited to mobile radio networks. The field is wide open and is currently under intense study due to its significance in both commercial and military applications.

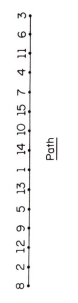

Path

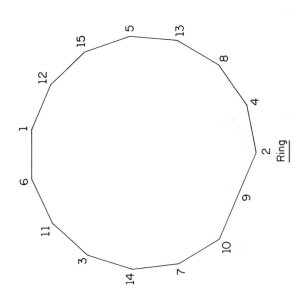

Ring

*Figure 12.3a Topologies of the networks on which the routing algorithms were simulated.*

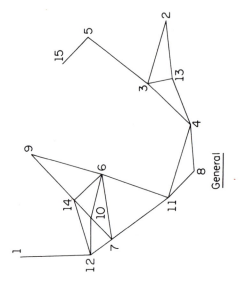

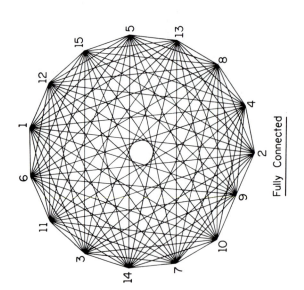

Fully Connected

General

*Figure 12.3a Topologies of the networks on which the routing algorithms were simulated (cont.).*

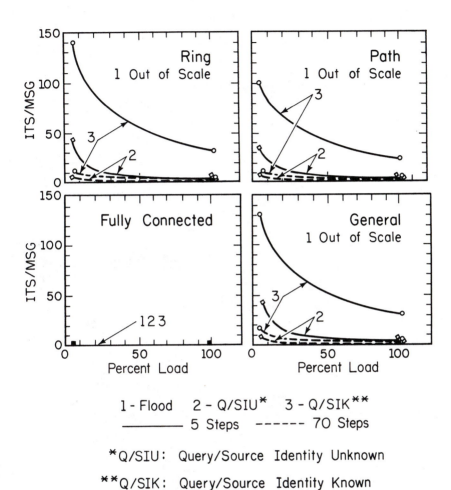

*Figure 12.3b Overhead performance as a function of load, parameterized by duration.*

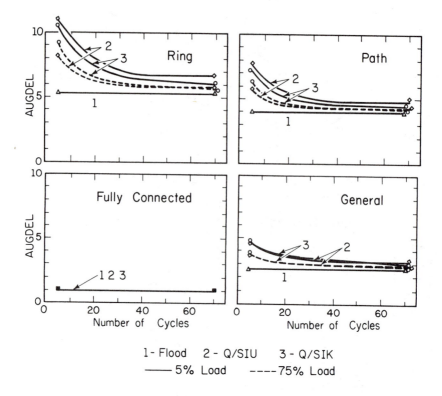

*Figure 12.3c Delay performance as a function of duration, parameterized by load.*

## 12.6 Conclusion

In this brief essay an introduction to the routing problems was presented. The main analytical approaches were surveyed and a commentary on practical aspects of routing schemes permitted a transition to the area of nonanalytical approaches with special emphasis on the case of radio networks. The routing problem is only a small part of the overall design of communication networks. It remains generally unsolved and challenging, even though it has seen more successful solution attempts than any other aspect of networking.

## References

[1]  L. Fratta, M. Gerla and L. Kleinrock, The flow deviation method - an approach to store-and-forward communication network design, *Networks,* Vol. 3, pp. 97-133, 1973.

[2]  L. Kleinrock, *Communication Nets,* New York, NY: McGraw-Hill, 1964.

[3]  J.R. Jackson, Networks of waiting lines, *Operations Research,* Vol. 5, pp. 518-521, 1957.

[4]  N. Abramson, The ALOHA system - another alternative for computer communications, *AFIPS Conference Proceedings,* FJCC 37, pp. 281-285, 1970.

[5]  L. Kleinrock, *Queueing Systems,* Vol. II, New York, NY: Wiley-Interscience, 1976.

[6]  R.G. Gallager, A minimum delay routing algorithm using distributed computation, *IEEE Trans. Comm.,* Vol. COM-25, pp. 73-85, 1977.

[7]  A. Ephremides, Extension of an adaptive distributed routing algorithm to mixed media networks, *IEEE Trans. Comm.,* Vol. COM-26, pp. 1262-1266, 1978.

[8]  D.P. Bertsekas, A class of optimal routing algorithms for communication networks, *Proc. 5th Intl. Conf. Comp. Comm.,* pp. 71-76, 1980.

[9]  D.P. Bertsekas, Projected Newton methods for optimization problems with simple constraints, *SIAM Jour. Cont. Opt.,* Vol. 20, pp. 221-246, 1982.

- 324 -

[10]  R.G. Gallager and S.J. Golestaani, Flow control and routing algorithms for data networks, *Proc. 5th Intl. Conf. Comp. Comm.*, pp. 779-784, 1980.

[11]  D. Bertsekas, Dynamic behavior of shortest path routing algorithms for communication networks, *IEEE Trans. on Auto. Cont.*, Vol. AC-27, pp. 60-74, 1982.

[12]  P. Merlin and A. Segall, A failsafe distributed routing protocol, *IEEE Trans. Comm.*, Vol. COM-27, pp. 1280-1287, 1979.

[13]  A. Segall and B. Awerbuch, A reliable broadcast protocol, *Proc. of INFOCOM*, pp. 103-107, 1983.

[14]  F. Zerbib and A. Segall, A distributed shortest path protocol, LIDS-P-1102 report, MIT, June, 1981.

[15]  J. Hagouel, Source routing and a distributed algorithm to implement it, *Proc. of INFOCOM*, pp. 115-123, 1983.

[16]  A.E. Baratz and J.M. Jaffe, Establishing virtual circuits in large computer networks, *Proc. of INFOCOM*, pp. 311-318, 1983.

[17]  M. Weber and A. Ephremides, A simulated performance study of some distributed routing algorithms for mobile radio networks, *Proc. Conf. Inform. Sci. Sys.*, Johns Hopkins University, 1983.

[18]  J.E. Wieselthier, D.J. Baker, A. Ephremides and D.N. McGregor, Preliminary system concept for an HF intra-task force communication network, NRL Report 8637, 1983.

[19]  D.J. Baker and A. Ephremides, The architectural organization of a mobile radio network via a distributed algorithm, *IEEE Trans. Comm.*, Vol. COM-29, pp. 1694-1701, 1981.

[20]  D.J Baker, A. Ephremides and J.E. Wieselthier, A distributed algorithm for scheduling the activation of links in a self-organizing, mobile, radio network, *Proc. of the ICC*, Philadelphia, PA, June, 1982.

[21]  A. Ephremides, Distributed protocols for mobile radio networks, *Proc. of NATO Advanced Study Institute on the Impact of Processing Techniques to Communications*, Chateau Bonas, France, July, 1983.

# 13

# Theoretical Analysis of Slotted ALOHA, CSMA, and CSMA-CD Protocols

**Yih-Chyun Jenq**

*Techtronix Applied Research Laboratories*
*Beaverton, Oregon*

## 13.1 Introduction

During the past ten years, the development of random access methods in the packet-switching (broadcasting) multi-user communications environment has been an active research topic [1-11]. A typical system consists of many users trying to send packets to a central station through a common channel. The original research began with the ALOHA scheme, where each individual user can access the channel whenever he has packets to be transmitted; if more than one user is attempting to transmit at the same time, packets collide and have to be retransmitted at a later time. This scheme is simple; no coordination among users is required . However, the maximum achievable channel utilization is only about 18 percent. Therefore, researchers have been trying to improve the channel utilization. One improvement is to synchronize all users so that the partial overlapping of colliding packets is eliminated and the maximum achievable channel utilization is raised to about 37 percent. This synchronous scheme is called slotted ALOHA. The next improvement is trying to avoid packet collision by enabling a user to "sense" the channel. When a user has a packet to transmit, he first listens to the channel. If the channel is sensed idle, the packet is transmitted. If, on the other hand, the channel is sensed busy, the packet transmission is delayed to a later time. In this way the chance of packet collision is greatly reduced. This scheme is called the carrier sense multiple access (CSMA) scheme. In a CSMA scheme, packet collisions can still happen. Since a user can listen to the channel, he knows if he has collided with the others. If a packet collision occurs, it is reasonable to abort the transmission before it is completed. In this way the collision-time duration can be shortened and the channel utilization can be further improved. This scheme is called CSMA with collision detection (CSMA-CD).

Besides the channel utilization, the stability of these schemes has also been investigated extensively. Various retransmission control methods have also been proposed to stabilize the system. The dynamic behavior of these systems is typically demonstrated through numerical examples or simulations. In this chapter we use a systematic theoretical approach to study the dynamic properties of slotted ALOHA, CSMA, and CSMA-CD schemes. Models of the three protocols are described in Section 13.2. In Section 13.3 we derive channel utilization functions in a simple and systematic way. In Section 13.4 we prove that all three protocols have the same stability property, namely, the system can only have either one stable equilibrium point or three equilibrium points with the first one and the third one stable and the second one unstable. We also derive some system properties which can be used to help in selecting proper retransmission probabilities to achieve a desirable system performance objective (such as eliminating bistability). Conclusions are given in Section 13.5.

## 13.2 Models

### 13.2.1 Slotted ALOHA

Consider a slotted time axis as shown in Figure 13.1.

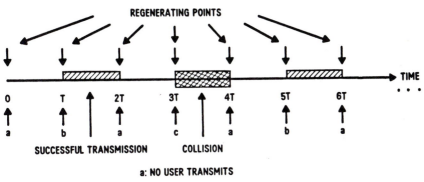

Figure 13.1 Slotted ALOHA protocol.

The slot time is the same as the packet time $T$, which is the time it takes to finish transmitting a packet. Users start transmission only at the beginning of a slot (i.e., the system is clocked). At the beginning of each slot, each user is either in the origination mode or in the retransmission mode. A user is in the retransmission mode if he has a collided packet waiting for retransmission. Otherwise, a user is in the origination mode. In our slotted ALOHA model, a user in the origination mode will try a slot with probability $p_0$, while a user in the retransmission mode will try a slot with probability $p_r$.

We assume that there are $N$ users in the system. Let $x(t), t = 0, T, 2T, \ldots$, be the number of users in the retransmission mode at the time instant $t$. The quantity $x(t)$ can assume one of the $(N+1)$ possible values $\{0, 1, 2, \ldots, N\}$, and is considered as the state variable of the system. Because of the memoryless assumption, the process is a finite-state Markov chain.

## 13.2.2 CSMA

We now consider a slotted time axis as shown in Figure 13.2.

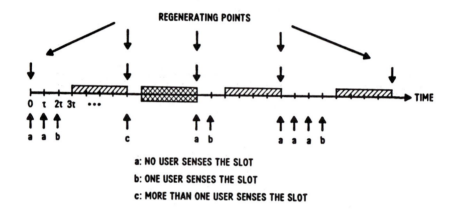

*Figure 13.2 CSMA protocol.*

The slot time $\tau$ is the time it takes to finish sensing a slot. If a user senses that the channel is idle, he transmits a packet at the beginning of the next slot (i.e., he transmits immediately after he finishes sensing an idle channel). If a user senses a busy channel, he will sense the next slot with certain probability. At the beginning of each slot, each user, similar to slotted ALOHA, is either in the origination mode or in the retransmission mode. If the last slot sensed by a user was busy, he is in the retransmission mode. Otherwise, the user is in the origination mode. A user is in the origination mode immediately after completing a successful transmission and a user is in the retransmission mode immediately after a collision.

In our CSMA model, a user in the origination mode will sense a slot with probability $q_0$, while a user in the retransmision mode will sense a slot with probability $q_r$. A user in the process of transmitting a packet does not sense the channel. It takes $1/a$ slots to finish transmitting a packet, i.e., $\tau = aT$, and there are $N$ users in the system. It is not difficult to see that those time instants when the transmission of a packet is just completed (either a success or a collision) form a set of regenerating points. Suppose that $t_i, i = 1, 2, \ldots$, are those regenerating points, and let $y(t_i)$ be the number of users in the retransmission mode at time $t_i$; then $y(t_i)$ is a finite-state Markov chain with state space $\{0, 1, 2, \ldots, N\}$. It is noted that the $(t_{i+1} - t_i)$'s no longer have a constant value $T$ as in the slotted ALOHA case where $t_i = iT$.

### 13.2.3 CSMA-CD

The model of CSMA-CD is the same as CSMA except that when a user finds that his packet has collided with the other packets, he aborts the transmission. We assume that it takes $a'/a$ slots for a user to recognize a collision and abort the transmission. A typical histogram is shown in Figure 13.3.

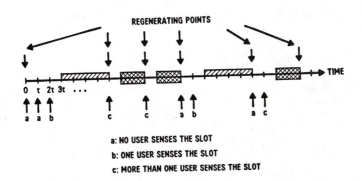

*Figure 13.3 CSMA-CD protocol*

Again, it is easy to see that $x(t_i)$ is a Markov chain, where $x(t_i)$ is the number of users in the retransmission mode at time instant $t_i$.

The origination probabilities $p_0$ and $q_0$ are usually determined by users' behavior. The quantity $p_0$ can be considered as the probability that a user would generate a new packet in a slot of duration $T$ (packet time) and $q_0$ can be considered the probability that a user would generate a new packet in a sensing slot time $\tau$. It is easy to see that for CSMA and CSMA-CD to be efficient, we must have $T \gg \tau$, hence we can expect $q_0 \ll p_0$. The quantities $p_r$ and $q_r$ can be controlled by the system designer. They should be carefully selected to achieve high utilization and stability.

## 13.3 Channel Utilization and Packet Delay

A general approach to calculate the channel utilizations and packet delays of the three protocols described in the preceding section is as follows. First, a sequence of time instants where the state of the system (i.e., the number of users in the retransmission mode) forms a Markov chain is determined. These time instants are the regenerating points as mentioned in the preceding section (see Figures 13.1 to 13.3). The cycle length is defined as the interval between consecutive regenerating points. Next, the channel utilization $u(n)$ conditioned on the state $n$, $n = 0,1,...,N$, is determined. The channel utilization $\bar{u}$ is given by

$$\bar{u} = \sum_{i=1}^{N} u(i)\pi(i),$$

where $\Pi = [\pi(0), \pi(1),...,\pi(N)]$ is the stationary probability distribution function of the system state. In principle, $\Pi$ can be obtained by solving the equation $\Pi = \Pi P$, $\sum_{i=1}^{N} \pi(i) = 1$, where $P$ is the transition probability matrix of the Markov chain. The mean delay $\bar{D}$ is, by Little's law, given by $\frac{1}{\bar{u}} \sum_{i=1}^{N} \pi(i)i$.

The performance of these protocols will be investigated by analyzing the conditional channel utilization $u(n)$. Channel utilization (sometimes called channel throughput) is defined as the percentage of time when the channel is utilized effectively. Ineffective time is when either the channel is unattempted and therefore goes unused, or is attempted by more than one user at the same time and therefore results in a collision.

To find the conditional channel utilization, we examine the cycles (time duration between two successive regenerating points) which begin with the system at state $n$. Then we derive the expected value of the cycle length. Since there is exactly one transmission (either a success or a collision) in one cycle, the expected length of effective time in a cycle is simply the probability that exactly one user tries in that cycle conditioned that there was at least one trial multiplied by the packet transmission time $T = \tau/a$. The channel utilization is simply the ratio of the expected length of the effective time to the expected cycle length. We now examine the performance of the three protocols individually.

### 13.3.1 Slotted ALOHA

In this case the cycle length is a constant $T$ and the expected length of the effective time is

$$[(N-n)p_0(1-p_0)^{N-n-1}(1-p_r)^n + np_r(1-p_r)^{n-1}(1-p_0)^{N-n}]T.$$

Therefore, the conditional channel utilization is

$$u_{s-ALOHA}(n) = (N-n)p_0(1-p_0)^{N-n-1}(1-p_r)^n$$
$$+ np_r(1-p_r)^{n-1}(1-p_0)^{N-n}. \qquad (13.1)$$

For the case with large user population, i.e., for large $N$, equation (13.1) can be approximated as follows. We let $\lambda_0 = Np_0$ and $\lambda_r = Np_r$ be constants and take the limit of (13.1) by allowing $N$ to go to infinity. Thus we have

$$u_{s-ALOHA}(\nu) = \lambda(\nu)e^{-\lambda(\nu)} \qquad (13.2)$$

where $\nu = n/N$ and

$$\lambda(\nu) = \lambda_0(1-\nu) + \lambda_r\nu. \qquad (13.3)$$

Equations (13.2) and (13.3) have an intuitively appealing explanation. The quantity $\lambda_0(1-\nu) = (N-n)p_0$ is the channel traffic intensity due to users in the origination mode and $\lambda_r \nu = n p_r$ is the traffic intensity due to users in the retransmission mode. Therefore, $\lambda(\nu) = \lambda_0(1-\nu) + \lambda_r \nu$ is the total traffic intensity. Equation (13.2) simply says that the channel traffic is approximated by a Poisson process with intensity $\lambda(\nu)$. We will see later that this approximation also applies to CSMA and CSMA-CD.

### 13.3.2 CSMA

From Figure 13.2 we see that a cycle for CSMA consists of a few contiguous idle sensing slots and a sensed slot followed by a transmission slot. Hence the expected length of a cycle is

$$\frac{(1-q_0)^{N-n}(1-q_r)^n}{1 - (1-q_0)^{N-n}(1-q_r)^n} \tau + \tau + T \qquad (13.4)$$

The expected length of the effective time in a cycle conditioned on state $n$ is the probability that exactly one user tries given that there was at least one trial multiplied by $T$, i.e.,

$$\frac{[(N-n)q_0(1-q_0)^{N-n-1}(1-q_r)^n + nq_r(1-q_r)^{n-1}(1-q_0)^{N-n}] \cdot T}{[1 - (1-q_0)^{N-n}(1-q_r)^n]}$$

$$(13.5)$$

Hence, by dividing expressions (13.5) by (13.4), we have the conditional channel utilization

$$u_{CSMA}(n) =$$

$$\frac{(N-n)q_0(1-q_0)^{N-n-1}(1-q_r)^n + nq_r(1-q_r)^{n-1}(1-q_0)^{N-n}}{1 - (1-q_0)^{N-n}(1-q_r)^n + a} \qquad (13.6)$$

Using the same limiting process as in slotted ALOHA, (13.4) through (13.6) can be approximated, for large $N$, by the following three expressions, (13.7) through (13.9), respectively.

$$\frac{e^{-\gamma(\nu)}}{1 - e^{-\gamma(\nu)}} \tau + \tau + T, \qquad (13.7)$$

$$\frac{\gamma(\nu)e^{-\gamma(\nu)}}{1 - e^{-\gamma(\nu)}}T, \qquad (13.8)$$

and

$$u_{CSMA}(\nu) = \frac{\gamma(\nu)e^{-\gamma(\nu)}}{1 - e^{-\gamma(\nu)} + a}, \qquad (13.9)$$

where

$$\gamma(\nu) = \gamma_0(1-\nu) + \gamma_r\nu \qquad (13.10)$$

and

$$\gamma_0 = Nq_0, \quad \gamma_r = Nq_r, \quad \nu = n/N$$

### 13.3.3 CSMA-CD

The CSMA-CD case is different from CSMA only in the expected length of a cycle. A collision results in a transmission length $a'\tau/a$, while a successful transmission lasts $T = \tau/a$. Hence the expected length of a cycle is

$$\frac{Q_0}{1 - Q_0}\tau + \tau + \left[\frac{Q_1}{1 - Q_0}(\tau/a) + \frac{1 - Q_0 - Q_1}{1 - Q_0}(a'\tau/a)\right] \qquad (13.11)$$

where

$$Q_0 = (1-q_0)^{N-n}(1-q_r)^n$$

and

$$Q_1 = (N-n)q_0(1-q_0)^{N-n-1}(1-q_r)^n + nq_r(1-q_r)^{n-1}(1-q_0)^{N-n}.$$

From (13.5) and (13.11), we have

$$u_{CSMA-CD}(n) = \frac{Q_1}{a + a'(1-Q_0-Q_1) + Q_1} \qquad (13.12)$$

Similarly to the previous cases, equation (13.12) can be approximated for large $N$ by

$$u_{CSMA-CD}(\nu) = \frac{\gamma(\nu)e^{-\gamma(\nu)}}{a + a'(1-e^{-\gamma(\nu)}-\gamma(\nu)e^{-\gamma(\nu)}) + \gamma(\nu)e^{-\gamma(\nu)}} \qquad (13.13)$$

Notice that if $a' = 1$, (13.13) is reduced to (13.9), as it should be. For comparison, we plot (13.2), (13.9), and (13.13) in Figures 13.4 and 13.5 with different parameters $a$ and $a'$.

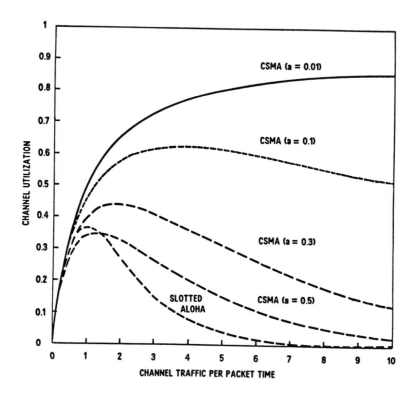

*Figure 13.4 Channel utilization of slotted ALOHA and CSMA.*

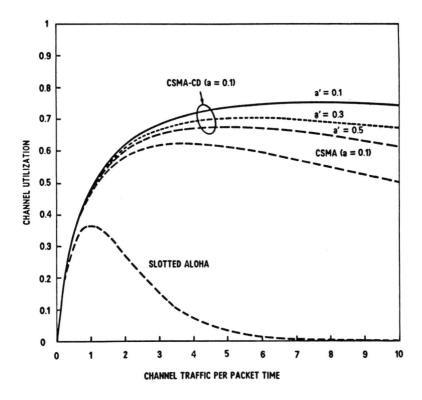

*Figure 13.5 Channel utilization of CSMA-CD*

Equation (13.2) was first obtained by Roberts [1], (13.9) was derived by Klein-rock and Tobagi [9], and (13.13) was derived by Tobagi and Hunt [11], all using an infinite population model and Poisson assumption of the channel traffic. (We use a finite population model.)

## 13.4 Stability and Retransmission Control

In the preceding section we derived the channel utilization as a function of channel traffic intensity, which is, in turn, a function of the system state $n$ (or $\nu = n/N$). However, given a system configuration $(N, p_0, p_r)$ or $(N, q_0, q_r)$, we are unable to determine the average utilization of the system without explicitly computing the probability distribution function $\{\pi(n), n = 0, 1, \ldots, N\}$. In this section we use the principle of flow balance to study the dynamics of these channel access protocols. We will be able to estimate mean channel throughput and packet delay without going through extensive computations. We also examine the stability and retransmission control problems.

The basic idea of the flow balance principle is as follows [3-5,7,8]. Suppose that the system is at state $n$, and let $PF_{in}(n)$ and $PF_{out}(n)$ be, respectively, the mean number of new packets flowing into the system (packets generated by users in the origination mode) and the mean number of packets flowing out of the system (successfuly transmitted packets) in a cycle. If $PF_{in}(n) > PF_{out}(n)$, then the system tends to drift to a higher ($>n$) state. If $PF_{in}(n) < PF_{out}(n)$, then the system tends to drift to a lower ($<n$) state. If $PF_{in}(n) = PF_{out}(n)$, then the state $n$ is an equilibrium state. An equilibrium state can be either stable or unstable. If a small perturbation tends to drive the system away from an equilibrium state, that state is an unstable equilibrium state. Otherwise, that equilibrium state is stable. If a system has only one stable equilibrium point, say $n^*$, then the system tends to stay at that state for a long period of time. Therefore, it is reasonable to use $PF_{in}(n^*) = PF_{out}(n^*)$ as a first-order approximation to the mean channel utilization (throughput) $\bar{u}$, and to use $n^*/PF_{in}(n^*)$ as an appoximation for packet delay $\bar{D}$.

Carleial and Hellman [3] introduced the concept of expected drift in their study of the finite population slotted ALOHA model. Jenq [7] proved that the expected drift $d(n)$ is equal to $PF_{in}(n) - PF_{out}(n)$. Hence the two approaches are equivalent.

The stability and dynamic properties of the slotted ALOHA protocol have been established by Jenq [7,8] using a finite population model. For the sake of completeness, those results are reestablished here in a somewhat simpler way.

*13.4.1 Slotted ALOHA*

For slotted ALOHA, $PF_{in}(n)$ and $PF_{out}(n)$ are given, respectively, by

$$PF_{in,s-ALOHA}(n) = (N-n)p_0 \qquad (13.14)$$

and

$$PF_{out,s-ALOHA}(n) = (N-n)p_0(1-p_0)^{N-n-1}(1-p_r)^n$$
$$+ np_r(1-p_r)^{n-1}(1-p_0)^{N-n} \qquad (13.15)$$

Using the Poisson approximation, we have

$$PF_{in,s-ALOHA}(\nu) = \lambda_0(1-\nu), \quad 0 \leq \nu \leq 1 \qquad (13.16)$$

and

$$PF_{out,s-ALOHA}(\nu) = \lambda(\nu)e^{-\lambda(\nu)}, \quad 0 \leq \nu \leq 1 \qquad (13.17)$$

where $\lambda(\nu) = \lambda_0(1-\nu) + \lambda_r\nu$. From (13.16) and (13.17) we observe:

1. $PF_{in,s-ALOHA}(0) = \lambda_0 > \lambda_0 e^{-\lambda_0} = PF_{out,s-ALOHA}(0)$ for $\lambda_0 > 0$.

2. $PF_{in,s-ALOHA}(1) = 0 < \lambda_r e^{-\lambda_r} = PF_{out,s-ALOHA}(1)$ for $\lambda_r > 0$.

3. Let $f(x) = xe^{-x}$; then $f(x)$ is concave for $0 \leq x \leq 2$, convex for $x > 2$, and assumes its maximum value $f(1) = e^{-1}$ at $x = 1$.

4. If $\lambda_r$ is a constant independent of $\nu$, then $PF_{out,s-ALOHA}(\nu)$ is simply a segment of the function $f(x) = xe^{-x}$, $\lambda_0 \leq x \leq \lambda_r$. Therefore, it should have one of the following three possible shapes: (a) concave, (b) convex, and (c) concave first and then convex.

From (1) and (2), we conclude that the number of equilibrium points is odd. From (4) and the fact that $\lambda_0(1-\nu)$ is a straight line we conclude that the slotted ALOHA system can have either one stable equilibrium point or three equilibrium points with the first and the third points stable and the second point unstable. The latter case is the well-known bistable phenomenon of the ALOHA protocol. It is also clear from these observations how one can properly select $\lambda_r$ to avoid bistability and adjust the system performance. If $\lambda_r$ can be made a function of state $\nu$ (or equivalently $n$), then the optimal choice is $\lambda_r = [1 - (1-\nu)\lambda_0]/\nu$ which maintains $\lambda(\nu)$ to be 1– the point which maximizes the packet outflow $PF_{out,s-ALOHA}(\nu) = \lambda(\nu)e^{-\lambda(\nu)}$. More detailed discussion and more examples can be found in [7,8]. A typical numerical example is given in Figure 13.6.

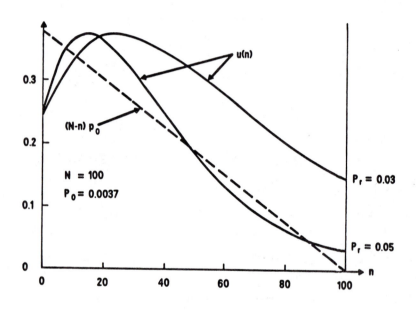

*Figure 13.6 Stable and bistable behavior of slotted ALOHA*

In this example ($N = 100$ and $p_0 = 0.0037$), if $p_r$ is 0.05, we have a bistable system; if $p_r$ is reduced to 0.03, we have a stable system with fairly small backlog.

## 13.4.2 CSMA

The expected number of output packets in a cycle for CSMA is the probability that exactly one user senses a slot given that there is at least one trial:

$$PF_{out,CSMA}(n) = [(N-n)q_0(1-q_0)^{N-n-1}(1-q_r)^n$$
$$+ nq_r(1-q_r)^{n-1}(1-q_0)^{N-n}]/[1 - (1-q_0)^{N-n}(1-q_r)^n] \quad (13.18)$$

Using a large population (Poisson) approximation, (13.18) becomes

$$PF_{out,CSMA}(\nu) = \frac{\gamma(\nu)e^{-\gamma(\nu)}}{1 - e^{-\gamma(\nu)}}, \quad 0 \le \nu \le 1 \quad (13.19)$$

where $\gamma(\nu) = \gamma_0(1-\nu) + \gamma_r\nu$. A plot of the function $g(x) = xe^{-x}/(1 - e^{-x})$ is shown in Figure 13.7. It is noted that $g(0) = 1$ and $g(x)$ is a decreasing and convex function of $x$. Since $PF_{out,CSMA}(\nu)$ is just a segment of the function $g(x)$, $\gamma_0 \le x \le \gamma_r$, it is also a decreasing and convex function of $\nu$.

The expected number of input packets in a cycle is (see Appendix A for derivation)

$$PF_{in,CSMA}(n) = (N-n)[1 - (1-q_0)^{1/a}]$$
$$+ \frac{(N-n)q_0(1-q_0)^{1/a}}{1 - (1-q_0)^{N-n}(1-q_r)^n} \quad (13.20)$$

Again, with a large population approximation, (13.20) becomes

$$PF_{in,CSMA}(\nu) = \gamma_0(1-\nu)/a + \frac{\gamma_0(1-\nu)(1-q_0)^{1/a}}{1 - e^{-\gamma(\nu)}}, \quad 0 \le \nu \le 1 \quad (13.21)$$

where $\gamma(\nu) = \gamma_0(1-\nu) + \gamma_r\nu$. It is also shown in Appendix A that (a) $PF_{in,CSMA}(\nu)$ is a convex function of $\nu$. (b) $PF_{in,CSMA}(0) > PF_{out,CSMA}(0)$; and (c) $PF_{in,CSMA}(1) = 0 < PF_{out,CSMA}(1)$. From these results and the fact that $PF_{out,CSMA}(\nu)$ is convex, we conclude that CSMA has exactly the same stability property as slotted ALOHA. A numerical example is shown in Figure 13.8 to illustrate three possible solutions: (1) one desirable (low delay and high throughput) stable equilibrium point, (2) bistable situation, and (3) one undesirable (high delay and low throughput) stable equilibrium point.

Another property of $PF_{in,CSMA}(\nu)$ is useful for the system designer. From (13.21), we have

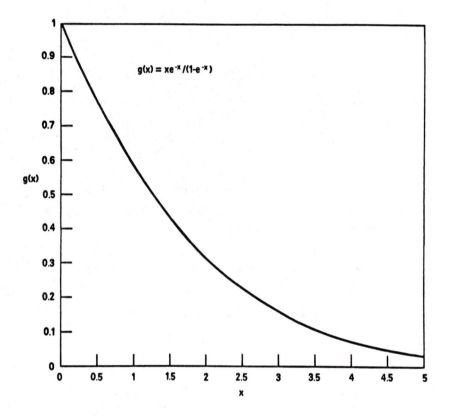

*Figure 13.7 Expected packet outflow PF$_{out}$ of CSMA and CSMA-CD.*

$$PF_{in,CSMA}(\nu) = (1-\nu)[\gamma_0/a + \frac{\gamma_0(1-q_0)^{1/a}}{1 - e^{-[\gamma_0(1-\nu) + \gamma_r\nu]}}, \quad 0 \le \nu \le 1 \quad (13.22)$$

For a CSMA system of practical interest (say, with achievable channel utilization > 80 percent), $1/a$ is on the order of about 100. Therefore, as long as $\nu$ is not too close to zero (say, $\nu > 0.1$), $\gamma_0/a$ is much greater than $\gamma_0(1-q_0)^{1/a}/[1 - e^{-\gamma(\nu)}]$, and hence $PF_{in,CSMA}(\nu)$ is approximately a linear function $(1-\nu)\gamma_0/a$ of $\nu$ with slope $-\gamma_0/a$. This fact can be seen in Figure

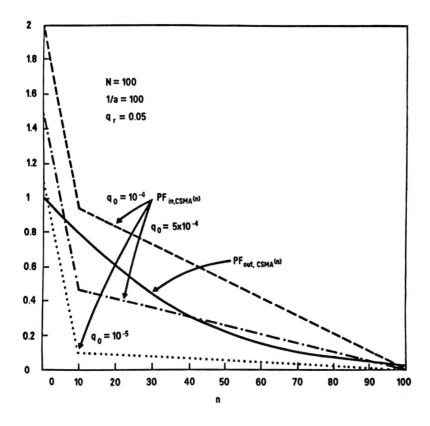

*Figure 13.8 Stable and bistable behavior of CSMA.*

13.8. This observation greatly simplifies the selection of the retransmission probability $q_r$ to meet the system design requirements, because now $q_r$ has effect
only on $PF_{out,CSMA}(\nu)$ and not on $PF_{in,CSMA}(\nu)$ as in the slotted ALOHA
case. Thus, once $PF_{in,CSMA}$ is determined (through $N$, $q_0$, and $a$), $q_r$ can
then be chosen such that $PF_{out,CSMA}$ has a desirable behavior without affecting $PF_{in,CSMA}$.

### 13.4.3 CSMA-CD

The CSMA-CD protocol has the same $PF_{out}$ as CSMA:

$$PF_{out,CSMA-CD}(n) = PF_{out,CSMA}(n). \tag{13.23}$$

The expected number of input packets in an interval is (see Appendix B for derivation)

$$PF_{in,CSMA-CD}(n) = (N-n)[1 - (1-q_0)^{a'/a}]$$
$$+ \frac{(N-n)q_0(1-q_0)^{a'/a}}{1 - (1-q_0)^{N-n}(1-q_r)^n} + R \tag{13.24}$$

where

$$R = \frac{(N-n)[(1-q_0)^{a'/a} - (1-q_0)^{1/a}]}{1 - (1-q_0)^{N-n}(1-q_r)^n} [nq_r(1-q_r)^{n-1}(1-q_0)^{N-n}$$
$$+ (N-n-1)q_0(1-q_0)^{N-n-1}(1-q_r)^n]. \tag{13.25}$$

Notice that if $a' = 1$, then $PF_{in,CSMA-CD}(n) = PF_{in,CSMA}(n)$. By the large population approximation, we have

$$PF_{in,CSMA-CD} \approx$$
$$\gamma_0(1-\nu)\left[\frac{a'}{a} + \frac{(1-q_0)^{a'/a}}{1 - e^{-\gamma(\nu)}} + \frac{\gamma(\nu)e^{-\gamma(\nu)}}{1 - e^{-\gamma(\nu)}}(1/a - a'/a)\right] \tag{13.26}$$

It is shown in Appendix B that $PF_{in,CSMA-CD}(\nu)$ has the same three properties as $PF_{in,CSMA}(\nu)$ and therefore we conclude that CSMA-CD has exactly the same stability property as slotted ALOHA and CSMA.

### 13.5 Conclusions

In this chapter we have used the average cycle length as the common basis for the analysis of the performance of slotted ALOHA, CSMA, and CSMA-CD channel access protocols. Channel utilizations have been derived in a systematic way using a finite poulation model and new theoretical results have been derived for the stability of these schemes. It has been proved that all three protocols could have the bistable behavior. Numerical examples have been used to demonstrate performances. The results can be used to provide design guides for choosing system parameters such as user population size $N$ and retransmission probabilities $p_r$ and $q_r$ to achieve a stable system with good performance.

## Appendix A

### Derivation of $PF_{in,CSMA}(n)$ and its Properties

The derivation of (13.20) is as follows: The quantity $PF_{in,CSMA}(n)$ is the expected number of new packets generated in an interval conditioned on the system being in state n. A cycle consists of a few idle sensing slots and a sensed slot followed by a transmission time $T$. Obviously, there is no packet generated during those idle sensing slots and the system stays at state $n$. Let $A$ denote the event that at least one user senses a slot and $B_k$ denote the event that there are precisely $k$ users in the origination mode generating new packets and sense slots. If $k$ out of $(N-n)$ users in the origination mode sense the slot, then there are $\{k + (N-n-k)[1-(1-q_0)^{1/a}]\}$ new packets generated in a cycle. Thus we have

$$PF_{in,CSMA}(n) = \sum_{k=0}^{N-n} \Pr\{B_k|A\}(k + (N-n-k)[1-(1-q_0)^{1/a}]), \quad (13.A1)$$

where the conditional probability $\Pr\{B_k|A\}$ is given by

$$\Pr\{B_k|A\} = \Pr\{B_kA\}/\Pr\{A\}$$

$$= \Pr\{B_kA\}/[1 - (1-q_0)^{N-n}(1-q_r)^n]. \quad (13.A.2)$$

By definition of $B_k$ and some reasoning, we have

$$\Pr\{B_0A\} = (1-q_0)^{N-n}[1 - (1-q_r)^n]$$

$$= (1-q_0)^{N-n} - (1-q_0)^{N-n}(1-q_r)^n \quad (13.A.3)$$

and

$$\Pr\{B_k A\} = \binom{N-n}{k} q_0^k (1-q_0)^{N-n-k}, \quad k = 1,2,\ldots,N-n \quad (13.A.4)$$

After substituting (13.A.2), (13.A.3), and (13.A.4) into (13.A.1) and performing some algebraic manipulation, we have

$$PF_{in,CSMA} = (N-n)[1 - (1-q_0)^{1/a}] + \frac{(N-n)q_0(1-q_0)^{1/a}}{1 - (1-q_0)^{N-n}(1-q_r)^n}, \quad (13.A.5)$$

which is (13.20).

We now show that $PF_{in,CSMA}(\nu)$ of (13.21) is convex. Since $\gamma_0(1-\nu)/a$ is linear, it is sufficient to show that

$$\gamma_0(1-\nu)(1-q_0)^{1/a}/(1-e^{-\gamma(\nu)})$$

is convex. Let $h_1(\nu) = \gamma_0(1-\nu)(1-q_0)^{1/a}$ and $h_2(\nu) = 1 - e^{-\gamma(\nu)}$, then we have $h_1 > 0$, $h_1' < 0$, $h_1'' = 0$, $h_2 > 0$, $h_2' > 0$ (assuming that $q_r > q_0$), and $h_2'' < 0$. With the conditions above, it is straightforward to show that $(h_1/h_2)'' > 0$. Therefore, $PF_{in,CSMA}(\nu)$ is convex.

The remaining two properties, $PF_{in,CSMA}(0) > PF_{out,CSMA}(0)$ and $PF_{in,CSMA}(1) < PF_{out,CSMA}(1)$, are relatively trivial after some reasoning. (They can also be proved mathematically.)

## Appendix B

### Derivation of $PF_{in,CSMA-CD}(n)$

The derivation of (13.24) is as follows. The derivation is similar to the one in Appendix A. Let $A$ be the event that at least one user senses a slot, $B_k$ be the event that $k$ users from origination mode sense a slot, and $C_k$ be the event that k users in retransmission mode sense a slot. If there is only one user sensing, then the following transmission is successful and will last $\tau/a$ long. If there are more than one users sensing a slot, then the following transmission is unsuccessful and will last only $a'\tau/a$ long. Thus $PF_{in,CSMA-CD}(n)$ is given by

$$PF_{in,CSMA-CD}(n) = \Pr\{B_0C_1|A\}(N-n)[1 - (1-q_0)^{1/a}]$$

$$+ \Pr\{B_1C_0|A\} \{1 + (N-n-1)[1 - (1-q_0)^{1/a}]\}$$

$$+ \sum_{j=1}^{N-n} \sum_{k=1}^{n} \Pr\{B_jC_k|A\} \cdot \{j + (N-n-j)[1-(1-q_0)^{1/a'}]\} \quad (13.B.1)$$

where the conditional probability $\Pr\{B_jC_k|A\}$ is given by

$$\Pr\{B_jC_k|A\} = \Pr\{B_jC_kA\}/\Pr\{A\}$$

$$= \Pr\{B_jC_k\}/\Pr\{A\}$$

$$= \Pr\{B_j\}\Pr\{C_k\}/\Pr\{A\}, \quad j \neq 0, k \neq 0 \quad (13.B.2)$$

From the definitions of $B_j$ and $C_k$, we have

$$\Pr\{B_j\} = \binom{N-n}{j}q_0^j(1-q_0)^{N-n-j}, \quad 0 < j < N-n \quad (13.B.3)$$

and

$$\Pr\{C_1\} = \binom{n}{k}q_r^k(1-q_r)^{n-k}, \quad 0 < k < n. \quad (13.B.4)$$

By substituting (13.B.2) through (13.B.4) into (13.B.1), and after some tedious algebraic manipulations, we have (13.24).

The proof of the convexity property of $PF_{in,CSMA-CD}(\nu)$ is the same as that of $PF_{in,CSMA}(\nu)$ and hence is omitted.

## References

[1]   N. Abramson and F.F. Kuo, Eds., *Computer-Communication Networks*, Englewood Cliffs, NJ: Prentice-Hall, Chapter 13, 1973.

[2]   R. Metcalfe, Steady state analysis of a slotted and controlled ALOHA system with blocking, *Proc. 6th Hawaii Int. Conf. Sys. Sci.*, January, 1973.

[3]   A.B. Carleial and M.E. Hellman, Bistable behavior of ALOHA-type

systems, *IEEE Trans. Comm.,* Vol. COM-23, pp. 401-410, 1975.

[4]   L. Kleinrock and S.S. Lam, Packet switching in a multiaccess broadcasting channel, *IEEE Trans. Comm.,* Vol. COM-23, pp. 410-423, 1975.

[5]   S.S. Lam and L. Kleinrock, Packet switching in a multiaccess broadcasting channel: Dynamic control procedures, *IEEE Trans. Comm.,* Vol. COM-23, pp. 891-904, 1975.

[6]   G. Fayolle, E. Gelenbe and J. Labetoulle, Stability of optimal control of switching broadcast channel, *Jour. ACM,* Vol. 24, pp. 375-386, 1977.

[7]   Y.-C. Jenq, On the stability of ALOHA system, *IEEE Trans. Comm.,* Vol. COM-28, pp. 1936-1939, 1980.

[8]   Y.-C. Jenq, Optimal retransmission control of slotted ALOHA systems, *IEEE Trans. Comm.,* Vol. COM-29, pp. 891-895, 1981.

[9]   L. Kleinrock and F.A. Tobagi, Packet switching in radio channels: Part I- CSMA and their throughput-delay characteristics, *IEEE Trans. Comm.,* Vol. COM-23, pp. 1400-1416, 1975.

[10]  F.A. Tobagi and L. Kleinrock, Packet switching in radio channel: Part IV - Stability considerations and dynamic control in CSMA, *IEEE Trans. Comm.,* Vol. COM-25, pp. 1103-1119, 1977.

[11]  F.A. Tobagi and V.B. Hunt, Performance analysis of carrier sense multiple access with collision detection, *Computer Networks,* Vol. 4, pp. 245-259, 1980.

# 14

# Image Compression via Self-Error-Correcting Two-Dimensional Coding

Morton E. Kanefsky

*Department of Electrical Engineering*
*University of Pittsburgh*
*Pittsburgh, Pennsylvania*

## 14.1 Introduction

A major problem of the predictive source coding of images is the inevitable fact that errors often propagate and destroy large portions of the reconstructed image. While this occurs for all source coding techniques, including information reducing but synchronous DPCM, it is particularly troublesome for information preserving, asynchronous, predictive techniques. There have been many efforts to deal with this problem, including, as often employed in facsimile coding, dividing the image into segments that are alternatively source encoded and then uncompressed so that significant distortions can be limited to only one segment. All such efforts cause a reduction of the efficiency of the code. This chapter explores the possibility of an efficient source coding technique that is self-error-correcting.

In order to explain the basic idea, let us consider (as an analogy) the concept of convolutional coding, which is an error-correcting channel encoding scheme. The very structure of a convolutional encoder imposes two properties on the code. First, decision errors tend to propagate and cause many subsequent errors. Second, it is possible to reject decoded signals that are grossly in error as a result of a previous decision error. These two properties enable a tree searching decoding algorithm that corrects transmission errors. Although this idea seems clear to us now, the concept of convolutional encoding was not evident until the encoder structure and its properties were studied.

Interestingly, all predictive source coding techniques satisfy the first of the above two properties. Indeed, that is precisely the problem inherent in predictive source coding. If an encoding algorithm is devised that has the second property, then a tree searching, self-error-correcting procedure should be possible. I believe that a proposal for facsimile encoding to the CCITT Study Group XIV (Contribution No. 82) from the Federal Republic of Germany [1] has the potential to satisfy the second property.

This predictive source encoder for binary data, henceforth called the German encoder, employs a unique type of run-length encoding. Rather than encoding the run lengths between prediction errors, the runs are encoded separately for each Markov mesh [2,3] source state, and, further, different coding tables are used depending on the source state. The reason for this technique is to enable one to take advantage of the typical kinds of nonstationarities that appear in facsimile by associating the coding tables with the states. This algorithm, which is quite efficient, if a bit cumbersome for typical facsimile, will be discussed in more detail in Section 14.3. The interesting point is that by modifying the coding tables, which will cause a slight degradation in efficiency, it should be possible to determine quickly when errors are made. If so, backtracking and using a tree searching technique could correct them.

It is speculated that there are only two types of errors. One type of error causes a small local disturbance that does not propagate and which may not be correctable. The other error temporarily causes a slight shift in the reconstructed image but eventually reaches a point where it degrades rapidly. The error must be identified quickly after degradation begins. This is essential because a tree searching algorithm would get out of hand if one has to backtrack too far. These ideas will be considered more fully in Section 14.4.

These procedures will be discussed in connection with binary or facsimile data. There are a number of ways that it can be extended to general multilevel images. One method, called differential bit plane coding [4], involves encoding the bit planes [5] separately. This method has two drawbacks, however. The sum of the entropies of the bit planes can be on the order of twice that of the image entropy [4], which means that the compressibility is greatly reduced. Also, while coding algorithms geared to nonstationary facsimile may be quite efficient for the most significant bit plane, other algorithms, such as the Gordon block algorithm [4,6], may be more efficient for less significant planes.

Another approach to multilevel image compression is one based on the model of a nonstationary mean. Many recent papers dealing with image modeling, or prediction are based on this kind of model [7,8,15]. Suppose that an image is partitioned into a modest number of regions each having an apparent constant mean value. Such a partitioning is shown in Figure 14.1, where there are three such regions, including the background. The hatched regions represent the transition regions between the neighborhoods of different intensity. The total image is represented by:

1.  The average intensity values of the identified regions.

2.  The binary partitioning image.

3.  The difference signal (mean subtracted) where some standard interpolation is used over the hatched or transitional regions.

The binary partitioning image can be greatly compressed by the German algorithm. If the difference is nearly white, it can be effectively source encoded with a Huffman code. Transmission errors in the Huffman code will be limited to a local region of the reconstructed image and will not propagate.

If small errors that do not propagate can be tolerated, the Huffman code can be truncated. If, on the other hand, the difference signal has substantial spatial dependence, some other source code, such as DPCM, is required. Perhaps the DPCM prediction can be restarted at every region edge. This chapter does not address this problem, however, nor the image partitioning problem. Only the source encoding of a binary image, whether facsimile or a bit-plane or partitioning image, will be considered.

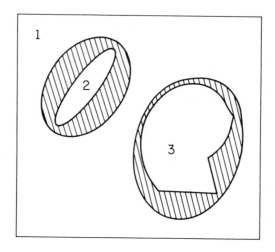

*Figure 14.1  Partitioning image*

## 14.2 Image Modeling

Spatial-domain predictive techniques, similar to DPCM, are commonly used for information-preserving source coding. These procedures often employ linear prediction algorithms which minimize the mean-square error. In the two-dimensional case, the past of an image pixel can be defined in an obvious way. Thus if $x_{ij}$ is an image pixel, where $i$ indicates the image row or line and $j$ the column, a linear estimate can be found from

$$\hat{x}_{ij} = \sum_{m=1}^{M} a_{0m} x_{i,j-m} + \sum_{n=1}^{N} \sum_{m=-M'}^{M} a_{nm} x_{i-n,j-m} \qquad (14.1)$$

For this special case

$$\hat{x}_{ij} = a_{01} x_{i,j-1} + a_{10} x_{i-1,j} + a_{11} x_{i-1,j-1} \qquad (14.2)$$

The optimum coefficients (which achieve the smallest mean-square error possible with a linear estimate) can be found for an arbitrary two-dimensional spatial corelation function [9]. For the more general case, finding optimum coefficients is quite difficult unless one makes assumptions such as factorable spatial correlation. While identifying appropriate values of $M$, $N$, $M'$ may not be possible, the prediction accuracy based on small values for these parameters should be adequate to obtain good compression. An important problem is that linear minimum mean-square estimation cannot be argued to be optimum for typical images. The assumption of Gaussian statistics for an image (necessary for the optimality of the linear minimum mean-square-error criterion) cannot be reconciled with the observed preponderance of black and white over gray points in many images. It is known [10] that the luminance of most pictures does not approximate a Gaussian process. Therefore, linear estimates are not really optimum, particularly near important image features such as edges. A nonlinear decision-oriented, rather than minimum mean square error, prediction seems reasonable. If we are dealing with images that are already digitized, a two-dimensional Markov model will lead naturally to a decision-oriented approach [11]. The natural two-dimensional extension of the Markov model is the Markov mesh model [2], which is based on a state-to-element transition probability that readily enables a maximum likelihood prediction. The array $X_{ab}$ of Figure 14.2 corresponds to the "past" of the image (relative to the data point $x_{ab}$) when scanned in the normal manner. The array $Z_{ab}$ is the entire image (past and future), excluding the data point $x_{ab}$. In a manner that is analogous to a one-dimensional Markov process, the Markov mesh is defined by the relationship

$$P(x_{ab} | X_{ab}) = P(x_{ab} | S_{ab}) \qquad (14.3)$$

where $S_{ab}$ is the state of the image. The probabilities of the state are

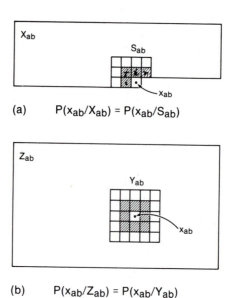

(a)     $P(x_{ab}/X_{ab}) = P(x_{ab}/S_{ab})$

(b)     $P(x_{ab}/Z_{ab}) = P(x_{ab}/Y_{ab})$

*Figure 14.2 The Markov mesh model.*

uniquely specified by the initial border and the transition matrix $P(x_{ab}|S_{ab})$. After an initial transient the state probabilities become independent of the border. A consequence of this definition is that each data point depends on a local neighborhood [2], or more precisely

$$P(x_{ab}|Z_{ab}) = P(x_{ab}|Y_{ab}) \tag{14.4}$$

where $Y_{ab}$ is a neighborhood surrounding (past and future) $x_{ab}$. In particular, if the state is specified by the shaded region in Figure 14.2a, which defines a second-order mesh, $x$ depends on the neighborhood indicated by the shaded region in Figure 14.2b. The order of the Markov mesh is arbitrarily defined according to the number and location of pixels in the state.[1] The more pixels

---

[1]The original reference [2] considers only left sector states. The state specified in Figure 14.2 comes from the generalization in [12].

in the state, the higher the order.

Although all of these ideas are analogous to a one-dimensional Markov process, a state-to-state transition matrix cannot be found, which is why the model cannot be called a Markov process. In the one-dimensional case when dealing with data, the Markov model and the entropy can be computed from the statistic

$$F_n = -\sum_{B_n} \sum_x P(B_n)P(x|B_n)\log_2 P(x|B_n) \qquad (14.5)$$

where $B_n$ represents the previous $n$ elements. It is known from Shannon's original work that $F_n$ converges monotonically to the entropy as $n$ is increased, and this statistic can be used to determine the order of the Markov process as well as the entropy. This is directly analogous to the two-dimensional Markov mesh, where the entropy is given by

$$H = -\sum_S \sum_X P(s)p(x|S)\log_2 p(x|S) \qquad (14.6)$$

The fact that, in one dimension, $p(x|B_n)$ can be trivially converted to state-to-state transition probabilities whereas in two dimensions this cannot be achieved is interesting but not significant for our purposes.

The states can be easily ordered. Using the notation of Figure 14.2a, the state number can be defined as (for a second-order mesh)

$$S = i + Lj + L^2k + L^3m \qquad (14.7)$$

where $0 \le i,j,k,m \le L-1$ and $L$ is the number of quantized levels of the image. The order of a Markov mesh model for real images can be identified from (14.6) by increasing the presumed order of the state until convergence is reached [12]. In the identification procedure, the state-to-element transition probability matrix is also generated. From the transition matrix, the maximum transition probability given each state determines the maximum likelihood (ML) prediction.

As an example, consider the simulated, nonstationary binary image of Figure 14.3. This is a $64 \times 64$ image with 41 per cent of the pixels being 1. Evaluating (14.6) for various assumed orders ($n$), while ignoring the apparent

```
00000000000000000000000000000000000000000000000000000000000000000
00000000000000000000000000000000000000000000000000000000000000000
00000000000000000000000000000000000000000000000000000000000000000
00000000000000000000000000000000000000000000000000000000000000000
00000000000000000000000000000000000000000000000000000000000000000
000000000000000000001111111100000000000000000011111000000000000
000000000000000000011111111110000000000000000111111110000000000
000000000000000000111111111110000000000000001111111111100000000
000000000000000011111111111111000000000000011111111111100000000
0000000000000001111111111111110000000001111111111111111100000000
0000000000000001111111111111111100000011111111111111111100000000
0000000000000001111111111111111101011111111111111111100000000
00000000000000111111111111111111111111111111111111111000000000
0000000000000111111111111111111111111111111111111111110000000000
000000000000011111111111111111111111111111111111111110000000000
000000000000011111111111111111111111111111111111111100000000000
00000000000001111111111111111111111111111111111110000000000
000000000000011111111111111111111111111111111111000000000000
00000000000001111111111111111111111111111111111000000000000
0000000000000011111111111111111111111111111111000000000000
00000000000000011111111111111111111111111111110000000000000
000000000000000011111111111111111111111111111000000000000
0000000000000000011111111111111111111111111111000000000000
0000000000000000001111111111111111111111111111000000000000
0000000000000000000111111111111111111111111111000000000000
00000000000000000001111111111111111111111110000000000000
0000000000000000000011111111111111111111111000000000000
000000000000000000011111111111111111111111100000000000
00000000000000000011111111111111111111111110000000000000
0000000000000000011111111111111111111111110000000000000
0000000000000000111111111111111111111111110000000000000
000000000000000111111111111111111111111111100000000000
00000000000001111111111111111111111111111110000000000000
0000000000011111111111111111111111111111110000000000000
0000000000111111111111111111111111111111110000000000000
000000000011111111111111111111111111111111100000000000
00000000011111111111111111111111111111111110000000000
000000001111111111111111111111111111111111110000000000
00000001111111111111111111111111111111111111000000000
0000000111111111111111111111111111111111111110000000000
000000111111111111111111111111111111111111111000000000
00000111111111111111111111111111111111111111110000000000
0000011111111111111111111111111111111111111111000000000
0000011111111111111111111111111111111111111111100000000
0000011111111111111111110000000001111111111111111100000000
000001111111111111111110000000000001111111111111111100000000
00001111111111111111000000000000000001111111111111111100000000
0000111111111111000000000000000000000011111111111111100000000
0000111111111110000000000000000000000001111111111111110000000
000011111111100000000000000000000000000011111111111111110000000
000001111110000000000000000000000000000001111111111111110000000
00000011100000000000000000000000000000000111111111111110000000
00000000000000000000000000000000000000001111111111111100000000
00000000000000000000000000000000000000011111111111000000000
00000000000000000000000000000000000000011111111000000000000
00000000000000000000000000000000000000001111000000000000
00000000000000000000000000000000000000000000000000000000000000000
00000000000000000000000000000000000000000000000000000000000000000
00000000000000000000000000000000000000000000000000000000000000000
00000000000000000000000000000000000000000000000000000000000000000
```

*Figure 14.3 A simulated image.*

nonstationarities, gives the values plotted in Figure 14.4. The entropy of the image is approximately 0.1 bit/pixel. According to Shannon's noise-free capacity theorem, this implies a compressibility (an upper bound on the achievable compression ratio) of 10.

While the order of the image is higher, the assumption that the image is of order 2 appears quite reasonable. One would expect, however, that the compressibility based on predictions from second-order states is 9 ($1/H_2 = 1/0.112$). The state probabilities and transition matrix determined for the second order mesh [13] is given in Table 14.1 together with the ML prediction.

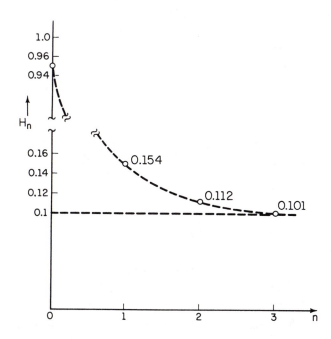

*Figure 14.4 Model identification.*

*Table 14.1. Second-order Markov mesh model.*

| State no. | P(s) | P(0|s) | P(1|s) | ML Pred. | Germ. Pred. |
|---|---|---|---|---|---|
| 0 | 0.54 | 1.00 | 0 | 0 | 0 |
| 1 | 0.02 | 0.68 | 0.32 | 0 | 1 |
| 2 | 0.01 | 1.00 | 0 | 0 | 0 |
| 3 | 0 | ? | ? | ? | 0 |
| 4 | 0 | ? | ? | ? | 0 |
| 5 | 0.01 | 0.49 | 0.51 | 1 | 1 |
| 6 | 0+ | 1.00 | 0 | 0 | 0 |
| 7 | 0.01 | 0.50 | 0.50 | ? | 1 |
| 8 | 0.01 | 0.56 | 0.44 | 0 | 0 |
| 9 | 0+ | 0 | 1.00 | 1 | 1 |
| 10 | 0.01 | 0.51 | 0.49 | 0 | 0 |
| 11 | 0+ | 0 | 1.00 | 1 | 1 |
| 12 | 0 | ? | ? | ? | 1 |
| 13 | 0.01 | 0 | 1.00 | 1 | 1 |
| 14 | 0.02 | 0.29 | 0.71 | 1 | 0 |
| 15 | 0.36 | 0.01 | 0.99 | 1 | 1 |

## 14.3 The German Algorithm.

The encoder proposed by the Federal Republic of Germany begins with an *ad hoc* prediction algorithm that is virtually identical to ML prediction based on the Markov mesh model. The prediction is based on the four surrounding pixels that correspond to a second order mesh plus a fixed prediction table. This table is listed in Table 14.1. It is not known whether this table is based on a study of typical facsimile images or was arrived at intuitively. As we shall see the compression is nearly the same for either prediction table. This strongly suggests that a fixed prediction table is quite viable. In fact, if the 16 bits required to encode the ML predictions are added to the encoded signal based on the ML predictions, the compression is often smaller than that obtained by the fixed table suggested by the German code.

The run lengths of correct predictions are encoded via encoding tables that are truncated Huffman codes. However, unlike typical run length encoding, that runs are associated with the state rather than their location in the image. For example, the eight runs associated with state 0 end at the indicated locations in Figure 14.3. Note that for this particular state, one anticipates long runs. This technique requires that both the encoder and decoder keep, in a memory stack, the states encountered plus the run length for each state. In the absence of transmission errors, the state of the reconstructed image is always the same as the state of the transmitted image and decoding is possible.

The advantage of this unusual run-length technique comes from the recognition that the run-length statistics depend on the state. Thus different coding tables can be used for different states which are more nearly matched to the correct statistics. The German proposal suggests six different coding tables [1]. Once again, it is not known whether these tables are based on typical facsimile images or were arrived at intuitively. For the tables corresponding to states 0 and 15, which typically have long runs, run lengths up to 64 are encoded in Huffman codes and longer runs have an identifiable prefix followed by an 11-bit binary encoded run length. The remaining 14 states are divided into four tables whose codes are truncated at length 32. Longer runs, if they occur, use prefixes and 11-bit run lengths, as before.

The German code was evaluated for the simulated 64×64 image. It was assumed that the first row and first column were zero and the remaining 63×63 image was encoded. Using the prediction and encoding tables suggested, the image consisted of 144 runs and was compressed into 493 bits. This corresponds to a compression ratio (63×63/493) of 8.05 or an efficiency (8.05/9) of nearly 90 percent. If the prediction table is replaced by the ML predictions, the image requires 491 bits (or 507 bits if the ML predictions are included). As indicated earlier, the fixed prediction table seems appropriate.

This same image was encoded using the IBM proposal [14] and the block Gordon algorithm. The IBM code required 595 bits, which corresponds to a compression ratio of 6.88. This can be improved by changing the encoding tables to one that is matched to the statistics of this image, but 90 percent efficiencies cannot be acheived [13]. The Gordon algorithm, which is quite efficient for stationary images, did worse, requiring 689 bits.

Let us now consider the effects of a transmission error which are quite serious for all asynchronous predictive techniques. In Figure 14.5, a bit error in the code for the seventh run of state 0 causes this long run to be interpreted two pixels too long. The first box indicates where this run should have ended while the second box indicates where this run now ends. Immediately after the first error occurs, the receiver "sees" the wrong state (state 8 instead of state 9). If this state is in the memory queue, the subsequent reconstructed image may appear as a shifted version of the original image. Indeed, this kind of shifted reconstruction may go on for a few lines. Eventually, however, a state will appear that is not in the queue. For our example in Figure 14.5, this occurs at the second box because the erroneous state (state 1) that appears had previously completed a run and was cleared in the memory queue. When this happens, the decoder determines the new run length from the coding tables and the subsequent code. If, as is likely, the wrong table is used (i.e., the next correct run corresponds to a state that uses a different coding table than state 1), then synchronization is lost and the rest of the reconstructed image is meaningless, as seen in Figure 14.5.

## 14.4 Error Correction Modifications

Suppose that the run-length codewords contain some information about the state. Such information is redundant in the absence of errors and must cause a decrease in the compression. For example, if the codewords were increased on the average by one bit, the image in Figure 14.3 would require 493 + 144 bits, which corresponds to a compression ratio of 6.23. However, in the presence of a transmission error, the decoder can detect any error by comparing this information with the state of the previously reconstructed image. After detecting such an error, the decoder could determine the last run that was completed and consider different possible run lengths. The decoding would then continue, along separate paths, for each of these possibilities. Similar to tree

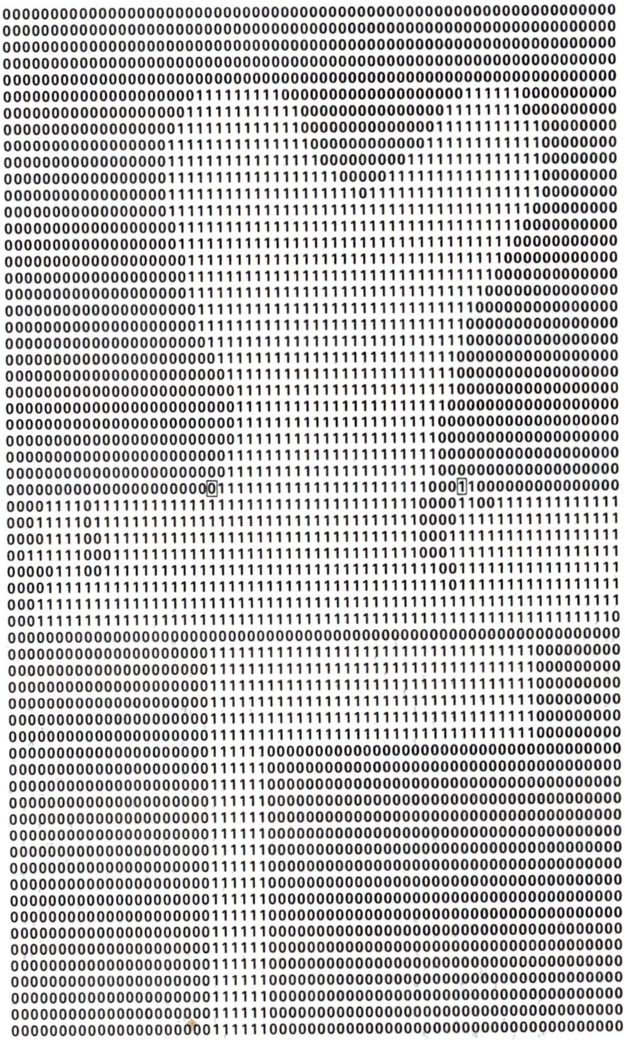

```
000000000000000000000000000000000000000000000000000000000000
000000000000000000000000000000000000000000000000000000000000
000000000000000000000000000000000000000000000000000000000000
000000000000000000000000000000000000000000000000000000000000
000000000000000000000000000000000000000000000000000000000000
000000000000000011111111100000000000000000111110000000000
000000000000000011111111111100000000000000001111111000000000
000000000000000011111111111110000000000000001111111111100000
00000000000000001111111111111100000000000011111111111100000
00000000000000001111111111111110000000001111111111111100000
000000000000000011111111111111111011111111111111111100000000
000000000000000011111111111111111111111111111111111110000000
000000000000000011111111111111111111111111111111111110000000
000000000000000011111111111111111111111111111111100000000000
000000000000000001111111111111111111111111111111100000000000
000000000000000001111111111111111111111111111111110000000000
000000000000000001111111111111111111111111111111100000000000
000000000000000001111111111111111111111111111111100000000000
000000000000000000111111111111111111111111111100000000000000
000000000000000000011111111111111111111111111100000000000000
000000000000000000011111111111111111111111111100000000000000
000000000000000000001111111111111111111111111100000000000000
000000000000000000001111111111111111111111111100000000000000
000000000000000000000111111111111111111111111100000000000000
000000000000000000000111111111111111111111111100000000000000
000000000000000000000011111111111111111111111100000000000000
0000000000000000000000[0]11111111111111111111000[1]1000000000000000
000011110111111111111111111111111111111111110000110011111111111111
000111110111111111111111111111111111111111110000111111111111111111
000111110011111111111111111111111111111111110001111111111111111111
001111110001111111111111111111111111111111110001111111111111111111
000011100111111111111111111111111111111111111001111111111111111111
000011111111111111111111111111111111111111111011111111111111111111
000111111111111111111111111111111111111111111111111111111111111111
000111111111111111111111111111111111111111111111111111111111111110
000000000000000000000000000000000000000000000000000000000000000000
000000000000000000011111111111111111111111111111111111000000000
000000000000000000011111111111111111111111111111111111000000000
000000000000000000011111111111111111111111111111111111000000000
000000000000000000011111111111111111111111111111111111000000000
000000000000000000011111111111111111111111111111111111000000000
000000000000000000011111000000000000000000000000000000000000
000000000000000000011111000000000000000000000000000000000000
000000000000000000011111000000000000000000000000000000000000
000000000000000000011111000000000000000000000000000000000000
000000000000000000011111000000000000000000000000000000000000
000000000000000000011111000000000000000000000000000000000000
000000000000000000011111000000000000000000000000000000000000
000000000000000000011111000000000000000000000000000000000000
000000000000000000011111000000000000000000000000000000000000
000000000000000000011111000000000000000000000000000000000000
000000000000000000011111000000000000000000000000000000000000
000000000000000000011111000000000000000000000000000000000000
000000000000000000011111000000000000000000000000000000000000
000000000000000000011111000000000000000000000000000000000000
000000000000000000001111000000000000000000000000000000000000
```

*Figure 14.5 A transmission error example.*

searching algorithms, a wrong path will soon be determined when the decoder detects a state error. For the error example shown in Figure 14.5, the paths corresponding to all possible, but wrong, run lengths of state 0 will be immediately detected as wrong and discarded. Of course, not all errors are so easily detected and a general tree searching algorithm has not yet been devised. Such a general algorithm may correct the image at the point where a state error is detected, leaving previous local errors or image shifts uncorrected.

To implement these ideas, it is necessary to modify the coding tables so that the codewords contain adequate state information without significantly decreasing the compression efficiency. A brute-force example is to force a two-bit prefix to every codeword that corresponds to the $i$ and $m$ bits of the state (see Figure 14.2a), or its inverse, by adding one bit. This prefix is chosen because an error that has just occurred will affect the $i$ bit, whereas an error on the preceding line due to an image shift will affect the $m$ bit. Such a modification will allow state errors to be detected easily but will reduce the compression efficiency. Although the resulting compression ratio of 6.23 may be acceptable considering the error correction capability, it is short of the 8.05 compression ratio achieved for the error-free case. Hopefully, coding tables can be found that are more efficient than this brute-force method.

The ideas discussed in this section are still speculative. We are presently attempting to implement a correcting algorithm, based on the two-bit prefix idea, that will correct all (or nearly all) types of errors. When this is accomplished, the concept will be proven and efforts can shift to efficiency considerations.

## References

[1]   CCITT Study Group XIV, Federal Republic of Germany, Two-dimensional coding scheme, Contribution No. 82, 1979.

[2]   K. Abend, T.J. Harley and L.N. Kanal, Classification of binary random patterns, *IEEE Trans. Inform. Theory*, Vol. 11, pp. 538-544, 1965.

[3]   M. Kanefsky, Modeling and simulation of two-dimensional pictures, *Proc. of the Sixth Pittsburgh Conf.*, pp. 471-473, Apr. 1975.

[4]    M. Kanefsky and C.B. Fong, Predictive source coding techniques using maximum likelihood prediction for compression of digitized images, *IEEE Trans. Inform. Theory.* Vol. IT-30, pp. 722-727, Sept., 1984, to appear.

[5]    J.W. Schwartz and R.C. Barker, Bit-plane encoding: a technique for source encoding, *IEEE Trans. Aero. Elec. Sys.,* Vol. AES-2, pp. 385-392, 1966.

[6]    C.B. Fong and M. Kanefsky, An efficient source coding technique for random binary images, *Proc. Conf. Inform. Sci. Sys.,* Johns Hopkins University, pp. 309-314, March 1981.

[7]    P. Maragos, R.M. Mersereau and R.W. Schafer, Some experiments in ADPCM coding of images, *ICASSP '82 Conf. Rec.,* 1982.

[8]    D.K. Mitrakos and A.G. Constantanides, Composite source coding technique for image bandwidth compression, *ICASSP '82 Conf. Rec.,* 1982.

[9]    M. Strinzis and R. Feick, ARMA models of bivariate processes, *Pittsburgh Conf. on Modeling and Simulation,* 1976.

[10]   A.N. Netravlis and J.O. Limb, Picture coding, *Proc. IEEE,* Vol. 68, pp. 366-406, 1980.

[11]   M. Kanefsky and M. Strinzis, A decision theory approach to picture smoothing, *IEEE Trans. Comp.,* Vol. C-27, pp. 32-36, 1978.

[12]   A.P. Sahasrabudhe, Identification of a Markov mesh model and its applications to discrete image processing, Ph.D Dissertation, Univ. of Pittsburgh, 1979.

[13]   Seminar on Information Theory at the Univ. of Pittsburgh, Winter, 1982.

[14]   Pennebaker, Goertzel and Mitchell, Recent advances in data-conversion facsimile techniques, *J. Appl. Phot. Engr.,* 1980.

[15]   C.W. Therrien, An estimation theoretic approach to terrain image segmentation, *Computer Vision, Graphics and Image Proc.,* Vol. 22,pp. 313-36, 1983.

# 15

# Vector Quantization

Peter F. Swaszek

*Department of Electrical Engineering*
*University of Rhode Island*
*Kingston, Rhode Island*

## 15.1 Introduction

Quantization is of ubiquitous need in information-processing systems. We typically model information-bearing signals as being analog in nature, while most of our processing of the signals is digital. As examples, consider the following. Digital communication systems encode samples of an input signal into a bit stream of finite length: finite due to bandwidth constraints. Various signal-processing techniques have their mathematical operations implemented on digital computers, finite binary representations being used for the data values. Hence an efficient method of transforming continuously valued signals into discretely valued signals is both desirable and necessary to ensure good system performance. Often such signals exist on a continuum of time. Here, however, we will assume that a sampling of the signal has already occurred and will employ the information-theoretic model of a discrete-time, continuously valued vector random process. With this assumption, the problem of interest is to in some way decide how to "round" a vector observation to one of $N$ values.

Quantization is this process of "rounding" a continuously valued random variable. By vector quantization, we mean the mapping of a vector of random variables rather than just one. Scalar quantization (length 1 vectors) has received much attention in the engineering and statistical literature. For an overview, see the excellent review article by Gersho [1]. Research has included asymptotic performance for a variety of error criteria and sources, small-$N$ performance for the mean-square-error criterion, and various other subjects from robustness of the design to source mismatch to "quantization error" spectra.

Vector quantization is a much more recent research area. Although the groundwork was laid twenty years ago by Zador and others, many of the available results have been attained in the last eight years. The interest in vector quantization resides in the fact that additional gain in performance is achievable over scalar quantization even when the input vector consists of independent elements. To demonstrate this fact, consider the following argument. Vector quantization of a length $k$ vector induces a partitioning of the $k$-dimensional input space into $N$ mutually exclusive, exhaustive regions called the quantization regions and a mapping of each of these regions into a particular value called the output point. Scalar quantization consists of the partitioning of the real line into intervals, the only region of interest. For a sequence of $k$ inputs, scalar quantization can be envisioned as a partitioning of the $k$-space into parallelepipeds, with perpendicular sides due to the scalar interval partitioning. From this observation, scalar quantization is seen to be a special case of vector quantization with the regions constrained. Since adding a constraint to a design problem can never increase the performance, we see that scalar quantization can never outperform optimum vector quantization.

As a numerical example, consider the minimum mean-square-error (MSE) quantization of a vector composed of two independent Gaussian random variables, each with zero mean and unit variance. Quantization to $N = 16$ levels for this case means separation of the Euclidean plane into 16 regions. For scalar quantization, we apply separate scalar quantizers to each of the two components having $N_x$ and $N_y$ levels, respectively, with $N_x N_y = 16$. A simple symmetry or variational argument demonstrates that the MSE is minimized by dividing the levels equally, four to each rectangular coordinate (see Figure 15.1).

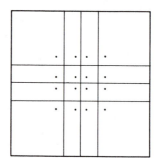

outputs $\pm$ 1.5104 $\pm$ 0.4528
breakpoints 0.0 $\pm$ 0.9816
MSE = 0.2350 from Max [2]

*Figure 15.1 Rectangular quantizer.*

A vector quantizer for the same source with better performance is depicted in Figure 15.2 (discussed in detail in Section 15.5). Both figures display the quantization pattern on the $(-4\sigma, 4\sigma)$ section of the plane along with pertinent data.

This chapter is a summary of results on the design and analysis of vector quantizers with emphasis on the MSE criterion. Section 15.2 presents definitions and several interesting facts on the design and implementation of optimum vector quantizers. Section 15.3 considers asymptotic MSE performance of optimum vector quantizers for the cases of constrained output entropy and constrained number of levels. Section 15.4 develops further results on implementation of vector quantizers through a discussion of companding and

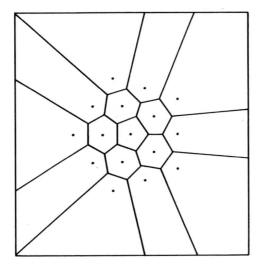

output radii 0.8725, 1.7123, 2.0177
angles equally distributed on $[0,2\pi)$
MSE $= 0.2172$

*Figure 15.2 Vector quantizer.*

the design of uniform quantizers. Section 15.5 explores a different avenue of interest in vector quantizing: the design of suboptimum vector quantizers. The reference list is partitioned to coincide with the subjects in each section.

## 15.2 Definitions

In general, a quantizer is a mapping of an input signal into a value which is in some way a close approximation to the input. The input space will be the $k$-dimensional Euclidean space $\mathbb{R}^k$ with the input data a $k$-dimensional vector $\underline{x}$. Occasionally, the input signal will naturally fall into a group of length $k$, as for example with positional coordinates. We are not constrained by this, however, and define a length $k$ vector as an ordered set of $k$ input variables, whether they occur concurrently, sequentially, or both. The source is further specified statistically by its probability density function $p(\underline{x})$; the exact form of $p(\underline{x})$ will be assumed to be known and to be continuous on $\mathbb{R}^k$. Generalizations to other cases can be found in the literature (see the references). The output space is defined to be $N$ distinct points in $\mathbb{R}^k$. This mapping is noninvertible in the sense that many points in the original space are mapped to a particular output point. We will denote the process of quantizing an input $\underline{x}$ as $Q(\underline{x})$ or $\hat{\underline{x}}$.

Let $E(\cdot)$ be the expectation operator. The performance measure of interest in this chapter will be the mean-square error (MSE), defined by

$$\begin{aligned} \text{MSE} &= E\{[\underline{x} - Q(\underline{x})]^T[\underline{x} - Q(\underline{x})]\} \\ &= \int_{\mathbb{R}^k} [\underline{x} - Q(\underline{x})]^T[\underline{x} - Q(\underline{x})]p(\underline{x}) \; d\underline{x} \end{aligned} \tag{15.1}$$

If we think of $\underline{e} = Q(\underline{x}) - \underline{x}$ as a noise vector added to the input, then the MSE is the noise power. Other performance criteria may be employed, but the large majority of results exists for MSE. Also, most of the results presented here for MSE generalize directly to mean $r$th error.

A $k$-dimensional, $N$-level vector quantizer is defined by the set $\{S_i, \underline{y}_i, i = 1,2,\ldots,N\}$, where the $S_i$ are the quantization regions and the $\underline{y}_i$ are the output points associated with these regions. The operation of the quantizer is to map every point in $S_i$ into $\underline{y}_i$. Clearly, the $S_i$ should be disjoint regions which cover the input space

$$S_i \cap_{i \neq j} S_j = \varnothing; \quad \bigcup_{i=1}^{N} S_i = \mathbb{R}^k$$

Using these facts, the mean-square error associated with a vector quantizer can be written as

$$MSE = \sum_{i=1}^{N} \int_{S_i} [\underline{x} - \underline{y}_i]^T[\underline{x} - \underline{y}_i]p(\underline{x}) \; d\underline{x}$$

Several approaches in the design of the vector quantizer can be taken from the foregoing expression for the error.

Initially, let us assume that the $S_i$ are fixed regions in the input space and try to optimize over the choice of $y_i$. Taking derivatives with respect to the $y_i$, equating to zero, and manipulating yields

$$y_i = \int_{S_i} \underline{x} p(\underline{x}) \, d\underline{x} \; / \int_{S_i} p(\underline{x}) \, d\underline{x} \qquad (15.2)$$

This expression states that each output should be the centroid of its associated region. Intuitively, mean-square error is an inertial measure of each quantization region and, from mechanics, we know that the inertia is minimized at the region's centroid. This result can be generalized to other error criteria, the solution being a generalized centroid.

The derivative operation above is a vector derivative yielding $k$ equations, one for each coordinate of the output point. Sufficiency of this solution is demonstrated by considering the matrix of second partial derivatives of the MSE with respect to the $y_i$. The only nonzero elements in this matrix are the diagonal terms, 2 Prob[$\underline{x} \in S_i$]. From this fact we see that the matrix is positive definite and that the condition of centroidal output points above is necessary and sufficient to minimize MSE for fixed quantization regions.

For a quantizer with the output values defined as centroids of the region, several expressions simplify. Since the definition of a centroid implies that $E\{\underline{x}^T Q(\underline{x})\} = E\{Q(\underline{x})^T Q(\underline{x})\}$, the resulting MSE is

$$\begin{aligned}
\text{MSE} &= E\{[\underline{x} - Q(\underline{x})]^T [\underline{x} - Q(\underline{x})]\} \\
&= E\{\underline{x}^T \underline{x}\} - 2E\{\underline{x}^T Q(\underline{x})\} + E\{Q(\underline{x})^T Q(\underline{x})\} \\
&= E\{\underline{x}^T \underline{x}\} - E\{Q(\underline{x})^T Q(\underline{x})\},
\end{aligned}$$

and the MSE is the difference between the input and output variances. Further manipulations yield

$$E\{\underline{x}\} = E\{Q(\underline{x})\}; \text{ input and output have equal means}$$

$$E\{\underline{x}^T [Q(\underline{x}) - \underline{x}]\} = - \text{ MSE}; \text{ input and noise are negatively correlated}$$

$$E\{Q(\underline{x})^T [Q(\underline{x}) - \underline{x}]\} = 0; \text{ output and noise are uncorrelated.}$$

Most of these results are familiar from applications of the orthogonality principle in linear minimum mean-square estimation.

For a second argument, assume that the output points, the $y_i$, are fixed. Consider a point $\underline{x}$ in the input space. The differential error contributed by an input of this value is proportional to the squared distance from this point to its associated output value. Since there are $N$ output points, this error takes one of $N$ possible values. To minimize the total MSE, the error associated with any point in the input space should be minimized; hence an input point should be mapped to the ouput point that is closest to it:

$$Q(\underline{x}) = y_i \quad \text{such that} \quad |\underline{x} - \underline{y_i}| < |\underline{x} - \underline{y_j}| \quad \forall j \neq i$$

With this result, each quantization region, $S_i$, is the set of all input points closer to $y_i$ than any other output point:

$$S_i = \bigcap_{\substack{j=1 \\ j \neq i}}^{N} \{\underline{x} : |\underline{x} - \underline{y_i}| < |\underline{x} - \underline{y_j}|\} \quad \forall i = 1,2,\ldots,N \qquad (15.3)$$

This definition is sometimes called Dirichlet or nearest-neighbor partitioning, and the regions are known as the Voronoi regions of the output points. At points in the input space where two output values are equally distant, we will use the convention that the points are mapped to the output with the smallest subscript.

With these Dirichlet partitions, the regions are seen to be the intersections of half-spaces. Half-spaces are convex regions and since the intersection of convex regions is again convex, the quantization regions, the $S_i$, are also convex and in fact are simply connected regions. Also, this condition is necessary and sufficient to minimize the MSE for fixed outputs. The argument above can be simply generalized to $r$th power and other error functionals which are monotonically increasing functions of the absolute value of the distance. For all of these functionals, the nearest-neighbor type of assignment of output points still holds and the regions are assigned as above.

We now consider the implementation of vector quantizers with regions defined as Dirichlet partitions of the output points. An obvious implementation is to compute the distance from the input to each of the $y_i$ and pick the minimum. This scheme requires computing $N$ distances and sorting $N$ values for a total of $Nk$ multiplications, $N(2k-1)$ additions, and $N-1$ scalar comparisons. Another implementation can be found by considering the partitioning of $\mathbb{R}^k$ as described in (15.3). From this result, $S_i$ and $S_j$ are seen to be divided by $\{\underline{x}:|\underline{x} - \underline{y}_i| = |\underline{x} - \underline{y}_j|\}$, a hyperplane that perpendicularly bisects the line segment connecting $\underline{y}_i$ and $\underline{y}_j$. The $N-1$ tests of $\underline{y}_i$ versus other outputs can be written as algebraic comparisons

$$Q(\underline{x}) = \underline{y}_i \quad \text{if} \quad \underline{a}_{ij}{}^T \underline{x} + \underline{b}_{ij} > 0 \quad \forall j \neq i$$

with $\underline{a}_{ij} = \underline{y}_i - \underline{y}_j$ and $\underline{b}_{ij} = 1/2[y_i^T y_i + y_j^T y_j]$. The alternative implementation is as follows. For each $\underline{y}_i$, compute the $N-1$ algebraic tests versus each of the other $\underline{y}_j$. If any of these $N-1$ tests fail, then $\underline{x} \notin S_i$.

Initially, it seems that the second implementation would require the evaluation of $N(N-1)/2$ such algebraic comparisons. Further examination, however, shows that many of these comparisons are redundant. Actually, comparisons need be made only with other regions which are adjacent to $S_i$ (share a hyperplane of dimension $k-1$). For the case of $k = 1$, scalar quantization, this is easily seen; each interval (region) need only be compared with the intervals on each side, not all the other intervals. In $k$ dimensions, the number of comparisons varies from region to region, depending on its number of adjacent regions. To detect nonadjacent regions, let $l_i = \min|y_i - y_j|$, $j \neq i$. Region $S_i$ about $\underline{y}_i$ and region $S_j$ about $\underline{y}_j$ cannot be adjacent if $|\underline{y}_i - \underline{y}_j| > 2l_i$. This criterion removes many of the redundant tests, but its usefulness is limited by the fact that the redundant tests are not well ordered; hence a table of relevant tests would be needed and the complexity of the implementation returns.

In the paragraphs above, we have described necessary and sufficient conditions for the region (Dirichlet partitions) and output value (centroid) selection if the other is fixed. When both are unknown, the arguments above become necessary conditions for a local minimum. Equations (15.2) and (15.3) may be used iteratively to converge to a local minimum of MSE. The iterative design method is to select an initial set of outputs and to employ (15.3) to select the regions optimally. This set of output values and regions has a distortion, call it $D_1$. Usually, however, (15.2) is not satisfied, the original outputs not being the centroids of the generated regions. Holding the regions fixed and redefining the outputs by (15.2) yields a new solution with error smaller than $D_1$, say $D_2$. Similarly, (15.3) is now probably not satisfied, the old regions not being Dirichlet partitions of the new output points. Hence, reapplying (15.3) will reduce the error below $D_2$. This iterative scheme (a multidimensional extension of Lloyd's Method I) converges to a local minimum of MSE due to the fact that the MSE is strictly reduced by each application of (15.2) or (15.3) and that the MSE is bounded below by zero, being the integral of a positive quantity. This design algorithm can also be used wth a set of training data if the source density is unavailable, the designed quantizer converging to a locally optimum quantizer as the number of training vectors goes to infinity.

### 15.3 Optimum Performance

In this section, upper bounds on the MSE performance of optimum vector quantizers are presented for two cases: first, when the output entropy is constrained, and second, when the number of output values is fixed. Both cases are of interest; the first naturally applies to coding of the data, the second to finite word-length problems. Finally, we relate a lower bound to the MSE for the fixed $N$ case.

Define a random quantizer as a mapping of $\mathbb{R}^k$ into a set of $N$ output points which are chosen by independent sampling of a density function $l(\underline{x})$ on $\mathbb{R}^k$. Let the region boundaries be the Dirichlet partitions of this output configuration. Also, assume that $N$ is large and that $l(\underline{x})$ is smooth. Below, we consider the MSE performance of this random quantizer. Since it is random, the resulting performance is also a random variable. We will compute the mean of this variable with the knowledge that at least one quantizer (the optimum quantizer) exists which has performance better than this mean.

For the random quantizer, the probability of an output point being within a hypersphere of radius $r$ about a point $\underline{x}$ can be approximated by $l(\underline{x})r^k B_k$, where $r^k B_k$ is the volume of the hypersphere ($B_k = \pi^{k/2}/\Gamma[1+k/2]$). For the entire quantizer, the probability that the closest output is at distance $r$ is the derivative of the probability that all $N$ outputs are at least a distance $r$

away. In terms of the probability above, this is

$$p(r) \approx \frac{d}{dr}[1 - l(\underline{x})r^k B_k]^N$$

$$= Nkl(\underline{x})B_k r^{k-1}[1 - l(\underline{x})B_k r^k]^{N-1}.$$

The MSE of the random quantizer is the square of this distance averaged over all of the random variables ( $\underline{x}$ and $r$)

$$\text{MSE} = E(r^2) = \int\limits_{\mathbb{R}^k} \int\limits_{0}^{\infty} r^2 \, p(r)p(\underline{x}) \, dr \, d\underline{x}.$$

Substituting $p(r)$, changing variables to $t(\underline{x}) = l(\underline{x})B_k r^k$, and noting that $t(\underline{x})$ is a probability, $0 < t(\underline{x}) < 1$, yields

$$\text{MSE} \approx NB_k^{-2/k} \int\limits_{\mathbb{R}^k} l(\underline{x})^{-2/k}p(\underline{x}) \int\limits_{0}^{1} t(\underline{x})^{2/k}[1 - t(\underline{x})]^{N-1} \, dt(\underline{x})d\underline{x}$$

$$\approx \Gamma[1+2/k]B_k^{-2/k} N^{-2/k} E\{l(\underline{x})^{-2/k}\} \qquad (15.4)$$

where we have used the fact that the interior integral is a beta function and that for large $N$, $\Gamma(N)/\Gamma(N+1+2/k) \approx N^{-1-2/k}$. For notational ease, let $\Gamma[1+2/k]B_k^{-2/k} = D(k)$.

Henceforth, we consider two cases of interest: the fixed output entropy quantizer and the fixed $N$ quantizer. The two results on upper-bounding the optimum MSE by random quantizers are typically called Zador's bounds. For the fixed-entropy case, define the output entropy $H_Q$:

$$H_Q = -\sum_{i=1}^{N} P(\underline{y}_i) \, \log P(\underline{y}_i); \quad P(\underline{y}_i) = \int\limits_{S_i} p(\underline{x}) \, d\underline{x}$$

For large $N$ and some small-region $S$, the probability of an input to the quantizer occurring within that region can be approximated by the product of the density at a point $\underline{x}$ in $S$ and the volume of $S$:

$$P(\underline{x} \in S) \approx p(\underline{x}) \, \text{vol}(S).$$

Now, consider the outputs distributed throughout $\mathbb{R}^k$. The probability that any one occurs in $S$ is $l(\underline{x}) \, \text{vol}(S)$ and the expected number of outputs occurring in $S$ is $N$ times this probability. Letting the region $S$ be the $i$th quantization region $S_i$, we have

$$P(S_i) \approx l(\underline{y_i}) \, \text{vol}(S_i) \quad \text{or} \quad \text{vol}(S_i) \approx 1/N \, l(\underline{y_i}).$$

where the second expression is due to the fact that any one output occurs in $S_i$. Combining these expressions yields

$$P(\underline{x} \in S_i) \approx p(\underline{y_i})/N \, l(\underline{y_i})$$

and the entropy can be written as

$$H_Q = -\sum_{i=1}^{N} [p(\underline{y_i}) \log p(\underline{y_i})]/N \, l(\underline{y_i}) - \sum_{i=1}^{N} [p(\underline{y_i}) \log 1/nl(\underline{y_i})]/N \, l(\underline{y_i})$$

Since $N$ is assumed large, the sums can be approximated by integrals:

$$H_Q \approx -\int_{\mathbb{R}^k} p(\underline{x}) \log p(\underline{x}) \, d\underline{x} - \int_{\mathbb{R}^k} p(\underline{x}) \log[1/N \, l(\underline{x})] \, d\underline{x}$$

$$= H_p + E\{\log [N \, l(\underline{x})]\}$$

where $H_p$ is the source entropy. Returning to (15.4), the MSE for the random quantizer can be written as the exponent of the log

$$\text{MSE} \approx D(k) \, E\left[\exp\left(-\frac{2}{k}\log N \, l(\underline{x})\right)\right]$$

Since $\exp(-\underline{x})$ is convex, we apply Jensen's inequality to yield

$$E\left[\exp\left(-\frac{2}{k} \log N \, l(\underline{x})\right)\right] > \exp\left[-\frac{2}{k} E\{\log N \, l(\underline{x})\}\right]$$

with equality if $l(\underline{x})$ is constant. Hence the random quantizer's MSE is smallest with $l(\underline{x})$ constant, i.e., uniform quantization. Combining yields the upper bound

$$\text{MSE}_{\text{fixed entropy}} < D(k) \exp\left[-\frac{2}{k}E\{\log N l(\underline{x})\}\right]$$

$$= D(k)\exp\left[-\frac{2}{k}(H_Q - H_p)\right]$$

For the fixed-$N$ case, we return to (15.4) and bound $E\{l(\underline{x})^{-2/k}\}$ through Hölder's inequality

$$E\{l(\underline{x})^{-2/k}\} > \left[\int_{\mathbb{R}^k} p(\underline{x})^{k/(k+2)} \, d\underline{x}\right]^{(k+2)/k} = \|p(\underline{x})\|_{k/(k+2)}.$$

We have equality if

$$l(\underline{x}) = p^{1/(k+2)}(\underline{x}) \Big/ \int_{\mathbb{R}^k} p^{1/(k+2)}(\underline{x}) \, d\underline{x}.$$

Hence the optimum quantizer's MSE is upper bounded by

$$\text{MSE}_{\text{fixed}N} < D(k)\|p(\underline{x})\|_{k/(k+2)}N^{-2/k}. \tag{15.5}$$

A secondary result on fixed $N$ quantization is established as follows. Considering each region separately and assuming that $N$ is large, the error associated with $S_i$ can be approximated by

$$\text{MSE}_i = \int_{S_i} |\underline{x} - \underline{y}_i|^2 p(\underline{x})d\underline{x}$$

$$\approx D(k)N^{-2/k} \int_{S_i} l(\underline{x})^{-2/k}p(\underline{x}) \, d\underline{x}$$

$$= D(k)N^{-2/k}l(\underline{y}_i)^{-2/k}p(\underline{y}_i) \, \text{vol}(S_i)$$

Using the fact that $\text{vol}(S_i) \approx 1/N l(\underline{y}_i)$, we can simplify this expression to $\text{MSE}_i = D(k)N^{-(k+2)/k}$, which is a constant independent of $i$. Hence, for the optimum, fixed-$N$ case, each region contributes equal MSE.

Let us now consider a fixed-$N$ optimum quantizer and derive a lower bound on the MSE. From (15.2), the MSE is a sum which for large $N$ and smooth $p(\underline{x})$ can be approximated by

$$\text{MSE} = \sum_{i=1}^{N} \int_{S_i} |\underline{x} - \underline{y}_i|^2 p(\underline{x}) d\underline{x}$$

$$\approx \sum_{i=1}^{N} p(\underline{y}_i) \int_{S_i} |\underline{x} - \underline{y}_i|^2 \, d\underline{x}$$

$$= \sum_{i=1}^{N} p(\underline{y}_i) I(S_i)$$

where $I(S_i)$ is the inertia of the $i$th quantization region. For a fixed volume, $\text{vol}(S_i)$, the inertia is a minimum if the region is a hypersphere,

$$I(S_i) > \frac{k}{(k+2)\pi} \, \Gamma^{2/k} [1 + k/2] \text{vol}(S_i)^{1+2/k}.$$

We also have the constraint that the total probability is constant

$$\int_{\mathbb{R}^k} p(\underline{x}) \, d\underline{x} \approx \sum_{i=1}^{N} p(\underline{y}_i) \text{vol}(S_i) = 1$$

Employing Hölder's inequality for sums and approximating the sum with an integral yields the lower bound:

$$\text{MSE}_{\text{fixed}N} > \frac{k}{(k+2)\pi} \, \Gamma^{2/k} [1+k/2] \|p(\underline{x})\|_{k/(k+2)} N^{-2/k} \qquad (15.6)$$

The upper and lower bounds on MSE for fixed $N$ presented in (15.5) and (15.6) allow an examination of the performance of optimum quantizers as the dimension varies. As $k$ grows toward infinity, the bounds converge.

## 15.4 Companding

For scalar quantization, Bennett [19] introduced the compandor model for both implementation and analysis of nonuniform quantizers. This model consisted of three devices in series: a compressor nonlinearity $g$ mapping the range of the input onto the unit interval [0,1], an $N$-level uniform (equal step size) quantizer on [0,1], and an expandor nonlinearity $g^{-1}$ mapping the quantized values back into the range of the input. Any $N$-level scalar quantizer can be implemented by the appropriate choice of the compressor $g$. The multidimensional extension of companding employs vector nonlinearities $g$ and $g^{-1}$ which map to and from the unit hypercube $\prod_{i=1}^{k} [0,1]$, and a uniform quantizer $Q_U$ implemented on the unit hypercube (see Figure 15.3).

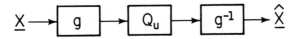

*Figure 15.3. Companding scheme.*

For the analysis of this system, we employ the additive noise model often used for scalar uniform quantizer analysis. In the scalar case, the uniform quantizer is replaced by an additive noise source; the noise is assumed to be independent of the input and uniformly distributed on $[-\Delta/2, \Delta/2]$, where $\Delta$ is the step size of the uniform quantizer. For the multivariate version, we will assume that the uniform quantizer on $\prod_{i=1}^{k} [0,1]$ is a tesselation of a space-filling polytope $P$ and that the effect of the quantizer is the addition of a noise vector $\underline{e}$, independent of the input vector and uniformly distributed over $P$, $p(\underline{e}) = 1/\mathrm{vol}(P) = N$.

Rewriting the expression for the MSE using these two models gives

$$\mathrm{MSE} = \int_{\mathbb{R}^k} \int_P \{\underline{x} - g^{-1}[g(\underline{x}) + \underline{e}]\}^T \cdot \{\underline{x} - g^{-1}[g(\underline{x}) + \underline{e}]\} p(\underline{x}) p(\underline{e}) \, d\underline{e} \, d\underline{x}$$

Assuming that the number of levels $N$ is large (or $|\underline{e}|$ is small), expand $g^{-1}$ into a Taylor series and keep only the first $k+1$ terms:

$$\text{MSE} \approx \int_{\mathbb{R}^k} \int_P g^{-1\prime}(\underline{x})^T \underline{ee}^T g^{-1\prime}(\underline{x}) p(\underline{x}) p(\underline{e}) \, d\underline{x} \, d\underline{e}$$

where $g^{-1\prime}(\underline{x})$ is the matrix of the partial derivatives of $g^{-1}$ with respect to the $x_i$. Several facts allow the simplification of this expression: $\underline{e}$ and $\underline{x}$ are independent, $E(\underline{ee}^T) = I(P)$ the inertia of the polytope $P$, and $S(\underline{x}) = g^{-1\prime}(\underline{x})^T g^{-1\prime}(\underline{x})$ is a symmetric matrix. By these facts and a matrix identity, the MSE is

$$\text{MSE} \approx I(P) \, E\{S(\underline{x})\} = I(P) \, E\{\text{trace } S(\underline{x})\}.$$

We know that the first term is due to the quantization region $P$ and that the second term is due to the compressor function $g$ alone. This expression is a multidimensional extension of Bennett's equation, allowing MSE evaluation of various compressors with a known source. To minimize the MSE, we must minimize both of these terms independently over the choice of $P$ and $g$.

Letting $l_i^{-2}(\underline{x})$ represent the eigenvalues of $S(\underline{x})$; then

$$E\{\text{trace } S(\underline{x})\} = \sum_{i=1}^{k} \int l_i^{-2}(\underline{x}) p(\underline{x}) \, d\underline{x}$$

However, we have the constraint

$$\int_{\mathbb{R}^k} |g'(\underline{x})| \, d\underline{x} = \int_{\mathbb{R}^k} \prod_{i=1}^{k} 1/l_i(\underline{x}) \, d\underline{x} = 1$$

due to the fact that $g(\underline{x})$ maps to the unit hypercube. A simple variational or symmetry argument demonstrates that for minimum MSE the $1/l_i(\underline{x})$ should be equal ($S(\underline{x})$ has equal eigenvalues), and

$$E\{\text{trace } S(\underline{x})\} = k \int_{\mathbb{R}^k} l^{-2}(\underline{x}) p(\underline{x}) \, d\underline{x}$$

This same form was minimized in Section 15.3, with the result that

$$l_i(\underline{x}) = \frac{p(x)^{1/(k+2)}}{\int_{\mathbb{R}^k} p(\underline{x})^{1/(k+2)} \, d\underline{x}} \tag{15.7}$$

and

$$E\{\text{trace } S(\underline{x})\} = \|p(\underline{x})\|_{k/(k+2)}.$$

We now need to solve for the first term, $I(P)$, which depends upon the shape of $P$. One difficulty of implementing multivariate compandors is that $P$ must be chosen so that it fills $\prod_{i=1}^{k} [0,1]$ without overlap. As a simple example, consider the use of a smaller hypercube for the region $P$. Clearly, $N$ such smaller hypercubes will completely fill the unit hypercube if the cubes are of side length $N^{-1/k}$. For the outputs at the center of these small hypercubes, the second moment is $I(P) = k/12N^{2/k}$. These small hypercubes fill the unit hypercube without overlap for any dimension, resulting in upper bounds for both $I(P)$ and the minimum MSE:

$$\text{MSE}_{\text{min}} < \frac{k}{12} \|p(\underline{x})\|_{k/(k+2)} N^{-2/k}.$$

We note that using the hypercube quantizer, the MSE is equivalent to scalar quantization if the input vector has independent rectangular coordinates, $p(\underline{x}) = p(x_1)p(x_2)\cdots p(x_k)$.

Employing different region shapes on $\prod_{i=1}^{k} [0,1]$ can yield smaller values of $I(P)$, hence lower MSE. Let the minimum value of $I(P)$ over all polytopes be of the form

$$\min_{P} I(P) = kC(k)N^{-2/k}$$

where $N$ is the number of regions in the hypercube, $k$ is the dimension of the hypercube, and $C(k)$ is a constant called the dimensionless second moment. This form makes sense since if $N$ of the regions fill $\prod_{i=1}^{k} [0,1]$, then as $N$ increases, the width of each region decreases as $N^{-1/k}$, and the second moment decreases as $(N^{-1/k})^2$. The foregoing hypercube value of $I(P)$ upper-bounds $C(k)$ by $1/12$. Exact values for $C(k)$ are not known for all $k$. In fact, minimum values are known only for the $k = 2$ and $k = 3$ cases. For $k = 2$, the hexagon is the best two-dimensional region which tiles the space, while for $k = 3$, the truncated octahedron has minimum $I(P)$. For

$3 < k < 10$, lattice structures have been analyzed for their Dirichlet polytope $P$ and its inertia $I(P)$. Several root lattices have been considered due to their ease of implementation as the uniform vector quantizer.

It is well known from mechanics that the region which minimizes the second moment for fixed volume is the hypersphere. Unfortunately, the hypersphere does not cover space without overlap, but it does provide a lower bound on the possible value of $C(k)$:

$$\frac{1}{(k+2)\pi} \Gamma^{2/k}(1+k/2) < C(k)$$

We note that with this lower bound on $C(k)$, the lower bound on the MSE of the companding scheme matches the lower bound on MSE derived through the use of the random quantizer in Section 15.3.

Vector companding is not without its difficulties. In particular, to apply the compandor system, complete knowledge of the multivariate statistical structure of the source is necessary. In this sense, scalar quantization is robust in that it only requires the marginal densities of the source. Also, the optimum uniform quantizer on the unit hypercube is needed. This is known only for small $k$. Finally, since the compandor system maps regions of the input space into congruent regions on the unit hypercube, both of which satisfy the Dirichlet partitioning and centroid outputs expressions, the compressor $g$ must be a conformal mapping. For this to be true for the optimal compressor, severe restrictions upon the source pdf exist. In the two-dimensional case, $p(\underline{x})$ must satisfy Laplace's equation. For $k > 2$, $p(\underline{x})$ must be either constant or a Pearson II form.

Another necessity for a successful compandor model implementation is the construction of real-time uniform vector quantizers. Simple implementations do exist for the root lattices. Also, a method called prequantization has been described for implementing the uniform quantizers with $k = 2, 3, 4$. This prequantization method consists of two parts. First, a real-time block quantizer is chosen which has the correct set of output values, but simpler-to-implement, incorrect region boundaries. The second part is a "prequantizer" which distorts the input so that the optimum region boundaries are mapped to the simpler suboptimum boundaries.

**15.5 Suboptimum Vector Quantizers**

Unfortunately, the optimum vector quantizers discussed in the preceding sections are either not defined for all dimensions or are difficult to implement; hence simpler suboptimum designs are needed. Suboptimum vector quantizers are defined as those systems that have better performance than scalar rectangular coordinate quantizers. Three such schemes are discussed below. They include block quantizing of correlated Gaussian vectors, spherical coordinate quantizing of spherically symmetric sources, and Dirichlet rotated polar quantizing of circularly symmetric sources.

**15.5.1** *Block Quantization of Correlated Sources*

In 1963, Huang and Schultheiss considered the minimum MSE quantization of a correlated Gaussian vector $\underline{x}$ of length $k$ with correlation matrix $M_{\underline{x}}$. The quantization scheme was chosen to be the following: a linear operator $P$ which transforms $\underline{x}$ into a vector $\underline{y}$ of uncorrelated (hence independent) Gaussian variables, a bank of $k$ scalar Lloyd-Max quantizers for a Gaussian variate, and another linear operator $R$ to recorrelate the quantized vector $\hat{\underline{y}}$. The optimization included selection of the matrix operators $P$ and $R$ as well as the allocation of levels to each of the separate scalar quantizers, $N_i$, such that $\prod_{i=1}^{k} N_i = N$. Application of the orthogonality principle demonstrates that the optimum choice of $R$ is $R = P^{-1}$. Further use of matrix identities shows that the optimum choice of $P$ is $P = U^T$, where $U$ is the orthogonal matrix which diagonalizes the matrix $M_{\underline{x}}$, so that the diagonal elements are the eigenvalues of $M_{\underline{x}}$, ordered greatest to least. It was also shown that the levels should be divided among the scalar quantizers for $\underline{y}$ according to

$$N_i = N^{1/k} + 1/2 \, \log_2 \sigma_i / |M_{\underline{x}}|^{1/k}; \quad i = 1,2,\dots,k$$

where $\sigma_i$ is the variance of the $i$th component of $\underline{x}$. Although this design was suboptimum from the start due to the system constraint, it gave good performance with simple implementation.

**15.5.2** *Spherical Coordinate Quantization*

For data from a spherically symmetric source, several authors have considered the advantages of quantization of the input's spherical coordinate representation rather than its rectangular coordinate representation. Interest began with polar quantizing of the independent, bivariate Gaussian source and was quickly generalized to other circularly symmetric bivariate and spherically symmetric densities. Once the source is available in spherical coordinates, this quantization scheme processes each coordinate with a separate scalar quantizer. Doing so defines the quantization regions as the intersections of nonzero width spherical shells with pyramids of apex zero (see Figure 15.4 for $k = 2$ and $k = 3$ examples). The minimization of the MSE includes the design of the scalar quantizers for each of the spherical coordinates together with the allocation of levels to each quantizer.

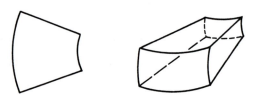

*Figure 15.4 Spherical regions for $k = 2$ and $k = 3$*

In the general $k$-dimensional case, the spherical coordinates include the magnitude $r$ and $k-1$ angles $\phi_j$. If they are not available as such, the spherical coordinate representation can be computed from the rectangular coordinate representation $\underline{x} = [x_1, x_2, \ldots, x_k]^T$ through the following transformations:

$$r = \left[ \sum_{i=1}^{k} x_i^2 \right]^{1/2} ; \quad \phi_j = \tan^{-1}\left[ \frac{x_{j+1}}{\left( \sum_{i=1}^{j} x_i^2 \right)^{1/2}} \right]$$

where $r \in [0,\infty)$, $\phi_1 \in [0,2\pi)$, and $\phi_j \in [-\pi/2, \pi/2]$, $j = 2,3,\ldots,k-1$. The sources under study are those that display spherical symmetry. The $k$-variate density function in rectangular coordinates for these sources is a function of a quadratic form, $p(\underline{x}) = f((\underline{x}^T\underline{x})^{1/2})$, and has contours of constant density which are hyperspheres in the $k$-dimensional space. For such a source, the rectangular coordinates are uncorrelated, but not independent. The only exception to this is the multivariate independent Gaussian source. Applying the transformations above, the density function of the source in spherical coordinates is

$$p(\underline{x}) \to \frac{2\pi^{k/2}r^{k-1}}{\Gamma[k/2]}f(r) \prod_{i=1}^{k-1} \frac{\Gamma[(j+1)/2]}{\Gamma[1/2]\Gamma[j/2]} \cos^{j-1}\phi_j.$$

We notice that the spherical coordinates are independent random variables.

The MSE can be written in terms of the spherical coordinate representation of the source as

$$\text{MSE} = \int_0^\infty [r^2 + \hat{r}^2 - 2r\hat{r}M_{k-1}]f_k(r) \, dr \qquad (15.8)$$

Here $f_k(r)$ is the magnitude density and $M_{k-1}$ is defined sequentially by

$$M_j = \int [\sin \phi_j \sin \hat{\phi}_j + M_{j-1} \cos \phi_j \cos \hat{\phi}_j]f(\phi_j) \, d\phi_j$$

where $f(\phi_j)$ is the $j$th angle density, the integral is over the range of $\phi_j$, and $M_0 = 1$. The MSE is minimized by maximizing each $M_j$ term over the $\phi_j$ quantizer and by minimizing (15.8) over the magnitude quantizer. For small $N$, the solution involves taking partial derivatives of the $M_j$ or the MSE with respect to the parameters of the scalar quantizer, as is typical of the Max-Lloyd solution. For large $N$, we can employ a scalar compandor model with the additive noise assumption. This yields the $M_j$ and MSE as functions of the $k$ compressor functions and the factorization of the levels to each of the spherical coordinate quantizers.

The resulting $N$-level quantizer which minimizes the MSE under this configuration can be described as follows. The magnitude should be processed with the compressor, which is matched in the minimum MSE sense to the magnitude density function, except that the output values are scaled by $M_{k-1}$; the longitude (uniformly distributed angle) should be processed by a uniform quantizer; and the $k-2$ latitudes require minimum MSE compressors for their respective densities. For the allocation of levels to each quantizer, we have the constraint that the product of the number of levels in each quantizer, $N_r N_1 \cdots N_{k-1}$, must be no greater than $N$. Asymptotic analyses have shown that the optimum allocation is unequal (versus equal in rectangular coordinates), with the longitude receiving the largest share. All, however, receive levels at the rate $N_i = B_i N^{1/k}$, where $B_i$ are a set of constants, $\prod_{i=1}^{k} B_i = 1$. The asymptotic MSE which results from this quantization scheme is

$$\text{MSE} = k \, 12^{-1/k} \left[ \frac{2k}{k-1} C_{k-1} \right]^{(k-1)/k} \| f_k(r) \|_{1/3}^{1/k} N^{-2/k}$$

where $C_{k-1}$ is a constant defined sequentially by ($C_1 = \pi^2/6$)

$$C_j = j \left[ \frac{\pi \Gamma[(j+1)/2]}{24\Gamma[j/2]} \right]^{1/j} \left[ \frac{\Gamma[(j+2)/6]}{\Gamma[(j+5)/6]} \right]^{3/j} \left[ \frac{jC_{j-1}}{j^2-1} \right]^{(j-1)/j}$$

Several variations of this technique have also been analyzed. In a much earlier paper, Dunn considered a similar scenario, except that the quantizer had only one magnitude value and all the regions had different combinations of angle values. This scheme had the advantage that the quantization regions were still Dirichlet partitions of the output values (which is not true for the regular spherical quantizers). Also, the regions were equiprobable, which boded well for coding of the outputs. Unfortunately, limiting the magnitude quantization to one value does not yield very good MSE performance except for very small $N$. For small $N$ and $k = 2$, Wilson let the number of phase regions vary from magnitude ring to magnitude ring, with the total number of phase regions summing to $N$. This scheme provided very good results with the

Gaussian source for small $N$; the region in which rectangular quantizers out-perform polar quantizers. Recently, the spherical quantizers have been analyzed under the constraint that the scalar quantizers be uniform in nature with good results for small $k$.

### 15.5.3 *Dirichlet Polar Quantizers*

Let us consider an extension of the above-described spherical coordinate quantizers for the bivariate ($k = 2$) case. Specifically, a change of variables to polar coordinates is effected and the magnitude and phase are quantized separately. Unfortunately, with respect to the conditions derived in Section 15.2, which are necessary for a local minimum of MSE, these quantizers are not optimum. In particular, the regions are partial annuli for all polar quantiz-ers, delimited by rays of constant angle and arcs of constant radius. These partial annuli are not convex regions.

In Section 15.2 it was suggested that (15.2) and (15.3) could be applied to a set of outputs to iterate toward a local minimum of MSE. The resulting quantizer will vary depending upon the initial output point pattern. A rec-tangular starting pattern produces a rectangular quantizer, since the partitions will move perpendicularly. A polar initial pattern produces a system of tra-pezoids fanning out from the origin. Unfortunately, this design has only slight gain in performance over polar quantizers for small $N$ and the two converge as $N$ increases. Instead, consider a polar quantizer where every other magni-tude ring has been rotated by $\pi/N_\phi$ radians. This new pattern, when applied as a starting point for the iterative method with (15.2) and (15.3), will yield a quantization pattern quite different from the trapezoids mentioned above. The optimized quantizer will still display circular symmetry, but the regions are now often hexagonal. This Dirichlet rotated polar quantizer (DRPQ) has been demonstrated to perform well for the Gaussian case for small $N$. In particular, the vector quantizer in Figure 15.2 was designed by this method.

Other research on these DRPQs includes numerical examples when a cen-tral region was present (since the origin has highest probability) and a real-time implementation. For other circularly symmetric sources, the same design methodology holds. Unfortunately, as of yet there are no asymptotic performance results for the DRPQ. An upper bound, however, does exist. Let $p(x,y)$ be the bivariate density function of the source. If we approximate the regions of this DRPQ by hexagons which trisect the phase quantizations, then the MSE can be bounded

$$\text{MSE}_{DRPQ} < \frac{10\pi^2}{9\sqrt{3}N} \left[ \int_0^\infty x^3 p(x,0) \, dx \right]^{1/3} \left[ \int_0^\infty x^{1/2} p^{1/3}(x,0) \, dx \right]^3$$

The asymptotic analysis for this bound employs a compandor model for the spacing of the magnitude rings. For the least upper bound, the compressor is the minimum MSE magnitude density compressor. With the Gaussian source, the value of this bound is $4.763/N$. Numerical examples of the Gaussian DRPQs have a MSE value of approximately $4.2/N$.

### 15.6 Final Comments

This chapter has presented an overview of results in minimum MSE quantization of vector sources. The author acknowledges that MSE is not the only criterion of interest, but also feels that from studying MSE, we can develop intuition about the problem and its solution. For results with other criteria, the interested reader is pointed to the references at the end of the chapter. The reference section also cites several applications of vector quantizers to problems of engineering and statistical interest.

An appropriate final discussion would be a comparison of the gains of performance of the techniques examined. Figure 15.5 displays the coefficient of MSE, defined by

$$\text{coef MSE} = \frac{1}{k} \lim_{N \to \infty} \text{MSE} \; N^{-2/k}$$

for the independent Gaussian source versus dimension. Included are the upper and lower bounds of performance, the spherical coordinate values, the companding MSE values with the known minimum $C(k)$ uniform quantizers for $1 < k < 10$, and the DRPQ value and bound for $k = 2$. Note that the block quantizers of Huang and Schultheiss are equivalent to rectangular

($k = 1$) quantizers for the independent Gaussian source.

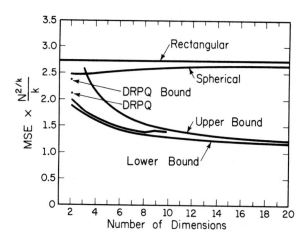

*Figure 15.5 Comparison of MSE for the independent Gaussian source.*

## References

[1] A. Gersho, Principles of quantization, *IEEE Trans. Circ. Sys.,* Vol. CAS-25, pp. 427-437, 1978.

[2] J. Max, Quantizing for minimum distortion, *IEEE Trans. Inform. Theory,* Vol. IT-6, pp. 7-12, 1960.

[3] E.F. Abaya and G.L. Wise, Convergence of vector quantizers with applications to the design of optimal quantizers, *Proc. Allerton Conf. Comm. Cont. Comp.,* University of Illinois, pp. 79-88, 1981.

[4] E.F. Abaya and G.L. Wise, On the existence of optimal quantizers, *IEEE Trans. Inform. Theory,* Vol. IT-28, pp. 937-940, 1982.

[5] D.T.S. Chen, On two or more dimensional optimum quantizers, *IEEE Int'l Conf. ASSP,* pp. 540-643, 1977.

[6]   N.C. Gallagher and J.A. Bucklew, Properties of minimum mean square error block quantizers, *IEEE Trans. Inform. Theory,* Vol. IT-28, pp. 105-107, 1982.

[7]   A. Gersho, On the structure of vector quantizers, *IEEE Trans. Inform. Theory,* Vol. IT-28, pp. 157-166, 1982.

[8]   R.M. Gray, J.C. Kieffer and Y. Linde, Locally optimum block quantizer design, *Inform. Cont.,* Vol. 45, pp. 178-198, 1980.

[9]   Y. Linde, A. Buzo and R.M. Gray, An algorithm for vector quantizer design, *IEEE Trans. Comm.,* Vol. COM-28, pp. 84-95, 1980.

[10]  J. Menez, F. Boeri and D.J. Esteban, Optimum quantizer algorithm for real time block quantizing, *Proc. Int'l Conf. ASSP,* pp. 980-984, 1979.

[11]  J.A. Bucklew, Upper bounds to the asymptotic performance of block quantizers, *IEEE Trans. Inform. Theory,* Vol. IT-27, pp. 577-581, 1981.

[12]  J.A. Bucklew and G.L. Wise, Multidimensional asymptotic quantization theory with r-th power distortion measures, *IEEE Trans. Inform. Theory,* Vol. IT-28, pp. 239-247, 1982.

[13]  P. Elias, Bounds and asymptotes for the performance of multivariate quantizers, *Ann. Math. Statist.,* Vol. 41, pp. 1249-1259, 1970.

[14]  A. Gersho, Asymptotically optimal block quantization, *IEEE Trans. Inform. Theory,* Vol. IT-25, pp.373-380, 1979.

[15]  M.P. Schützenberger, On the quantization of finite dimensional messages, *Inform. Cont.,* Vol. 1, pp. 153-158, 1958.

[16]  Y. Yamada, S. Tazaki and R.M. Gray, Asymptotic performance of block quantizers with difference distortion measures, *IEEE Trans. Inform. Theory,* Vol. IT-26, pp. 6-14, 1980.

[17]  P. Zador, *Development and Evaluation of Procedures for Quantizing Multivariate Distributions,* Stanford University Dissertation, Department of Statistics, 1963.

[18]  P.L. Zador, Asymptotic quantization error of continuous signals and the quantization dimension, *IEEE Trans. Inform. Theory,* Vol. IT-28, pp. 139-149, 1982.

[19]   W.R. Bennett, Spectra of quantized signals, *Bell Sys. Tech. Jour.*, Vol. 27, pp. 446-472, 1948.

[20]   J.A. Bucklew, Companding and random quantization in several dimensions, *IEEE Trans. Inform. Theory*, Vol. IT-27, pp. 207-211, 1981.

[21]   J.A. Bucklew, A note on optimal multidimensional compandors, *IEEE Trans. Inform. Theory*, Vol. IT-29, pp. 279, 1983.

[22]   J.H. Conway and N.J.A. Sloane, Voronoi regions of lattices, second moments of polytopes, and quantization, *IEEE Trans. Inform. Theory*, Vol. IT-28, pp. 211-226, 1982.

[23]   J.H. Conway and N.J.A. Sloane, Fast quantizing and decoding algorithms for lattice quantizers and codes, *IEEE Trans. Inform. Theory*, Vol. IT-28, pp. 227-232, 1982.

[24]   L. Fejes Toth, Sur la representation d'une population infinie par un nombre finie d'elements, *Acta Mathematica*, Magyar Tudomanyos Akademia Budapest, Vol. 10, pp. 299-304, 1959.

[25]   D.J. Newman, The hexagon theorem, *IEEE Trans. Inform. Theory*, Vol. IT- 28, pp. 137-139, 1982.

[26]   K.D. Rines and N.C. Gallagher, Jr., The design of multidimensional quantizers using prequantization, *Proc. Allerton Conf. Comm. Cont. Comp.*, pp. 446-453, 1979.

[27]   K.D. Rines and N.C. Gallagher Jr., The design of two dimensional quantizers using prequantization, *IEEE Trans. Inform. Theory*, Vol. IT-28, pp. 232-239, 1982.

[28]   K.D. Rines, N.C. Gallagher Jr. and J.A. Bucklew, Nonuniform multidimensional quantizers, *Proc. Princeton Conf. Inform. Sci. Sys.*, Princeton University, pp. 43-46, 1982.

[29]   K. Sayood and J.D. Gibson, An algorithm for designing vector quantizers, *Proc. Allerton Conf. Comm., Cont., Comp.*, pp. 301-310, 1982.

[30]   J.A. Bucklew and N.C. Gallagher Jr., Quantization schemes for bivariate Gaussian random variables, *IEEE Trans. Inform. Theory*, Vol. IT-25, pp. 537-543, 1979.

[31]  J.A. Bucklew and N.C. Gallagher Jr., Two-dimensional quantization of bivariate circularly symmetric densities, *IEEE Trans. Inform. Theory*, Vol. IT-25, pp. 667-671, 1979.

[32]  W.J. Dallas, Magnitude-coupled phase quantization, *Appl. Optics*, Vol. 13, pp. 2274-2279, 1974.

[33]  J.G. Dunn, The performance of a class of n dimensional quantizers for a Gaussian source, *Proc. Columbia Symp. Signal Tran.*, New York, pp. 76-81, 1965.

[34]  R.M. Gray and E.D. Karnin, Multiple local optima in vector quantizers, *IEEE Trans. Inform. Theory*, Vol. IT-28, pp. 256-261, 1982.

[35]  J.J.Y. Huang and P.M. Schultheiss, Block quantization of correlated Gaussian random variables, *IEEE Trans. Comm. Sys.*, Vol. CS-11, pp. 289-296, 1963.

[36]  W.A. Pearlman, Polar quantization of a complex Gaussian random variable, *IEEE Trans. Comm.*, Vol. COM-27, pp. 892-899, 1979.

[37]  P.F. Swaszek, Further notes on circularly symmetric quantizers, *Proc. Conf. Inform. Sci. Sys.*, Johns Hopkins University, pp. 794-800, 1983.

[38]  P.F. Swaszek, Uniform spherical coordinate quantizers, *Proc. Allerton Conf. Comm., Cont. Comp.*, pp. 491-500, 1983.

[39]  P.F. Swaszek and J.B. Thomas, Optimum circularly symmetric quantizers, *J. Franklin Inst.*, Vol. 313, pp. 373-384, 1982.

[40]  P.F. Swaszek, Asymptotic performance of optimal circularly symmetric quantizers, submitted for publication.

[41]  P.F. Swaszek and J.B. Thomas, Multidimensional spherical coordinates quantization, *IEEE Trans. Inform. Theory*, Vol. IT-28, pp. 570-576, 1983.

[42]  P.F. Swaszek and T. Ku, Asymptotic performance of unrestricted polar quantizers, *Proc. Princeton Conf. Inform. Sci. and Sys.*, pp. 581-586, 1984.

[43]  M. Tasto and P.A. Wintz, Note on the error signal of block quantizers, *IEEE Trans. Comm.*, Vol. COM-21, pp. 216-219, 1973.

[44] S.G. Wilson, Magnitude/phase quantization of independent Gaussian variates, *IEEE Trans. Comm.*, Vol. COM-28, pp. 1924-1929, 1980.

[45] A. Buzo, A.H.Gray, Jr., R.M. Gray and J.D. Markel, Speech coding based upon vector quantization, *IEEE Trans. Acoust., Speech, Sig. Proc.*, Vol. ASSP-28, pp. 562-574, 1980.

[46] N.C. Gallagher, Jr., Quantizing schemes for the discrete Fourier transform of a random time series, *IEEE Trans. Inform. Theory*, Vol. IT-24, pp. 156-163, 1978.

[47] A. Habibi and P.A. Wintz, Image coding by linear transformation and block quantization, *IEEE Trans. Comm.*, Vol. COM-19, pp. 50-62, 1971.

[48] J. MacQueen, Some methods for classification and analysis of multivariate observations, *Proc. 5th Berkeley Symp. Math. Stat. and Prob., Vol. 1*, Berkeley, CA: Univ. of California Press, pp. 281-297, 1967.

[49] W.A. Pearlman, Optimum fixed level quantization of the DFT of achromatic images, *Proc. Allerton Conf. Comm. Cont. and Comp.*, pp. 313-319, 1979.

[50] D. Pollard, Quantization and the method of $k$-means, *IEEE Trans. Inform. Theory*, Vol. IT-28, pp. 199-205, 1982.

# 16

# The Chinese Remainder Theorem and Applications

Jack Keil Wolf

*Department of Electrical Engineering and Computer Science*
*University of California, San Diego*
*La Jolla, California*

## 16.1 Introduction

A number of common mathematical techniques in signal processing and data transmission have as their common basis an ancient number-theoretic theorem known as the Chinese remainder theorem. The scope of problems to which this applies is very wide. It includes cryptography, error control coding, fault-tolerant systems, and certain aspects of signal processing. In this chapter we present various versions of this theorem and discuss some of the problems

This work was supported by the Air Force Office of Scientific Research under grant AFOSR-82-0061.

to which it can be applied.

We begin with the simple example of Figure 16.1.

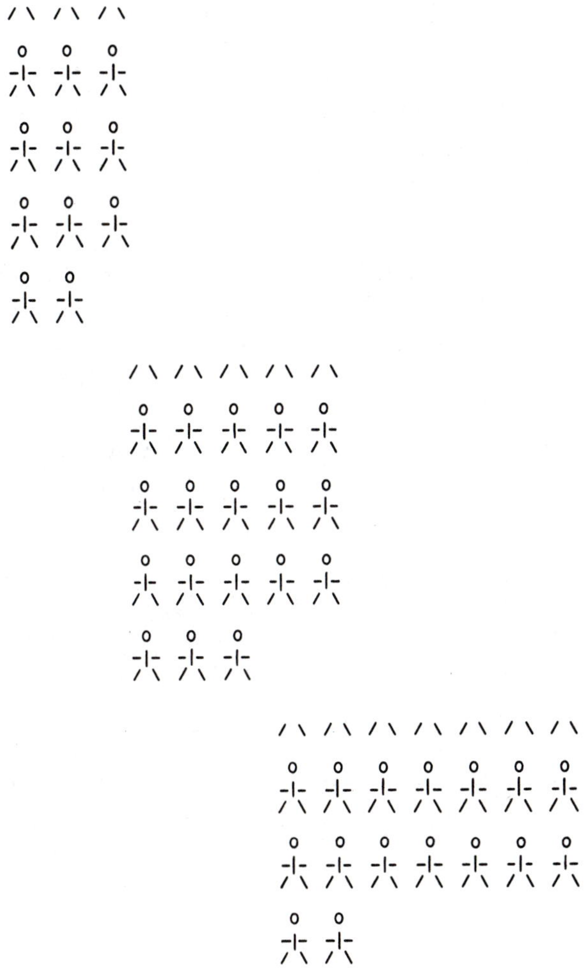

```
/ \  / \  / \
 o    o    o
-|-  -|-  -|-
/ \  / \  / \
 o    o    o
-|-  -|-  -|-
/ \  / \  / \
 o    o    o
-|-  -|-  -|-
/ \  / \  / \
 o    o
-|-  -|-
/ \  / \


            / \  / \  / \  / \  / \
             o    o    o    o    o
            -|-  -|-  -|-  -|-  -|-
            / \  / \  / \  / \  / \
             o    o    o    o    o
            -|-  -|-  -|-  -|-  -|-
            / \  / \  / \  / \  / \
             o    o    o    o    o
            -|-  -|-  -|-  -|-  -|-
            / \  / \  / \  / \  / \
             o    o    o
            -|-  -|-  -|-
            / \  / \  / \


                        / \  / \  / \  / \  / \  / \  / \
                         o    o    o    o    o    o    o
                        -|-  -|-  -|-  -|-  -|-  -|-  -|-
                        / \  / \  / \  / \  / \  / \  / \
                         o    o    o    o    o    o    o
                        -|-  -|-  -|-  -|-  -|-  -|-  -|-
                        / \  / \  / \  / \  / \  / \  / \
                         o    o
                        -|-  -|-
                        / \  / \
```

*Figure 16.1 Our three observations of the first-grade class.*

Suppose we know that there are fewer than 100 children in the first grade of a school and we are able to observe them at several times during the day through small windows. We are unable to see (and count) the entire class but rather can see only the children in the last few rows of the class. The first time we see that the children are arranged in a formation of three columns and that there are only two children in the last row. The second time, we see that the formation has five columns and that there are only three children in the last row. The last time we see that the children form seven columns with only two children in the last row. We believe that in each case all rows but the last are full. The question is to determine the number of students in the class from these three observations.

We, of course, could test all positive integers less than 100 to see if there were one or more solutions consistent with our observations. However, we are interested in a more general (and more elegant) approach. As we shall see, this is provided to us by the Chinese remainder theorem. Returning to the example, let us denote by $x$ the number of students in the class and by $a$, $b$ and $c$ the number of students in the last row for our three observations. Then the following linear congruences describe our knowledge:

$$x \equiv a \text{ modulo } 3, \quad x \equiv b \text{ modulo } 5, \quad x \equiv c \text{ modulo } 7 \qquad (16.1)$$

where for our specific observations $a = 2$, $b = 3$, and $c = 2$. A formula which gives the unique solution to the foregoing set of linear congruences for arbitrary $a, b$ and $c$ is

$$x = (70a + 21b + 15c) \text{ modulo } 105 \qquad (16.2)$$

For $a = 2$, $b = 3$, and $c = 2$ this equation yields the unique solution $x = 23$. How the constants 70, 21 and 15 are related to the numbers 3, 5, and 7 will be discussed later.

Before delving into the details of the Chinese remainder theorem, it is interesting to review its history as researched by one my graduate students, Howard Ma [1]. The theorem was recorded in the chapter "Tai Yen Chiu Yi Shu" ("Method of Unifying the Universe") in the book *Sun Tsu Suan Ching* (Sun Tsu Arithmetic Book) believed to be written circa 500 BC by Sun Tsu.

A solution to the specific congruencies of Figure 16.1 was given by Hsin Tsai-Wei, a famous author during the Ming dynasty (1368 AD to 1643 AD), in the following poem

*Three men walk together, their chance of reaching seventy so slight.*
*Among the five plum trees, twenty-one blossoms did they yield.*
*Seven sons at mid-month, happily did reunite.*
*Divide this sum by 105, the answer is revealed.*

Note how the pairs of numbers in the first three lines of the poem (3,70), (5,21), and (7,15) (midmonth = 15) correspond to the constants in the congruences and in the reconstruction formula for $x$. A formal proof of the Chinese remainder theorem was published by Euler in 1734.

In the next section we give one form of the Chinese remainder theorem (for integers). We will use the following notation. Assume that $m$ is a positive integer. The linear congruence

$$x \equiv y \text{ modulo } m, \qquad (16.3)$$

read "$x$ is congruent to $y$ modulo $m$", is used to indicate that $(x - y)$ is divisible by $m$ without remainder. On the other hand, the equation

$$x = (y \text{ modulo } m) \qquad (16.4)$$

read "$x$ is equal to the value of $y$ taken modulo $m$", means that $x - y$ is divisible by $m$ without remainder and that $x$ is in the range 0 to $m - 1$. Clearly, (16.4) implies (16.3) but not vice versa. Sometimes we will employ the shorthand notation $\langle y \rangle_m$ for $(y \text{ modulo } m)$. Thus either notation is used to denote the remainder obtained by dividing $y$ by $m$, where this remainder must lie in the range 0 to $m - 1$. Later we will use the same notation for polynomials with coefficients from a field.

## 16.2 The Chinese Remainder Theorem for Integers

Let $m_0, m_1, \ldots, m_{k-1}$ be a set of pairwise prime positive integers and $M = \prod_{i=0}^{k-1} m_i$. Let $a_0, a_1, \ldots, a_{k-1}$ be any set of integers. Define $t_i = M/m_i$, $i = 0, 1, \ldots, k-1$. Finally let $u_i$, $i = 0, 1, \ldots, k-1$, be such that

$$t_i u_i \equiv 1 \quad \text{modulo } m_i \qquad (16.5)$$

Then we have the

*Chinese Remainder Theorem:* The set of linear congruences

$$x \equiv a_i \quad \text{modulo } m_i, \quad i = 0, 1, \ldots, k-1 \qquad (16.6)$$

has the unique solution $\hat{x}$ in the range $0 \le \hat{x} < M$

$$\hat{x} = \left( \sum_{i=0}^{k-1} a_i u_i t_i \right) \text{ modulo } M \qquad (16.7)$$

*Proof:* First we show that the set of linear congruences has at most one solution in the range 0 to $M-1$ by assuming that there are two distinct solutions to the congruences and proving a contradiction. If $x_1$ and $x_2$, $0 \le x_1 < x_2 \le M-1$, both satisfy the congruences

$$x \equiv a_i \text{ modulo } m_i, \quad i = 0, 1, \ldots, k-1 \qquad (16.8)$$

then $x_3 = x_2 - x_1$, $(1 \le x_3 \le M - 1)$ must satisfy the congruences

$$x_3 \equiv 0 \text{ modulo } m_i, \quad i = 0, 1, \ldots, k-1 \qquad (16.9)$$

But then $x_3$ would have to be divisible by $m_1$, and by $m_2, \ldots$, and by $m_k$. Since $m_1, m_2, \ldots, m_k$ have no common factors, $x_3$ must be divisible by the product $M = \prod_{i=0}^{k-1} m_i$. But since $x_3$ is greater than 0 and less than $M$, this cannot be the case. Thus we have our contradiction and have proved that there cannot be two or more solutions. We next show that

$$\hat{x} = \left( \sum_{i=0}^{k-1} a_i u_i t_i \right) \text{ modulo } M \qquad (16.10)$$

is a solution to the congruences and falls in the proper range. The modulo $M$ operation ensures that $\hat{x}$ falls in the range 0 to $M - 1$, so that we must only demonstrate that $\hat{x}$ satisfies the congruences. First note that

$$\langle \hat{x} \rangle_{m_j} = \sum_{i=0}^{k-1} \langle a_i u_i t_i \rangle_{m_j} \text{ modulo } m_j \tag{16.11}$$

But

$$\langle a_i u_i t_i \rangle_{m_j} = \begin{cases} 0, & i \neq j \\ \langle a_j \rangle_{m_j}, & i = j \end{cases} \tag{16.12}$$

since $\langle t_i \rangle_{m_j} = 0$ for $i \neq j$ and $\langle u_i t_i \rangle_{m_j} = 1$ for $i = j$. Thus

$$\langle \hat{x} \rangle_{m_j} = \langle a_j \rangle_{m_j} \tag{16.13}$$

or

$$\hat{x} \equiv a_j \text{ modulo } m_j, \quad j = 0, 1, \ldots, k-1. \tag{16.14}$$

Q.E.D.

Note that for the example presented in Section 16.1, $m_0 = 3$, $m_1 = 5$, $m_2 = 7$, so that $M = \prod_{i=0}^{k-1} m_i = 105$ and $t_0 = 105/3 = 35$, $t_1 = 105/5 = 21$, and $t_2 = 105/7 = 15$. Then one set of solutions for $u_0$, $u_1$, and $u_2$ are $u_0 = 2$, $u_1 = 1$, and $u_2 = 1$ since

$$2 \cdot 35 \equiv 1 \quad \text{modulo } 3$$

$$1 \cdot 21 \equiv 1 \quad \text{modulo } 5$$

$$1 \cdot 15 \equiv 1 \quad \text{modulo } 7.$$

Thus we have the formula (16.2) for the solution to the congruence given in (16.1).

One application of the Chinese remainder theorem for integers is to justify a critical step in proving the validity of the Rivest-Shamir-Adelman (RSA) encryption algorithm [2]. For lack of space we avoid a full description of the algorithm and merely jump to a crucial point in the proof. We have two primes $p$ and $q$ with $n = pq$. Furthermore, we have two positive integers $e$ and $d$ such that

$$\langle ed \rangle_{(p-1)(q-1)} = 1$$

The proof of the validity of this procedure requires us to demonstrate that for any nonzero $Q$ less than $n$ and relatively prime to $n$ that

$$\langle Q^{ed} \rangle_n = Q$$

One method of proof involves first showing that

$$\langle \langle Q^{ed} \rangle_n \rangle_p = \langle Q^{ed} \rangle_p = \langle Q \rangle_p$$
$$\langle \langle Q^{ed} \rangle_n \rangle_q = \langle Q^{ed} \rangle_q = \langle Q \rangle_q$$

But now the Chinese remainder thorem immediately gives us our desired result since $Q$ and $\langle Q^{ed} \rangle_n$ are both positive integers less than $n$ having the same residues modulo $p$ and modulo $q$. By the uniqueness of the solution to these congruences, we then find that $Q$ and $\langle Q^{ed} \rangle_n$ must be equal. More will be said about applications of the Chinese remainder theorem to cryptography in a later section.

## 16.3 The Chinese Remainder Theorem for Polynomials

Most of our applications require us to extend the notion of the Chinese remainder theorem to polynomials with coefficients from a field. In what follows all coefficients are assumed to have coefficients from this field, denoted $F$. We begin with $k$ polynomials $m_0(x), m_1(x), \ldots, m_{k-1}(x)$ of degrees $d_0, d_1, \ldots, d_{k-1}$, respectively. These polynomials are assumed to be pairwise relatively prime—that is, no two of them have a common factor of degree greater than zero. Define

$$M(x) = \prod_{i=0}^{k-1} m_i(x)$$

and

$$t_i(x) = M(x)/m_i(x), \quad i = 0,1,\ldots,k-1$$

Finally, let $u_i(x)$, $i = 0,1,\ldots,k-1$, be such that

$$t_i(x)u_i(x) \equiv 1 \quad \text{modulo} \ m_i(x)$$

Then we have the

*Chinese Remainder Theorem for Polynomials:* The set of linear congruences

$$I(x) \equiv a_i(x) \ \text{modulo} \ m_i(x), \quad i = 0,1,\ldots,k-1$$

has the unique solution $\tilde{I}(x)$, with $\deg \tilde{I}(x) < \deg M(x)$, given as

$$\tilde{I}(x) = \left( \sum_{i=0}^{k-1} a_i(x)u_i(x)t_i(x) \right) \ \text{modulo} \ M(x)$$

The proof of this theorem is omitted since it closely resembles the proof of the previous theorem.

Several well-known tools of signal processing are the Chinese remainder theorem in disguise. Among these are the Lagrange interpolation formula and the discrete Fourier transform. We begin with a discussion of the

*Lagrange Interpolation Formula:* We are given a real or complex-valued polynomial function $H(z)$ of a real or complex variable $z$ the values of which are known at $k$ distinct points $z_0, z_1, \ldots, z_{k-1}$ to be $H(z_0), H(z_1), \ldots, H(z_{k-1})$. Then there is one and only one polynomial of degree $k-1$ or less that is consistent with these values.

*Proof:* Let $m_i(z) = (z - z_i)$, $i = 0,1,\ldots,k-1$, $z_i \neq z_j$, and use the Chinese remainder theorem, Q.E.D.

The interpolation formula which gives $H(z)$ at any other value of $z$, say $z = z'$, is then

$$H(z') = \sum_{i=0}^{k-1} \left( \prod_{j \neq i} \frac{z' - z_j}{z_i - z_j} \right) H(z_i) \tag{16.15}$$

since

$$\langle H(z)\rangle_{(z-z_i)} = H(z_i)$$

We next consider the

*Discrete Fourier Transform* [4]: Given a set of real or complex numbers $h_0, h_1, \ldots, h_{k-1}$. The $k \times k$ discrete Fourier transform yields another set of complex numbers $H_0, H_1, \ldots, H_{k-1}$, which are related by the formulas

$$H_j = \sum_{i=0}^{k-1} h_i W_k^{ij}, \quad j = 0,1,\ldots,k-1 \tag{16.16}$$

and

$$h_i = \frac{1}{k} \sum_{j=0}^{k-1} H_j W_k^{-ij}, \quad i = 0,1,\ldots,k-1 \tag{16.17}$$

where $W_k$ is the $k$th complex root of unity

$$W_k = e^{-\frac{2\pi \sqrt{-1}}{k}}$$

*Proof of* (16.17): Let

$$h(z) = \sum_{i=0}^{k-1} h_i z^i \tag{16.18}$$

Using the Lagrange interpolation formula with $z_j = W_k^j$, $j = 0,1,\ldots,k-1$, yields the equation

$$h(z) = \sum_{j=0}^{k-1} h(W_k^j) W_k^j (z^{k-1} + W_k^j z^{k-2} + \cdots + W_k^{(k-1)j})/k \tag{16.19}$$

Denoting $h(W_k^j)$ by $H_j$, we then have from (16.18) that

$$H_j = \sum_{i=0}^{k-1} h_i W_k^{ij} \tag{16.20}$$

which is (16.16). Furthermore, (16.19) and (16.18) yield the formula

$$h_{k-i} = \frac{1}{k} \sum_{j=0}^{k-1} H_j W_k^{ij} \tag{16.21}$$

or

$$h_i = \frac{1}{k} \sum_{j=0}^{k-1} H_j W_k^{-ij} \qquad (16.22)$$

which is (16.17).

## 16.4 The Chinese Remainder Theorem with Redundant Remainders

We now discuss a version of the Chinese remainder theorem that leads to some very interesting applications in error control and in fault-tolerant systems. Although we could state the needed result for both integers and polynomials, we will limit ourselves to the latter. The basic idea is that if there are more remainders than the number which are required to reconstruct the original polynomial, then we are able to reconstruct the polynomials even if some of the remainders are lost and others are in error provided that we are left with enough "good" remainders. We begin with $n$ pairwise relatively prime polynomials $m_0(x), m_1(x), \ldots, m_{n-1}(x)$ of degrees $d_0, d_1, \ldots, d_{n-1}$, respectively. Let $d_0 \le d_1 \le \cdots \le d_{n-1}$ and let $L = \sum_{i=0}^{k-1} d_i$ for some $k \le n$. Let $I(x)$ be any polynomial of degree $L-1$ or less and consider the set of $n$ congruences

$$I(x) \equiv a_i(x) \quad \text{modulo} \quad m_i(x), \quad i = 0, 1, 2, \ldots, n-1.$$

Let $E$ and $T$ be mutually exclusive subsets of the set $\{0, 1, 2, \ldots n-1\}$ of cardinality $e$ and $t$ respectively. The set $E$ will denote the indices of the residues which are in error, and the set $T$ will denote the indices of the lost residues. The idea will be to reconstruct $I(x)$ from a set of residues $b_i(x)$, $i = 0, 1, 2, \ldots, n-1$, defined as

$$b_i(x) = \begin{cases} \varnothing, & i \in E \\ \sigma_i(x), & i \in T \\ a_i(x), & i \notin E \cup T. \end{cases} \qquad (16.23)$$

Here $\varnothing$ is the null symbol representing lost residues and the $\sigma_i(x)$ ($i \in T$) represent residues which are in error [i.e., $\sigma_i(x) \ne a_i(x)$ for $i \in T$]. Given the set $b_0(x), b_1(x), \ldots, b_{n-1}(x)$ it is immediately apparent which residues have been lost but it is not apparent which residues are in error. We now prove the following:

*Theorem:* $I(x)$ can be reconstructed from the $b_i(x)$, $i = 0, 1, \ldots, n-1$, provided that $e + 2t \leq n - k$.

*Proof:* We can take care of the lost residues by replacing $n$ by $n - e = n'$. Now we must show that we can reconstruct $I(x)$ from $t$ faulty residues and $(n' - t)$ good ones provided that $2t < n' - k$. Because of the restriction on the degree of $I(x)$, this polynomial can be correctly reconstructed from any set of $k$ of the correct residues. Our reconstruction procedure will be to compute $I(x)$ from each of the

$$\binom{n'}{k}$$

choices of $k$ residues from the $n'$ unerased residues and then choose which $I(x)$ that has the most votes. Since there are $(n' - t)$ "good" residues, there will be at least

$$\binom{n' - t}{k}$$

votes for the correct $I(x)$. We complete the proof by showing that any other $I(x)$ cannot receive that many votes. Let us consider a vote which results in some other $I(x)$. It must contain at least one faulty $\sigma_i(x)$ and at most $(k-1)$ "good" $a_i(x)$. Consider a specific set of $(k-1)$ "good" $a_i(x)$ such that when one chooses $k$ $b_i(x)$ from the union of this set and the set of "bad" $\sigma_i(x)$, it produces a wrong $I(x)$. There are at most

$$\binom{t + k - 1}{k}$$

ways of choosing $k$ items from the total of $t + (k - 1)$ items. It may be possible that all of these will produce the same $I(x)$ but that no other set of $k$ $b_i(x)$ will produce the same $I(x)$ since then we would have at least $k$ "good" $a_i(x)$, consistent with the wrong $I(x)$. Furthermore, note that

$$\binom{t+k-1}{k} < \binom{n'-t}{k}$$

if $t+k-1 < n'-t$ or equivalently if $2t < n'-k$. Q.E.D.

## 16.5 Applications of the Chinese Remainder Theorem with Redundant Remainders

### 16.5.1 Reed-Solomon Codes [5]:

Consider a finite field $F$ having an element $\alpha$ of order $n$. Let $A_0, A_1, \ldots, A_{k-1}$ be arbitrary elements from this field and let

$$a_j = \sum_{i=0}^{k-1} A_i \alpha^{ij}, \quad j = 0, 1, \ldots, n-1 \qquad (16.24)$$

Let $b$ be an $n$-vector having $e$ null components, $t$ components of which are arbitrary with the remaining components being equal to the corresponding components of the vector $a$.

*Theorem:* The vector $a$ can be obtained from the vector $b$ if $2t + e \le n - k$.

*Proof:* Define $A(z) = \sum_{j=0}^{n-1} A_j z^j$ and let $m_i(z) = (z - \alpha^i)$, $i = 0, 1, \ldots, n-1$. Then note that

$$A(z) \equiv a_j \quad \text{modulo } m_j(z), \quad j = 0, 1, \ldots, n-1$$

From the preceding section, $A(z)$ can be reconstructed from the $a_j$ even if $t$ are in error and $e$ are missing provided that $2t \le n - k$. Once $A(z)$ is known, then so are the $\{A_i\}$ and then the $\{a_i\}$. Q.E.D.

### 16.5.2 Discrete Fourier Transform Codes [6]:

Let $a = (a_0, a_1, \ldots, a_{n-1})$ be a set of complex n numbers having the property that its discrete Fourier transform $A_0, A_1, \ldots, A_{n-1}$ is such that $A_k = A_{k+1} = \cdots = A_{n-1} = 0$. Let $b$ be an $n$-vector where $n - e$ nonnull components are a set of complex numbers, $t$ of which are arbitrary, and the remaining $(n - e - t)$ equals the corresponding components of $\underline{a}$.

*Theorem:* $\underline{a}$ can be recovered from $\underline{b}$ if $2t + e \leq n - k$.

*Proof:* Same as for Reed-Solomon codes.

It is interesting that a more powerful version of this theorem "almost always" holds. That is, if $t + e \leq n - k - 1$, then for almost all choices for the positions and values of the errors $\underline{a}$ can be recovered from $\underline{b}$. The reason this is true is that for all but very special choices for the t arbitrary components, every different set of $k$ components involving one of the arbitrary components will yield a distinct vector $\underline{a}$, while every set of $k$ components involving the $(n - t - e)$ "correct" components will yield the same (and correct) $\underline{a}$. Thus as long as $n - t - e$ exceeds $k$, we will have a number of votes for one $\underline{a}$, the correct one, while any incorrect $\underline{a}$ will have at most one vote.

An application of discrete Fourier codes is the transmission of analog (i.e., continuous amplitude) signals over an impulsive noise channel. Here we assume that we begin with a discrete-time sequence of real or complex numbers whose discrete Fourier transform has $(n - k)$ zeros in consecutive positions. After transmission over an additive impulsive noise channel, the received discrete time sequence equals the transmitted sequence in $(n - t)$ of its components and equals the transmitted sequence plus impulses in $t$ of its components. If the number of impulses, $t$, is no more than $(n - k)/2$, then these impulses can always be located, and their values calculated. Then the impulses can be subtracted from the received sequence, yielding an exact copy of the transmitted sequence. The calculation of the position of the impulses and their values can actually be accomplished by solving a set of nonlinear equations. When one takes the DFT of the received sequence and examines those components where the transmitted sequence's DFT were all zeros, the resulting values of the components are due to the noise impulses alone. Equations can be written relating the positions and values of the impulses to those component values and these equations can be solved if the number of impulses, $t$, is no more than $(n - k)/2$.

More interestingly, one can almost always remove the $t$ impulses provided that $t$ is less than $(n - k)$, an improvement by a factor of 2 in the number of impulses that can be removed. Now, however, one needs to use the voting procedure discussed above– a very complex procedure if $n$ and $k$ are large.

Finally, it is to be noted that these procedures also work if there are errors on these components which are not affected by impulses provided that these errors are small enough.

### 16.5.3 *Goppa Codes* [5]:

Let the coefficients of $I(x)$, which are the information symbols to be encoded, be symbols from $GF(q)$. Let $G(x)$ be a particular polynomial from $GF(q)$ and let $f(x) = G(x)I(x)$. Let

$$a_i(x) = f(x) \text{ modulo } m_i(x), \quad i = 0,1,\ldots,n-1$$

Let $G$ be a ("good") subset of $(0,1,\ldots,n-1)$ of cardinality $n-t$, let $b_i(x) = a_i(x)$ for $i \in G$, and let $b_i(x)$ be arbitrary for $i \notin G$. Then $I(x)$ can be recovered from the $n$ $b_i(x)$ provided that:

1.  $G(x)$ is relatively prime to all $m_i(x)$, $i = 0,1,\ldots,n-1$.
2.  $G(x)$ has degree at least equal to the sum of any $2t$ $m_i(x)$.

If all the $m_i(x)$ have the same degree $b$, then $\deg[G(x)] \geq 2tb$.

For Goppa codes, the $m_i(x)$ are chosen to equal $(x - \beta^i)$, $i = 1,2,\ldots,n-1$, and $m_0(x) = x$, where $\beta$ is a primitive element of $GF(2^h)$ and $n = 2^h$.

We do not prove the foregoing result, but it should not be difficult to believe that its proof follows directly from the theorem of the preceding section.

### 16.5.4 *Cryptographic Key Storage* [7]:

Assume that a cryptographic key is a binary $s$ vector so that it can be represented as a symbol from $GF(2^s)$. Assume that we wish to give information about this key to $n$ people so that any $k$ or more people can reconstruct the key with their information but that the information possessed by fewer than $k$ people gives no knowledge of the key. One method of accomplishing this task is as follows. Let $I(x)$ be a polynomial of degree $k-1$ or less with coefficient from $GF(2^s)$ and having its zero order coefficient equal to the key. Let $\alpha$ be an element if $GF(2^s)$ of order $n$ or greater. Give the following information to the $i$−th person for $i = 0, 1, ..., n-1$: $\langle I(z) \rangle_{(z-\alpha^i)} = I(\alpha^i)$. If one has fewer than $k$ of the $I(\alpha^i)$, there are multiple solutions. Furthermore, the zero-order coefficient of these multiple solutions takes on the $2^s$ values from $GF(2^s)$ with equal multiplicity. The Chinese remainder theorem with redundant remainders allows for some of the information to be lost and others to be tampered with.

## 16.6 Other Applications

Space precludes a more complete explanation of the applications of the Chinese remainder theorem. Any scheme that uses residues, interpolation, or the discrete Fourier transform is a candidate. For example, it has been suggested that one could build an entire computer utilizing residue arithmetic. In such a machine one would represent numbers by remainders calculated from the Chinese remainder theorem. This has been referred to as the Sino representation [8]. Then when one adds two numbers, one adds their remainders, and when one multiplies two numbers, one multiplies their remainders. The remainders calculated modulo $m_i$ are added or multiplied modulo $m_i$. If such a machine were built with redundant remainders, the machine would have fault-tolerant properties and could produce correct results even if a limited number of components failed. This idea could be applied to the design of digital filters where addition and multiplication were performed using the Sino representation. Similarly, if one expands the dimensionality of a vector when taking the discrete Fourier transform, the resultant vector is redundant and has fault tolerant properties. Still another application is in the storage of information in a distributed system. Here one could have faulty memories and lost data and still be able to reconstruct the original information. It is the contention of this chapter that this technique is a very general one and will become more important in future systems.

## References

[1] Editorial Board Chun-Hua Book Company, *The Sea of Chinese Terminology (Tz-Hai)*, Vol. 1, 2nd Edition, Chun-Hua Book Company, pp. 865-867, 1967.

[2] R.L. Rivest, A. Shamir and L.M. Adelman, A method for obtaining digital signatures and public-key cryptosystems, *Comm. ACM*, Vol. 21, pp. 120-126, 1978.

[3] F.B. Hildebrand, *Introduction to Numerical Analysis*, New York, NY: McGraw-Hill, 1956.

[4] M. Schwartz and L. Shaw, *Signal Processing, Discrete Spectral Analysis and Estimation*, New York, NY: McGraw-Hill, pp. 28-33, 1975.

[5] R.E. Blahut, *Theory and Practice of Error Control Codes*, Reading, MA: Addison-Wesley, pp. 207-247, 1983.

[6] J.K. Wolf, Redundancy, the discrete Fourier transform and impulsive noise cancellation, *IEEE Trans. Comm.*, Vol. COM-31, pp. 458-461, 1983.

[7] A. Shamir, How to share a secret, *Comm. ACM*, Vol. 222, pp. 612-613, 1979.

[8] J.H. McClellan and C.M. Rader, *Number Theory in Digital Signal Processing*, Englewood Cliffs, NJ: Prentice-Hall, p. 22, 1979.

# 17

# Detection of Complex Sinusoids by the Pisarenko Method

**Kung Yao**

*Electrical Engineering Department*
*University of California at Los Angeles*
*Los Angeles, California*

## 17.1 Introduction

Modern detection, estimation, and signal processing problems not only share common mathematical tools and optimization techniques but also need digital computers and processors for practical realizations. In off-line applications, the available computational resources can be quite substantial. Thus, all sorts of classically known numerical analysis and optimization techniques are being considered for implementations. On the other hand, for real-time on-

This work is partially supported by the Electronics Program of the Office of Naval Research.

board applications, computationally intensive optimum solutions as well as lesser computationally demanding but nevertheless high-performance suboptimum solutions are of interest.

In this chapter we consider the detection of complex sinusoids in the presence of white Gaussian noise. The amplitudes are assumed to be deterministic but unknown. The frequencies are also assumed to be deterministic, unknown, and can be closely spaced. The phases are assumed to be either random or unknown.

In Section 17.2 we formulate this problem as a binary hypothesis detection problem based on the DFT (or FFT) technique. The minimum frequency difference of two complex sinusoids with equal amplitudes but arbitrary phases that can be detected under the "3-dB criterion" is obtained. In Section 17.3, we consider the Pisarenko method and summarize some relevant analytical results related to the binary hypothesis problem. In Section 17.4 we introduce the generalized trace method as a computationally tractable technique of performing rank determination for the binary hypothesis detection problem. In Section 17.5 various numerical results illustrating the use of the generalized trace method based on the observed data are given. Our new technique is better than the classical DFT technique by approximately a factor of 2 to 3.

### 17.2 Problem Formulation and Classical DFT/FFT Results

Consider a binary hypothesis-testing problem where under $H_j$, $j = 0,1$, the observed data are given for $n = 0,1,...,N-1$ by

$$x_n = \begin{cases} A_0 e^{i(2\pi f_0 n + \phi_0)} + q_n, & H_0 \\ A_0 e^{i(2\pi f_0 n + \phi_0)} + A_1 e^{i(2\pi f_1 n + \phi_1)} + q_n, & H_1 \end{cases} \quad (17.1)$$

where $A_0$ and $A_1$ are deterministic but unknown real-valued amplitudes, $f_0$ and $f_1$ are deterministic but unknown frequencies in the interval $[0,1]$, $\phi_0$ and $\phi_1$ are uncorrelated and uniformly spaced r.v.'s in $[0,2\pi]$ and $\{q_n\}$ is a sequence of zero mean white Gaussian r.v.'s of variance $\sigma^2$ and also uncorrelated with $\phi_0$ and $\phi_1$.

If the phases $\phi_0$ and $\phi_1$ are fixed and known and $A_0$, $A_1$, $f_0$, and $f_1$ are also assumed to be known, then the LR receiver (see [1]) consists of two correlators utilizing the two deterministic sequences under $H_0$ and $H_1$. However, under the assumptions of (17.1) stated above, a conventional approach is to use Fourier analysis such as a DFT or an FFT on the data $\{x_n, \ n = 0,...,N-1\}$ to determine whether there are one or two complex sinusoids. We want to consider the Fourier method in this section and indicate the smallest frequency difference resolvable under this classical approach. We shall consider the limiting case of large SNR where $\{q_n\}$ can be assumed to be absent. The processed data $\{y_n, \ n = 0,1,...,N-1\}$ are obtained by windowing the observed data $\{x_n, \ n = 0,...,N-1\}$ by

$$y_n = x_n w_n, \quad n = 0,...,N-1 \tag{17.2}$$

We shall consider the uniform and Chebyshev window weights.

Consider the output $Y(k)$ in the Fourier transform domain with an input $\{x_n\}$ given by (17.1) and (17.2). Then

$$Y(k) = \sum_{n=0}^{N-1} x_n w_n e^{-i2\pi nk/N}, \quad 0 \le k < N; \tag{17.3}$$

(17.3) either represents a $z$-transform with $z = e^{i2\pi k/N}$ and $k$ as a real-valued number in $[0,N]$ or it represents a DFT (or an FFT) with integral $k$ in $[0,N-1]$. In either case, if we ignore $q_n$, (17.3) can be expressed as

$$Y(k) = A_0 e^{i\phi_0} W(k/N - f_0), \quad H_0, \ 0 \le k \le N \tag{17.4a}$$

or

$$Y(k) = A_0 e^{i\phi_0} W(k/N - f_0) + A_1 e^{i\phi_1} W(k/N - f_1), \quad H_1, \ 0 \le k < N \tag{17.4b}$$

where

$$W(k/N) = \sum_{n=0}^{N-1} w_n e^{-i2\pi nk/N}, \quad 0 \le k < N \tag{17.5}$$

is the transform of the window weights and will be called the *spectral window function*. Then

$$|Y(k)|^2 = A_0^2 |W(k/N - f_0)|^2, \quad H_0, \ 0 \le k < N \qquad (17.6a)$$

$$|Y(k)|^2 = A_0^2 |W(k/N - f_0)|^2 + A_1^2 |W(k/N - f_1)|^2$$

$$+ A_0 A_1 [e^{i(\phi_0 - \phi_1)} W(k/N - f_0) W^*(\frac{k}{N} - f_1) \qquad (17.6b)$$

$$+ e^{-i(\phi_0 - \phi_1)} W^*(\frac{k}{N} - f_0) W(k/N - f_1)], \quad H_1, \ 0 \le k < N$$

Consider a uniform window of unity weights. Then its spectral window function by direct evaluation is given by

$$W(k/N) = e^{-i\pi(N-1)k/N} \ \mathrm{ssin}_N k/N, \quad 0 \le k < N, \qquad (17.7)$$

where we have used the notation

$$\mathrm{ssin}_N x = \sin \pi N x / \sin \pi x. \qquad (17.8)$$

For the uniform window, (17.6a) and (17.6b) become

$$|Y(k)|^2 = A_0^2 \ \mathrm{ssin}_N^2(k/N - f_0), \quad H_0, \ 0 \le k < N \qquad (17.9a)$$

and

$$|Y(k)|^2 = A_0^2 \ \mathrm{ssin}_N^2(k/N - f_0) + A_1^2 \ \mathrm{ssin}_N^2(k/N - f_1)$$

$$+ 2 A_0 A_1 \cos(\phi_0 - \phi_1 + (N-1)\pi(f_0 - f_1))$$

$$\cdot \ \mathrm{ssin}_N(k/N - f_0) \ \mathrm{ssin}_N(k/N - f_1), \quad H_1, \ 0 \le k < N. \qquad (17.9b)$$

For a Chebyshev window of length $N$ and mainlobe peak-to-sidelobe-peak ratio of $10^\alpha$, the spectral window function is given by

$$W(k/N) = e^{-i\pi(N-1)k/N} \ T_{N-1}(\beta \cos \pi k/N) \qquad (17.10)$$

where $T_n(\cdot)$ is the Chebyshev polynomial [2] and

$$\beta = \cosh[(1/N - 1) \cosh^{-1} 10^\alpha]. \qquad (17.11)$$

Then (17.6a) and (17.6b) become

$$|Y(k)|^2 = A_0^2 T_{N-1}^2(\beta \cos \pi(k/N - f_0)), \quad H_0, \ 0 \le k < N \qquad (17.12a)$$

and

$$|Y(k)|^2 = A_0^2 T_{N-1}^2(\beta \cos \pi(k/N - f_0)) + A_1^2 T_{N-1}^2(\beta \cos \pi(k/N - f_1))$$

$$+ 2A_0 A_1 \cos(\phi_0 - \phi_1 + (N-1)\pi(f_0 - f_1)) T_{N-1}(\beta \cos \pi(k/N - f_0))$$

$$\cdot T_{N-1}(\beta \cos \pi(k/N - f_1)), \quad H_1, \; 0 \le k < N. \quad (17.12b)$$

Under hypothesis $H_0$, the square of the magnitude of the spectral window function, $|Y(k)|^2$, takes on a large value at $k/N = f_0$ as seen in (17.6a). For the uniform window, $|Y(k)|^2$ in (17.9a) is well known to have uniformly spaced nulls at positive and negative integral multiples of $1/N$ centered about $f_0$ and the first sidelobe peak's magnitude is 13.1 dB from the mainlobe peak centered at plus and minus $1.43/N$ about $f_0$. For the Chebyshev window, $|Y(k)|^2$ in (17.12a) has $(N-1)$ nulls and $(N-2)$ interior sidelobe peaks. By the minimax property of a Chebyshev window, all the sidelobe peaks have the same magnitude values of $1/10^\alpha$ of that of the mainlobe peak. Thus the distinguishing feature of $|Y(k)|^2$ under $H_0$ is that it has a single large peak.

Under hypothesis $H_1$, the response of $|Y(k)|^2$ in (17.6b) in general and (17.9b) and (17.12b) for the two specific windows can be quite involved. It not only depends deterministically on $A_0$, $A_1$, $f_0$, and $f_1$, but also on the realizations of the r.v.'s $\theta_0$ and $\theta_1$. There are many ways in which it is not easy to distinguish $H_1$ from $H_0$ from the observations of $|Y(k)|^2$. Clearly, if $A_1 \ll A_0$, then $|Y(k)|^2$ in (17.6b) is similar to that in (17.6a). Even if $A_1$ is comparable to $A_0$, then $|Y(k)|^2$ still need not be particularly different between (17.6a) and (17.6b) if the frequency $f_1$ is too close to the frequency $f_0$. The random behavior of the two phases $\theta_0$ and $\theta_1$ further complicates this problem.

A simple criterion to determine two complex sinusoids is to find two relatively distinct and large peaks in $|Y(k)|^2$. The two peaks can be considered to be distinct if a valley of sufficient dip exists between them. A commonly used 3-dB criterion in continuous-time spectral analysis is to require the dip to be equal or less than half of the smaller of the two peaks in the spectral domain. However, for a DFT or an FFT implementation, the observed $|Y(k)|^2$ are restricted to integral values. In order to understand the difference between the continuous-time and discrete-time spectral analysis based on the 3-dB criterion, consider a simple example with a uniform window and two unit amplitude sinusoids with frequencies $f_0 = 0$ and $f_1 = 2/N$ and

$$\cos(\phi_0 - \phi_1 + (N-1)\pi(f_0 - f_1)) = -1.$$

A plot of $|Y(k)|^2$ from (17.9b) is given in Figure 17.1.

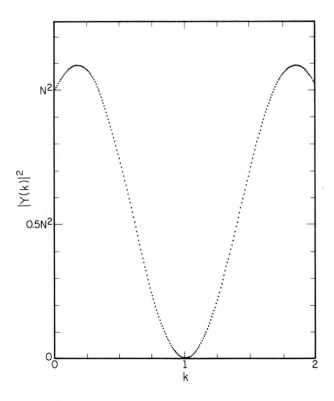

Figure 17.1 $|Y(k)|^2$ versus k for continuous values of k

Since $\text{ssin}_N \, n/N = 0$, for all nonzero integers, direct evaluations show that $|Y(0)|^2 = |Y(2)|^2 = N^2$ and $|Y(1)|^2 = 0$. Thus the dip at $k = 1$ is indeed less than 3 dB as compared to the peaks at $k = 0$ and $k = 2$. Now, suppose that we take $f_0 = -0.3/N$ and $f_1 = 1.7/N$. Graphically, this is equivalent to moving the curve $0.3/N$ unit to the left in Figure 17.1 as shown in Figure 17.2.

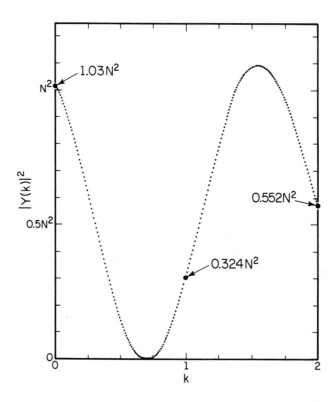

*Figure 17.2 $|Y(k)|^2$ versus $k$ for integral values of $k$*

It is simple to show that $|Y(0)|^2 \approx 1.03N^2$, $|Y(1)|^2 \approx 0.324N^2$, and $|Y(2)|^2 \approx 0.552N^2$. Thus the dip of $|Y(k)|^2$ at $k = 1$ is no longer less than half of the peak at $k = 2$. Thus, for a uniform window, two complex sinusoids with $A_0 = A_1$ and a frequency difference of $f_1 - f_0 = 2/N$ is not detectable under the 3-dB criterion by using the DFT spectral technique.

From this simple example it becomes clear that in order to apply the 3-dB criterion for a DFT or an FFT implementation, we require the two peaks with a dip of 3 dB or more to be valid for all possible translations of $k$ values which have integral differences. Specifically, $|Y(k)|^2$ is declared to be from hypothesis $H_1$ if

$$|Y(k')|^2 \geq 2|Y(k)|^2 \text{ and } |Y(k'')|^2 \geq 2|Y(k)|^2 \qquad (17.13)$$

where $0 \leq k' \leq k < k'' \leq N-1$ and

$$f_0 < k/N < f_1, \quad (k'' - k) \in I, \quad (k - k') \in I. \qquad (17.14)$$

In (17.14), while $k'$, $k$, and $k''$ are real-valued, we require their differences to be in the set of integers $I$. The first condition of (17.14) imposes this 3-dB criterion dip to be applied to the two large peaks and not applied to the sidelobe peaks. We also note that the condition of (17.14) does not necessarily require $(k'' - k)$ and $(k - k')$ to be unit integers. Indeed, we can have $0 \leq k' \leq k_1 \leq k_2 \leq k'' \leq N-1$, where

$$k'' - k_2 = k_2 - k_1 = k_1 - k' = 1 \qquad (17.15)$$

in which (17.13) is satisfied for each $k = k_i$, $i = 1, 2$.

The basic problem of interest in determining hypothesis $H_1$ by the 3-dB criterion under a DFT or an FFT implementation is to find the minimum frequency difference $|f_1 - f_0|$, where $f_0$ and $f_1$ can have arbitrary real values in the set $[0, 1)$, $A_0$ and $A_1$ can take arbitrary real values in $[0, 2\pi)$, such that (17.13) and (17.14) are satisfied. Unfortunately, the problem stated above does not appear to have a simple analytically tractable solution for arbitrary positive $A_0$ and $A_1$. However, by imposing $A_0 = A_1$ in the problem above, symmetric conditions can be used to simplify the analysis greatly.

To find the minimum frequency difference $\Delta = |f_0 - f_1| = D/N$, denote $f_1 = K_1/N$, $f_0 = K_0/N$, and $D = K_1 - K_0$. Detailed analysis show that the critical equality constraints of (17.13) are satisfied if $K_0$ and $K_1$ are placed symmetric to $k'$ and $k''$ with

$$\cos(\phi_0 - \phi_1 + (N-1)\pi(f_0 - f_1)) = -1$$

in (17.9b) or (17.12b). Without loss of generality, we can take $k' = 0$, $k_1 = 1$, $k_2 = 2$, and $k'' = 3$. The symmetry condition yields

$$K_0 = (3-D)/2 \quad \text{and} \quad K_1 = (3+D)/2 \tag{17.16}$$

From $|Y(0)|^2 = 2|Y(1)|^2$ and $|Y(3)|^2 = 2|Y(2)|^2$ of (17.12), the minimum $D$ for the uniform window is given as the solution of

$$f(D) = (\text{ssin}_N((3+D)/2N) - \text{ssin}_N((3-D)/2N))^2$$

$$- 2(\text{ssin}_N((D-1)/2N) - \text{ssin}_N((D+1)/2N))^2 = 0, \tag{17.17}$$

and for the Chebyshev window is given as the solution of

$$0 = h(D)$$

$$= (T_{N-1}(\beta \cos \pi(3 + D)/2N) - T_{N-1}(\beta \cos \pi(3-D)/2N))^2$$

$$- 2(T_{N-1}(\beta \cos \pi(D-1)/2N) - T_{N-1}(\beta \cos \pi(D+1)/2N))^2 \tag{17.18}$$

In Table 17.1, the minimum frequency difference $\Delta$ for uniform and Chebyshev windows as functions of the window length $N$ are given. In the Chebyshev window case, the corresponding optimum sidelobe levels are also given.

As can be seen, $\Delta$ is not particularly sensitive to the window length or the type of window. In summary, for two complex sinusoids of equal amplitudes, regardless of the random phases and actual frequency locations, as long as the frequency difference is greater than $\Delta$ of about $2.4/N$, there is a dip of at least 3 dB between two peaks at the outputs of the DFT located on integral values. In practice, in the presence of random additive noise and unequal amplitudes, the minimum frequency difference needed for declaring hypothesis $H_1$ would be greater than $2.4/N$.

*Table 17.1 Minimum Frequency Difference $\Delta$ for Uniform Window and Chebyshev Window.*

| Uniform Window | | Chebyshev Window | |
|:---:|:---:|:---:|:---:|
| $N$ | $\Delta$ | $\Delta$ | dB |
| 8 | 2.407 | 2.382 | 33 |
| 16 | 2.390 | 2.370 | 33 |
| 32 | 2.386 | 2.358 | 35 |
| 64 | 2.385 | 2.352 | 37 |
| 128 | 2.385 | 2.349 | 37 |
| 256 | 2.385 | 2.347 | 38 |
| 512 | 2.385 | 2.346 | 38 |
| 1024 | 2.385 | 2.346 | 38 |
| 2048 | 2.385 | 2.346 | 38 |

## 17.3 The Pisarenko Method

Consider a sequence of observed data

$$x_n = s_n + q_n, \quad n = 0, 1, \dots \tag{17.19}$$

where the signal is given by

$$s_n = \sum_{j=0}^{r-1} A_j e^{i(2\pi f_j n + \phi_j)} \tag{17.20}$$

with $A_j$ being unknown real-valued amplitudes, $f_j$ being unknown frequencies in $[0,1)$, $\phi_j$ being uncorrelated and uniformly spaced r.v.s in $[0, 2\pi)$, and $q_n$ being zero-mean, white Gaussian r.v.s of variance $\sigma^2$ and also uncorrelated to $\phi_j$. The correlation matrix of $x = (x_0, \dots, x_{N-1})'$ is given by

$$R = E\{xx^*\} = P + \sigma^2 I_N \tag{17.21}$$

$$P = \sum_{j=0}^{r-1} P_j \qquad (17.22)$$

$$P_j = \rho_j e_j e_j^*, \quad \rho_j = A_j^2 \qquad (17.23)$$

$$e_j = (1, e^{i2\pi f_j}, \ldots, e^{i2\pi(N-1)f_j})', \quad j = 0, \ldots, r-1 \qquad (17.24)$$

We note the expectation $E\{\cdot\}$ in (17.21), is taken to be that of statistical ensemble averaging. Later, we shall be concerned with the practical time-averaging aspect of this problem.

In the model of (17.19) and (17.20), there are two basic problems of interest. One problem is to find an efficient and unbiased estimator for the sinusoidal frequencies $\{f_0, f_1, \ldots, f_{r-1}\}$. In the standard Pisarenko approach to this problem [3], the components of an eigenvector corresponding to the minimum eigenvalue of the correlation matrix $R$ of (17.21) are used as coefficients of an $(N-1)$st-degree complex polynomial in $Z$. The roots of this polynomial on the unit circle agree with the original sinusoidal frequencies $\{f_0, f_1, \ldots, f_{r-1}\}$. Considerable numerical instability is encountered in the actual solution of this problem by the standard Pisarenko approach [4].

In this chapter we are concerned with the detection or classification of the number of sinusoids $r$ in the observed data. The actual frequencies $\{f_0, f_1, \ldots, f_{r-1}\}$ are obtained reliably by some estimation procedure, when r is available. However, one would expect a reliable method of obtaining just the number $r$ to be computationally less costly than that of reliably determining the values of $\{f_0, f_1, \ldots, f_{r-1}\}$. We shall consider one such approach in the next section. While our approach is quite different from the original Pisarenko estimation problem, we make use of the algebraic structure of the correlation matrix $R$ of (17.21) to (17.24). We summarize these results below.

*Lemma 1:* Let $\{f_0, f_1, \ldots, f_{r-1}\}$ be distinct real numbers on $[0,1)$. Then $\{e_0, e_1, \ldots, e_{r-1}\}$ are $r$ linearly independent vectors in $\mathbb{R}^N$ for $r \le N$, where $e_j$ is defined in (17.24).

*Lemma 2:* For $P_j, j = 0, 1, \ldots, r-1$, defined in (17.23), the range of $P_j$ is a one-dimensional space spanned by $e_j$ in $\mathbb{R}^N$.

*Lemma 3:* The matrix $P$ defined in (17.22) is an $N \times N$ hermitian matrix with rank $r$ or a null space of dimension $(N - r)$. Thus if $r < N$, then $P$ is a singular matrix.

*Lemma 4:* The correlation matrix $R$ of (17.21) with $\sigma^2 > 0$ is a positive-definite matrix with minimum eigenvalue $\sigma^2$ of multiplicity $\nu = N - r$. The eigenspace $E_0 \subset \mathbb{R}^N$ corresponding to $\sigma^2$ is the orthogonal subspace of the linear span of $\{e_0, e_1, \ldots, e_{r-1}\}$. That is, $u \in E_0$ satisfies $e_j^* u = 0$, $j = 0, 1, \ldots, r - 1$.

From Lemma 4, if $R$ is available, then the minimum eigenvalue $\sigma^2$ and its multiplicity $\nu$ is computable. Then the number of sinusoids $r = N - \nu$. In general, the evaluation of the minimum eigenvalue $\sigma^2$ and its multiplicity $\nu$ is computationally costly and quite numerically unstable. In practice, errors in the matrix $R$ usually lead to an unreliable estimate of the multiplicity. On the other hand, since the noise $q_n$ is assumed to be white, a good estimation of the noise variance $\sigma^2$ is often quite feasible. This means that $P$ can be assumed to be available. From Lemma 3, any computationally efficient method of rank determination of $P$ can be used to determine the number of sinusoids $r$. In the next section we use the general trace approach to solve this approach.

## 17.4 The Generalized Trace and Rank Determination

In the preceding section we have seen that the detection problem of interest reduces to the problem of rank determination of the matrix $P$. While the concept of the rank of a matrix is elementary and is discussed in every linear algebra book, the actual numerical evaluation of the rank of a given matrix is more complicated. It is generally recognized that the singular value decomposition approach represents the most advanced and reliable method of numerically evaluating the rank of a matrix [4,5]. Unfortunately, SVD is generally complicated to implement [6,7] and can require a fair amount of active workspace. Thus, whereas SVD may be ideal for sophisticated high-performance off-line applications, it is generally not suitable for real-time on-board detection, estimation, and signal processing tasks.

We consider the use of the generalized trace method for rank determination of the nonnegative definite matrix $P$. This method needs only modest computational efforts and will be seen to be quite efficient for detecting closely spaced complex sinusoids.

The nonnegative definiteness of a complex-valued $N \times N$ matrix $P$ is defined in terms of the quadratic form $x'Px$ being nonnegative for all complex valued $N$-dimensional column vectors $x$. While the definition above is useful, it does not yield a constructive manner to establish the non-negative definiteness of the matrix. The use of principal minors provides direct verification of the nonnegative definiteness of this property. A *minor* of order $m$ of $P$ is the determinant of an $m \times m$ submatrix taken from $P$ with $1 \leq m \leq N-1$. A *principal minor* of $P$ is a minor whose elements are taken from the diagonal elements of $P$. Then it can be shown [8] that a matrix is nonnegative definite if and only if all its principal minors are nonnegative. Now, we want to determine the rank of the matrix $P$. It is clear that if all $m$th-order minors of a matrix $P$ are zero, then so are all higher orders. However, the rank of a matrix is equal to the highest order of nonzero minors of the matrix. This leads to Lemma 5.

*Lemma 5:* $P$ is an $N \times N$ nonnegative definite matrix of rank $r$ if and only if all principal minors of order $r+1$ of $P$ are zero while at least one principal minor of order $i$ for each $i = 1,2,\ldots,r$ is positive.

In practice, for a given order, we would like to use as many principal minors of that order as possible in order to reduce the maximum uncertainty in the determination of the rank of the $P$ matrix. A *generalized trace of order* $i$ of the matrix $P$, denoted by $\text{Tr}_i(P)$, is the sum of all the principal minors of order $i$ of $P$. Lemma 5 can be restated in terms of generalized traces as given in Lemma 6.

*Lemma 6.* $P$ is an $N \times N$ nonnegative definite matrix of rank $r$ if and only if the generalized traces $\text{Tr}_i(P)$ of $P$ satisfy

$$\text{Tr}_i(P) > 0, \quad i = 1,2,\ldots,r \tag{17.25}$$

and

$$\mathrm{Tr}_i(P) \;=\; 0, \quad i \;=\; r+1,\ldots,N-1 \qquad\qquad (17.26)$$

In theory, from Lemma 6, we only care about $\mathrm{Tr}_r(P)$ and $\mathrm{Tr}_{r+1}(P)$. Suppose that we consider the idealized matrix $P$ of (17.24) as given by $R - \sigma^2 I_N$. The nonnegative definite correlation matrix $R$ is obtained under the assumption of using statistical ensemble averaging of the random phases in (17.21). The white noise variance $\sigma^2$ is also assumed to be known through perfect measurements.

In Table 17.2, we considered the generalized trace of orders 1 to 4 for three complex sinusoids (i.e., $r = 3$) with frequencies of (0.1, 0.11, 0.12), $\rho_1 = \rho_2 = \rho_3 = 1$, in the absence of noise. As can be seen, $\mathrm{Tr}_i(P)$, $i = 1,2,3$, are positive and $\mathrm{Tr}_4(P) = 0$. Clearly, a larger-dimensional $N$ permits a sharper discrimination of a positive $\mathrm{Tr}_3(P)$ from a zero $\mathrm{Tr}_4(P)$. In Table 17.3 we consider the sensitivity effect of imperfect canceling of the white noise from the correlation matrix $R$. The data consists of two real-valued sinusoids and $N=5$ [i.e., $e_i = (1, \cos 2\pi f i,\ldots,\cos 8\pi f i)'$, $i = 1,2$] of frequencies (0.1,0.2), $\rho_1 = \rho_2 = 1$, with a white noise $\sigma^2 = 0.5$. Generalized traces of orders 1 to 5 for values of estimated $\sigma^2$ from 0.48 to 0.52 are tabulated. As can be seen, for $\sigma^2 = 0.5$, there is perfect canceling, and $\mathrm{Tr}_3 = \mathrm{Tr}_4 = \mathrm{Tr}_5 = 0$. As $\sigma^2$ deviates further from $\sigma^2 = 0.5$, $\mathrm{Tr}_3$ also deviates from zero and the chance of not classifying $r = 2$ also increases. In practice, the possible nonwhiteness of the noise, the statistical variations in the sample correlation matrix, cross correlation between the signal and noise, and statistical variations in the random phases all contribute to errors in ways to be considered in the next section.

Table 17.2 *Generalized Trace of Orders* 1 *to* 4 *of Matrix P for Sinusoids of* $r=3$ with $(f_0, f_1, f_2) = (0.1, 0.11, 0.12)$ *and* $\rho_1 = \rho_2 = \rho_3 = 1$ *in the Absence of Noise*

| $N$ | $Tr_1$ | $Tr_2$ | $Tr_3$ | $Tr_4$ |
|---|---|---|---|---|
| 1 | 6 | 0.0237 | - | - |
| 2 | 9 | 0.142 | 2.46E-7 | - |
| 3 | 12 | 0.471 | 4.90E-6 | 0 |
| 4 | 15 | 1.18 | 4.28E-5 | 0 |
| 5 | 18 | 2.45 | 2.39E-4 | 0 |
| 6 | 21 | 4.56 | 9.97E-4 | 0 |
| 7 | 24 | 7.77 | 3.40E-3 | 0 |
| 8 | 27 | 12.4 | 9.97E-3 | 0 |
| 9 | 30 | 18.8 | 2.59E-3 | 0 |
| 10 | 33 | 27.4 | 6.14E-2 | 0 |

Table 17.3 *Effect of Mismatch for Various Values of* $\sigma^2$ *on Generalized Trace of Orders* 1 *to* 5 *for Real-Valued Sinusoids of* $r = 2$ *with* $(f_0, f_1) = (0.1, 0.2)$ *and* $\rho_1 = \rho_2 = 1$ *and White Noise* $\sigma^2 = 0.5$

| $\sigma^2$ | $Tr_1$ | $Tr_2$ | $Tr_3$ | $Tr_4$ | $Tr_5$ |
|---|---|---|---|---|---|
| 0.48 | 5.10 | 5.65 | 0.327 | 6.46E-3 | 4.28E-5 |
| 0.49 | 5.05 | 5.45 | 0.161 | 1.60E-3 | 5.30E-6 |
| 0.495 | 5.03 | 5.35 | 0.0795 | 3.96E-4 | 6.59E-7 |
| 0.5 | 5.00 | 5.25 | 0 | 0 | 0 |
| 0.505 | 4.98 | 5.15 | -0.078 | 3.91E-4 | -6.53E-7 |
| 0.51 | 4.95 | 5.05 | -0.155 | 1.56E-3 | 5.20E-6 |
| 0.52 | 4.90 | 4.85 | -0.303 | 6.14E-3 | -4.12E-5 |

## 17.5 Numerical Results and Conclusions

As noted in Section 17.3, the idealized correlation matrix $R$ given by (17.21) was obtained from the observed data vector $x$ by statistical ensemble averaging over the random phases $\phi_j$ and random noises $q_n$. In practice, we observe only $N$ values of the data $\{x_n, \quad n = 0, 1, \ldots, N-1\}$ and have to use some form of time averaging technique to approximate the idealized correlation matrix $R$. Let the observed data $x_n$ be given by (17.19) and the signal $s_n$ be given by (17.20). In the case of $r = 2$, then (17.19) reduces to (17.1). The time-averaged sample autocorrelation function of $\{x_n, \quad n = 0, \ldots, N-1\}$ is given by either

$$R_0(m) = r_{xx^*}(m)/(N - m), \qquad m = 0, 1, \ldots \qquad (17.27a)$$

or

$$R_1(m) = r_{xx^*}(m)/N, \qquad m = 0, 1, \ldots \qquad (17.27b)$$

where

$$r_{xx^*}(m) = \sum_{n=0}^{N-m-1} x_{m+n} x_n^*, \qquad m = 0, 1, \ldots \qquad (17.28)$$

The sample autocorrelation of (17.27a) is unbiased, while that of (17.27b) is biased but has a smaller mean-square error [10]. In either case, the crucial time-averaging operation is performed in (17.28). Since $x_n$ consists of a signal term $s_n$ and a noise term $q_n$, then (17.28) can be expressed as

$$r_{xx^*}(m) = r_{ss^*}(m) + r_{qs^*}(m) + r_{sq^*}(m) + r_{qq^*}(m) \qquad (17.29)$$

where in the right hand side of (17.29) the first term is the desired signal sample autocorrelation, the second and third terms are the signal and noise sample cross correlations, and the fourth term is the sample noise autocorrelation. Even in the absence of noise (or high SNR), when the last three terms on the right-hand side of (17.29) vanish (or become small), the term $r_{ss^*}(m)$ is not a deterministic function, but depends on the realizations of the random phases $\phi_0$ and $\phi_1$ under hypothesis $H_1$. Specifically, by direct evaluation

$$r_{ss}*(m) = (N - m)[A_0^2 e^{i2\pi f_0 m} + A_1^2 e^{i2\pi f_1 m}]$$

$$+ 2A_0 A_1 e^{i\pi m(f_0 + f_1)}[\cos(\phi_1 - \phi_0 + (N-1)\pi(f_1 - f_0))]$$

$$\cdot \text{ssin}_{N-m}(f_1 - f_0), \qquad m = 0,1,\dots \qquad (17.30)$$

where $\text{ssin}_N(\cdot)$ is defined in (17.7). In (17.29), since $\cos(\cdot)$ can vary from $-1$ to $1$, the statistical variation of $r_{ss}*(m)$ due to $\phi_0$ and $\phi_1$ can be significant if the magnitude of the $\text{ssin}_N(\cdot)$ term is not negligible. This phenomenon was noted as a factor in the limitation of the Pisarenko method for the estimation of the sinusoidal frequencies [11].

In Table 17.4 we have tabulated various numerical evaluations of unnormalized magnitudes of sample autocorrelation of the signal $r_{ss}*(m)$ of (17.29) for two complex sinusoids. In all cases, the observed data length $N = 110$ and $f_0 = 0.201$, while in case A, $f_1 = 0.20784$ yields $\Delta f = 0.75/N$, and in case B, $f_1 = 0.21464$ yields $\Delta f = 1.5/N$. The amplitudes $A_0 = A_1 = 1$. In Table 17.4 the ratio of the maximum to minimum $|r_{ss}*(m)|$ is about 2 for case A, while it reduces to about 1.5 for case B.

Table 17.4 Unnormalized Magnitudes of Sample Autocorrelation Sequences $r_{ss}*(m)$ of Equation (17.29) with No Windowing for Two Complex Sinusoids of Unity Amplitudes and Dimension 110

| | Case A: $\Delta = 0.75/N$ | | Case B: $\Delta = 1.5/N$ | |
|---|---|---|---|---|
| | Min. | Max. | Min. | Max. |
| $|r_{ss}*(0)|$ | 154 | 286 | 173 | 267 |
| $|r_{ss}*(1)|$ | 151 | 285 | 171 | 264 |
| $|r_{ss}*(2)|$ | 147 | 285 | 169 | 262 |
| $|r_{ss}*(3)|$ | 143 | 284 | 166 | 259 |
| $|r_{ss}*(4)|$ | 140 | 283 | 163 | 255 |

In Table 17.5, the generalized traces $\text{Tr}_i(P)$ of an $M \times M$ matrix $P = R - \sigma^2 I_M$ are evaluated, where

$$R = \begin{bmatrix} R_0(0) & R_0(1) & \cdot & \cdot & \cdot & R_0(M-1) \\ \cdot & \cdot & \cdot & \cdot & \cdot & \cdot \\ \cdot & \cdot & \cdot & \cdot & \cdot & \cdot \\ R^*_0(M-1) & R^*_0(M-1) & \cdot & \cdot & \cdot & R_0(0) \end{bmatrix}$$

and $R_0(m)$ is given by (17.27A). We used $M = 8$. In the case of a single complex sinusoid with no noise, $\text{Tr}_i(P)$ is independent of the phase $\phi_0$. Indeed, $\text{Tr}_1(P) = 8$ and $\text{Tr}_2(P) \leq \text{Tr}_3(P) \leq 0$, yielding the correct decision of a single complex sinusoid of $r = 1$. At 20 dB SNR, $7.9 \leq \text{Tr}_1(P) \leq 8.1$ and $.03 \leq \text{Tr}_2(P) \leq 0.14$, may still be able to predict a correct value of $r = 1$. On the other hand, at 10 dB SNR, $7.7 \leq \text{Tr}_1(P) \leq 8.3$ and $0.09 \leq \text{Tr}_2(P) \leq 0.45$ may yield an erroneous predicted value of $r = 2$. In the case of two complex sinusoids, under case A of $\Delta f = 0.75/N$, even in the absence of noise, the fact that $\text{Tr}_3(P)$ can attain 0.78 may lead to an erroneous prediction of $r = 3$. On the other hand, in case B of $\Delta f = 1.5/N$, we can predict $r$ correctly with great certainty at $\infty$ dB and 20 dB and probably even at 10 dB SNR. In practice, the actual magnitudes of $A_0$ and $A_1$ are unknown. If each $A_i$ is multiplied by a constant $c$, then $r_{ss^*}(m)$ of (17.30) is multiplied by $c^2$. In the absence of noise, $R_0(m)$ or $R_1(m)$ of (17.27a) and (17.27b) and thus $P$ are multiplied by $c^2$. However,

$$\text{Tr}_i(c^2 P) = c^{2i} \text{Tr}_i(P), \quad i = 1,2,\ldots \tag{17.31}$$

From (17.31), it becomes clear that the rank determination of the sample correlation matrix should be based not so much on $\text{Tr}_i(\cdot)$ but on the normalized generalized trace $\text{Tr}'_i(\cdot)$ given by

$$\text{Tr}'_1(P) = \text{Tr}_1(P) \cdot (M/\text{Tr}_1(P))$$

$$\text{Tr}'_2(P) = \text{Tr}_2(P) \cdot (M/\text{Tr}_1(P))^2$$

$$\text{Tr}'_3(P) = \text{Tr}_3(P) \cdot (M/\text{Tr}_1(P))^3 \tag{17.32}$$

*Table 17.5 Generalized Traces for One and Two Complex Sinusoids*

$$r = 1$$
$$f = 0.201$$

|          | ∞dB     | 20 dB  | 10 dB  |
|----------|---------|--------|--------|
| $Tr_1(P)$ | 8.0     | 8.0    | 8.1    |
| $Tr_2(P)$ | 1.6E-14 | 0.03   | 0.09   |
| $Tr_3(P)$ | 1.9E-24 | 1.2E-4 | 0.001  |

$$r = 2$$
Case A: $\Delta = 0.75/N$

| ∞dB | | 20dB | | 10dB | |
|------|------|------|------|------|------|
| Min. | Max. | Min. | Max. | Min. | Max. |
| 17 | 21 | 17 | 21 | 17 | 21 |
| 0.50 | 7.3 | 0.67 | 7.3 | 1.0 | 7.3 |
| 0.006 | 0.78 | 0.008 | 0.78 | 0.01 | 0.76 |

$$r = 2$$
Case B: $\Delta = 1.5/N$

| ∞dB | | 20dB | | 10dB | |
|------|------|------|------|------|------|
| Min. | Max. | Min. | Max. | Min. | Max. |
| 16 | 19 | 15 | 20 | 14 | 20 |
| 2.1 | 2.4 | 2.1 | 2.4 | 2.1 | 3.4 |
| 0.006 | 0.07 | 0.01 | 0.07 | 0.07 | 0.17 |

*Table 17.6 Normalized Generalized Traces for One and Two Complex Sinusoids*

$$r = 1$$
$$f = 0.201$$

| | $\infty$dB | 20dB | | 10dB | |
|---|---|---|---|---|---|
| | | Min. | Max. | Min. | Max. |
| $Tr'_1(P)$ | 8 | 8 | 8 | 8 | 8 |
| $Tr'_2(P)$ | 1.6E-14 | 0.03 | 0.14 | 0.09 | 0.41 |
| $Tr'_3(P)$ | 1.9E-24 | 1E-4 | 7E-4 | 1E-3 | 7E-3 |

$$r = 2$$
Case A: $\Delta f = 0.75/N$

| $\infty$dB | | 20dB | | 10dB | |
|---|---|---|---|---|---|
| Min. | Max. | Min. | Max. | Min. | Max. |
| 8 | 8 | 8 | 8 | 8 | 8 |
| 0.11 | 1.1 | 0.15 | 1.1 | 0.23 | 1.1 |
| 6E-4 | 4E-2 | 8E-4 | 4E-2 | 2E-3 | 4E-2 |

$$r = 2$$
Case B: $\Delta f = 1.5/N$

| $\infty$dB | | 20dB | | 10dB | |
|---|---|---|---|---|---|
| Min. | Max. | Min. | Max. | Min. | Max. |
| 8 | 8 | 8 | 8 | 8 | 8 |
| 0.36 | 0.58 | 0.36 | 0.58 | 0.36 | 1.1 |
| 2E-3 | 5E-3 | 2E-3 | 5E-3 | 5E-3 | 3E-2 |

In Table 17.6, the normalized generalized traces $Tr'_i(\cdot)$ of these results given in Table 17.5 are shown. As can be seen, a threshold of 0.145 on $Tr'_2(P)$ is sufficient to yield error-free prediction between one or two complex sinusoids when the SNR is 20 dB and higher. On the other hand, at SNR = 10 dB, a threshold of 0.35 could lead to small probability of errors for case B and larger probability of errors for case A.

In conclusion, we have seen that the Pisarenko method can be used with generalized trace functions for a computationally tractable approach in the detection of closely spaced complex sinusoids with unknown amplitudes and phases. This minimum frequency difference in this approach is about two to three times smaller than the classical DFT approach. Various extensions and improvements are possible and a more detailed analysis will be presented in a future work.

## References

[1]   C.W. Helstrom, *Statistical Theory of Signal Detection*, 2nd ed., Oxford, England: Pergammon Press, 1968.

[2]   M. Abramowitz and I.A. Stegun, *Handbook of Mathematical Functions*, Washington, D.C.: National Bureau of Standards, 1964.

[3]   V.F. Pisarenko, The retrieval of harmonics from a covariance function, *Geophy. J. R. Astro. Soc.*, Vol. 33, pp. 347-366, 1973.

[4]   G.E. Shilov, *Linear Algebra*, Englewood Cliffs, NJ: Prentice-Hall, 1971.

[5]   G.H. Golub and C. Reinsch, Singular value decomposition and least squares solutions, *Numer. Math.*, Vol. 14, pp. 403-420, 1970.

[6]   B.T. Smith, *Matrix Eigensystem Routines - Eispack Guide*, Heidelberg, Germany: Springer-Verlag, 1976.

[7]   C.L. Lawson and R.J. Hanson, *Solving Least Squares Problems*, Englewood Cliffs, NJ: Prentice-Hall, 1976.

[8]   I.V. Proskuryakov, *Problems in Linear Algebra*, Moscow, USSR: Mir Publications, 1978.

[9]   S.R. Searle, *Matrix Algebra Useful for Statistics,* New York, NY: Wiley, 1982.

[10]  G.M. Jenkins and D.G. Watts, *Spectral Analysis and Its Applications,* San Francisco, CA: Holden-Day, 1968.

[11]  T.J. Ulrych and R.W. Clayton, Time series modelling and maximum entropy, *Physics of the Earth and Planetary Interiors,* Vol. 12, pp. 188-200, 1976.

# Index

identification, 226
in detection-estimation, 31
performance versus complexity, 126
robust location estimation, 135
series expansions in, 47, 66
Polyspectra, 203
p-point classes, 135
Predictive source coding, 348
Prequantization, 328
Prohorov neighborhoods, 134

Quantization,
in detection of known low-pass
signals, 82-90
in detection of narrowband signals,
90-98
in detection of random signals,
98-107
MMSE, 73, 370-374
Nyquist sampling theorem in, 113
random, 370
rectangular, 364
vector, 362-389
Quantizer-detectors, 72-110
correlator, 84
envelope correlator, 97
cross-correlation array, 104
narrowband correlator, 95

Random coding, 255
Random fields, 14, 16, 230-243
Brownian sheet, 16
Gaussian, 283
Gibbs distribution, 266-298

Markov, 231, 270
Markov mesh, 267, 276-282, 352-356
multiparameter Brownian motion, 232
multiparameter Ornstein-Uhlenbeck
process, 10
multiparameter Wiener process, 234
Slepian field, 16
Ratio threshold mitigation technique, 262
Rectangular lattice, 269, 272
Rice's function, 13
Rivest-Shamir-Adelman encryption
algorithm, 395-396
Robust procedures,
in hypothesis testing, 132-135
in matched filtering, 147-150
in parameter estimation, 135-136
in quadratic receivers, 150-151
in signal detection, 49, 131-156
correlator-limiter, 139
dependent noise, 144-146
limiter-correlator, 141
sequential, 143, 181-183
Routing algorithms, 299-324
alternate, 301-302, 306
centralized, 301
distributed, 301, 306, 308
dynamic, 301
fixed, 301-302, 308
flooding, 313
flow balance principle, 336
Gallager's algorithm, 305, 311
Merlin and Segall, 311-312, 315-316
quasi-static, 301, 306, 308
retransmission control, 336-342